Interceptive Actions in Sport

When playing and watching sport, we have all been impressed by the ability of athletes to co-ordinate their actions with respect to important objects and surfaces in the environment. Interceptive actions are common to everyday life and many sports. Examples include catching, hitting and striking stationary and moving projectiles, as well as tackling sprinting players and running towards targets in space. This book explores how these fascinating movements are performed.

It is the first book to offer a comprehensive review of current theoretical research on interceptive actions, as well as demonstrating the connections between theory and practice for a wide range of key sport skills. Contributions from experts all over the world cover sports such as cricket, soccer, tennis, volleyball, golf, long jumping and triple jumping.

Interceptive Actions in Sport offers a wealth of theoretical material, as well as unique analysis of dynamic interceptive actions in practice. It will be essential reading for anybody with an interest in motor control and skill acquisition, and will be of interest to students and practitioners in sport psychology, movement science and coaching science.

Keith Davids is at the School of Physical Education, University of Otago, New Zealand. **Geert Savelsbergh** is at the Department of Exercise and Sport Science, Manchester Metropolitan University. **Simon J. Bennett** is at the Department of Optometry and Neuroscience, University of Manchester Institute of Science and Technology. **John Van der Kamp** is at the Faculty of Human Movement Science, Vrije Universiteit of Amsterdam.

Interceptive Actions in Sport

Information and movement

**Edited by Keith Davids,
Geert Savelsbergh, Simon J. Bennett
and John Van der Kamp**

London and New York

First published 2002
by Routledge
11 New Fetter Lane, London EC4P 4EE

Simultaneously published in the USA and Canada
by Routledge
29 West 35th Street, New York, NY 10001

Routledge is an imprint of the Taylor & Francis Group

Typeset in Times by
HWA Text and Data Management, Tunbridge Wells
Printed and bound in Great Britain by
TJ International Ltd, Padstow, Cornwall

British Library Cataloguing in Publication Data
A catalogue record for this book is available from the British Library

Library of Congress Cataloging in Publication Data
A catalog record for this book has been requested

ISBN 0–415–24152–9 (hbk)
ISBN 0–415–24153–7 (pbk)

Contents

Tables

Figures

Contributors

J. Gregory Anson School of Physical Education, University of Otago, New Zealand

Roger Bartlett The Centre for Sport and Exercise Science, Sheffield Hallam University, UK

Sam Beak Department of Exercise and Sport Science, Manchester Metropolitan University, UK

Nicolas Benguigui Centre de Recherche en Sciences du Sport, Université Paris-Sud, France

Simon J. Bennett Department of Optometry and Neuroscience, UMIST, UK

Michael P. Broderick Department of Health and Human Performance, Auburn University, USA

Chris Button Department of Physical Education, Sport and Leisure Studies, University of Edinburgh, UK

James H. Cauraugh Motor Behaviour Laboratory, Department of Exercise and Sport Science, University of Florida, Gainesville, USA

Keith Davids School of Physical Education, University of Otago, New Zealand

Digby Elliott Department of Kinesiology, McMaster University, Hamilton, Canada

Paul Glazier School of Sport, PE and Recreation, University of Wales Institute, Cardiff, UK

Craig Handford Department of Physical Education, Sports Science and Recreation Management, Loughborough University, UK

Christopher M. Janelle Motor Behaviour Laboratory, Department of Exercise and Sport Science, University of Florida, Gainesville, USA

Damian Keil Department of Exercise and Sport Science, Manchester Metropolitan University, UK

Michel Laurent UMR Mouvement et Perception, Faculté des Sciences des Sports, Université de la Méditerranée, Marseille, France

Jon Law School of Sport and Exercise Sciences, University of Birmingham, UK

Adrian Lees Research Institute for Sport and Exercise Sciences, Liverpool John Moores University, UK

François-Xavier Li School of Sport and Exercise Sciences, University of Birmingham, UK

Brian K.V. Maraj Perceptual Motor Behavior Laboratory, University of Alberta, Edmonton, Canada

Richard Masters Physical Education and Sports Science Unit, University of Hong Kong, China.

Jon Maxwell Neuroscience Research Institute, Aston University, Birmingham, UK

Claire F. Michaels Department of Psychology, University of Connecticut, Storrs, USA and Faculty of Human Movement Science, Vrije Universiteit, Amsterdam, Netherlands

Gilles Montagne UMR Mouvement et Perception, Faculté des Sciences des Sports, Université de la Méditerranée, Marseille, France

Hubert Ripoll Equipe Expertise, Mémoire, Motivation, Université de la Méditerranée, Marseille, France

Shannon D. Robertson Department of Exercise Science and Physical Education, Arizona State University, Tempe, USA

Geert Savelsbergh Department of Exercise and Sport Science, Manchester Metropolitan University, UK and Faculty of Human Movement Science, Vrije Universiteit, Amsterdam, Netherlands

Mark A. Scott Research Institute for Sport and Exercise Sciences, Liverpool John Moores University, UK

Janet Starkes Department of Kinesiology, McMaster University, Hamilton, Canada

Jeffrey Summers School of Psychology, University of Tasmania, Hobart, Australia

Martin A. Tayler School of Psychology, University of Tasmania, Hobart, Australia

Jean Jacques Temprado UMR Mouvement et Perception, Faculté des Sciences des Sports, Université de la Méditerranée, Marseille, France

Luc Tremblay Department of Kinesiology, McMaster University, Hamilton, Canada

Yvonne Turrell School of Sport and Exercise Sciences, University of Birmingham, UK

John Van der Kamp Faculty of Human Movement Science, Vrije Universiteit, Amsterdam

Cornelia Weigelt Institut für Arbeitsphysiologie, Universität Dortmund, Germany

A. Mark Williams Research Institute of Sport and Exercise Sciences, Liverpool John Moores University, UK

Frank T.J.M. Zaal Faculty of Human Movement Science, Vrije Universiteit, Amsterdam, Netherlands

Preface

Interceptive actions play a significant role in human behaviour and are integral to successful performance in many different contexts including sport and physical activity. Interceptive actions can be defined as those activities that involve relative motion between an actor (or body parts of an actor) and an object, surface, opening, target, implement, land feature or projectile. An underlying principle in all of these tasks is that the actor (or limb segment or implement) has to be in the right place at the right time, often while imparting an appropriate amount of force in a movement (e.g. Savelsbergh and Bootsma, 1994; Williams, Davids and Williams, 1999). In everyday life, activities such as walking up and down stairs, crossing roads, jumping onto surfaces, shaking hands, sitting on a chair, driving a car and riding a bicycle represent just a few of the common interceptive actions which are important to humans.

In similar vein, interceptive actions have received significant attention in the research areas of psychology, sports science, movement science, the neurosciences, physical education, physiotherapy and coaching science. These actions are particularly prevalent in sports and physical activities and include running to hit the take-off board in the long jump approach, kicking a ball, reaching to catch a ball, landing on skis on a snowy slope, grasping a bar in a gymnastics, placing feet on the poolside during a tumble-turn, and striking a ball in tennis, golf and cricket. From a broader perspective in psychology, they have represented a useful vehicle for developing our theoretical understanding of the relationship between perception and action in goal-directed behaviour. The chapters in this book, by established and emerging scientists from the academic disciplines of sport and movement science, represent selected examples of work from a variety of theoretical perspectives including cognitive science, Gibsonian (1979) ideas on direct perception and dynamical pattern theory exemplified in the work of Kelso (e.g. 1995) and Edelman (1992).

Structure and organisation

Due to the intertwined nature of processes of perception and action during tasks involving interceptive timing behaviour, there are many ways of providing structure and organisation in this book for the reader. The chapters in the book break down loosely into two sections. Outside these sections, Chapter 1 starts by attempting to summarise the contributions of each chapter to the book and to signal the relevance of separate areas of interest to the literature on interceptive actions. After this chapter, in the first part of the book, eleven chapters provide a historical perspective on research on interceptive actions. They trace the development of the theoretical work through the initial impetus derived from the cognitive science research paradigm, to the excitement of the new arrival with plenty to say on information and movement during interceptive tasks: ecological psychology. An additional chapter examines the link between behavioural and neuroscientific research on perception and action during interceptive tasks, providing an integrative modelling perspective for readers. In the second part, the chapters focus on research examining co-ordination and control of movements during specific interceptive actions in a variety of sport contexts. The main tasks examined in this book include: catching, hitting, kicking, and stepping and locomoting on and towards targets or surfaces in the environment.

Our colleagues contributing to this book have been given the brief of providing comprehensive and comprehensible reviews of the literature on interceptive actions. They have been admirable in completing the task of bringing together relevant research findings and sign-posting new areas for future research. This book provides a rich and detailed mix of material, with different chapters adopting a theoretical, practical or integrated approach. In each chapter, the authors have been given the freedom to explore their area of expertise either by reviewing the past and present theoretical developments in the literature or by examining the potential of extant research for practical applications. As can be seen, the result is that many chapters attempt to provide links with existing theoretical frameworks for studying interceptive actions and to examine practical applications for teachers, coaches and therapists. Even the chapters with a more practical slant direct the reader's attention to the theoretical research base for guidance. The outcome is a very broad coverage of the many different types of interceptive actions performed in sport contexts.

In successfully performing a metaphorical interceptive action of 'hitting' a deadline for publishing an edited text such as this, co-operation from key individuals is paramount. For their professional approach in listening to our advice and revising initial chapter drafts, we would like to thank our contributing authors, expert colleagues in the study of interceptive actions. I acknowledge the support of the Department of Exercise and Sport Science at Manchester Metropolitan University in providing me with the space and time to coordinate the efforts of the editorial team in pulling together the material in this book. The editorial team would also like to thank our publishers, Routledge, Taylor and Francis, and particularly Simon Whitmore, for their organisational efforts on our behalf. Finally, I can think of few better places to edit a text than Brisbane, Australia. Particular thanks go to my mother Pearl Jannette Davids, one of Brisbane's finest, for providing nurture and nature in support of my work.

Keith Davids
Brisbane, Australia, June 2001

References

Edelman, G. (1992). *Bright Air, Brilliant Fire: On the Matter of Mind*. New York: Penguin.

Gibson, J.J. (1979). *The Ecological Approach to Visual Perception*. Boston: Houghton Mifflin.

Kelso, J.A.S. (1995). *Dynamic Patterns: The Self-organization of Brain and Behavior*. Cambridge: MIT Press.

Savelsbergh, G.J.P. and Bootsma, R.J. (1994). 'Perception–action coupling in hitting and catching', *International Journal of Sport Pyschology* **25**, 331–43.

Williams, A.M., Davids, K. and Williams, J.G. (1999). *Visual Perception and Action in Sport*. London: Routledge.

1 Interceptive actions in sport

Theoretical perspectives and practical applications

Keith Davids, Geert Savelsbergh,
Simon J. Bennett and John Van der Kamp

Interceptive actions are common in everyday life and are instrumental in helping humans to adapt to their complex and uncertain environments. The range of interceptive actions includes both fine and gross motor responses, performed under a variety of conditions in static and dynamic environments, embracing discrete and continuous tasks. They include mundane tasks like picking up a cup, placing a foot on a kerb when crossing the road, sitting down gently on a chair, or shaking hands with a friend. They are important in many contexts involving rapid aiming movements with different parts of the body such as when playing the piano, typing on a computer keyboard, or placing the foot on the brake of a car. Other interceptive actions require the use of hand-held implements, for example using tools or wielding a fly swat. Indeed, some of the most fascinating insights into motor control processes, such as Bernstein's (1967) influential observations on movement variability, have been made using putatively mundane interceptive tasks like hammering a nail (see Figure 1.1).

Interceptive actions in sport

Sport is an exciting, real-world context for studying processes of movement co-ordination, control and perception because it encompasses virtually all of the current topics engaging the curiosity of psychologists, movement scientists, vision scientists, neuropsychologists and biomechanists. In this opening chapter, we highlight why interceptive actions are critical to successful performance in a wide variety of sports. We discuss why there is a need for a book bringing together world-class experts engaged in studying processes of perception and movement under the unique task constraints of interceptive actions in sport. Examples of interceptive actions in sport include: catching a ball in Australian rules football or lacrosse; hitting a ball in hockey, cricket or tennis; putting a golf ball; landing after a triple salto; tackling a dribbling player in soccer; running towards a take-off board in the long and triple jumps; landing on a moving skate- or snow-board after a jump; contacting the chest area of an opponent with an épee in fencing; and grasping a high bar in a full circle gymnastics manoeuvre.

Figure 1.1 Bernstein's (1967) classic image of the movement trajectories of a repetitive
hammering task. Note the patterned trajectories are similar but not identically
overlaid. Even in the most mundane of interceptive movements, there are slight
functional variations in the movement pattern that allows the performer to achieve
the goal of hammering in a nail.

The role of perceptual and movement systems in interceptive tasks

A common underlying principle in interceptive actions is that they involve co-
ordination between the performer's body, parts of the body or a held implement,
and an object, surface, gap, or target area in the environment. That is, they typically
involve two types of co-ordination processes. First, like many complex actions,
interceptions involve a high level of co-ordination between body parts, joints or
limb segments. Co-ordination, in this respect, refers to the efficient and effective
patterning of skeleto–muscular components to achieve the task goal of interception.
The second co-ordination process involved is between key limbs (or even the
whole body) and a target object or surface in the environment (Turvey, 1990).
With respect to the latter type of co-ordination process, interceptive movements
typically require a limb segment or held implement to be in the right place at the
right time, often with an additional constraint of imparting a controlled amount of
force into an intentional collision with an object or a surface (Savelsbergh and
Bootsma, 1994).

To achieve a high level of co-ordination between body segments, and timing
and force control under the severe task constraints of sport, performers need access
to a rich variety of information such as sight of a take-off board, the sound of a
ball hitting a bat, and proprioceptive and haptic information from wielding rackets
or from the soles of the feet contacting a balance beam in gymnastics. In co-
ordinating movement with important environmental events or objects, cooperation

between the performer's perceptual sub-systems and movement sub-systems is paramount (e.g. Turvey, 1990). In fact, a highly specialised relationship between these sub-systems has evolved over an extensive period of time for all biological species to support performance of a number of different functional interceptive actions (Turvey, 1990).

The idea of the co-evolution of the perceptual and motor systems in biological species is gaining further support due to an increasing amount of integrative modelling between psychologists, movement scientists and neuroscientists. For example, recent evidence suggests that at least three different types of looming sensitive neurons have evolved in birds, functionally differentiated by the time course of their activation relative to the moment of collision with an object (Sun and Frost, 1998). It now seems that one class of neurons provides time-to-contact (Tc) information with looming objects. However, rotundal neurons in the nervous systems of pigeons do not show activation in simulated conditions when the bird is apparently moving towards an object along the same flight path. This finding suggests that Tc information, produced through self-generated motion, may be perceived in a brain structure distinct from those involved in the pick-up of information about looming objects. Further work from an integrated modelling perspective (see Keil and Bennett, Chapter 12, this volume, also Davids, Williams, Button and Court, 2001) is needed to reveal the exact nature of the specialised relationships that exist between perceptual and motor systems during interceptive actions in different biological species including humans.

Ongoing research is revealing that informational support for the performance of interceptive actions is available through the tight integration of the perceptual and movement systems, not just at the beginning, but also during and after performance. It is not surprising that a major emphasis of most chapters is on reviewing research aimed at identifying the key sources of information used in supporting interceptive movements. It is to this feature of interceptive actions that we now turn in our overview.

Information sources for interceptive movements

Previous studies have implicated a large variety of multi-modal information sources used in supporting interceptive movements. Chapter 5 by Robertson, Tremblay, Anson and Elliott, Chapter 10 by Button, and Chapter 11 by Davids, Bennett and Beak together discuss how visual, tactile, kinaesthetic, vestibular and auditory receptors provide the performer with specific information about forces, position and motion of the body and various body segments relative to important surfaces and objects during interceptive movements. Additionally, within a single modality such as vision, there is typically a variety of different sources available for the performer to pick up and use. Information for interceptive movements can be obtained from the *environment* (e.g. from accretion and deletion of background texture or from the focus of expansion information (Gibson, 1979)), from the *object* or *surface* to be acted upon by the performer (e.g. from an approaching ball or the wall of the swimming pool when performing a tumble turn), or the *limb* and/or *implement* used in contacting a moving projectile (e.g. foot or racket). These information sources are specifically discussed in the chapters by Benguigui, Ripoll and Broderick (8), Montagne and Laurent (7), Button (10), Michaels and Zaal (9), Davids, Bennett and Beak (11), Scott (20), and Maraj (21).

The psychophysical paradigm and perception for movement

The chapters by Benguigui and colleagues and by Keil and Bennett refer to early research on perceptual processes that typically occurred in the psychophysical laboratory. The aim of this work was to identify laws describing threshold limitations and detection capacities of individuals in highly controlled experimental settings. This psychophysical paradigm has dominated vision research for over a century and is still prevalent in the study of perceptual processes today (Harris and Jenkin, 1998).

Current support for the psychophysical paradigm

It has been proposed that the problem of identifying visual information sources used in interceptive timing cannot be resolved theoretically, but only through rigorous psychophysical experimentation and follow-up, field-based studies of perceptual–motor performance (e.g. see Regan, 2000; Regan and Gray, 2000). For example, although many potential information sources have been identified in previous psychophysical experiments, Regan and co-workers have argued that they need to be tested in field-based research in sport and related physical activities, such as flying aircraft. In interceptive timing tasks, Regan and Gray (2000) proposed that a potentially useful approach is to break the task problem into two questions: (i) how does the performer estimate an object's motion in depth?; and (ii) how does the performer estimate Tc with the object?

A 'psychophysically based rational approach' has been proposed for the task of designing field studies to examine Tc and motion in depth information, based on the hypothesis that the sources of information, important in visually guided movements, are processed independently of one another and independently of all other sources of visual information. According to this approach, the performance of each individual participant on a perceptual–motor task selected for isolating a specific information source could then be correlated with ranked performance on a psychophysical task emphasising the pick-up of that particular information source. Logically, if one varies the information source available to the performer, then rank order and performance on the motor task should vary too. In this way, vision scientists could logically develop and validate different psychophysical tests that could be used to predict performance on different perceptual motor tasks. In fact, such a hypothesis, although logical, is a rather contentious issue, due to perceived weaknesses of the traditional theoretical rationale behind the use of psychophysical techniques, which we discuss next.

Difficulties with the psychophysical paradigm

Lately some doubts have been raised over whether psychophysical techniques actually allow us to understand how humans *use* the information sources they pick up for the regulation of movements. This dissatisfaction was exemplified in a recent text on vision and action edited by Harris and Jenkin (1998), in which a critical attack on the artificiality of the standard methods of the psychophysical paradigm was sustained. They pointed out that the psychophysical approach for studying processes of perception is rather *reductionist* and was established in an attempt to make psychology respectable as a science in the late nineteenth century. More recently, many researchers of perceptual processes are adopting a more *functional* approach in emphasising the inextricable relationship between vision and action. According to Harris and Jenkin (1998) 'Vision in the real world is an interactive, multisensory process' (p. 1), typically emphasising an active process of exploration and the co-ordinated use of eye, head and neck muscles.

The recent emphasis on the entwined, co-evolved relationship between perception and movement systems of the human performer fits well with the functional perspective of ecological psychology, famously captured by James Gibson's (1979) reference to acting to perceive and perceiving to act during goal-directed behaviour. Gibson (1979) alluded to the process of perception as the perception of events in the environment, involving the perception of changes over space and time in the optic array. This functional view of human perception and movement contrasts markedly with a major contention of the psychophysical paradigm: that human observers are capable of being aware of their surroundings in minute detail, leading to the potential to develop measurable laws of perception. Harris and Jenkin (1998) refer to such a view of the human observer as the 'Grand Illusion' in psychology. Their arguments suggest that we need to increase our understanding of the large variety of human visual processes, some of which underpin conscious perception, and others that do not. Vision may be better analysed as a bundle of processes that support various functional human behaviours in a variety of contexts.

Issues with the 'psychophysically based rational approach'

The more general arguments raised by the critics of the psychophysical tradition, can be allied to two main difficulties with accepting the hypotheses behind the psychophysically based rational approach of Regan and colleagues. First, the correlations obtained between the psychophysical tests and performance on specific perceptual motor tasks, although statistically significant, have been unconvincing. For example, it has been noted that: 'Inter-pilot differences in the performance of the flying tasks gave moderate correlations with inter-pilot differences in the expanding flow pattern and changing-size tracking laboratory tasks (significant correlations ranged from $r = 0.67$ to 0.71)'. (Regan and Gray, 2000, p. 102). The justification for interpreting these moderate correlations values as support for the psychophysically based rational approach to studying interceptive timing behaviour was based on the fact that no correlations were found with other variables considered to be less relevant. The absence of statistical effects in some pairings does not logically imply the existence of a strong causal effect between other pairings.

A second difficulty with accepting the psychophysically based rationale is captured in Chapter 12 by Keil and Bennett. For Keil and Bennett, there is little reference to the benefits of integrating behavioural findings from psychological experiments with relevant neuroscientific data. In fact, Regan (2000) has asserted the independence of the psychophysical paradigm from validation by neurophysiological research. Keil and Bennett point out that, in contrast, over the past decade there has been a growing awareness of the value of an integrated modelling approach in which theoretical work in psychology is used to direct and support neuroscientific effort in localising brain activity associated with performance of cognitive, perceptual and motor activities (e.g. Nelson, 1995). The goal of an integrative modelling approach has been described as an attempt to integrate theory and methodology for interpreting how cognitive, perceptual and motor functions map onto specific central nervous system locations, with a view to mapping sets of the psychological operations/locations onto 'system level' models of particular tasks (see Parsons, 2001). In recognising the significance of this approach, some investigators have referred to the importance of a multi-level analysis of perceptual, cognitive and motor behaviour (e.g. Kandel, Schwartz and Jessell, 2000; Keil, Holmes, Bennett, Davids and Smith, 2000).

Distinctions in task constraints of psychophysical and field-based studies of perceptual processes

Disquiet with the psychophysical paradigm for studying processes of perception under a full range of task constraints is also voiced elsewhere in this book. In Chapter 8, Benguigui, Ripoll and Broderick argue that the implementation of classical psychophysical techniques may not provide enough relevant insights into the study of interceptive movements in real world tasks. According to Benguigui and colleagues, this tendency may be the reason for the equivocality in previous literature on sensitivity to perception of object acceleration. Some psychophysical evidence, based on computer-controlled simulation studies, exists for the capacity of humans to detect changes in object velocity, as long as the difference between initial and final velocity (the so called 'velocity ratio') exceeds 20 per cent of the mean velocity value.

Such experimental analyses are useful in telling us something about discrimination thresholds. However, we still do not understand a lot about how people *use* information on acceleration to regulate their attempts to intercept objects, or even whether they can. Under simulated motion conditions participants are typically required to make perceptual judgements to discriminate between object trajectory characteristics, rather than to perform movements in order to intercept objects in motion. But previous studies of movement timing in children and adults have revealed that skill-based or developmental differences only seem to emerge under specific experimental task constraints, (e.g. when motion properties of the object to be actually intercepted are similar to those of specific sports or physical activities undertaken by participants) (Benguigui and Ripoll, 1998). This experimental trend may have occurred because, with practice under specific task constraints, performers develop a tight coupling between perceptual and motor systems to support interception (Tresilian, 1995).

The suggestion by Benguigui and colleagues of an inherent bias in previous simulation studies of perception of object acceleration resonates clearly with the views of Harris and Jenkin (1998) on the methodological biases of traditional studies of perceptual processes. The conclusion is that more research is needed to understand the nature of the multiple sources of information used to constrain natural interceptive actions. The nature and use of information sources differ when anticipating, judging or discriminating simulated motions, compared with when actually moving to intercept; distinctions captured well in the chapter by Benguigui and colleagues. The issue of how information and perceptual strategies differ as a function of task constraints in investigations of interception is considered in more detail next.

Receptor and perceptual anticipatory processes

Tresilian (e.g. 1994, 1995) has outlined a number of key differences between traditional laboratory methodologies for studying processes of perception and movement, and the task constraints of natural interceptive movements such as catching, batting or running towards a take-off board. For example, an inordinate emphasis on the use of simulated motion has led to the popularity of coincident timing tasks in which participants have to typically *predict* when a (suddenly occluded) object/image will arrive at a designated target point. The task constraints of motion prediction paradigms emphasise the significance of *perceptual anticipation* processes in studying how predictive visual timing processes are used for interception. In perceptual anticipation tasks, participants are permitted to see only a part of the trajectory of the object image on the computer screen, for example, and are required to predict the arrival time of the object image at a designated target point. Those task constraints require them to represent part of the approach trajectory of an object image in short term memory to predict its time to arrival at a target location (e.g. see Todd, 1981; Bootsma and Oudejans, 1993). This traditional emphasis in designing studies to investigate predictive visual processes fitted well with the dominant theoretical view of hierarchically-organised perceptual and movement systems (see Poulton, 1957; Williams, Davids and Williams, 1999). From this perspective, the performer is highly dependent on accurate perception of spatio–temporal characteristics of projectile motion in order to programme the movement of an effector towards a predicted future contact point.

These task constraints differ considerably from those involved in most natural interceptive actions where the emphasis is on *receptor anticipation* processes (Poulton, 1957; Williams, Davids and Williams, 1999; Davids, Kingsbury, Bennett and Handford, 2001). Under the task constraints of a natural interceptive action like ball catching or cricket batting, participants are typically able to continuously regulate movements by viewing the ball until it arrives at the location of the hands or the bat, and do not need to perceptually construct the ball's flight path from earlier remembered information from ball flight. This view of the task constraints of natural interceptive actions fits well with the concept of perception–movement coupling in ecological psychology, which promotes a strategy of prospective control of movement. Prospection is based on a heterarchical view of the performer, and an integrated relationship between movement and perceptual systems. It involves a close and continuous coupling of movement and perceptual systems founded on the relationship between the instantaneous states of the performer and environment during task performance (Montagne, Laurent, Durey and Bootsma, 1999).

One possibility is that the different constraints of motion prediction and natural interceptive tasks might imply the existence of different control mechanisms for successful completion of each type of task. For example, the slower velocities used in perceptual anticipation tasks (typically >1 s) might permit the perceptual construction of the stimulus trajectory for prediction of future contact points. In natural interceptive actions, however, movement execution times are typically more brief (e.g. 300 ms for one-handed catching at 10 m/s (Alderson, Sully and Sully, 1974)), facilitating the development of strategies of continuous regulation or perception-movement coupling (Tresilian, 1995; Bootsma, Fayt, Zaal and Laurent 1997).

Evidence for functional relevance of natural interceptive actions

Extant data suggest that performers find the task constraints of natural interceptive actions more functionally relevant than psychophysically-based experiments. In computer simulation studies, participants usually underestimate time to arrival of a stimulus object at a designated location point on the monitor screen. The amount of underestimation increases with increasing time to arrival (e.g. see data from Schiff and Detwiler, 1979; McLeod and Ross, 1983; Schiff and Oldak, 1990, and Kaiser and Mowafy, 1993). Tresilian (1994) has calculated that the average underestimate of reported time to arrival in these tasks is around 60 per cent of actual time to arrival at the point of execution of the button press, with the standard deviation (SD) of the estimates being 50 per cent. These error margins and levels of variability suggest that participants are not familiar with these task constraints and rarely come across them in the real world. In contrast, data on timing from adults and infants suggest that the large amount of variability in estimated time to arrival is often not observed in natural tasks such as fast interceptive actions (see section below on spatio–temporal constraints of interceptive movements which documents the results of several studies of interceptive actions in sport). Tresilian (1995) highlighted the fact that 'the variability (standard deviation of response times) of responses in CA [coincidence anticipation] tasks is some five or six times greater than that observed in IAs [interceptive actions] performed under the same stimulus conditions' (p. 237; see also data from Bootsma (1989) and Davids, Kingsbury, Bennett and Handford (2001)).

This trend in the data is particularly apparent when skilled performers are studied (see Chapter 17 by Handford). It calls into question the use of motion prediction tasks for investigating interceptive timing movements because of the novelty of these task constraints. As outlined by Handford, practice at an interceptive action should typically lead to decreased variability in performance as a perception–movement coupling is first established and then refined by the athlete (see also Tresilian, 1995).

In summary, we have considered how task constraints may influence the nature of the information sources and control mechanisms used by performers. These arguments need to be understood in relation to the growing awareness of the need for an integrative approach to validating theoretical models of the performance of interceptive actions. In the chapters by Keil and Bennett and by Benguigui and colleagues, examples of how an integrative modelling approach may benefit understanding of interceptive actions are provided. They survey current neuroscientific evidence for the existence of multiple visual systems (see also Harris and Jenkin, 1998), which might underpin the use of different information sources and control mechanisms by performers. Next we consider how differences in task constraints may be understood in relation to the existence of multiple visual systems in humans.

Multiple visual systems: implications for interceptive actions

The basic point to understand is that many visual sub-systems might have evolved because humans need the flexibility to perform different types of activities. From a Gibsonian standpoint, a functional task-based distinction may be the rationale for the existence of different visual systems (Gibson, 1979). According to Harris and Jenkin (1998), functional divisions do not require that the visual system rigorously compartmentalises visual processes by information sources. For example, there may be many centres in the brain that make use of stereopsis information in performing different types of tasks such as 3-D object recognition, reaching and grasping, and control of locomotion towards targets in space. However, this level of duplication does not signify redundancy in the movement system. The stereopsis process might be used by humans to extract different types of visual information to perform a variety of tasks.

In interceptive actions, the flexibility of the human performer is predicated on the likelihood that there are many different sources of perceptual information available to support timing behaviour under different task constraints (Savelsbergh and Van der Kamp, 2000; Tresilian, 1999). We have explored some of these task constraints above (e.g. relative judgement, prediction motion and interceptive actions). The nature and range of these task and informational constraints are quite extensive in the context of interceptive actions. They include differences in background reference points and surface texture, object speeds, size, shape, distances, and use of implements with different inertial characteristics.

Perhaps this is why existing research indicates that people are, generally, remarkably good at performing interceptive actions. From the initial grasping lunges of a young infant to the smooth and efficient performances of skilled athletes, evidence suggests a refined capacity to perform these skills with a great degree of success. For instance, Von Hofsten (1983) has shown that infants aged around nine months display an intra-individual mean timing error of only 4.4 ms against an average reach time of 479 ms, when reaching for objects moving past them at 45 cm s⁻¹.

These findings fit neatly with Gibson's (1979) argument that visual information is continuously available to be picked up from the environment to support different types of movements and is 'usually perceivable directly, without an excessive amount of learning' (p. 143). The implication for this book is that these data may indicate a fundamental human capacity to perform interceptive movements. It is possible that, as individuals become more skilled, they may be able to exploit this fundamental capacity to perform interceptive movements in more complex and dynamic environments. Could this explanation account for how skilled athletes develop such elegantly refined timing skills, necessary for success at the highest levels of performance?

Spatio–temporal constraints of interceptive movements

During interceptive actions performers have to satisfy both temporal *and* spatial constraints on movement patterns. That is, one could organise the most fluent and beautifully timed pattern of movements, in which the limb segments are co-ordinated in proper relation and sequence, but if the location of the movement endpoint varies by a few centimetres, the task goal may not be achieved. Regan (1997) exemplified this point in estimating that skilled cricketers facing fast bowling speeds of 160 km h⁻¹ need to be able to perceptually discriminate the spatial traject-ories in depth of balls to a precision of 0.5 degrees. This level of required accuracy in task performance is also exemplified in Chapter 20 by Scott on the long jump approach phase. He discusses initial research by Lee, Lishman and Thomson (1982) who found that elite jumpers often demonstrated an inter-trial error margin of around 8 cm in placing the foot on the take-off board at the end of a 40-metre run up.

Failure to intercept can also occur if one makes the mistake of being in the right place but at the wrong time. Indeed, the margin of timing failure in many interceptive movements can be extremely small, as evidenced in studies of catching and hitting tasks. For instance, Alderson, Sully and Sully (1974) showed that errors could occur if skilled catchers varied the timing of hand closure around a ball during the grasp phase by around 16 ms. Response timing precision at the point of movement execution in cricket batting is even more demanding. Regan (1997) has demonstrated that accurate timing of a cricket stroke can have a margin of failure of around ± 2.5 ms at the point of movement execution.

Force control and interceptive movements

However, being in the right place at the right time is only a part of the challenge for many sport performers. The importance of force control, whilst recognised in key definitions, is rarely addressed in studies of interceptive movements. In this book, Chapter 18 by Li and Turrell, Chapter 19 by Glazier, Davids and Bartlett, and Chapter 6 by Masters, Law and Maxwell, provide overviews of current literature on grip force and force control. These are defined as important characteristics in the performance of striking tasks involved in cricket, tennis and golf. As Li and Turrell explain, under such task constraints, good control of an implement enhances stroke accuracy and is predicated on adequate grip force control. For example, when batting in cricket, as Glazier, Davids and Bartlett point out, it is apparent that the player's grip on the bat handle represents the surface of the interface between the player and implement. Good quality control of the ball during a cover drive depends on the ability to produce an appropriate level of grip force to counter the load force produced by the cricket ball contacting the surface of the bat. If the ball is successfully intercepted on the centre of percussion of the bat, then no excessive forces are transferred to the hands, resulting in little or no post-impact reactive grip forces for the batter to deal with. Striking the ball off-centre on the bat requires a refined modulation of the relationship between grip force and loading force. Skilled use of vision for placing the bat at the right place and at the right time will contribute to the accuracy of strike, resulting in little need to use energy and muscular forces to modulate grip. Even under more static task constraints, such as in golf putting, accurate force control of the implement mediates successful striking performance. For example, Masters, Law and Maxwell calculate that golfers need to adhere to maximum velocity constraints of 4.3 ft/s for a golf ball travelling over a hole, if it is to successfully fall in.

To summarise the first part of this introductory overview, we have begun by highlighting the prevalence of interceptive actions in everyday life activities and in sport, exemplified by the exacting perceptual–motor demands of many tasks such as catching, hitting and running towards targets. In order to successfully perform these actions, it is clear that performers need information to regulate their movements. The chapters in this book discuss some of the current theoretical explanations for how sport performers attempt to satisfy these exacting spatio–temporal task constraints. Two main frameworks are addressed in the book, and in the rest of this chapter we provide a brief summary of these major theoretical perspectives for the reader.

Different perspectives on interceptive actions

Cognitive science interpretations

How can we theoretically model the performance of interceptive actions in sport? The traditional view is that the visual system requires mediation by a high-level internal mechanism that generates perceptual and motor representations for predicting interceptive timing (e.g. Regan, 2000; Smeets, Brenner, Trebuchet and Mestre, 1996). In many chapters the traditional emphasis on the role of advance information sources in interceptive timing movements is explored. This approach is typically adopted in research on interceptive actions from a cognitive science perspective. For example, in Chapter 2, Williams and Starkes focus on the role of cognitive factors in skilled performance of interceptive movements, particularly anticipatory processes. They refer to the extensive programme of work undertaken during the past three decades using various forms of film occlusion technique to examine accuracy and response speed in groups of experts and novices in a variety of interceptive tasks, including many ball sports. A consistent finding has been that the expert advantage is based on a high level of domain-specific knowledge, amongst other factors.

Williams and Starkes take a selected look at research proposing various ways in which the expert's task-specific knowledge base may provide performance advantages. Expertise in interceptive actions is examined with reference to both historical and contemporary literature, starting with a discussion of important findings from classic studies by Hubbard and Seng (1954) and the programme of work by Whiting and colleagues (e.g Whiting, 1968, 1969; Whiting, Alderson and Sanderson, 1973) in the UK just over a decade later. The latter programme used interceptive movements as a task vehicle for studying the information process- ing capacities of the human performer, investigating such questions as the signal- to-noise ratio in perceiving information for movement, the minimal amount of information that skilled performers need to successfully intercept a ball and the time during the trajectory when they need that information (for an overview see Williams, Davids and Williams, 1999). Although Williams and Starkes discuss some of the main developments in the cognitive science literature on interceptive movements, such as the operational timing hypothesis, the major focus of their chapter is on the relationship between anticipation and successful performance of interceptive movements. In their chapter, the potential benefits of pattern recogni- tion skills, advance cue utilisation and the effective use of subjective probabilities by highly skilled performers are considered.

Visual search behaviours in information pick-up

Cauraugh and Janelle in Chapter 3 pick up this particular line of analysis and extend it to the study of visual search behaviours in skilled racket games players. They pose the question: why do skilled racket games players seem to have all the time they need to execute appropriate movements? Analysing eye movement behaviour in badminton, squash and tennis, they discuss the strategies that permit skilled performers to make quick and accurate decisions in selecting and initiating appropriate motor responses. Their integrated review of literature summarises the current state of knowledge concerning anticipation and decision-making in racket sports. Extant data on visual search strategies and cue utilisation findings are outlined. Accordingly, reliable differences reported among athletes at various levels of expertise are highlighted, and implications of these findings for training of perceptual skills are discussed.

Cauraugh and Janelle highlight the fact that the questions of where, when and how racket games players look for visual information for action have received a considerable amount of attention in the literature on perceptual and motor processes in sport. Their conclusion is in line with that of Land and McLeod (2000) who argued that looking in the right way, in the right place and at the right time is a fundamental ingredient for successful performance of interceptive actions, particularly those involving high levels of projectile velocity as a critical feature of the task constraints. The difficulty in understanding how task constraints influence visual search behaviour has been compounded by the fact that much of the previous and existing research on control of gaze has tended to emphasise perceptual task constraints, to the exclusion of movement, and has been dominated by laboratory-based studies (see Williams and Davids, 1998). For these reasons, it is not readily apparent whether the gaze behaviours observed in the laboratory would appear under the task constraints of natural interceptive actions.

Visual search during natural interceptive actions

The study of cricket batting by Land and McLeod (2000) is an exception to this tendency. They argued that, because previous research has implicated the fovea and parafovea in the pick-up of information about ball approach in cricket, it was important to know where batsmen look when facing fast bowling. To answer this question, they examined eye movements from three mixed ability batsmen when facing fast bowling. Balls were delivered from a bowling machine at 25 m s^{-1}. Key findings indicated that the fovea was directed to the ball the moment it appeared from the mouth of the ball machine, at the bounce point, and for about 200 ms after the bounce. For the final part of trajectory, approach the eyes 'loosely' tracked the ball (implying a 'washing' of the ball's image across the retina), confirming data from other studies of gaze control during natural interceptive actions discussed in the chapter by Cauraugh and Janelle (e.g. Bahill and LaRitz, 1984; Ripoll and Fleurance, 1988; Singer *et al.*, 1998). Land and McLeod (2000) found that a large saccade was used to move the direction of gaze from the mouth of ball machine to the bounce point before the ball arrived there. Apparently, the fovea 'lay in wait' (p. 1,341) for the ball. This eye movement was called an 'anticipatory saccade', and has been reported in studies of table tennis and baseball. This finding also fits well with existing work on expert table tennis players by Ripoll and Fleurance (1988). Eye movement analysis during stroke performance revealed that the eyes and head were placed in a stable position fixated on the point between the final bounce and the point of bat–ball contact. This strategy for picking up key information from the final phase of ball flight was called 'eye–head stabilisation'. A similar visual strategy, termed 'quiet eye', allowing performers to fixate a target early and stabilise gaze on a critical location point immediately prior to the onset of movement, has been observed in a basketball-shooting task by Vickers (1996). Clearly, there is a need for further studies on the visual search behaviours of skilled performers of interceptive actions so that we can identify the patterns that facilitate the pick-up of key sources of optical information during actual performance.

But it is important to not just investigate the eye movement behaviours of skilled performers. The skill level analysis by Land and McLeod (2000) revealed broadly similar patterns of visual search between performers, but there were some key differences to reflect different abilities. The batsman with the lowest skill level started saccades too late and was more variable in the timing of the saccade than the high and intermediate skill level performers. The main difference between the lower skill level player and the other two players was the speed and variability of commencing the initial saccade. The most skilled performer used an optimal mix of smooth pursuit and saccadic eye movements to watch the ball.

Because all the batsmen did not watch the ball between release and bounce, the authors argued that image expansion information could not have been used for estimating time to contact. However, this conclusion is somewhat contradictory since the authors believed that information from the bounce point was most crucial for stroke making against fast bowling in cricket. Saccades before this point are geared toward ensuring that the fixation point matched the bounce point as soon as possible. The bounce point was seen as being crucial to the discontinuity of the ball's velocity, and performers fixated on the ball for over 200 ms after this point, a value entirely within the limits of using retinal image expansion information for visual timing of the stroke. Could this visual search strategy have been a function of the task constraints captured in the amount of deviation that is possible when a cricket ball moves off the seam after contact with the ground? This is a question discussed in Chapter 19 by Glazier, Davids and Bartlett. Although the answer is unclear from the data on cricket batting, Glazier and colleagues point out that Land and McLeod (2000) did not actually rule out the use of image expansion and binocular disparity *after* the bounce as late sources of information used for timing the stroke. Their conclusion was that cricket batsmen are able to pick up and use a number of visual information sources in deciding where and when to initiate the stroke in relation to ball trajectory and bounce. This conclusion fits well with extant data in ecological psychology (e.g. Savelsbergh and Van der Kamp, 2000) and is a critical feature of skilled behaviour resulting from learning. The skill differences noted in the study by Land and McLeod (2000) raise some pertinent issues about learning to perform interceptive actions. That is an important issue that we examine next.

Learning interceptive actions: cognitive science interpretations

The issue of learning of interceptive actions is examined from a cognitive science perspective in a number of chapters. For example, in Chapter 2 Williams and Starkes briefly discuss the nature of the information sources that performers learn to pick up and use to ensure successful performance. They outline how athletes learn how to interpret contextual information as situational probabilities of events in sport contexts.

Skill differences in the pick-up and use of sensory information to support interceptive actions in other sports is also discussed in some detail in Chapter 5 by Robertson, Tremblay, Anson and Elliott. They focus on the outcomes from a research programme on the gymnastics task of locomoting across a balance beam. During this task the performer has to accurately place a foot on the balance beam, while the head is oriented away from the support surface. Examining research on performance under two different conditions, on a balance beam and on the floor, Robertson and colleagues show how skilled gymnasts can learn to use tactile information from receptors in the feet to perform these tasks, thus becoming less dependent on visual information as they become more skilful. They argue that multiple sensory systems are involved in this type of interceptive locomotion task and learners become increasingly attuned to multiple information sources to support performance. They cannot remain dependent on visual information alone for accurate foot placement on the support surface because the required head and body orientation of aesthetic gymnastic manoeuvres prohibits looking directly at the beam.

Vision and proprioception during learning

The relationship between multiple information sources during the performance of interceptive actions with lower limb segments is discussed further in Chapter 4 by Williams and Weigelt. They review research on the role of vision and proprioception in interceptive actions. They provide a critical overview of research on vision and proprioception in catching and other upper limb interceptive movements before discussing data from some recent studies involving lower limb tasks, such as kicking a ball. Although several methodological variations in the literature contribute to some differences between studies, generally, it does appear that having sight of the hand is helpful during one-handed catching. However, several studies have shown that the relative importance of vision and proprioception during interceptive movements interacts with performer skill level and the spatio–temporal constraints of the task (e.g. Davids, Palmer and Savelsbergh, 1989). For instance, in contrast to one-handed catching, having sight of the effector does not facilitate performance in tennis volleying or when catching using a baseball glove rather than a bare hand (e.g. Fischman and Mucci, 1989). Moreover, as suggested in Chapter 5 by Robertson and colleagues, skilled and inexperienced performers of interceptive actions also seem to become less reliant on visual proprioception as task accuracy requirements decrease. In lower limb tasks like controlling a soccer ball, Williams and Weigelt argue that vision of the ball during the final 115 ms prior to foot/ball contact is more important than having sight of the effector. Although performers seem able to position the foot accurately using proprioception, the ability to extract and use visual information from ball trajectory, possibly in conjunction with the foot, is crucial for successful performance. The need for further research, to corroborate these tentative findings, is highlighted by Williams and Weigelt.

Verbal instructions and implicit learning of interceptive movements

While Robertson and colleagues briefly touched on a cognitive analysis of the strategies used by learners and skilled athletes to process multiple information sources for performance of interceptive actions, the issue of processing strategies is dealt with in greater detail by Masters, Law and Maxwell in Chapter 6. They question the traditional emphasis in sport on large amounts of verbal instructions, as well as the strategy of verbalisation of performance by learners. They make the case for implicit learning of interceptive movements, focusing on research evidence supporting the significance of an 'external' focus of attention. They also point to the inappropriateness of learners developing a conscious 'over-awareness' of movement during practice. Their arguments refer to recent literature on feedback in which Wulf and colleagues have demonstrated that a qualitative focus on internally-based statements i.e. feedback emphasising awareness of the movement of specific body parts, may be detrimental to learning (e.g. Wulf, McNevin, Fuchs, Ritter and Toole, 2000).

An interesting feature of the work on implicit motor skill learning by Masters and colleagues is use of interceptive tasks such as golf putting as a vehicle for examining skill acquisition processes. With reference to the implicit learning literature, they identify two avenues of research, one focused on the acquisition of information about environmental features, the other on knowledge about the motor pattern itself. Empirical findings from their own studies, reviewed in Chapter 6, add to a growing body of data highlighting the benefits of an external focus on feedback and instructions and an emphasis on discovery learning. According to Masters and colleagues, if learners acquire skill in interceptive movements by focusing on a large pool of rules and knowledge about how to execute such movements, they can default to a conscious type of control when performance is disrupted by intervening factors such as anxiety. There are many problems with movements that are consciously regulated, discussed in some detail by Masters and colleagues. For them, a better approach is to avoid the development of verbalisable information for controlling interceptive actions by emphasising implicit learning techniques.

Implicit learning occurs in practice contexts where individuals are not formally exposed to verbal instructions to perform an interceptive movement in a particular manner. The argument proposed by Masters and colleagues is that exposing learners to too many verbal instructions leads to them 'investing' attention and effort in acquiring *verbal knowledge* that might interfere with the sequencing of motor commands for controlling movements. They point out how these findings concur with criticisms of an 'internal' focus of attention. Taken together, these findings provide some support for the relative efficacy of discovery learning of interceptive tasks, compared to more formal prescriptive approaches where coaches may instruct learners in a step-by-step procedure.

To summarise so far, cognitive science approaches to the acquisition and performance of interceptive actions emphasise the role of perceptual and motor representations in predicting the point of contact with an object or surface. Advance information can be used to predict time of arrival at the point of interception, and the initiation of an internal representation of an interceptive movement. Multiple sources of information can be used to predict timing of actions after extensive task experiences.

In the following section we examine an alternative framework for understanding processes of perception and movement in interceptive actions. It encompasses ecological psychology and dynamical systems theory and, for ease of communication, these ideas have been integrated into one framework entitled the ecological approach (see Williams, Davids and Williams, 1999). The ecological approach to studying interceptive actions can be considered as an umbrella theoretical framework that includes Gibson's (e.g. 1979) theory of direct perception, Bernstein's (1967) insights on co-ordination and control, and variant hybrids related to dynamical systems theory (for a review see Williams, Davids and Williams, 1999).

The ecological approach

Co-ordinating interceptive movements with respect to objects and surfaces in the environment

Direct perception

In research on direct perception, there is not as great an emphasis on investigating the *amount* of visual information needed to perform an interceptive task. Rather, explanations are based on the idea that there is already rich structure in the optical information available for pick-up in the environment by an organism equipped with appropriate perceptual systems. With reference to vision, James Gibson emphasised that direct perception 'is the activity of getting information from the ambient array of light. I call this a process of information pickup that involves the exploratory activity of looking around, getting around, and looking at things' (1979, p. 147). Thus, the main emphasis is on the *nature* of the information sources used to support action.

Chapter 7 by Montagne and Laurent, Chapter 8 by Benguigui, Ripoll and Broderick, and Chapter 9 by Michaels and Zaal review the first-generation theoretical models of interceptive timing movements by James Gibson's (e.g. 1979) followers, such as Lee (e.g. 1976, 1980; Lee and Young, 1985). Lee demonstrated how, in principle, the support for interceptive timing could be based on the pick-up of time-to-contact (Tc) information provided by optic variables, such as tau, rather than the computation of physical variables such as absolute distance and velocity of approach of a ball (see Williams, Davids, Burwitz and Williams, 1992, for a basic review).

It is now well accepted that the original formulations of the concept of tau are currently being subjected to some revision in the ecological psychology literature (e.g. see Tresilian (1999) and Wann (1996) for extensive reviews). The chapter by Montagne and Laurent discusses a re-conceptualisation of tau and increasing awareness of the need to identify variables other than 'visual tau' in accounts of interceptive timing. It is clear that this important theoretical progression is being based on studies of interceptive movements.

Multiple sources of information and the degrees of freedom problem

In fact, there have been some cogent arguments that a variety of information sources may be used to provide a platform for the flexible adaptations needed by skilled athletes during performance of interceptive actions.

For example, Savelsbergh and Van der Kamp (2000) used the task vehicle of interceptive actions to respond to recent criticisms of extant research on tau by revisiting previous data from a number of studies. They outlined a Gibsonian-inspired framework for interpreting discrepancies in the literature, including differences between binocular and monocular viewing conditions and the size–arrival effect (for overviews see Williams, Davids and Williams, 1999; Van der Kamp, Savelsbergh and Smeets, 1997; DeLucia and Warren, 1994). It is now becoming apparent that monocular tau is not the only optical information source for co-ordinating and controlling interceptive actions.

The literature reveals a variety of information sources for timing behaviour, including monocular tau, tau-function of disparity, optical size, looming or relative rate of constriction, and relative distance between object and observer (zeta-ratio) (see Bootsma and Oudejans, 1993; Tresilian, 1994; Laurent, Montagne and Durey, 1996; Wann, 1996). Spatial information sources include vertical optical acceleration, binocular information for motion in depth, and rates of accretion and decretion of optical texture elements (see Beverley and Regan, 1973; Fitch and Turvey, 1978; Michaels and Oudejans, 1992; Peper, Bootsma, Mestre and Bakker, 1994; Oudejans, Michaels, Bakker and Davids, 1999). This range of optical (and other) sources of information for regulating timing and spatial adaptations is highly functional since it can support the goal-directed behaviour of skilled athletes under a variety of performance settings and different task constraints.

Savelsbergh and Van der Kamp (2000) argued that performers of interceptive actions need to learn to exploit a variety of information sources available to support performance. The task for learners is to establish a reliable information–movement coupling, and then search for other available sources during practice under the typical range of task constraints experienced during interceptive tasks such as ball games and long jumping. This practice strategy enhances flexibility of perceptual behaviour and mirrors the Bernsteinian (1967) perspective on coping with the multitude of movement system degrees of freedom. A similar explanation exists for the task of learning to cross a balance beam (see the discussion of low level and higher order afference offered in Chapter 5 by Robertson and colleagues). It seems that, at first, coaches and athletes need to discover the basic sources of information available for regulating interceptive movements, before later engaging in variable practice to discover a wider variety of useful informational constraints.

Multiple information sources for interceptive movements: recent models

In Chapter 7 Montagne and Laurent review the progress of recent models of interceptive timing that emphasise the role of multiple information sources, such as the dipole model (Rushton and Wann, 1999) and the required velocity model (e.g. Peper, Bootsma, Mestre and Bakker, 1994; Bootsma, Fayt, Zaal and Laurent, 1997; Montagne, Fraisse, Ripoll and Laurent, 2000).

Dipole model

Rushton and Wann (1999) proposed that several different types of optical information unequivocally specify the same physical property (e.g. the first-order temporal relation), and that there are specific information-combining laws governing an observer's access to that property. Although this relationship may seem ambiguous and maladaptive, the reverse is actually true. Rushton and Wann (1999) proposed the 'security principle' to explain how an observer might select between information sources specifying a relevant physical property. They argued that the information source supporting the earliest response would permit the most optimal adaptation for the performer in an uncertain environment.

This theoretical argument received some support in a study of locomotor pointing (placing the foot on a visible target in the environment during walking) by de Rugy, Montagne, Buekers and Laurent (e.g. 2000, 2001). They studied time to passage (TTP) to visible floor targets using a virtual reality set up. They were interested in whether two different sources, target expansion and eye-direction (to target) information, would prove equally useful for an actor. Their data suggested that the contribution of target expansion information was equal to eye-direction information early in the approach, but became negligible towards the end of the walk. Despite crucial differences in gait close to the target line, participants showed the same pointing performance. These findings are in line with Rushton and Wann's (1999) 'security principle' argument. It can be concluded that performers have different ways of accessing relevant physical properties of the environment (in that study, TTP) during interceptive actions, particularly, as Gibson (1979) stated, those invariant variables that are 'commensurate with the body of the observer himself' (p. 143). When the system is confronted with conflicting information sources, the source providing the basis for the earliest response will be taken, helping resolve potential conflict. These findings help explain the principles behind the selection of information from the many perceptual degrees of freedom available to support interceptive movements.

Required velocity model

In Chapter 7, Montagne and Laurent discuss results from their own experiments supporting the notion of laws of control, obtained by manipulating the variables that determine the required velocity of a limb for intercepting a moving object. Performance of interceptive actions requires participants to regulate the amount of acceleration of a limb towards an object/target, on the basis of the optically-specified differential between required velocity and current velocity (e.g. Bootsma, Fayt, Zaal and Laurent, 1997; Montagne, Laurent, Durey and Bootsma, 1999; Peper, Bootsma, Mestre and Bakker, 1994).

Prospective vs. predictive control strategies

Earlier in this chapter we discussed the basic differences between predictive visual timing and prospective control as perceptual strategies for performing interceptive actions. There has been a traditional emphasis on prediction in control strategies for catching because of the belief that the extent and duration of interceptive movements need be planned in advance, based on (perceptually-acquired) knowledge of initial conditions and the point of interception (e.g. Regan, 1997; Regan and Gray, 2000; Saxberg, 1987). There are a number of logical problems with this view of movement control in interceptive actions, including an inordinate need for the perceptual system to be highly precise, the need for the postulation of dedicated internal structures (e.g. Bahill and Karnavas, 1990; McBeath, Shaffer and Kaiser, 1995) and the lack of attention to the influence of unexpected changes in flight trajectory (Montagne, Laurent, Durey and Bootsma, 1999). Montagne and Laurent's chapter discusses how a prediction-based strategy might be viewed as computationally burdensome and not very robust. In contrast, they propose 'prospective control' as a better strategy, emphasising a close and continuous coupling between information and movement. The importance of this relationship has been emphasised by Montagne, Laurent, Durey and Bootsma (1999) who argued that 'The circular causality relations between information and movement can be described formally by laws of control, which relate generic kinetic properties of movement to generic kinematic properties of perceptual flow' (p. 87). They argued that the velocity of the movement required for interception at each instance is equal to the ratio of the distance that an intercepting effector has to cover, divided by the first-order time-to-contact.

Tests of the validity of the prospective basis of the required velocity model have been thin on the ground, but the data have provided some strong support. Montagne, Laurent, Durey and Bootsma (1999) were interested in the presence of movements, particularly reversal movements when the hand was positioned at the actual point of interception to begin with. Data showed that the reversal rate was higher for a perpendicular ball trajectory (ball travelling straight to hand), than for two-angled approaches. This finding would not be expected with a predictive strategy in which no movement need be planned in perpendicular trajectory conditions because the hand was already at the appropriate location for interception (movement reversals occurred in over 50 per cent of these trials). Furthermore, Montagne, Laurent, Durey and Bootsma (1999) argued that there was a pattern to the reversals in which the number of left–right reversals was higher for outward ball trajectories and right–left reversals greater for inward trajectories.

Kinematics of interceptive movements analysed by Montagne, Laurent, Durey and Bootsma (1999) provided support for the 'prospection' hypothesis. Despite all ball trajectories heading towards the same interception point, different kinematic profiles were found for different combinations of angle of approach and hand start positions. These data showed that the difference between the required and current velocity of the hand converges to zero as the time remaining to ball–hand contact decreases. The findings fit neatly with the prospective control strategy. The approach to zero in this relationship does not happen suddenly in a short time period, due to the potential for perturbation to the sensitive grasp phase of the catching movement. The results of Montagne, Laurent, Durey and Bootsma (1999) showed that the convergence to zero between current and required velocity happens around 300 ms before ball–hand contact, regardless of initial start conditions. This strategy allowed the performer's hand to reach the interception point at the same time as the ball. As Montagne and Laurent argue, however, the required velocity model needs refinement through further experimentation. Indeed, some tests of the model have accounted for only 55 per cent of the observed total variance in the data (see Montagne, Cornus, Glize, Quaine and Laurent, 2000).

Challenges for the modelling of a prospective control strategy

An interesting feature of the data in the Montagne, Laurent, Durey and Bootsma (1999) study concerns the high level of inter-individual variability in the approach to the task of intercepting the ball. Sometimes movement reversals did not occur when the ball was on an inward and outward trajectory, and in the perpendicular condition, approximately 30 per cent of trials involved reversals when the hand was already at the interception point. To explain these findings, the authors argued that prospective strategies should not be viewed as deterministic in prescribing behaviour. Prospective strategies can be applied in different ways depending on the performer's intentions, a subject that is discussed in more detail in Chapter 13 by Button and Summers. Furthermore, the task constraints were not severe in the Montagne, Laurent, Durey and Bootsma (1999) study and the total number of trials performed on this novel task was only 45 per participant. These factors may have encouraged some amount of task exploration by the participants.

A key question, raised in Chapter 19 by Glazier and colleagues, is whether the model can be generalised to other interceptive task constraints. These include when both temporal and spatial constraints are varied, for example under higher velocity conditions, when participants have to perform different types of interceptive actions, perhaps using different effector systems, and when the moving object's speed varies due to acceleration (the type of task constraints discussed in the chapter by Benguigui and colleagues). The latter generalisation is important to study because, whenever the velocity of a moving object varies, TC_1 and the real time-to-contact differ. Because of this apparent discrepancy, some authors have questioned whether TC_1 is used to control goal-directed interceptive actions in the real world. Despite this argument, the existence of a difference between TC_1 and real time-to-contact does not necessarily indicate that successful interceptive strategies do not involve TC_1. This conclusion can be drawn because TC_1 allows performers not to rely solely on real time-to-contact information (Lee *et al.*, 1983), an argument supported by Peper, Bootsma, Mestre and Bakker's (1994) experiment with non-constant velocities. Despite the need for more work, the extant data suggest that TC_1 is a relevant property of the actor–environment system that constrains the kinematics of an interceptive movement when a projectile is approaching the performer.

Taking a running jump

Not all the chapters focusing on optical sources of information for co-ordinating interceptive actions deal with the case of approaching objects, such as in ball games. Chapter 20 by Scott and Chapter 21 by Maraj examine the long jump and triple jump as interceptive actions involving locomotion of a performer towards important surfaces in the environment. As noted earlier, the task of locomotor pointing has proved to be a valuable tool in laboratory studies of visuo–motor control of locomotion (e.g. de Rugy, Montagne, Buekers and Laurent, 2000, 2001). In the main horizontal jumps, locomotor pointing involves placing the foot on the take-off board, a target area of 20 cm width. Athletes attempt to strike the take-off board with their leading foot prior to initiating the flight phase. The task constraints of the long jump run-up phase dictate that, in the final stride, the jumper needs to place the foot close to the leading edge of the take-off board with as much horizontal velocity as possible.

Regulation of gait in the approach phase of the jumps

Interesting questions concern the control mechanisms and the information sources used to regulate gait in the run-up phase of the horizontal jumps. Early ideas proposed by Lee, Lishman and Thomson (1982) suggested how light reflected from the take-off board in long jumping could be used as information to adjust flight times in regulating the stride pattern in the approach phase. As Scott points out in Chapter 20, Lee, Lishman and Thomson (1982) were quite specific in their views about the key optical information source used by jumpers to regulate gait in judging time to contact with the board. It has since become apparent that Lee, Lishman and Thomson (1982) were arguing for a form of local tau (Tresilian, 1990, 1991) by suggesting that 'time-to-contact is specified directly by a single optical parameter, the inverse of the relative rate of dilation of the image of the board' (p. 456).

Maraj and Scott both highlight a plethora of studies on the long jump approach phase endorsing the view of a two-phase approach indexed by ascending and descending trends in variability of footfall placements between trials. Scott indicates that within this body of work there exist different opinions on why there may be two phases in the approach, and most recently whether they exist at all. Apart from the practical interest of how long jumpers cope with the problem of running to jump from a finite target area, these studies are also imbued with considerable theoretical curiosity. First, there is the pertinent issue whether the two phases signal different control mechanisms at work. Second, there is a related issue concerning the information sources used to regulate gait during the approach phase in order to spatially and temporally co-ordinate the strike and take-off phase of the jump.

Initial attempts to investigate information for regulating gait

Some previous interpretations of the initial phase of the approach run have proposed that the low levels of inter-trial variability in footfall placement may indicate a pre-programming control mechanism that helps the skilled athlete to stereotype a large portion of the approach (e.g. Lee, Lishman and Thomson, 1982; Berg, Wade and Greer, 1994). The descending variability evidenced in the second phase of the run up has been interpreted as evidence for the implementation of a visual regulation strategy as the athlete approaches the take-off board. In support of this view, the data overviewed in Chapter 21 by Maraj show different patterns of footfall placements over trials when the take-off board was present or removed. However, the literature has shown a large amount of within-individual (Lee, Lishman and Thomson, 1982) and between-individual (Berg, Wade and Greer, 1994) variability on the stride at which visual regulation was purported to take over from the pre-programming mechanism. These levels of variability call into question proposals for such a dichotomous explanation of gait control. This is an excellent example of how variability in movement behaviour can tell us something interesting about processes of perception and movement. At this point a brief detour would allow us to exploit the opportunity to discuss the importance of these observed levels of variability in performance.

New views on movement variability

In fact, the problem of how to interpret the meaning of inter- and intra-individual variability in performance measures has become particularly pertinent in the movement co-ordination literature in recent years (e.g. see chapter by Lees and Davids; Newell, 1986; Newell and Slifkin, 1998; Button and Davids, 1999; Slifkin and Newell, 1999). Technological advances in recording fine-grained data on complex movements in sport are revealing high levels of movement variability. For example, pattern-recognition algorithms, used in analysing national and international-class athletes performing relatively stable actions, such as discus and javelin throwing, have picked out performance 'clustering' showing high levels of intra-individual variability between different competitions, and even between training sessions (Bauer and Schöllhorn, 1997). Moreover, observed variability in joint angles and angular velocity data from the throws was higher in groups of international-level athletes compared to national competitors. The algorithm was even able to identify clusters associated with gender differences and national 'performance styles' of these tasks. The identification of clusters of within- and between-athlete performances was all the more striking when it is considered that the pattern-recognition algorithm only sampled the final 200 ms of the throws.

The previous tendency to ignore movement variability has been viewed as: (i) a legacy of the traditional tendency to rely on outcome measures and error scores from pooled group data; and, (ii) a function of the types of experimental tasks preferred in traditional laboratory studies of motor learning and control (e.g. tracking tasks) (Slifkin and Newell, 1999). This type of approach has been influential in the effort to establish laws of action that are generalisable, on the basis of sample parameters, to wider populations. However, it is becoming increasingly apparent that the existence of subtle variations over trials, and as performance conditions change, may be interpreted as more than mere system noise or error (Slifkin and Newell, 1999). In this respect, it is apparent that the statistical technique of pooling group data or blocking trials, to examine central tendencies and dispersion, may have limited value and may not permit insights into the way that individuals cope with the task of forming information–movement coupling during interceptive actions (see Newell, Liu and Meyer-Kress, 2001).

Continuous perception–movement coupling

So, although pooled data from previous studies of the long jump seemed to imply the implementation of a visual regulation strategy initiated at around four strides from the take-off board, the large amount of inter-individual variability noted may actually have indicated that different strategies were being used by performers (e.g. Montagne, Cornus, Glize, Quaine and Laurent, 2000). Moreover, due to the participants' initial start distance from the take-off board, and because the take-off board does not directly approach the eye, doubts exist over the validity of the original statement of Lee, Lishman and Thomson (1982) on the specific optical information source to regulate gait.

Prospective control of gait during the long jump approach phase

Scott summarises, in his chapter, recent methodological advances on the issue of the type of control strategy adopted by jumpers during the approach phase. Montagne *et al.* (2000) have advocated the use of a trial-by-trial method, rather than an inter-trial technique, for analysing variability in footfall placement in the approach phase. Maraj points out that the latter has been the generally accepted dependent variable for capturing performance on locomotor pointing tasks such as long jumping. The inter-trial technique has emphasised pooled data over trials, whereas the trial-by-trial approach involves a more rigorous analysis of individual trials. Various measures of footfall placement were made in the study by Montagne *et al.* (2000), including amount of adjustment made in each trial (the difference between the value of the current step and mean step length), amount of adjustment needed (the difference between the current toe–target distance and the mean toe–target distance) and coherence of the adjustment made. The latter is an interesting development related to the values of footfall placement at a given step number relative to the adjustment needed at the previous step number. In order to understand how participants were regulating action, the authors calculated the relationship between the step number at which regulation was initiated and the mean amount of adjustment needed during the remaining steps to the target.

Their evidence supported the utility of the continuous perception–movement coupling approach indicated by an inverse relationship between the amount of variability in footfall placement and the timing of the adjustment made by athletes during the run-up phase. The idea of a continuous perception–movement control strategy was supported by an analysis of the coefficients of determination plotted for the relationship between the amount of adjustment to gait produced and the amount needed for each trial, as jumpers neared the take-off board.

Potential information sources for specifying first-order time before passage over the take-off board

If a continuous perception–movement coupling strategy were available for use by a jumper, then it is still apparent that the sources of information used to support the existence of a prospective mode of control need to be investigated. In his chapter, Scott points out that we do not, as yet, understand the precise nature of important information sources used by jumpers to regulate gait in the approach phase.

Global tau　One possibility that Scott discusses is that global tau information, defined by Tresilian (1990, 1991) as the relative rate of expansion of the gap between the focus of expansion of the optic flow field and an environmental texture point (in this case the take-off board), could provide the source of information used to regulate gait when running to jump (for an explanation, see Williams, Davids and Williams, 1999). The findings of Maraj (1999), in which the take-off board was removed or present during triple jumping, may be explained by the board's use as a environmental texture element relative to a focus of expansion, as a form of global tau information.

Vertical axis information　Recently, de Rugy, Montagne, Buekers and Laurent (2000) have argued that there are at least four different sources of visual information that can specify time remaining before jumpers pass over the take-off board. They reviewed the progress of research on tau involving definitions related to the inverse of the relative rate of dilation of the retinal image of the object, as well as the inverse of the relative rate of the optical distance separating the object from the direction of motion (identified as global tau by Scott). In their paper, de Rugy, Montagne, Buekers and Laurent (2000) proposed a further definition related to the angle created by the vertical axis at the point of observation and the eye–object direction and its variation over time. The reason for the proposal of a further source of information to specify the physical property of time before passing over a take-off board is that there are limitations to the pick up and use of all the sources of information proposed in earlier work on tau.

The use of the vertical axis for providing information for timing relative approach is theoretically interesting because it provides optical gap information on the location of a specific target and the vertical axis at the point of observation. If the optical information sources available from direction of motion were not stable in the environment, then vertical axis information would be still available at constant approach velocity from extra-retinal sources such as the vestibular apparatus. The benefits of multi-modal and multiple sources of information have all been outlined earlier, but the main point is that they afford a high level of flexibility in dynamic performance contexts.

To summarise, the chapters discussed in this section all examine the nature of the co-ordination between the (limbs of the) performer and information sources in the complex, dynamic environments in which interceptive movements occur. There are also several other chapters in this book that overview how patterns of co-ordination can arise between movement system components during interceptive movements. We turn to this issue next.

Co-ordinating degrees of freedom in the movement system

Dynamical systems theory

Chapter 13 by Button and Summers, Chapter 14 by Tayler, Chapter 15 by Temprado, Chapter 16 by Lees and Davids, and Chapter 17 by Handford, highlight how the number of works devoted to the study of co-ordination in the movement system has increased considerably within the last two decades. The chapter by Button and Summers highlights how the application of principles of co-ordination dynamics to the study of movement systems emphasises an abstract, mathematical description of the kinematics (space-time displacements of limb segments) of movement behaviour (Beek, Peper and Stegeman, 1995). The relatively recent concern with human movement systems as dynamical systems, reflects the desire to understand the mechanisms involved in mastering the redundant degrees of freedom of the neuro–musculo–skeletal system during the process of assembling stable but flexible patterns of movement co-ordination. This issue in motor behaviour research has become known as 'Bernstein's problem' (see Bernstein, 1967). The quest to understand Bernstein's problem has led to many studies of co-ordination in interceptive actions, as this book demonstrates. From a dynamical systems theoretical perspective, many studies of interceptive actions have examined the involvement of self-organisation processes in the human movement system as a potential solution to Bernstein's (1967) problem.

Self-organisation in catching behaviour

Polman, Whiting and Savelsbergh (1996) have shown how self-organisation may help performers adapt to rapidly changing task constraints during interceptive actions. To examine the stability and flexibility of movement system dynamics during performance of a one-handed interceptive action, they manipulated timing of the grasp by springloading the fingers of the grasping hand of participants. They managed to perturb the grasp phase of the one-handed catching movement by attaching flexible wires to the fingers of a glove worn by participants in a springloaded system. Participants started with their fingers closed and were required to time the opening of their hand as a ball on a pendulum approached them. Two masses (0.6 kg and 1.6 kg) were used to manipulate the perturbing force to be resisted, in addition to a baseline (non-perturbed) condition. Significant differences observed between baseline and perturbed conditions were for two grasp variables: (i) the extent of the hand aperture at the time of catching (baseline less than both perturbed conditions); and (ii) the maximal closing velocity of the fingers (baseline condition significantly faster than the 0.6 kg condition only). By perturbing an element of the movement system (i.e. by adding weights to the fingers of the catching hand), Polman, Whiting and Savelsbergh (1996) managed to dissociate the time of maximal closing velocity of the grasp component of one-handed catching from the parameter of overall movement time.

Their data support the dynamical systems view that order is available for 'free' in the skeletomuscular system, which good catchers learn to exploit in the organisation of interceptive actions. A dynamical systems theoretical approach considers that the specific co-ordination pattern required in any environmental context emerges as a function of the existing task constraints (see Davids, Handford and Williams, 1994; Williams, Davids and Williams, 1999). For example, skilled performers learn to take advantage of key inherent biomechanical properties in the spring-like qualities of muscle and the self-organising relationship between arm and finger movements during one-handed catching.

Furthermore, it seems that emergent behaviour is not just a feature of one-handed interceptive movements. The first part of Chapter 14 by Tayler highlights how two-handed catching can be characterised by a bimanual co-ordinative structure, exemplifying what Bernstein (1967) called 'synergies' in the motor system. Synergies are solutions to the degrees of freedom problem faced by movement systems during goal-directed behaviour. Synergies involve movement system degrees of freedom being co-ordinated into greater structures that become increasingly stable with extensive task experience and practice. Tayler's analysis of extant data from skilled catchers reveals support for a co-ordinative structure model of bimanual co-ordination. The separate limbs involved in catching, although having to move different distances when catching to the side of the body's vertical midline, showed a highly stable synchronous inter-limb pattern of movement velocity and acceleration during two-handed catching of a tennis ball.

Learning interceptive movements: dynamical systems interpretations

Perceptual–motor landscapes

The study of emergent, self-organisation processes under constraints leads neatly to questions concerning development, learning and practice of interceptive movements. A key issue concerns the relationship between stability and flexibility of movement patterns during goal-directed behaviour. In the ecological approach, an interdisciplinary theoretical framework emphasises a neo-Darwinian perspective on processes of learning and development. The emphasis is on how functional, goal-directed patterns of behaviour are selected under constraint from a veritable landscape of perceptual–motor possibilities (Newell, 1986, 1991; Kauffmann, 1993; Turvey and Fitzpatrick, 1993; Thelen and Smith, 1994; Schmidt and Fitzpatrick, 1996; Fitzpatrick, 1998; Williams, Davids and Williams, 1999). The perceptual-motor landscape is a concept borrowed from evolutionary biology and has been applied to the study of how skilled behaviour evolves in learners (Thelen and Smith, 1994). It is considered equivalent to the hypothetical totality of unique co-ordination solutions available for each individual in specific performance contexts. The configuration of different physical and psychological characteristics, previous experiences and unique task constraints, leads to an emergent movement pattern for each individual as they search the perceptual–motor landscape for stable co-ordination solutions to an interceptive movement problem (Davids, Bennett, Handford and Jones, 1999).

The learning–development distinction

Broadly, a dynamical systems interpretation of movement skill acquisition suggests that the similarities between the development and learning of interceptive actions are more fundamental than the differences. The concept of self-organisation under constraints allows dynamical systems theorists to play down the differences between processes of learning and development. Although timescales of development and learning may differ, the same principles can explain change in the form of the dynamical movement system (Newell, Liu and Mayer-Kress, 2001). Changes to performance of interceptive actions during development and learning may both be best understood as a neo-Darwinian process due to the selection and use of information to regulate behaviour (Thelen and Smith, 1994; Davids, Bennett, Handford and Jones, 1999). The process of information-behaviour regulation is seen as being independent of the time-scale of analysis (i.e. developmental time vs. performance real-time). The dichotomy between development on the one hand and learning on the other, a manifestation of the traditional nature–nurture dichotomy, may be avoided (Newell and Van Emmerik, 1990).

Material in Chapter 12 by Keil and Bennett suggests that the dorsal stream has the heaviest involvement in the development and learning of interceptive movements. Given the nature of dorsal stream functioning, it is proposed that the development, learning and practice of interceptive movements is predominantly implicit, occurring without the concurrent acquisition of explicit knowledge, in agreement with the data presented and discussed in Chapter 6 by Masters, Law and Maxwell. This perspective leads neatly to the view that, during practice of interceptive actions, the role of the coach is primarily to facilitate the search for information and an appropriate co-ordination pattern by learners as outlined in Chapter 17 by Handford.

Development of stability in co-ordinative structures

The question of how co-ordination patterns become more stable with increasing task experience is taken up in the second part of Chapter 14 by Tayler. He points out that, until recently, there have been few previous studies of the development of bimanual co-ordination in children (for exceptions see Fitzpatrick, Schmidt and Lockman (1996) and Robertson (2001)). Tayler describes data from the study of the development of two-handed catching skill in children aged between five and eleven years of age. Typically, the limited amount of previous work on two-handed catching has focused on perceptual skill development as the reason for age group differences (e.g. Williams, 1992). The traditional emphasis on the role of predictive visual information for timing interceptive movements is influential here. It was argued that, as attentional and perceptual mechanisms develop, there is a concomitant improvement in the young child's ability to predict where and when a ball will arrive at the hands.

Tayler argues that the development of skill in two-handed catching may also depend on the capacity of the child to harness movement system degrees of freedom in achieving the task goal. This is typically achieved through the acquisition of a stable coupling between the two hands with practice. The acquisition of a co-ordinative structure has been shown to underpin skill differences in adults performing other interceptive movements such as the volleyball serve (see Chapter 15 by Temprado). Tayler shows how younger children can typically co-ordinate both limbs for successful completion of a two-handed catching task, as long as the ball is projected to a location which permits both limbs to move equal distances to the interception point. With even a limited amount of task experience it seems, children aged eleven years can cope with increasing complexity of task constraints and can stabilise a co-ordinative structure in which limbs move unequal distances to catch the ball. With increasing task experience and practice it seems that stable, functional bimanual co-ordinative structures can be acquired, although both limbs can be de-coupled when specific task constraints demand.

Discovery learning and self-organisation processes

In Chapter 17, Handford discusses how self-organisation processes in the movement system can be exploited by the learner when attempting to assemble a co-ordination solution for a given task goal. It is worth noting how the findings on implicit learning described by Masters and colleagues mirror experimental outcomes promoting the role of self-organisation processes during discovery-based practice in the dynamical systems literature. Handford argues that dynamical systems theory provides a fruitful framework for understanding the significance of a discovery learning strategy. The specific emphasis is on the search for the essential relationships between performer, environmental and task constraints. His chapter examines some strategies and practices for acquiring timing in discrete, self-paced interceptive skills, using the volleyball serve as an exemplar. The potential for a constraints-led approach to shed new light on contemporary principles of practice organisation is explored. Handford presents data, from research on the question of task decomposition for practice, that support the need to preserve essential information–movement relationships for successful transfer under changing task conditions. He concludes that a framework emphasising the manipulation of constraints may have much to offer in practice organisation under a variety of other task constraints in sport. Future research is encouraged to examine the possible impact in areas of skill acquisition such as instruction, observational learning and feedback provision.

Chapter 16 by Lees and Davids, and Chapter 15 by Temprado deal with the acquisition of co-ordination in interceptive movements. Lees and Davids highlight the significance of motor control and biomechanics in developing understanding of soccer kicking skills. It is argued that a dynamical systems interpretation of the processes of co-ordination and control in movements with multiple degrees of freedom signals a new era in the relationship between motor control and bio-mechanics. Biomechanical analyses of the forward motion of the kicking leg reveal the same proximo-distal sequence of joint involvement found in the study of other striking movements. In soccer kicking, a subtle co-ordination process allows the energy flows from the thigh to the shank and eventually the foot to be exploited so that the foot achieves peak linear velocity when it is adjacent to the ball. Lees and Davids discuss developmental analyses of the kicking action that support a Bernsteinian approach to restricting and exploiting movement system degrees of freedom. The authors point out that most previous studies of ball-kicking view skilled behaviour as synonymous with a high level of movement consistency. They argue that future research needs to vary task constraints and to examine skill development in longitudinal studies in order to understand the nature of the relationship between variability and consistency of performance as learners attempt to satisfy different task constraints during practice.

Self-paced extrinsic timing movements

Data from a comparison of the performance of self-paced, extrinsic timing movements in skilled and unskilled volleyball players have also been useful in providing a 'snap-shot' of the development of expertise (see Figure 1.2).

The chapters by Handford and Temprado are concerned with understanding of the acquisition of co-ordination in a special variety of interceptive movements: self-paced extrinsic timing tasks. They analyse co-ordination processes in volleyball underarm serving, as reflected in the intra-limb co-ordination of the serving arm. The strategy outlined in Temprado's chapter is based on identifying the essential variable(s) that characterise(s) co-ordination, and on determining whether the development of co-ordination consists of the transition of one stable state to another, or directly from disorder to a unique final ordered co-ordination state. In the context of interceptive actions in sport, the challenging task of modelling control parameters exemplifies the potential benefits of an interaction between the practical knowledge of the coach/player, and the theoretical knowledge of the sport scientist. Both types of knowledge can constrain the modelling process, adding to theory development and practical understanding.

In the chapter by Temprado, the co-ordination patterns of the skilled and unskilled servers are examined and found to qualitatively differ in the nature of the shoulder/wrist coupling (in-phase versus anti-phase) used by each group. It is suggested that the type of coupling between shoulder and wrist could be considered as an essential variable of intra-limb co-ordination in the volleyball serve. Moreover, the distribution of the different co-ordination patterns exhibited by each participant group revealed that the experts' pattern was not observed regularly in the initial repertoire of the novices. However, the novice pattern was sometimes apparent in the expert repertoire signalling that, under certain task constraints, experts can freeze system degrees of freedom as a solution to achieving a task goal (see Figure 15.3 in the chapter by Temprado). In this type of interceptive movement, skill acquisition seems to consist of the transition from one (stable) state of co-ordination to another, rather than the generation of a completely new pattern of co-ordination.

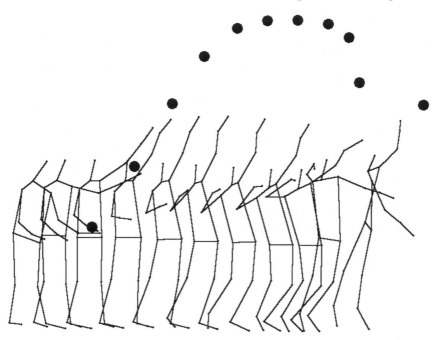

Figure 1.2 Stick figure analysis of the volleyball serve to exemplify a self-paced extrinsic timing task. The task is self-paced because the server initiates the multi-degree of freedom movement by tossing the ball into air above the serving arm. Extrinsic timing involves co-ordination and timing of the serving action with respect to the ball's trajectory. This is not a simple task as revealed by analysis of co-ordination of the whole movement pattern (see Chapter 17 by Handford and Chapter 15 by Temprado). The editors would like to acknowledge the help of Damian Kingsbury in providing the stick figure.

The influence of task and instructional constraints in the acquisition of skill in striking movements

The findings discussed in the chapter by Handford point up some interesting differences with the data of Temprado. Surprisingly, it is found that the general pattern of co-ordination in the data from *experts* in Handford's research programme corresponds with that of the *novices* described by Temprado. The analysis of Temprado also reveals weaker relationships between joint centres in his expert group, in particular for the shoulder–elbow pairing. Moreover, the coupling between the shoulder and wrist joint centres is reported as anti-phase, rather than in-phase as in Handford's work (see Davids, Bennett, Handford and Jones, 1999). Temprado also finds peak shoulder amplitude in skilled volleyballers to occur at an average of 38 per cent of total movement time compared to a mean of 77.4 per cent in the studies of Handford (see Davids, Bennett, Handford and Jones, 1999). It can be inferred from Handford's investigations that segments of the upper body are organised to act as a single co-ordinative structure, with the hip, shoulder, elbow and wrist moving in the same direction at the same time, and with similar velocity profiles. At first glance, such an interpretation is inconsistent with the results of Temprado, and the view that the release of degrees of freedom in expert performers permits the exploitation of inertial properties of the movement system. How can these unexpected differences between the analyses of skilled volleyballers be interpreted?

One argument for these findings, also discussed in the chapter by Lees and Davids, concerns the influence of task-specific constraints and the emergent characteristic of movement patterns. The task constraints utilised by Temprado required participants to hit a cylindrical target (30 cm diameter, 40 cm height) at a distance of 16 m on the other side of the net. At the same time, participants were instructed to keep the trajectory of the ball as close as possible to the net. There was a double spatial constraint for participants to satisfy: that of ensuring that the trajectory requirements were adhered to at the same time as conforming to the exacting accuracy requirements of hitting the cylinder. Indeed, Temprado, Della-Grasta, Farrell and Laurent (1997) observed that the experts in their study 'concentrated more heavily on the precision of the trajectory than on the force of the strike' (p. 660–1). Data on mean amplitude of service trajectory in the chapter by Temprado support the view that different emphases in instructional constraints could provide a rationale for the co-ordination differences observed between the groups of experts (see Newell, 1996). For example, although the target was placed 16 m away, both the experts and novices of Temprado tended to 'undershoot', with the mean amplitude of the expert trajectory being a surprisingly tentative 12.90 m. The co-ordination pattern selected by the experts under the specific instructional constraints with a double emphasis on accuracy, involved little input from the shoulder joint and a lot of late forward motion in the elbow and wrist joints.

In contrast, the task constraints described in Davids, Bennett, Handford and Jones (1999) required the assembly of a co-ordination solution to satisfy the requirements of accurately hitting a larger target area (1 × 1 m) with as much force as possible. Although the target distance (17 m) was roughly equivalent to that used by Temprado, the trajectory requirements were not emphasised. Rather velocity requirements were emphasised as part of the task constraints. Previous research has found that, under task constraints in which force production exceeds 65 per cent of maximum (e.g. with accuracy *and* velocity requirements in the volleyball serving task), there is a significant decrease in the variability of muscular force output, as well as lower levels of movement variability (e.g. Sherwood and Schmidt, 1980). These findings might explain why a more tightly coupled co-ordinative structure was selected by the experienced performers under the task constraints described in Handford's chapter. The specificity of task constraints may have led the participants to a different co-ordination solution that was functional under the specific experimental conditions imposed by instructions.

This view contrasts with the suggestion of a sequential transition between successively refined states of organisation in many of the major theories of skill acquisition and development. As argued by Corbetta and Vereijken (1999), motor learning and control theories have typically been predicated on the sequential nature of a succession of stages in which movement control becomes successively refined and differentiated. A comparison of the data from the studies described in the chapters of Temprado and Handford implies that the emphasis on understanding the acquisition and development of co-ordination under varying task constraints should be on nonlinear processes of change as adaptation rather than mere sequential elaboration over time. In order to verify these arguments, further work emphasising intra-group analyses with experts is needed to confirm how co-ordination solutions evolve as a function of specific task constraints.

Summary and conclusions

This overview chapter has shown that current research into interceptive movements is rich and vibrant, providing theoretical insights and implications for practical application. Regardless of the theoretical stance taken by authors of each chapter, it is apparent that successful performance of interceptive actions is dependent on the pick-up and use of information to support movement. From a traditional viewpoint a number of chapters have highlighted ongoing work on the nature of the perceptual and cognitive advantages enjoyed by skilled performers engaged in a variety of interceptive movements. Emphasis is on the skilled deployment of attentional, perceptual and cognitive (knowledge-based) processes as resources underlying successful performance. The link with the cognitive expertise literature is made apparent, and important ideas to emerge from this approach concern how expertise underpins visual search strategies to pick up information for action. Another important advantage is an implicit mode of learning, in which learners acquire interceptive movement repertoires without accumulating verbalisable rules or conscious knowledge of them.

Current theoretical interest in the behaviour of movement systems as dynamical, self-organising systems which rely on environmental energy flows, such as haptic, auditory and optical information, to support and guide performance and acquisition of interceptive movements, provides the background for a number of other chapters. These contributions pose some interesting new theoretical questions and raise some considerations on the role of the coach and how to practice interceptive movements.

Taken as a whole, the material presented in this book suggests that the sport sciences have an increasingly influential role to play in the development of adequate accounts of motor learning and control. Clearly, there is a need for future work using real-world behaviours, such as interceptive movements and other sport-related tasks, to further our understanding of the relationship between the perceptual systems and the movement systems during goal-directed activity. It is our hope that the chapters of this book provide a strong platform for the development of research programmes on interceptive actions in the coming years.

References

Alderson, G.J.K., Sully, D.J. and Sully, H.G. (1974). An operational analysis of a one-handed catching task using high speed photography. *Journal of Motor Behavior* **6**, 217–26.

Bahill, A.T. and Karnavas, W.J. (1990). The perceptual illusionof baseball's rising fastball and breaking curveball. *Journal of Experimental Psychology: Human Perception and Performance* **19**, 3–14.

Bahill, A.T. and LaRitz, T. (1984). Why can't batters keep their eyes on the ball. *American Scientist* **72**, 249–53.

Bauer, H.U. and Schöllhorn, W. (1997). Self-organizing maps for the analysis of complex movement patterns. *Neural Processing Letters* **5**, 193–9.

Beek, P.J., Peper, C.E. and Stegeman, D.F. (1995). Dynamical models of movement co-ordination. *Human Movement Science* **14**, 573–608.

Benguigui, N. and Ripoll, H. (1998). Effects of tennis practice on the coincidence-timing accuracy of adults and children. *Research Quarterly for Exercise and Sport* **69**, 217–23.

Berg, W.P., Wade, M.G. and Greer, N.L. (1994). Visual regulation of gait in bipedal locomotion: revisiting Lee, Lishman, and Thomson (1982). *Journal of Experimental Psychology: Human Perception and Performance* **20**, 854–63.

Bernstein, N.A. (1967). *The Co-ordination and Regulation of Novements*. Oxford: Pergamon Press.

Beverley, K.I. and Regan, D. (1973). Evidence for neural mechanisms selectively sensitive to the direction of movement in space. *Journal of Physiology* **235**, 17–29.

Bootsma, R.J. (1989). Accuracy of perceptual processes subserving different perception–action systems. *Quarterly Journal of Experimental Psychology* **41A**, 489–500.

Bootsma, R.J., Fayt, V., Zaal, F.T.J.M. and Laurent, M. (1997). On the information-based regulation of movement: things Wann (1996) may want to consider. *Journal of Experimental Psychology: Human Perception and Performance* **23**, 1282–9.

Bootsma, R.J. and Oudejans, R.R.D. (1993). Visual information about time to collision between two projectiles. *Journal of Experimental Psychology : Human Perception and Performance* **19**, 1041–52.

Button, C. and Davids, K. (1999). Interacting intrinsic dynamics and intentionality requires co-ordination profiling of movement systems. In *Studies in Perception and Action V* (edited by M.A. Grealy and J.A. Thomson). Mahwah, NJ: Lawrence Erlbaum Associates.

Corbetta, D. and Vereijken, B. (1999). Understanding development and learning of motor co-ordination in sport: the contribution of dynamical systems theory. *International Journal of Sport Psychology* **30**, 507–30.

Davids, K., Bennett, S.J., Handford, C. and Jones, B. (1999). Acquiring co-ordination in self-paced, extrinsic timing tasks: a constraints-led perspective. *International Journal of Sport Psychology* **30**, 437–61.

Davids, K., Handford, C.H. and Williams, A.M. (1994). The natural physical alternative to cognitive theories of motor behaviour: an invitation for interdisciplinary sports science? *Journal of Sports Sciences* **12**, 495–528.

Davids, K., Kingsbury, D., Bennett, S.J. and Handford, C. (2001). Information–movement coupling: implications for the organisation of research and practice during acquisition of self-paced extrinsic timing skills. *Journal of Sports Sciences* **19**, 117–27.

Davids, K., Palmer, D.R.P. and Savelsbergh, G.J.P. (1989) Skill level, peripheral vision and tennis volleying peformance. *Journal of Human Movement Studies* **16**, 191–202.

Davids, K., Williams, A.M., Button, C. and Court, M. (2001). An integrative modeling approach to the study of intentional movement behavior. In *Handbook of Sport Psychology* (2nd edn) (edited by R.N. Singer, H. Hausenblas and C. Janelle). New York: John Wiley & Sons.

DeLucia, P.R. and Warren, R. (1994). Pictorial and motion-based information for depth information during active control of self-motion: size-arrival effects on collision avoidance. *Journal of Experimental Psychology: Human Perception and Performance* **20**, 784–9.

de Rugy, A., Montagne, G., Buekers, M.J. and Laurent, M. (2000). The control of human locomotor pointing under restricted informational conditions. *Neuroscience Letters* **281**, 87–90.

de Rugy, A., Montagne, G., Buekers, M.J. and Laurent, M. (2001). Spatially constrained locomotion under informational conflict. *Behavioral Brain Research* **123**, 11–15.

Fischman, M.G. and Mucci, W.G. (1989). The influence of a baseball glove on the nature of errors produced in simple one-handed catching. *Research Quarterly for Exercise and Sport* **60**, 251–5.

Fitch, H. and Turvey, M.T. (1978). On the control of activity: some remarks from an ecological point of view. In *Psychology of Motor Behavior and Sport* (edited by D.H. Landers and R.W. Christina). Champaign, IL: Human Kinetics.

Fitzpatrick, P. (1998). Modeling co-ordination dynamics in development. In *Applications of nonlinear dynamics to developmental process modelling* (edited by K.M. Newell and P.C.M. Molenaar). Mahwah, NJ: Lawrence Erlbaum Associates.

Fitzpatrick, P., Schmidt, R.C. and Lockman, J.J. (1996). Dynamical patterns in the development of clapping. *Child Development* **67**, 1691–708.

Gibson, J.J. (1979). *The Ecological Approach to Visual Perception*. Boston: Houghton Mifflin.

Harris, L.R. and Jenkin, M. (eds) (1998). *Vision and Action*. Cambridge: Cambridge University Press.

Hubbard, A.W. and Seng, C.N. (1954). Visual movements of batters. *Research Quarterly* **25**, 42–57.

Kaiser, M.K. and Mowafy, L. (1993). Optical specification of time-to-passage: observer's sensitivity to global tau. *Journal of Experimental Psychology: Human Perception and Performance* **19**, 1028–40.

Kandel, E.R., Schwartz, J.H. and Jessell, T.M. (2000). *Essentials of Neural Science and Behavior*. London: Prentice Hall International.

Kauffmann, S.A. (1993). *The Origins of Order: Self-organisation and Selection in Evolution*. New York: Oxford University Press.

Keil, D., Holmes, P.S., Bennett, S.J., Davids, K. and Smith, N.C. (2000). Theory and practice in sport psychology and motor behaviour needs to be constrained by integrative modelling of brain and behaviour. *Journal of Sports Sciences* **18**, 433–43.

Land, M.F. and McLeod, P. (2000). From eye movements to actions: how batsmen hit the ball. *Nature Neuroscience* **3**, 1340–5.

Laurent, M., Montagne, G. and Durey, A. (1996). Binocular invariants in interceptive tasks: a directed perception approach. *Perception* **25**, 1437–50.

Lee, D.N. (1976). A theory of visual control of braking based on information about time-to-collision. *Perception* **5**, 437–59.

Lee, D.N. (1980). Visuo–motor co-ordination in space-time. In *Tutorials in Motor Behaviour* (edited by G.E. Stelmach and J. Requin). Amsterdam: North Holland.

Lee, D.N., Lishman, J.R. and Thomson, J.A. (1982). Regulation of gait in long jumping. *Journal of Experimental Psychology: Human Perception and Performance* **8**, 448–59.

Lee, D.N. and Young, D.S. (1985). Visual timing of interceptive movement. In *Brain Mechanisms and Spatial Vision* (edited by D. Ingle, M. Jeannerod and D.N. Lee). Dordrecht: Martinus Nijhoff.

Lee, D.N., Young, D.S., Reddish, D.E., Lough, S. and Clayton, T.M.H. (1983). Visual timing in hitting an accelerating ball. *Quarterly Journal of Experimental Psychology* **35a**, 333–46.

Maraj, B.K.V. (1999). Evidence for programmed and visually controlled phases of the triple jump approach run. *New Studies in Athletics* **14**, 51–6.

Mason, A.H. and Carnahan, H. (1999). Target viewing time and velocity effects on prehension. *Experimental Brain Research* **127**, 83–94.

McBeath, M.K., Shaffer, D.M. and Kaiser, M.K. (1995). How baseball outfielders determine where to run to catch fly balls. *Science* **268**, 569–72.

McLeod, R.W. and Ross, H.E. (1983). Optic-flow and cognitive factors in time to collision estimates. *Perception* **12**, 417–23.

Michaels, C.F. and Oudejans, R.R.D. (1992). The optics and actions of catching fly balls: zeroing out optical acceleration. *Ecological Psychology* **4**, 199–222.

Montagne, G., Cornus, S., Glize, D., Quaine, F. and Laurent, M. (2000). A perception–action coupling type of control in long jumping. *Journal of Motor Behavior* **32**, 37–43.

Montagne, G., Fraisse, F., Ripoll, H. and Laurent, M. (2000). Perception–movement coupling in an interceptive task: first-order time-to-contact as an input variable. *Human Movement Science* **19**, 59–72.

Montagne, G., Laurent, M., Durey, A. and Bootsma, R.J. (1999). Movement reversals in ball catching. *Experimental Brain Research* **129**, 87–92.

Nelson, C.A. (1995). The ontogeny of human memory: a cognitive neuroscience perspective. *Developmental Psychology* **31**, 723–38.

Newell, K.M. (1986). Constraints on the development of co-ordination. In *Motor Development in Children: Aspects of Co-ordination and Control* (edited by M.G. Wade and H.T.A. Whiting). Dordrecht: Nijhoff.

Newell, K.M. (1991). Motor skill acquisition. *Annual Review of Psychology* **42**, 213–37.

Newll, K.M. (1996). Change in movement and skill: learning, retention and transfer. In *Dexterity and its Development* (edited by M.L. Latash and M.T. Turvey). Mahwah, NJ: Lawrence Erlabaum and Associates.

Newell, K.M. and Slifkin, A.B. (1998). The nature of movement variability. In *Motor Behavior and Human Skill: A Multidisciplinary Perspective* (edited by J.P. Piek). Champaign, IL: Human Kinetics.

Newell, K.M., Liu, Y-T. and Mayer-Kress, G. (2001). Time scales in motor learning and development. *Psychological Review* **108**, 57–82.

Newell, K.M. and Van Emmerik, R.E.A. (1990). Are Gesell's developmental principles general principles for the acquisition of co-ordination? In *Advances in Motor Development Research III* (edited by J. Clark and J. Humphrey). New York: AMS Press.

Oudejans, R.R.D., Michaels, C.F., Bakker, F.C. and Davids, K. (1999). Shedding some light on catching in the dark: perceptual mechanisms for catching fly balls. *Journal of Experimental Psychology: Human Perception and Performance* **25**, 531–42.

Parsons, L.M. (2001). Integrating cognitive psychology, neurology and neuroimaging. *Acta Psychologica* **107**, 155–81.

Peper, C.E., Bootsma, R.J., Mestre, D.R. and Bakker, F.C. (1994). Catching balls: how to get the hand to the right place at the right time. *Journal of Experimental Psychology: Human Perception and Performance* **20**, 3, 591–612.

Polman, R.C.J., Whiting, H.T.A. and Savelsbergh, G.J.P. (1996). The spatio–temporal structure of control variables during catching in different load conditions. *Experimental Brain Research* **109**, 483–94.

Poulton, E.C. (1957). On prediction in skilled movements. *Psychological Bulletin* **54**, 467–78.

Regan, D. (1997). Visual factors in hitting and catching. *Journal of Sports Sciences* **15**, 533–58.

Regan, D. (2000). *Human Perception of Objects: Early Visual Processing of Spatial Form Defined by Luminance, Color, Texture, Motion and Binocular Disparity.* Toronto: Sinauer Associates.

Regan, D. and Gray, R. (2000). Visually guided collision avoidance and collision achievement. *Trends in Cognitive Sciences* **4**, 99–107.

Ripoll, H. and Fleurance, P. (1988). What does keeping one's eye on the ball mean? *Ergonomics* **31**, 1647–54.

Robertson, S.D. (2001). The development of bimanual skill: the search for stable patterns of co-ordination. *Journal of Motor Behavior* **33**, 114–26.

Rushton, S.K. and Wann, J.P. (1999). Weighted combination of size and disparity: a computational model for timing a ball catch. *Nature Neuroscience* **2**, 186–90.

Savelsbergh, G.J.P. and Bootsma, R.J. (1994). Perception–action coupling in hitting and catching. *International Journal of Sport Psychology* **25**, 331–43.

Savelsbergh, G.J.P. and Van der Kamp, J.G. (2000). Information in learning to co-ordinate and control movements: is there a need for specificity of practice? *International Journal of sport Psychology* **31**, 467–84.

Saxberg, B.V.H. (1987). Projected free fall trajectories. II. Human experiments. *Biological Cybernetics* **56**, 177–84.

Schiff, W. and Detwiler, M.L. (1979). Information used in judging impending collision. *Perception* **8**, 647–58.

Schiff, W. and Oldak, R. (1990). Accuracy of judging time-to-arrival: effects of modality, trajectory, and gender. *Journal of Experimental Psychology: Human Perception and Performance* **16**, 303–16.

Schmidt, R.C. and Fitzpatrick, P. (1996). Dynamical perspectives on motor learning. In *Advances in Motor Learning and Control* (edited by H.N. Zelaznik). Champaign, IL: Human Kinetics.

Schöner, G. (1990). A dynamic theory of co-ordination of discrete movement. *Biological Cybernetics* **63**, 257–70.

Sherwood, D.E. and Schmidt, R.A. (1980). The relationship between force and force variability in minimal and near-maximal static and dynamic contractions. *Journal of Motor Behavior* **12**, 75–89.

Singer, R.N., Williams, A.M., Janelle, C., Frehlich, S. Barber, D. and Boutchard, L. (1998). Visual search during 'live' on-court situations in tennis. *Research Quarterly for Exercise and Sport* **69**, 109–16.

Slifkin, A.B. and Newell, K.M. (1999). Noise, information transmission, and force variability. *Journal of Experimental Psychology: Human Perception and Performance* **25**, 837–51.

Smeets, J.B.J., Brenner, E., Trebuchet, S. and Mestre, D.R. (1996). Is judging time-to-contact based on tau? *Perception* **25**, 583–90.

Sun, H. and Frost, B.J. (1998). Computation of different optical variables of looming objects in pigeon nucleus rotundus neurons. *Nature Neuroscience* **1**, 296–303.

Temprado, J.J., Della-Grasta, M., Farrell, M. and Laurent, M. (1997). A novice–expert comparison of (intra-limb) co-ordination subserving the volleyball serve. *Human Movement Science* **16**, 653–76.

Thelen, E. and Smith, L.B. (1994). *A Dynamic Systems Approach to the Development of Cognition and Action.* Cambridge, MA: MIT Press.

Todd, J.T. (1981). Visual information about moving objects. *Journal of Experimental Psychology: Human Perception and Performance* **7**, 795–810.

Tresilian, J.R. (1990). Perceptual information for the timing of interceptive action. *Perception* **19**, 223–39.

Tresilian, J.R. (1991). Empirical and theoretical issues in the perception of time to contact. *Journal of Experimental Psychology: Human Perception and Performance* **17**, 865–76.

Tresilian, J.R. (1994). Approximate information sources and perceptual variables in interceptive timing. *Journal of Experimental Psychology: Human Perception and Performance* **20**, 154–73.

Tresilian, J.R. (1995). Perceptual and cognitive processes in time-to-contact estimation: analysis of prediction-motion and relative judgement tasks. *Perception and Psychophysics* **57**, 231–45.

Tresilian, J.R. (1999). Analysis of recent empirical challenges to an account of interceptive timing. *Perception and Psychophysics* **61**, 515–28.

Turvey, M.T. (1990). Co-ordination. *American Psychologist* **45**, 938–53.

Turvey, M.T. and Fitzpatrick, P. (1993). Commentary: development of perception–action systems and general principles of pattern formation. *Child Development* **64**, 1175–90.

Van der Kamp, J., Savelsbergh, G.J.P. and Smeets, J. (1997). Multiple information sources in interceptive timing. *Human Movement Science* **16**, 787–821.

Vickers, J. (1996). Visual control when aiming at a far target. *Journal of Experimental Psychology: Human Perception and Performance* **22**, 342–54.

Von Hofsten, C. (1983). Catching skills in infancy. *Journal of Experimental Psychology: Human Perception and Performance* **9**, 75–85.

Wann, J.P. (1996). Temporal judgement in ego-motion: is the tau-margin a specious theory? *Journal of Experimental Psychology: Human Perception and Performance Journal of Experimental Psychology: Human Perception and Performance* **22**, 1031–48.

Whiting, H.T.A (1968). Training in a continuous ball-throwing and catching task. *Ergonomics* **4**, 375–82.

Whiting, H.T.A (1969). *Acquiring Ball Skill: A Psychological Interpretation.* London: Bell.

Whiting, H.T.A., Alderson, G.J.K. and Sanderson, F.H. (1973) Critical time intervals for viewing and individual differences in performance of a ball-throwing task. *International Journal of Sport Psychology* **4**, 155–6.

Williams A.M., Davids, K., Burwitz, L. and Williams, J.G. (1992). Perception and movement in sport. *Journal of Human Movement Studies* **22**, 147–204.

Williams, A.M. and Davids, K. (1998). Visual search strategy, selective attention, and expertise in the sub-phases of soccer. *Research Quarterly for Exercise and Sport* **69**, 111–28.

Williams, A.M., Davids, K. and Williams, J.G. (1999). *Visual Perception and Action in Sport.* London: Routledge.

Williams, J.G. (1992). Catching action: visuomotor adaptatons in children. *Perceptual and Motor Skills*, **75**, 211–19.

Wulf, G., McNevin, N.H., Fuchs, T., Ritter, F. and Toole, T. (2000). Attentional focus in complex motor skill learning. *Research Quarterly for Exercise and Sport* **71**, 229–39.

2 Cognitive expertise and performance in interceptive actions

A. Mark Williams and Janet Starkes

If we watch a professional baseball batter connect in an effortless way with a 160 kph pitch, and the shortstop dive to field the powerful hit to the infield, the grace and fluidity of the players' movements clearly belies the difficulty of the task. An inexperienced baseball player simply cannot deal with pitches that fast. A novice infielder can neither judge where the ball will be hit to, nor get to it in time. The question addressed in this chapter is what happens in the development of skill that permits athletes to seemingly overcome severe spatio–temporal constraints to perform such remarkable interceptive actions.

In this chapter we attempt to trace what is known about the nature of expertise in interceptive actions. This is done by first examining issues related to success in catching, and second, anticipation in sport. Third, we present a critical analysis of the specificity of learning literature and the role of context. Towards the end of the chapter, we offer three potential future directions for research on expertise and performance in interceptive actions. First, we speculate what might constitute the minimal information sources for expert performance. This is followed by a discussion of the potential role of connectionist theories; and finally, we evaluate the need for semi-longitudinal research designs. In keeping with the historical nature of this review, the majority of the work presented adopts the traditional cognitive, information-processing perspective on interceptive actions in sport. This theoretical approach was prevalent with regard to the study of interceptive actions until the late 1980s, and remains the dominant paradigm in contemporary research on perceptual and decision-making skill in sport (e.g. see Starkes and Allard, 1993; Williams, Davids, and Williams, 1999).

Our historical analysis begins by reviewing the classic work of Hubbard and Seng (1954) on catching and progresses through the work of Whiting and colleagues, who were primarily interested in *how much* visual attention must be allocated to an approaching ball and *when* vision is most critical. As several chapters in this book attest, more recent work in this area has focused on the relative importance of motor programme versus continuous guidance control in interceptive actions, and we finish our retrospective analysis on this question.

A historical perspective on the role of cognitive expertise and performance in interceptive actions

Over the past twenty years a significant amount of research has determined that expert athletes have a number of perceptual and cognitive advantages, the result of years of training and competition in their sport. In this chapter we examine what aspects of cognitive expertise are most influential in interceptive actions. While the term interceptive actions can refer to 'closed' skills such a walking on a balance beam, grasping a cup, or hitting a golf ball as outlined in Chapter 1, we will focus on more dynamic and 'open' (Gentile, 1972; Poulton, 1957) skills such as batting in baseball or the return of serve in tennis. Cognitive expertise may play a greater role in more dynamic, unpredictable, time-constrained tasks and thus elicit the greatest advantages for skilled players.

The eye movements of baseball batters: Hubbard and Seng's 'classic' study

Perhaps the earliest researchers to look at the role of vision during interceptive actions were Hubbard and Seng (1954). In this study, the performance of professional baseball batters during practice was examined. Cinematography and electromyography were employed to study the batters' swing kinematics as well as their eye and head movements. Frame-by-frame film analysis showed that the start of the step was geared to the release of the ball while the finish of the step was more closely coupled to ball speed and tended to occur at a consistent time period prior to bat/ball contact. The start of the swing was also related to ball speed, with batters maintaining a fairly consistent swing duration across trials regardless of ball speed. Eye rather than head movements were employed to track the ball during flight. However, none of the batters tracked the ball until the point of bat/ball contact. Players stopped tracking the ball using foveal vision when it was between 2.4 to 4.5 m (60 to 240 ms) away from the plate. Either the batters thought that tracking the ball beyond this point did not provide useful information or the eyes were unable to physically track a ball moving with such high angular velocities. Hubbard and Seng (1954) suggested that the spatio–temporal parameters of the swing were programmed prior to the termination of ball tracking, although they did acknowledge the possibility that some modifications to the swing might be possible due to monitoring of the ball in peripheral vision as it crossed the plate.

Hubbard and Seng's findings (1954) were extended some thirty years later by Bahill and LaRitz (1984) using more sophisticated technology to monitor the visual behaviour of major league and college level baseball players during a simulated batting task. Although findings supported the earlier observations of Hubbard and Seng (1954), with no player visually tracking the ball through to bat contact, the major league player was able to track the ball for longer than the college level players. The college players typically tracked the ball until it was around 2.75 m from the plate, whilst the major league player kept up with the ball until it was almost 1.5 m in front of the plate before falling behind in his tracking. The major league batter's ability to track the ball for longer is consistent with Sanderson's (1981) suggestion that skilled players may be more 'velocity resistant' and capable of tracking the ball under less optimal conditions than their less skilled counterparts.

The primary restriction on the ability of players to track the ball throughout its flight appears to be the physical capacity of the visual system. Smooth pursuit eye movements are capable of a maximum angular velocity of 100 deg sec^{-1}, although the eye's ability to track begins to deteriorate at an angular velocity greater than 30 deg sec^{-1} (Rosenbaum, 1991). Since the angular velocities required to track a ball can often exceed 1000 deg sec^{-1}, an important physical constraint on eye movement behaviour in sport is identified (Haywood, 1984). At faster ball velocities, the suggestion is that skilled players do not attempt to track the ball during its entire flight path, preferring instead to employ anticipatory saccades to predict the future position of the ball (e.g. see Ripoll, Fleurance, and Cazeneuve, 1987; Ripoll, 1991; Williams, Singer, and Weigelt, 1998). Another suggestion is that experts may be better at extracting information from the final portion of the ball's flight using the 'image–retina' rather than 'eye–head' system (Haywood, 1984). When using the image–retina system the eyes are kept motionless as the ball moves across the retina, whereas with the eye–head system a combination of eye and head movements are employed to keep the ball stationary on the eye. An enhanced capability to suppress the vestibulo–ocular reflex during tracking may also contribute to the experts' increased tendency to employ the image–retina rather than eye–head system (Ripoll, Bard, and Paillard, 1986).

Keep your eye on the ball? The work of Whiting and colleagues

A common instruction when coaching is 'keep your eye on the ball'. Although several recent studies have shown that athletes are unable to track the ball until contact with a bat or an effector, perhaps the earliest systematic programme of work to address this issue was undertaken by Whiting and colleagues at the University of Leeds in England. The crucial questions revolved around *what* proportion of ball flight needs to be viewed for successful performance on an interceptive task and *when* this information needs to be extracted. The initial studies attempted to quantify the minimal amount of information needed to support the fine spatio–temporal requirements of catching (e.g. see Whiting, 1968, 1969). These studies typically used a throwing and catching task where participants had to intercept an object in flight and immediately re-direct it towards a target such as in baseball or cricket. In one study (Whiting, 1968), the ball was attached to a chain around a thin metal column that permitted a circular flight path. When thrown, the ball rotated around the column to be caught by the participant and was immediately propelled towards skittle targets. The task was performed under normal lighting conditions as well as in total darkness, while other conditions involved the occlusion of early, middle, and late segments of flight. Findings provided support for Hubbard and Seng's (1954) suggestion that it is not necessary to view the ball for its entire flight, with the best performance being observed when cues were available in the middle segment of flight.

In another study, Whiting (1970) allowed participants to manipulate whether they watched the ball or target at any given time. Following practice, participants tended to process visual cues earlier in flight and the ball needed to be illuminated for shorter periods of time, indicating that competent performance was based on fewer flight cues. The suggestion was that, through practice, participants learned the sequential dependencies of ball flight, invoking the use of inferential processes in perception and memory to anticipate the spatio–temporal characteristics of ball flight.

Further studies attempted to determine the exact viewing period required for successful performance and examined whether the magnitude of the period varied as a function of participants' skill level on the task. For example, Whiting, Gill and Stephenson (1970) investigated competent performers on a one-handed catching task in which a ball was propelled by a trampette over a 2.77 m distance. Full light and total darkness conditions were employed as well as five different viewing periods ranging from having sight of the initial 100 to 400 ms of the ball's flight. Not surprisingly, performance improved as the viewing period increased, although there was little difference in the number of catches made between the 300 and 400 ms conditions. As Figure 2.1 demonstrates, after an initial viewing period, in this instance 300 ms, vision of the remainder of the ball's flight was not essential for improving performance. In fact, skilled catchers recorded moderate levels of success even when only the initial 100 to 150 ms of the ball's flight was observed. These data were interpreted as evidence for the important role of cognitive processes during interceptive actions, particularly in time-stressed and visually-degraded environments.

Follow-up studies manipulated the length of the viewing and occlusion periods in an attempt to evaluate the prevalent cognitive notion that the human performer was a discrete sampler of environmental information (e.g. Sharp and Whiting, 1974; Sharp Farrally, Kingston, Laidler and Saunders, 1975; Whiting, Alderson, and Sanderson, 1973; Whiting and Sharp, 1973). Although a considerable amount of individual variation in catching performance was observed, a viewing period of 80 ms somewhere during the middle segment of ball flight appeared to provide sufficient information for reasonable catching performance. The length of this critical viewing period appeared to vary as a function of participants' skill level, the assumption being that successful performance was at least partially mediated by task-specific knowledge structures developed through experience (for more detailed and critical reviews, see Savelsbergh, 1990; Williams, Davids, Burwitz and Williams, 1992).

The operational timing hypothesis

Following successful perception of the spatio–temporal characteristics of ball flight, the next prediction necessary for sucessful performance of an interceptive task is

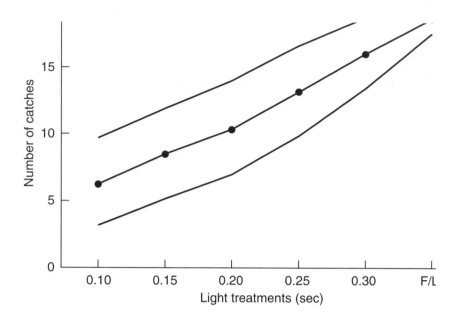

Figure 2.1 Number of catches by a group of skilled catchers as a function of viewing time. Mean data are represented by the circled line, standard deviations by the uncircled outer lines. The data clearly indicate that the longer the ball is viewed in flight the more successful the outcome. (Source: Whiting, H.T.A., Gill, E.B. and Stephenson, J.M. (1979). Critical time intervals for taking in flight information in a ball-catching task. *Ergonomics* **13**, 265–72).

when to initiate movement. Tyldesley and Whiting (1975) argued, like Hubbard and Seng (1954), that there is an inordinate degree of consistency in the movement patterns displayed by skilled sports performers. Their arguments were based on high-speed film analysis of novice, intermediate, and expert table tennis players performing forehand drives to a designated target area on the table. When displacement and velocity profiles from expert and intermediate players were subjected to within-participant analyses, remarkable levels of spatial and temporal precision and consistency were observed. As illustrated in Figure 2.2, the degree of consistency was particularly evident in the group of expert participants who maintained such a high degree of spatial consistency that the problem of playing the shot seemed to be reduced to solely one of timing. For the expert players, the degree of spatial variability at the key moments of movement initiation and bat–ball contact was very small, while the variability inherent in the action's timing was negligible (± 4ms). Such results have typically been interpreted as providing support for the role of highly consistent motor programmes in skill reproduction. The assumption being that these motor programmes needed only to be initiated at the right moment prior to bat/ball contact (Franks, Weicker and Robertson, 1985; see also van Soest and Beek, 1996). In contrast, novices showed poor consistency

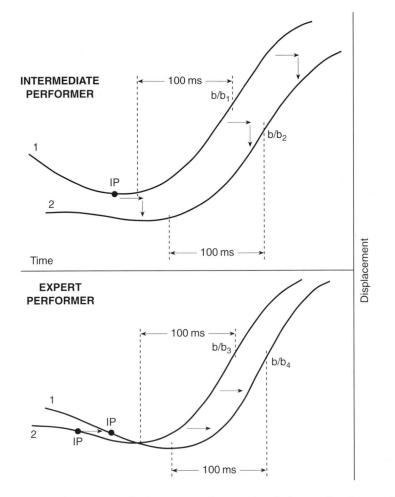

Figure 2.2 Movement displacement profiles over time for intermediate (top graph) and expert (lower graph) table tennis players performing a forehand drive to a standardised feed from a projection machine. The data are indicative of a high level of repeatability in the movement patterns of both groups. Note, however, that the more extensive practice of the expert affords a greater level of consistency for the temporal and spatial configuration of the drive at the initiation point (IP) and at bat–ball contact (BB) – unlike the intermediate who is merely temporally consistent in reproducing both points. Novice data, not reproduced here, showed little consistency of either spatial or temporal nature (Source: Tyldesley, D. and Whiting, H.T.A. (1975). Operational timing. *Journal of Human Movement Studies* **1**, 172–7).

of either a spatial or temporal nature, implying a role for more feedback-oriented control processes.

Tyldesley and Whiting (1975) argued that skilled performers reduce the degree of temporal uncertainty in interceptive tasks by practising an action until it has a highly consistent movement duration (termed 'operational timing'). Following practice, performers are assumed to develop motor programmes that are temporally consistent to the extent that the processing demands are reduced merely to predicting the moment of initiation (termed 'input timing'). According to this hypothesis, the performer needs to compute velocity and distance information from ball flight characteristics to correctly predict the initiation time of a movement with a known temporal duration. The key advantage of such an approach is that the problem of movement timing is simplified, thereby reducing the computational burden on performers.

Although the operational timing hypothesis is intuitively appealing, more recent data suggest that an explanation based upon continuous visual guidance may be more plausible. For example, Bootsma and van Wieringen (1990) replicated and extended Tyldesley and Whiting's (1975) study using five top table tennis players. High-speed film analysis of the forehand drive showed much higher temporal accuracy at the moment of bat/ball contact than at the initiation of the action, implying that the players did not fully rely on a consistent movement-production strategy. Their data showed that although the variability in movement time was relatively small (with standard deviation values ranging from 4.8 to 20.9 ms) the timing accuracy at bat/ball contact was considerably smaller with standard deviation values varying from 2.0 to 4.7 ms. Bootsma and van Wieringen (1990) proposed that such tasks are controlled through continuous visual guidance based upon the functional coupling between the optic variable *tau* (see Lee, 1976) and the mean velocity and acceleration of the bat during the drive. Variability in the time remaining prior to contact, specified by *tau*, is closely coupled to the variability inherent in the acceleration of the swing. Players are assumed to compensate for late initiation of the action through more rapid acceleration of the swing, while early initiation is compensated for by reducing bat acceleration (see also Laurent, Montagne and Savelsbergh, 1994; Matsuo and Kasai, 1994; Wallace, Stevenson, Weeks and Kelso, 1992). According to this approach, the spatio–temporal variability of the movement trajectories decreases monotonically from the initiation of the action to the moment of bat/ball contact in what has been called a 'funnel-like' fashion (cf. Bootsma and van Wieringen, 1990). Figure 2.3 illustrates the decrease in variability as contact nears.

In recent years, several researchers have attempted to determine the relative importance of motor programme versus continuous guidance control in interceptive actions, with varying degrees of success (for a more detailed and critical review, see Williams, Davids and Williams, 1999). The general consensus supports the use of a more flexible strategy based on perception–action coupling that allows movement time to be controlled by time-to-contact information (e.g. see Bootsma and Peper, 1992; Bootsma, Fayt, Zaal and Laurent, 1997; Tresilian, 1994, 1997). As discussed in Chapter 1, the information used to perceive time-to-contact is also presumed to come from many different sources of perceptual information (of which *tau* is only one). It is also argued that their use is task dependent and influenced by the information processing constraints of the nervous system (see Tresilian, 1999).

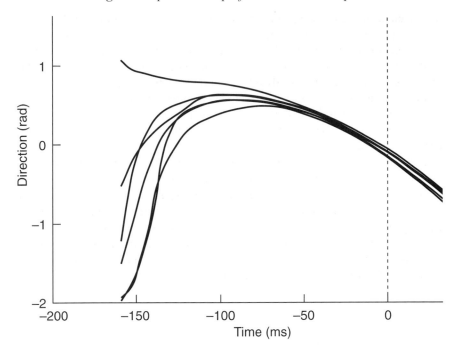

Figure 2.3 Decreasing variability of response as time to contact nears. (Source: Bootsma, R.J. and van Wieringen, P.C.W. (1990). Timing an attacking forehand drive in table tennis. *Journal of Experimental Psychology: Human Perception and Performance* **16**, 21–9).

Anticipation in sport: contemporary research on cognitive expertise and performance in interceptive actions

The effective processing of contextual information

Other evidence for expertise-based differences in interceptive actions is provided by research focusing on anticipation skill in sport. Several reviews have outlined the areas where perceptual/cognitive advantages are seen in expert athletes (e.g. Abernethy, 1994; Ripoll, 1991; Starkes and Allard, 1993; Starkes, Helsen and Jack, 2002; Williams, Davids and Williams, 1999). Skilled athletes do not possess better visual systems, or what is commonly referred to as 'visual hardware', than their less skilled counterparts (Helsen and Starkes, 1999; Starkes, 1987; Williams, Davids and Williams, 1999). Their advantage appears to lie in superior perceptual and cognitive skill within their sport; the so-called 'software' distinction (Starkes and Deakin, 1984). Research has shown that skilled athletes can readily recognise and recall offensive/defensive structure when viewing game play, even when viewing time is in the order of seconds. This superior pattern recognition ability has been demonstrated in many sports including basketball (Allard, Graham and Paarsalu, 1980; Millslagle, 1988), handball (Tenenbaum, Levy-Kolker, Bar-Eli and Weinberg, 1994), soccer (Williams and Davids, 1995), and field hockey (Starkes and Deakin, 1984).

It is also known that skilled athletes are able to use 'advance visual cues' to access information much earlier than novices. Using badminton as an example, advance visual cues comprise the information afforded in viewing the opponent's stance, body and racket position as s/he moves to return a shot. Expert players are able to make use of contextual information from these sources to improve prediction accuracy of where a shot will go, even prior to viewing contact with the bird. Experimentally, by using film- or video-based *temporal occlusion* techniques, one is able to 'black out' information at various points prior to, at, or after contact with the shuttlecock. A second technique, known as *spatial or event occlusion*, permits examination of specific visual cues, such as the racket, arm or lower body, to determine which cues provide the most meaningful information. Following the seminal work of Abernethy (e.g. 1986, 1988, 1990; Abernethy and Russell, 1987) many researchers have used the temporal occlusion method to determine how early visual information is used by experts and novices in interceptive tasks. In contrast, the spatial occlusion method has rarely been used (for a recent exception, see Williams and Davids, 1998).

Using advance visual cues, skilled athletes can decide more quickly and accurately what the next optimal offensive move is for an athlete in possession of the ball (Helsen and Pauwels, 1993; Starkes, 1987; Starkes and Lindley, 1994; Williams, Davids, Burwitz and Williams, 1994). Likewise, skilled baseball hitters can predict more readily where a pitch will be (Paull and Glencross, 1997), field and ice hockey players (Salmela and Fiorito, 1979; Starkes and Deakin, 1984) can predict more accurately where a shot will be placed on the net, and, finally, volleyball (Coelho and Chamberlin, 1991; Starkes, Edwards, Dissanayake and Dunn, 1995; Wright, Pleasants and Gomez-Meza, 1990), tennis (Goulet *et al.*, 1988; Isaacs and Finch, 1983; Jones and Miles, 1978), and badminton players (Abernethy, 1986, 1988; Abernethy and Russell, 1987) can more accurately predict the likely position of a serve or shot. In their early work on anticipation skill in ice hockey goalkeepers, Salmela and Fiorito (1979) also demonstrated that experts are more confident in their predictions compared with novice counterparts.

While early temporal occlusion research using film was often criticised for lack of ecological validity, recent work (Starkes, Edwards, Dissanayake and Dunn, 1995) has examined the prediction of actual volleyball serves on court (using liquid crystal occlusion goggles). The results from this on-court study replicated previous findings obtained in studies using two dimensional film displays. Interestingly, like Salmela and Fiorito's (1979) earlier findings, expert players' had greater confidence in their predictions. Players are both more accurate and confident as they are permitted to view contact and beyond.

Eye movement analyses demonstrate other advantages of skill in sport. In many situations expert athletes visually fixate on different information sources within a scene, and may have either many more fixations of shorter duration or fewer fixations of longer duration (Bard and Fleury, 1976, 1981; Helsen and Starkes, 1999; Neumaier, 1982; Williams and Davids, 1998). Presumably fewer, longer fixations might reflect more integrative viewing within one fixation or better selective attention, what Ripoll (1991) referred to as a more 'synthetic' search process.

Situational probabilities in interceptive actions

Situational probabilities may operate in two different ways to assist expert performance. They may reduce uncertainty by directing attention to that part of the scene in which the most useful visual cues are likely to occur. Probabilities may also prime certain components of long term memory towards information necessary to complete a subsequent action (Anderson, 1990). As well as their enhanced ability to extract task-specific contextual information from the display, research involving racket sports suggests that skilled performers are able to use their experience to assign subjective probabilities to those events likely to occur within any given situation (e.g. Alain and Proteau, 1977, 1980; Alain, Sarrazin and Lacombe, 1986; Alain and Sarrazin, 1990).

For example, Alain and Proteau (1980) examined the extent to which defensive players in various racket sports made use of situational probabilities to anticipate the shots available to their adversaries. The decision-making behaviour of squash, tennis, badminton, and racketball players was studied in the game situation by filming some of the rallies, allowing participants to view the film, and then asking them specific questions regarding shot selection during the rally. Players were asked to comment on the subjective probabilities they had assigned to their opponent's shots. The results showed that players evaluated the probability of each possible event that could occur and then used this information to maximise the efficiency of subsequent behaviour. Players' initial anticipatory movements were guided by their expectations with subsequent corrective or confirmatory movements being made on the basis of current information or contextual cues. Skilled racket sports players typically made an anticipatory response whenever the probability of success was greater than 0.7 (>70%) (see also Dillon, Crassini and Abernethy, 1989).

Alain and Girardin (1978) suggested that players' positions on the court prior to the impending shot might provide a key source of information when assigning subjective probabilities. However, although intuitively appealing, they failed to provide strong support for this assumption in the sport of racketball. Alain and Proteau (1980) argued that the speed and 'bouncy' nature of the ball could override the need for an uncertainty-based attacking strategy in racketball. The unique characteristics generated by the ball's resilience make it more difficult to play a decisive, point-winning shot when compared to other racket sports such as squash. This factor may reduce the need for players to make *a priori* decisions based on situational probabilities. It remains to be seen whether the on-court positions of players may provide relevant information for assigning shot probabilities in perhaps more strategically-oriented ball games such as tennis, badminton or squash.

A distinction may be made between 'general' and 'specific' situational probabilities (Williams, 2000). The former could include information such as the typical shots facing a squash player when retreating into the back court region (e.g. crosscourt or straight drive, boast) or the likely stroke played by a badminton player when returning a drop shot (e.g. lob or return drop shot). The latter relates to a player's knowledge of specific opponents' tendencies. For example, a particular player may prefer to play a crosscourt drive from the back of the squash court, whereas in badminton, a certain player may be more inclined to play a drop shot return. Clearly, both sources of information are important for skilled players since they have to play regularly against the same opponent as well as against a team or an opponent for the first time.

Paull and Glencross (1997) demonstrated that general situational probabilities are of benefit to baseball batters of varying skill levels. They provided expert and novice batters with strategic game information on cards prior to hitting. This information included the count of balls, strikes, batters out, the progressive score, total score, and safe hits recorded against the pitcher. The cards also showed a graphical representation of a baseball diamond with runners on base. These details provide only general situational probability information. Participants were prevented from using specific probability information because they were unfamiliar with the pitching tendencies/skills of the filmed pitchers. Expert and novices hitters were then shown an experimental video of pitches and required to simulate hitting with an instrumented bat. In order to consider the value of the strategic information, participants only received the game details prior to half the pitches; for the other half they received no information. Regardless of condition, expert players always predicted the path of the ball more accurately and responded more quickly. However, all players were able to make use of strategic information to improve accuracy of prediction and decrease decision time. The authors suggest that knowledge of game context and the probability of pitch types is fundamental to the sport of baseball and is probably learned very early in training. Further research is required to determine the situational probabilities employed by athletes when performing interceptive actions, how these vary with skill, and how such expectations constrain the effective pick-up of contextual information during skilful perception.

Specificity of learning and performance in interceptive actions: Proteau's specificity of learning hypothesis

One of the advantages of advance cue use in experts is that by using early information they are able to make movement decisions quickly and focus more effort on the interceptive part of the movement action. As a result, skilled athletes often appear to have 'all the time in the world', despite the severe time constraints of the task. Coaches have speculated that visual stimuli in the environment should be manipulated so as to 'force' trainees to use earlier information, or to use eye movement patterns that would facilitate pick-up of early information (e.g. see Starkes and Lindley, 1994; Williams and Grant, 1999). Alternatively, vision could be constrained in order to force athletes to rely on other sources of information, such as proprioception or audition. This is the case when basketball coaches force trainees to look up while dribbling the ball, or when ice hockey coaches insist that players not look at the puck while carrying it up the ice.

Proteau and colleagues (e.g. 1987, 1990, 1992), however, argued for specificity of learning. From aiming studies they provided evidence that learners do not typically progress from closed to open loop control, or from visual to more kinesthetically controlled movement. They suggested that learning could not progress as readily if relevant visual cues are manipulated or subtracted during learning. Williams, Davids and Williams (1999) compared data from a number of catching studies that either supported or refuted the specificity argument. They concluded that overall the results suggest that vision of the catching limb is '*helpful* for successful positioning of the arm in skilled catchers, but is *necessary* for unskilled performers' (p. 305). Furthermore, they argued that there is a lack of support for specificity (expert performance does not deteriorate in the absence of vision) in sport tasks such as the tennis volley (Davids, Palmer and Savelsbergh, 1989) and powerlifting (Bennett and Davids, 1995). In an attempt to reconcile these findings, Williams, Davids and Williams (1999) suggested that vision is of considerable advantage to skilled performers but they gradually learn not to be dependent upon it in skills that have low spatio–temporal constraints.

The role of context and ecological validity

The context and ecological validity of interceptive actions under study have also received considerable interest. Neisser (1976) was the one of the first to call for sensitivity to context and greater concentration on real world skills and environment. More recently, Ripoll's (1991) study of table tennis players has highlighted the important implications of context on the type of information used and one's resultant motor responses in returning a serve. Different visual information is attended to and response variability is much higher when players rally in a game than when they return shots in practice. Put simply, Ripoll suggested that different dimensions are operating at various times in a game. Prior to ball–racket impact, the decisions made are primarily semantic (strategic) in nature. Following interception, operations are largely sensorimotor and concerned with the execution of the movement. He proposed that the effect of expertise is likely to be seen both in the efficacy of decision-making prior to contact and in reduced variability and improved accuracy of the movement response.

Another finding that has been consistent across all of the work on cognitive expertise (not just in sport but in areas as diverse as chess, bridge, computer programming) is that the knowledge and performance advantages of experts are almost entirely domain specific. Performance changes are the result of years of training in a particular sport, not just a by-product of mere exposure to the domain (Allard, Deakin, Parker and Rodgers, 1993; Williams and Davids, 1995). Likewise, researchers have determined that there is an inherent link between knowledge structure, strategies chosen and one's physical skill. The strategies that athletes select reflect only those actions that they themselves can complete (French *et al.*, 1996). In other words, if you are unable to physically perform a skill, this skill will not be elicited in your repertoire of possible responses. All of which suggests that the study of cognitive expertise and performance in interceptive actions is likely to be extremely task-driven, specific to a sport and specific to one's own perceptual–motor skill level. Knowing this, it may be extremely difficult to derive common features that determine skill in interceptive actions across different domains, and for participants of varying skill levels.

Over the past decade there has also been a move towards increasing the ecological validity of laboratory tasks so that they are more representative of real world skills. There has also been a concomitant move toward more field-based research. Initially, cognitive expertise was assessed by laboratory tasks that involved slides, film, and eventually video of game situations. The next experimental development was to have participants perform with 'life-size' interactive video and actual motor responses (Helsen and Pauwels, 1993; Helsen and Starkes, 1999; Williams and Davids, 1998). In the past five years the experimental paradigm has advanced toward assessment of anticipation skill on the court/field.

The progression towards more field-based research has been made feasible through recent technological advances. Three examples will illustrate the move to more realistic assessment of cognitive expertise in interceptive actions. In the latest development in temporal occlusion studies, Starkes, Edwards, Dissanayake and Dunn (1995) were able to assess the use of advance cues in expert volleyball players when actual serves were visually tracked on court. Recently, Singer *et al.* (1998) monitored eye movements and motor responses on the tennis court during live game situations. Finally, Rodrigues, Vickers, and Williams (1999) have been able, by combining infra-red, video, and magnetic head tracking technologies, to examine the temporal and spatial coupling of eye, head, and arm movements in players returning a table tennis serve. Each of these studies is illustrative of the role that improving technologies can play in the assessment of real world skill.

Thus far, we have reviewed current understanding on how cognitive factors may contribute to skilled performance in interceptive actions. It appears that skilled performers have developed extensive task-specific knowledge bases that allow them to: a) use the sequential dependencies of flight to anticipate the ball's eventual position; b) employ appropriate eye and/or head movements to extract information from the ball's flight; c) produce reliable and consistent movement responses under either pre-programmed or continuous control modes; d) effectively process contextual information (i.e., advance visual cues, pattern recognition); and e) use their knowledge of situational probabilities to facilitate anticipation in interceptive tasks. In the final section of this chapter, we highlight three potential avenues for future research on cognitive expertise and performance in interceptive actions.

Future directions

What are the minimal essential sources of information for expert performance?

Abernethy has had a long-standing interest in the area of expert performance, and as evidenced from his work on temporal and spatial occlusion, has done much to characterise expert–novice differences. Given this background, it is not surprising that he has set out to determine the minimal essential information in any particular context that will produce the expert advantage. He suggested that the extreme time constraints in sports dictate that early information needs to be picked-up from opponents' preparatory actions, and that as a result perceptual skill may be closely linked to perception of the kinematics of the action viewed. While this idea was first generated from expert–novice differences in information processing, it is actually more consistent with ideas on perception of biological motion in ecological psychology. Abernethy (1993) proposed that the raw kinematics of an action may produce a 'feature-rich flow field' (p. 134) of optical information, that may be more readily used by experts.

Abernethy prepared point light displays (Johansson, 1973, 1975) of squash players hitting a ball. The motion of the lights represented the displacement-time records of movements from the joint centres of the opponent's body and racket head (Abernethy and Packer, 1989; Abernethy, 1993). Experimental results showed that experts were able to make shot predictions based on information derived from just point light information. While prediction levels for shot placement were degraded compared with the full vision condition, expert–novice differences were still apparent.

These findings suggest that kinematic information may be a valuable source and one that is available and extracted early, in order to enhance perception and decision-making. On the other hand, while the results indicate that experts are *able* to make use of this information, one cannot say whether experts *do* use this information to aid interceptive actions in the course of normal game play. Nevertheless, this is an intriguing finding and one that may serve to link the traditional findings on perceptual/cognitive expertise with perception/action approaches.

In a similar study, Ward, Williams, and Bennett (2002) examined the relationship between visual search strategy, anticipation, and biological motion perception in tennis. Experienced and inexperienced players were required to physically respond to tennis shots presented as 'normal' video clips and as point light images. Although the experienced group performed better than their inexperienced counterparts under both conditions, a decrement in performance was observed for both groups when viewing point light images. When viewing the point light video clips, participants employed fewer fixations (5.8 vs. 7.2) of longer duration (597 vs. 457 ms) to a smaller number of fixation locations (3.8 vs. 4.6) compared with the 'normal' film display. Further changes were apparent with regard to the areas of the display fixated, with a shift from proximal (trunk/hip) to more distal (arm/racket) cues under point light conditions. As observed in Figure 2.4, this shift in reliance on different sources of information was more pronounced in inexperienced rather than experienced players. These changes in visual behaviour as a result of the removal of structural/background information suggest that players may have employed a more 'synthetic' search strategy under point light compared with 'normal' viewing conditions. This is particularly the case for the experienced players, who fixated on more central or proximal areas than the inexperienced participants in the point light condition, maximising their potential to group or

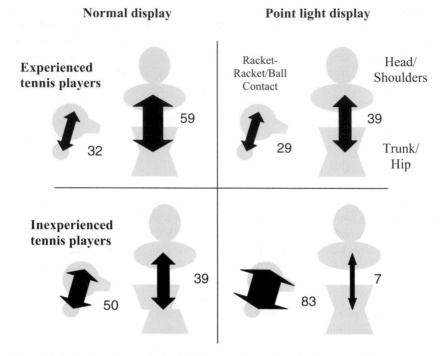

Figure 2.4 A schematic analysis of differences in search order between skill groups across viewing conditions. The direction of each arrow indicates the pattern of fixation behaviour, to and from specific areas of the display, while the number indicates the frequency. A thicker arrow represents a higher frequency of fixations. (Data from Ward, P., Williams, A.M. and Bennett, S.J (2002). Visual search and biological motor perception in tennis. *Quarterly for Sport and Exercise* **73**, 1, 107–12).

chunk information from peripheral areas of the display during single fixations. These differences in visual behaviour as a result of experience are consistent with Abernethy's proposal that anticipation skill is at least partly dependent on the perception of movement kinematics. The use of point light displays, perhaps coupled with event occlusion techniques, provides a potentially fruitful approach to identify the key invariants underlying perceptual skill in interceptive tasks.

Neural networks and symbolic connectionism

Neural network research has made great strides over the past ten years in describing motor control of aiming movements. Initially, most of the work centred on mapping the networks for relatively simple movement responses, such as moving a hand or tool to a stationary target. Neural networks have several advantages over traditional constructionist approaches. First, in neural networks movement control is parallel and distributed. In this way networks avoid two pitfalls of the constructionist approach, that of central control and serial processing of decisions.

In a neural network stimulus information enters the system and creates a *pattern of activation* across the units encompassed by the network. It is this pattern of activation that determines how an event or object is represented. Before a movement response is compiled, further computations are made and one's eventual response is based on the weight or strength of the connections within the system. Each new stimulus situation gives rise to new representations and, subsequently, alters the weights or strengths of the representations within the system. Initially when learning a new movement, the correct motor output may be produced only sporadically. Eventually, however, the system's weights for the correct response are altered to ensure more consistent and accurate performance. For obvious reasons, network modelling does have difficulties in explaining the generation of novel, more successful movement responses to stimuli.

One reason that network modelling is appealing is because it may bear resemblance to the architecture and neurophysiology of real systems. Bullock, Grossberg and Guenther (1996) provided a very detailed summary of their neural network research which models the computations and neurophysiological bases of movement control in animals, specifically their skill in reaching to targets in space. The authors offer a detailed description of how neural networks can represent a visually perceived target within a head-centred co-ordinate frame, transform this into a body-centred co-ordinate frame, form a spatial trajectory for hand movement, transfer this information into joint angle commands and, finally, produce movements. One subset of their computations, known as the direct model, can provide robust performance of movement trajectories with varying visual input, changes in degrees of freedom of joints, and changes in whether the end effector is the hand or a tool. They speculated that learning may occur when a body-centred representation of a three-dimensional target position is derived from a Vector Associative Map (VAM) (Gaudiano and Grossberg, 1991; Guenther, Bullock, Greve and Grossberg, 1994). They also suggested that the transformation from a head-centred representation to a body-centred representation is a complex process and one that is difficult to learn. This is in part because once the position of the target and body are known, a hand trajectory must be formulated based on spatial co-ordinates. Finally, their Vector Integration to Endpoint (VITE) model (Bullock and Grossberg, 1988) provides a neural network for trajectory formation.

Overall, Bullock, Grossberg and colleagues offer an elegant picture of inter-related neural networks that work together to allow both perception of a target and a motor response to reach for the target. The functional goal of the networks is to optimise performance over a wide range of reaching tasks. The authors also offered a discourse on the development of movement control. They addressed changes in movement performance through the learning of voluntary movements in infants, and suggested that spontaneous, non goal-directed, movements in infants, or 'motor babbling' provides a motor-to-spatial transformation that eventually, with practice, permits goal-directed reaching.

It will be interesting to see in future whether generated neural networks are able to produce skilled performances in complex environments equivalent to those seen in high level athletes. To date, most network analyses have been limited to situations where there is relatively little variability in target and performer positions and few time constraints. From a motor behaviour perspective, the tasks modelled to date have been relatively simple. A baseball example will serve to illustrate the current capabilities for modelling of interceptive actions. In the models of Bullock and Grossberg, the nature of an interceptive action is largely determined by the spatial location of the movement endpoint. Once the goal or movement endpoint is specified, the system essentially works backward to compute the most efficient movement to reach the target. If we imagine baseball to be similar to 'tee ball', the form of baseball played by young children, then networks would probably be able to model performance. If the ball is stationary on a tee, the endpoint is known and the effector can be modelled to contact this point in space. However, for real world pitches many variables help determine endpoint of the ball in space, some predictable (e.g. position of the fingers on the ball, angle of release, force imparted) some unpredictable (e.g. motor variability, wind). Dealing with these issues presents real difficulties for neural network modelling, even though such factors exemplify the constraints upon skilled performance in interceptive actions. It remains to be seen how realistic neural network simulations will be for skilled performance of complex movements, where the requirements of the response are always unique, and decisions must often be made with limited information, often under severe time constraints.

Unlike neural networks, connectionist modelling (McClelland and Rumelhart, 1981) is less concerned with either representing neurobiology *in vivo*, or technological applicability. It is more concerned with representing the semantic complexities of a task and how one's representation of a task changes with practice. Inherently, it has a closer link with traditional cognitive psychology. Holyoak's (1991) work, in particular, provides an important connection between a traditional cognitive psychology perspective of expert–novice differences, and network modelling. He suggests that most second generation findings in expertise research all point to domain specificity. Domain specificity means there are symbols, strategies and actions peculiar to a certain task. Because of specificity, he predicts that third generation expertise theory building will need to employ the strength of connectionist modelling, but not lose the importance of symbols. For this reason he proposes that the third wave of modelling is likely to employ what he terms, 'symbolic connectionism'.

The connectionist perspective has been ably described by Tienson (1990), and entails nodes and 'links' which are analogous to synaptic connections. The strength of connections between nodes is termed 'weight'. Higher weights indicate stronger signals, and/or connections with less resistance. Connectionist systems *learn* through the adjustment of weights. Unlike traditional information processing systems, but like neural networks, in connectionist models there is no central processing; there is simply simultaneous local processing throughout the entire system. Patterns of activation within a domain are formed and constantly updated. In the case of experts, their better memory for domain specific information (a robust finding for sport experts) can be characterised as symbols in active representations that are recreated, and whose weights are refined, each time they are accessed. As with neural networks, changing patterns of activation are the mechanism of learning. Some excitatory connections may be strengthened with learning, while the weights of other inhibitory links are weakened. If Holyoak (1991) is correct, 'symbolic connectionism' may play an important future role in describing the nature of expertise. Eventually, one may be able to determine the relative value of certain forms of practice, based on their efficacy for altering node links and weights. Likewise, the richness of symbols, their accessibility and their interconnectedness may prove valuable as potential measures of expertise.

Semi-longitudinal studies of expertise development

Within the expertise literature, there is a paucity of longitudinal and semi-longitudinal studies that examine the development of skill in interceptive actions. The proto-typical approach has been to use a cross-sectional design with skilled and less-skilled adult performers. Although there are several logistical problems with longitudinal designs (see Abernethy, Thomas and Thomas, 1993), this type of approach is essential to ensure that appropriate instructional interventions are employed to facilitate the acquisition and maintenance of expertise across the life span (Housner and French, 1994; McPherson, 1994). One approach would be to follow performers over the course of a season to determine changes in knowledge and skill level over a period of time (for an example, see French and Thomas, 1987). An initial cross-sectional analysis using large numbers of participants from various age groups could be followed by more detailed and protracted analyses of a smaller number of athletes or even a single performer (Housner and French, 1994).

Another alternative to the arduous process of longitudinal research has been suggested by Morris (2000). He proposed a quasi-longitudinal design based upon Régnier and Salmela's (1987) sliding populations approach. The sliding populations approach involves selecting a population 'pool' at each age group, for example, 10, 12, 14, 16 and 18 years of age. The pool must be large enough to ensure that it includes those performers at each age level who will become the elite at the next age group up and those who will not. At each age level, every performer is tested on those measures of interest using a 'detection instrument' (Régnier, Salmela and Russell, 1993). The suggestion is that each population pool (e.g. 10 years of age) should be followed through to the next age group (e.g. 12 years of age) and then re-tested using the same measures. This approach would provide quasi-longitudinal data on elite and sub-elite performers between 10 and 18 years within a two-year time period. Integrating cross-sectional and longitudinal research in this manner may provide a potentially useful approach, circumventing the problems involved when using either design in isolation.

Summary

In this chapter we have attempted to provide a historical review of cognitive research on interceptive actions in sport. Initially, we reviewed seminal work in this area by Hubbard and Seng (1954) as well as the first systematic programme of research on interceptive actions undertaken by Whiting and colleagues. Thereafter, we turned our attention to contemporary research on cognitive expertise in sport. Perceptual expertise in interceptive actions appears to be at least partly dependent on the development of task-specific cognitive knowledge structures accumulated through practice and experience. The ability to pick up advance visual cues, to have greater awareness of the events likely to unfold and to make more efficient use of eye and/or head movements are prerequisites for skilful performance on interceptive tasks. In the final section of the review we briefly highlighted some potential avenues for further investigative effort. The intention in this chapter was not to present an exhaustive review, but merely to provide a flavour of the wealth of knowledge accumulated during the last few decades by those working in the area of cognitive expertise and performance in interceptive actions in sport.

References

Abernethy, B. (1986). Visual search characteristics of expert and novice racket sport players. In J. Watkins, T. Reilly and C. Burwitz (eds), *Sports Science Common-Wealth and International Conference on Sport, Physical Education, Dance, Recreation and Health*. London: E & FN Spon.

Abernethy, B. (1988). The effects of age and expertise upon perceptual skill development in a racket sport. *Research Quarterly for Exercise and Sport* **59**, 210–21.

Abernethy, B. (1990). Anticipation in squash: differences in advance cue utilization between expert and novice players. *Journal of Sport Sciences* **8**, 17–34.

Abernethy, B. (1993). Searching for the minimal essential information for skilled perception and action. *Psychological Research* **55**, 131–8.

Abernethy, B. (ed.) (1994). Expert–novice differences in sport [Special Issue]. *International Journal of Sport Psychology* **25**(3).

Abernethy, B. and Packer, S. (1989). Perceiving joint kinematics and segment interactions as a basis for skilled anticipation in squash. In C.K. Giam, K.K. Cook and K.C. The (eds), *Proceedings 7th World Congress in Sport Psychology*. Singapore: International Society for Sport Psychology.

Abernethy, B. and Russell, D.G. (1987). Expert–novice differences in an applied selective attention task. *Journal of Sport Psychology* **9**, 326–45.

Abernethy, B, Thomas, K.T. and Thomas, J.T. (1993). Strategies for improving understanding of motor expertise (or mistakes we have made and things we have learned!) In J.L. Starkes and F. Allard (eds), *Cognitive issues in motor expertise*. Amsterdam: North Holland, SCAPPS.

Alain, C. and Girardin, Y. (1978). The use of uncertainty in racketball competition. *Canadian Journal of Applied Sport Sciences* **3**, 240–3.

Alain, C. and Proteau, L. (1977). Perception of objective probabilities in motor performance. In B. Kerr (ed.), *Human Performance and Behaviour*. Banff, Alberta: SCAPS.

Alain, C. and Proteau, L. (1980). Decision making in sport. In C.H. Nadeau, W.R. Halliwell, K.M. Newell and G.C. Roberts (eds), *Psychology of Motor Behavior and Sport*. Champaign, IL: Human Kinetics.

Alain, C. and Sarrazin, C. (1990). Study of decision-making in squash competition: a computer simulation approach. *Canadian Journal of Sport Science* **15**, 3, 193–200.

Alain, C., Sarrazin, C. and Lacombe, D. (1986). The use of subjective expected values in decision making in sport. In D.M. Landers (ed.), *Sport and elite performers*. Champaign, IL: Human Kinetics.

Allard, F., Deakin, J., Parker, S. and Rodgers, W. (1993). Declarative knowledge in skilled motor performance: byproduct or constituent? In J.L. Starkes and F. Allard (eds), *Cognitive Issues in Motor Expertise*. Amsterdam: North Holland.

Allard, F., Graham, S. and Paarsalu, M. (1980). Perception in sport: basketball. *Journal of Sport Psychology* **2**, 14–21.

Anderson, J.R. (1990). *Cognitive Psychology and its Implications* (3rd edition). New York: W.H. Freeman.

Bahill, A. and LaRitz, T. (1984). Why can't batters keep their eyes on the ball? *American Scientist* **72**, 249–53.

Bard, C. and Fleury, M. (1976). Analysis of visual search activity during sport problem situations. *Journal of Human Movement Studies* **3**, 214–22.

Bard, C. and Fleury, M. (1981). Considering eye movements as a predictor of attainment. In I.M. Cockerill and W.W. McGillivary (eds), *Vision and Sport*. Cheltenham: Stanley Thornes.

Bennett, S. and Davids, K. (1995). The manipulation of vision during the powerlift squat: exploring the boundaries of the specificity of learning hypothesis. *Research Quarterly for Exercise and Sport* **66**, 210–18.

Bootsma, R.J., Fayt, V., Zaal, F.T.J.M. and Laurent, M. (1997). On the information-based regulation of movement: what Wann (1996) may want to consider. *Journal of Experimental Psychology: Human Perception and Performance* **23**, 1282–9.

Bootsma, R.J. and Peper, L. (1992). Predictive visual information sources for the regulation of action with special emphasis on catching and hitting. In D. Elliott and L. Proteau (eds), *Vision and Motor Control*. Amsterdam: North Holland.

Bootsma, R.J. and van Wieringen, P.C.W. (1990). Timing an attacking forehand drive in table tennis. *Journal of Experimental Psychology: Human Perception and Performance* **16**, 21–9.

Bullock, D. and Grossberg, S. (1988). Neural dynamics of planned arm movements: emergent invariants and speed-accuracy properties during trajectory formation. *Psychological Research* **95**, 49–90.

Bullock, D., Grosssberg, S. and Guenther, F. (1996). Neural network modeling of sensory-motor control in animals. In H. Zelaznik (ed.). *Advances in Motor Learning and Control*. Champaign, IL: Human Kinetics.

Coelho, A. and Chamberlin, C.J. (1991). Decision-making in volleyball as a function of expertise. Paper presented at meeting of North American Society for Psychology of Sport and Physical Activity, Asilomar, CA, USA.

Davids, K., Palmer, D.R.P. and Savelsbergh, G.J.P. (1989). Skill level, peripheral vision and tennis volleying performance. *Journal of Human Movement Studies* **16**, 191–202.

Dillon, J.M., Crassini, B. and Abernethy, B. (1989). Stimulus uncertainty and response time in a simulated racket-sport task. *Journal of Human Movement Studies* **17**, 115–32.

Franks, I.M., Weicker, D. and Robertson, D.G. (1985). The kinematics, movement phasing and timing of a skilled action in response to varying conditions of uncertainty. *Human Movement Science* **4**, 91–105.

French, K.E. and Thomas, J.R. (1987). The relation of knowledge development to children's basketball performance. *Journal of Sport Psychology* **9**, 15–32.

French, K.E., Nevett, M.E., Spurgeon, J.H., Graham, K.C., Rink, J.E. and McPherson, S.L. (1996). Knowledge representation and problem solution in expert and novice youth baseball performance. *Research Quarterly for Exercise and Sport* **66**, 194–201.

Gaudiano, P. and Grossberg, S. (1991). Vector associative maps: unsupervised real-time error-based learning and control of movement trajectories. *Neural Networks* **4**, 147–83.

Gentile, A.M. (1972). A working model of skill acquisition with application to teaching. *Quest* **17**, 3–23.

Goulet, C., Fleury, M., Bard, C., Yerlès, M., Michaud, D. and Lemire, L. (1988). Analysis of visual cues from tennis serves. *Canadian Journal of Sport Sciences* **13**, 79–87.

Guenther, F.H., Bullock, D., Greve, D. and Grossberg, S. (1994). Neural representations for sensory-motor control, III: learning a body-centered representation of 3-D target position. *Journal of Cognitive Neuroscience* **6**, 341–58.

Haywood, K.M. (1984). Use of the image–retina and eye–head movement visual systems during coincidence-anticipation performance. *Journal of Sport Sciences* **2**, 139–44.

Helsen, W. and Pauwels, J.M. (1993). The relationship between expertise and visual information processing in sport. In J. Starkes and F. Allard (eds), *Cognitive Issues in Motor Expertise*. Amsterdam: North Holland.

Helsen, W.F. and Starkes, J.L. (1999). A multidimensional approach to skilled perception and performance in sport. *Applied Cognitive Psychology* **13**, 1–27.

Holyoak, K. (1991). Symbolic connectionism: toward third-generation theories of expertise. In K.A. Ericsson and J. Smith. (eds), *Toward a General Theory of Expertise*. Cambridge: Cambridge University Press.

Housner, L.D. and French, K.E. (1994). Future directions for research on expertise in learning, performance, and instruction in sport and physical activity. *Quest* **46**, 241–6.

Hubbard, A.W. and Seng, C.N. (1954). Visual movements of batters. *Research Quarterly* **25**, 42–57.

Isaacs, L.D. and Finch, A.E. (1983). Anticipatory timing of beginning and intermediate tennis players. *Perceptual and Motor Skills* **57**, 451–4.

Johansson, G. (1973). Visual perception of biological motion and a model for its analysis. *Perception and Psychophysics* **14**, 201–11.

Johansson, G. (1975). Visual motion perception. *Scientific American* **232**, 6, 76–88.

Jones, C.M. and Miles, T.R. (1978). Use of advance cues in predicting the flight of a lawn tennis ball. *Journal of Human Movement Studies* **4**, 231–5.

Laurent, M., Montagne, G. and Savelsbergh, G.J.P. (1994). The control and co-ordination of one-handed catching: the effect of temporal constraints. *Experimental Brain Research* **101**, 314–22.

Lee, D.N. (1976). A theory of visual control of braking based on information about time-to-collision. *Perception* **5**, 437–59.

Matsuo, T. and Kasai, T. (1994). Timing strategy of baseball-batting. *Journal of Human Movement Studies* **25**, 253–69.

McClelland, J.L. and Rumelhart, D.E. (1981). An interactive activation model of context effects in letter perception: Part 1. Account of basic findings. *Psychological Review* **88**, 375–406.

McPherson, S.L. (1994). The development of sport expertise: mapping the tactical domain. *Quest* **46**, 223–40.

Millslagle, D. (1988). Visual perception, recognition, recall and mode of visual search control in basketball involving novice and experienced basketball players. *Journal of Sport Behaviour* **11**, 32–44.

Morris, T. (2000). Psychological characteristics and talent identification in soccer. *Journal of Sports Sciences* **18**, 715–26.

Neumaier, A. (1982). The function of watching behavior in visual perception process in sport. *Sportwissenschaft* **12**, 78–91.

Neisser, U. (1976). *Cognition and reality*. San Francisco: W.H. Freeman.

Paull, G. and Glencross, D. (1997). Expert participation and decision making in baseball. *International Journal of Sport Psychology* **28**, 35–56.

Poulton, E.C. (1957). On prediction in skilled movements. *Psychological Bulletin* **54**, 467–78.

Proteau, L. (1992). On the specificity of learning and the role of visual information for movement control. In L. Proteau and D. Elliott (eds), *Vision and Motor Control*. Amsterdam: North Holland.

Proteau, L. and Cournoyer, J. (1990). Vision of the stylus in a manual aiming task: the effects of practice. *Quarterly Journal of Experimental Psychology* **42B**, 811–28.

Proteau, L., Marteniuk, R.G., Girouard, Y. and Dugas, C. (1987). On the type of information used to control and learn an aiming movement after moderate and extensive training. *Human Movement Science* **6**, 181–99.

Régnier, G. and Salmela, J.H. (1987). Predictors of success in Canadian male gymnasts. In B. Petiot, J.H. Salmela and T.B. Hoshizaki (eds.) *World Identification Systems for Gymnastic Talent*. Montreal, QC: Sport Psyche Editions.

Régnier, G., Salmela, J.H. and Russell, S.J. (1993). Talent detection and development in sport. In R. Singer, M. Murphey and L.K. Tennant (eds) *A Handbook of Research on Sports Psychology*. New York: Macmillan.

Ripoll, H. (1991). The understanding–acting process in sport: the relationship between the semantic and sensorimotor visual function. *International Journal of Sport Psychology* **22**, 221–43.

Ripoll, H., Bard, C. and Paillard, J. (1986). Stabilization of head and eyes on target as a factor in successful basketball shooting. *Human Movement Science* **5**, 47–58.

Ripoll, H., Fleurance, P. and Cazeneuve, D. (1987). Analysis of the visual strategies involved in the execution of forehand and backhand strokes in table tennis. In J.K. O'Regan and A. Levy-Schoen (eds), *Eye Movements: From Physiology to Cognition*. Amsterdam: Elsevier Science Publishing.

Rodrigues, S.T., Vickers, J.N. and Williams, A.M. (1999). Two visual systems and temporal pressure in table tennis. *Journal of Sport and Exercise Psychology* **21**, S91.

Rosenbaum, D.A. (1991). *Human Motor Control*. San Diego, CA: Academic Press.

Salmela, J.H. and Fiorito, P. (1979). Visual cues in ice hockey goaltending. *Canadian Journal of Applied Sport Sciences* **4**, 56–9.

Sanderson, F. H. (1981). Visual acuity and sports performance. In I.M. Cockerill and W.W. MacGillivary (eds.), *Vision and Sport*. Cheltenham: Stanley Thornes.

Savelsbergh, G.J.P. (1990) *Catching Behaviour: From Information-Processing to Ecological Psychological Explanation*. Amsterdam: Free University.

Sharp, R.H. and Whiting, H.T.A. (1974). Exposure and occluded duration effects in a ball-catching skill. *Journal Motor Behaviour* **6**, 3, 139–47.

Sharp, R.H., Farrally, M., Kingston, D., Laidler, A. and Saunders, J. (1975). Viewing time and occluded time as determinants of ball-catching success. *British Journal of Physical Education* **5**, 12–14.

Singer, R.N., Williams, A.M., Frehlich, S.G., Janelle, C.M., Radlo, S.J., Barba, D.A. and Bouchard, L.J. (1998). New frontiers in visual search: an exploratory study in live tennis situations. *Research Quarterly for Exercise and Sport* **69**, 290–6.

Starkes, J.L. (1987). Skill in field hockey: the nature of the cognitive advantage. *Journal of Sport Psychology* **9**, 146–60.

Starkes, J. and Allard, F. (eds) (1993). *Cognitive Issues in Motor Expertise.* Amsterdam: North Holland.

Starkes, J.L. and Deakin, J. (1984). Perception in sport: a cognitive approach to skilled performance. In W.F. Straub and J.M. Williams (eds.), *Cognitive Sport Psychology.* Lansing: Sport Science Associates.

Starkes, J.L. and Lindley, S. (1994). Can we hasten expertise by video simulations? *Quest* **46**, 211–22.

Starkes, J.L., Helsen, W.F. and Jack, R. (2001). Expert performance in sport and dance. In R.N. Singer, H.A. Hausenblas and C.M. Janelle (eds), *Handbook of Sport Psychology*, 2nd edition. New York: Macmillan

Starkes, J.L., Edwards, P., Dissanayake, P. and Dunn, T. (1995). A new technology and field test of advance cue usage in volleyball. *Research Quarterly for Exercise and Sport* **65**, 1–6.

Tenenbaum, G., Levy-Kolker, N., Bar-Eli, M. and Weinberg, R. (1994). Information recall of younger and older skilled athletes: the role of display complexity, attentional resources and visual exposure duration. *Journal of Sports Sciences* **12**, 529–34.

Tienson, J.L. (1990). An introduction to connectionism. In J.L Garfield (ed.), *Foundations of Cognitive Science.* New York: Paragon House.

Tresilian, J.R. (1994). Perceptual and motor processes in interceptive timing. *Human Movement Science* **23**, 1272–81.

Tresilian, J.R. (1995). Perceptual and cognitive processes in time-to-contact estimation: analysis of prediction–motion and relative judgement tasks. *Perception and Psychophysics* **57**, 231–45.

Tresilian, J.R. (1997). A revised tau hypothesis: consideration of Wann's analyses. *Journal of Experimental Psychology: Human Perception and Performance* **23**, 1272–81.

Tresilian, J.R. (1999). Visually timed action: time-out for 'tau'? *Trends in Cognitive Sciences* **3**, 301–10.

Tyldesley, D. and Whiting, H.T.A. (1975). Operational timing. *Journal of Human Movement Studies* **1**, 172–7.

van Soest, A.J. and Beek, P.J. (1996). Perceptual–motor coupling in the execution of fast interceptive actions. *Corpus, Psyche et Societas* **3**, 92–101.

Wallace, S.A., Stevenson, E., Weeks, D.L. and Kelso, J.A.S. (1992). The perceptual guidance of grasping a moving object. *Human Movement Science* **10**, 691–715.

Ward, P., Williams, A.M. and Bennett, S.J. (2002). Visual search and biological motor perception in tennis. *Research Quarterly for Sport and Exercise* **73**, 1, 107–12

Whiting, H.T.A. (1968). Training in a continuous ball-throwing and catching task. *Ergonomics* **11**, 375–82.

Whiting, H.T.A. (1969). *Acquiring Ball Skill: A Psychological Interpretation.* London: Bell.

Whiting, H.T.A. (1970). An operational analysis of a continuous ball throwing and catching task. *Ergonomics* **13**, 445–54.

Whiting, H.T.A. and Sharp, R.H. (1973). Visual occlusion factors in a discrete ball catching task. *Journal of Motor Behaviour* **6**, 1, 11–16.

Whiting, H.T.A., Alderson, G.J.K. and Sanderson, F.H. (1973). Critical time intervals for viewing and individual differences in performance of a ball-catching task. *International Journal of Sport Psychology* **4**, 155–6.

Whiting, H.T.A., Gill, E.B. and Stephenson, J.M. (1970). Critical time intervals for taking in flight information in a ball-catching task. *Ergonomics* **13**, 265–72.

Williams, A.M. (2000). Perceptual skill in soccer: implications for talent development and identification. *Journal of Sports Sciences* **18**, 737–50.

Williams, A.M. and Davids, K. (1995). Declarative knowledge in sport: a byproduct of experience or a characteristic of expertise. *Journal of Sport and Exercise Psychology* **17**, 259–78.

Williams, A.M. and Davids, K. (1998). Visual search strategy, selective attention, and expertise in soccer. *Research Quarterly for Exercise and Sport* **69**, 111–28.

Williams, A.M. and Grant, A. (1999). Training perceptual skill in sport. *International Journal of Sport Psychology* **30**, 194–220.

Williams, A.M., Davids, K. and Williams, J.G. (1999). *Visual Perception and Action in Sport.* London: Spon.

Williams, A.M., Singer, R.N. and Weigelt, C. (1998). Visual search strategy in live 'on-court' situations in tennis: an exploratory study. In A. Lees, I. Maynard, M. Hughes and T. Reilly (eds), *Science and Rackets II*. London: E & FN Spon.

Williams, A.M., Davids, K., Burwitz, L. and Williams, J.G. (1992) Perception and action in sport. *Journal of Human Movement Studies* **22**, 147–204.

Williams, A.M., Davids, K., Burwitz, L. and Williams, J.G. (1994). Visual search strategies in experienced and inexperienced soccer players. *Research Quarterly for Exercise and Sport* **65**, 127–35.

Wright, D., Pleasants, F. and Gomez-Meza, M. (1990). Use of advance cue sources in volleyball. *Journal of Sport and Exercise Psychology* **12**, 406–14.

3 Visual search and cue utilisation in racket sports

James H. Cauraugh and
Christopher M. Janelle

Dynamic interceptive actions in racket sports engage the performer in a series of perceptual and motor activities that generally occur in a predictable manner (Keele, Davidson and Hayes, 1998). Frequently, the sequence of shots during a rally demands that players make immediate decisions based on only partial stroke execution information from their opponent in order to anticipate the direction and force of an upcoming return. Other chapters have referred to the severe spatial and temporal constraints in many sports emphasising the use of interceptive actions (for example, see Chapter 1 and the chapters by Williams and Weigelt and by Williams and Starkes). Racket sport performers face just as severe task constraints. Indeed, many of today's highly-skilled tennis players serve and hit ground strokes at speeds over 160 km/h. Players preparing to receive such serves or volleys must begin anticipating and initiating movements very early to be in position to execute a return stroke, otherwise delays in the series of perceptual and motor processing activities prevent performers from being in the right place at the right time.

Given that highly-skilled racket players are adept at manipulating and disguising the characteristics of ground strokes, serves and volleys alike, opponents are faced with approaching stimuli from the ball that are extremely variable in direction, trajectory, and speed. The combination of these parameters dictates that expert racket players be capable of responding to a virtually unlimited array of stimulus combinations, under a wide variety of situational circumstances. How these individuals deal with these demanding task constraints remains an area of great interest to sport scientists, and is an issue of considerable debate among motor behaviourists interested in helping players acquire expertise in various racket sports.

Motor behaviourists and sport psychologists have been interested in identifying the visual cues and strategies used by high-level players to minimise delays in decision making and anticipation so as to assist performers. The assumption is that discovering and modelling successful perception and motor activity will better prepare players and minimise processing delays. Acknowledging the importance of identifying the most relevant environmental cues and ignoring irrelevant ones, substantial research has been directed toward determining the most critical visual cues on which to focus, as well as how experts and non-experts differ in the number and/or types of cues used. As William James noted as long ago as 1890, perceptual recognition of situations is a function of prior experience (James, 1890).

Establishing habits in visual search patterns that provide advance information (cues) about an upcoming stimulus, recognising these cues, and responding appropriately in the context of the goal of the task, involves many experiences from previous racket sport situations. Indeed, Helsen and Starkes (1999) argued that many racket sport decisions are multidimensional, and require a clear distinction on the perception–action link.

Scope of the review

In this integrated review of literature, the primary focus is on research emanating from an information processing framework (i.e. indirect perception). According to this view, stimuli acquired from the environment are processed through stimulus identification, response selection, and response programming stages. Within this conceptual approach, the quality of performance is reflected in the speed and accuracy by which the acquired information is coded and paired with appropriate motor responses. Topics include attentional/visual search strategies, decision making, anticipatory behaviour, and training capabilities. Leading questions directing this critical review include: (a) what is the consensus of visual search patterns used by highly-skilled racket sport players?; (b) do visual search patterns, decision making, and anticipatory behaviour of highly-skilled racket sport players (experts) differ from lesser-skilled players?; (c) can visual search patterns, decision making, and anticipatory behaviour be learned?; and (d) what are some future directions for research in visual search anz cue utilisation for racket sports?

Characteristics of the visual system

In attempting to answer the above questions, an overview of the visual system is beneficial. The visual system is the dominant sensory receptor with specific characteristics and capabilities. Inherent physical limitations of the visual system affect one's capability to intercept an approaching tennis ball, table tennis ball, racket ball, squash ball, or shuttlecock. The most relevant limitation is the speed with which the eye can move. Moreover, as an object approaches, the cerebellum is activated. Specifically, the cerebellum predicts the trajectory and velocity of an approaching ball/shuttlecock while activating feed-forward control in assisting with programming the appropriate movements (Leonard, 1998).

The traditional coaches' trusted reminder to 'keep your eyes on the ball' is not as easy as it seems. In the chapter by Williams and Starkes, the seminal work of Hubbard and Seng (1954) is discussed. They investigated the visual search charac-teristics of 24 collegiate and 54 professional baseball batters using a combination of electromyography, photographs, and cinematography. Electromyography measures indicated that no batter was able to continuously pursuit track (i.e. smooth pursuit eye movements) a pitch to the point of contact. This limitation of the ocular–motor system was attributed to the speed with which the eye can move while maintaining acuity. They estimated that the line of gaze was decoupled from the ball at between 60 to 240 ms prior to contact. At the time of contact, pursuit tracking was no longer feasible due to the ball velocity being too great to maintain acuity. Therefore, one interpretation from an information processing perspective is that the temporal and spatial accuracy of the bat swing was programmed based on information acquired by the cerebellum prior to this decoupling zone. Furthermore, Hubbard and Seng (1954) suggested that minor alterations in swing parameters might be possible due to monitoring from peripheral vision as the ball crossed the plate.

Ripoll and Fleurance (1988) reported similar results in a study of eye tracking in table tennis. Five expert table tennis players' visual search patterns were examined while participating in a live table tennis situation involving three strokes (backhand, forehand-topspin, and forehand). Visual search findings indicated that only the first part of the ball's trajectory was actually tracked. Additionally, the eye–head co-ordination strategy (i.e. tendency to keep the eye stable in the orbit at table tennis bat and ball contact) dominated the visual search characteristics. This was especially true when the ball was moving toward the body, as during the backhand, the image was constantly viewed with the eye–head orienting system dominant. They concluded that fixing the head and eye in a place approximately where contact will occur is a more appropriate strategy because the need to follow the ball with the image–retina system (i.e. eye is rotating within its socket at the point-of-contact) is eliminated. This strategy also minimises the potential detrimental effects of the blurring that can occur due to the attempt to pursuit track a ball that is beyond the psychophysical limitations of the visual system.

Taken together, it appears that participants in sports that require visual search and gaze control, adopt search strategies to comply with the limitations imposed by the visual system. A commonality among the above studies is that when participants pursuit track, they decouple the line of sight before actual contact with the arriving object. Therefore, any visual input that occurs after this point is modulated by peripheral sources. Assuming, from an information processing viewpoint, that an open-loop control process guides the initiation and execution of responses in this context, adjustments following the point at which line of sight is decoupled from the object probably have little effect on the overall quality of the movement.

Visual search: obtaining advance information for anticipation

If a player is capable of acquiring advanced cues, much of the response selection processing that is required can be accomplished prior to viewing the stimulus (i.e. ball flight characteristics). Of particular interest in the visual search literature has been the measurement of fixation characteristics such as locations and durations. A fixation is typically defined as a pause in time during which point of gaze is maintained for 90 ms or more (e.g. see Williams, Davids and Williams, 1999). Fixations tend to be distributed across the visual scene through saccades. The blurring of images that occurs during saccades is known as saccadic suppression, a phenomenon that precedes saccades by approximately 30–40 ms due to unknown reasons. Accordingly, it is often suggested that slower search rates (fewer fixations for longer durations) tend to be most advantageous due to enhanced opportunities for information acquisition. Further, a coherent representation of the visual field or situation may accrue among experts because of their ability to chunk information effectively, thus requiring fewer fixations. An assumption inherent in examining eye movements as an index of visual attention allocation is that fixations depend on the most appropriate point for the pick-up of the most information relevant to task performance. However, this issue remains a source of debate (along with others) that is beyond the scope of this chapter. For a thorough discussion on this topic, see Abernethy (1988) and Williams and Grant (1999).

In recent years, the visual search activity of athletes has been examined as a means of discriminating performance expertise in sport tasks (e.g. Abernethy, 1990; Goulet, Bard and Fleury, 1989; Helsen and Pauwels, 1990; Singer, Cauraugh, Chen, Steinberg, Frehlich and Wang 1994; Shank and Haywood, 1987; Williams, Davids, Burwitz and Williams, 1994). Specifically, researchers have attempted to outline the mechanisms and patterns that differentiate experts and novices in their ability to perceive and use vital information in the sport environment. The majority of research in this area has been concerned with the relationship between visual search and selective attention, and with the influence of these processes on decision making strategies and eventual performance (Helsen and Pauwels, 1992, 1993).

Visual search in racket sports

Visual search patterns of expert performers have been found to differ from novice performers in a wide variety of sports and sport simulations emphasising interceptive actions including baseball (Bahill and LaRitz, 1984; Shank and Haywood, 1987), basketball (Vickers, 1996), fencing (Bard, Guezennec and Papin, 1980), golf (Vickers, 1992, 1988), ice hockey (Bard and Fleury, 1981), soccer (Tyldesley, Bootsma and Bomhoff, 1982; Williams, Davids, Burwitz and Williams, 1994; Williams and Davids, 1998), table tennis (Ripoll and Fleurance, 1988), and volleyball (Ripoll, 1988; Sandu, 1982; Vickers and Adolphe, 1997).

Following Bard and Fleury's (1976) initial study on eye movements in sport, many researchers interested in attentional processing began asking questions concerning the nature of visual search in static slide presentations as well as in the context of more dynamic sports, such as badminton, squash, tennis, or table tennis. Perhaps most notable in the area of racket sports is the research conducted by Abernethy and colleagues (Abernethy, 1990; Abernethy and Russell, 1987a, 1987b). Through a systematic series of studies, they identified the most pertinent visual cues used by badminton and squash players as well as how visual search strategies differed among expert and novice players of these sports. The next sections highlight these studies in addition to more recent studies on tennis.

Visual search in badminton

Abernethy and Russell (1987a) examined how both temporal and spatial occlusion of various information sources affected the coincidental use of anticipatory cues by expert and novice badminton players. In two experiments, the task was to predict quickly and accurately the landing position of the opponent's stroke. In Experiment 1, temporal occlusion was used to selectively vary the duration of the stroke sequence that was viewed. Manipulations of temporal periods yielded differences in visual cue usage. Expert players were more capable of using information presented earlier in the display in comparison to novices. Similarly, the results of Experiment 2, in which spatial occlusion techniques were deployed, demonstrated that both experts and novices relied primarily on the playing side arm and racket regions for information pick-up. Additionally, when these cues were occluded, prediction accuracy was significantly adversely affected for experts, but not for novices.

Though arguably a subtle difference in the overall cue utilisation sequence employed by expert and novice players, the differential effect of occluding the racket and arm region for experts and novices has important implications. When the racket and arm regions were occluded, performance for experts significantly deteriorated, indicating that the additional information provided by the orientation of the arm along with the racket was critical for maintaining prediction accuracy in expert performers. Cues from the arm also occurred earlier in the sequencing of the serve, and therefore provided advance cues that the experts were apparently reliant upon. For novices, on the other hand, removal of this information was less detrimental, as they were presumably less attuned to arm and racket orientations for gathering prediction information. In turn, this finding suggests a critical coupling of biomechanical attributes (i.e. orientation of arm and racket) for decision making among expert players, which allows them to prepare a response in advance through receptor anticipation.

In a follow-up study, Abernethy and Russell (1987b) included occlusion techniques while also recording eye movements. Contrary to expectations, visual search patterns did not differ between experts and novices, for the most part. However, in line with the findings of their previous study, fixation patterns were centered on the arm and the racket-arm areas of the display. They also noticed a proximal to distal sequence of visual scanning, a finding that is consistent with the notion of a visual pivot, as espoused by Ripoll, Williams, and respective colleagues (e.g. Ripoll, Kerlirizin, Stein and Reine, 1995; Williams and Davids, 1998; Williams and Elliott, 1999).

Visual search in squash

Abernethy's (1990) studies on squash were similar to those on badminton. Players were required to view game situations presented through video, and to determine the direction and force of the opponent's shot. Consistent with the badminton findings, expert–novice differences emerged in the temporal occlusion performance of the groups. A second experiment was conducted in a squash court to determine whether the artificiality of the experimental setting and the two-dimensional film presentation influenced visual search strategies. As in previous work, it was again found that search patterns (fixation distribution, order, and duration) remained stable across the skill groups. These findings led Abernethy to conclude that the difference in anticipatory skill between groups is not a function of fixation on different cues but, rather, differences in processing the meaning of informational cues acquired from various locations.

Note that in each of the studies in which visual search patterns were evaluated, differences were evident in a few dependent measures. Although it could certainly be the case that search strategies are more similar than different among experts and novices, subtle differences in eye movements could be responsible for a significant amount of the variance between expert and novice performers. As will become evident in the following section, the predominance of evidence in the tennis context points to differences in search patterns as a significant means of differentiating experts and novices.

Visual search in tennis

Indirect measurement of visual search

Perhaps the first attempt to determine how tennis players use advanced cues to prepare a response was conducted by Jones and Miles (1978). Their work is often cited (along with that of Whiting and colleagues) as one of the pioneering efforts to implement temporal occlusion in an effort to determine the critical cues needed for effective decision making in an applied sport setting. Expert lawn tennis coaches (who were subdivided into top-grade coaches and other coaches) and novice undergraduates were presented film sequences of a tennis serve and asked to determine where the ball was going, as quickly and accurately as possible. Temporal occlusion was spaced at 336 ms after ball/racket contact, 126 ms after impact, and 42 ms before impact. Across skill levels, occluding the film prior to ball contact significantly impaired anticipatory performance, whereas prediction accuracy remained stable among the two temporal occlusion conditions post ball contact. However, significant between-group differences emerged in the 126 ms-after-contact and 42 ms-before-contact conditions. The top-grade coaches were more capable of responding accurately than the novices. Collectively, the results were some of the first, not only in tennis, but also in the context of reactive sports, to empirically document differences in cue usage proficiency among athletes of disparate skill levels.

Isaacs and Finch (1983) conducted a similar investigation on anticipatory accuracy using 34 beginning and 16 intermediate tennis players. Like Jones and Miles (1978), a temporal occlusion paradigm was arranged in which viewing was restricted to four time periods around ball and racket contact: (a) 10 ms prior to contact, (b) at contact, (c) 15 ms after contact, and (d) 30 ms after contact. Findings indicated that experts were superior at predicting the latitude of ball placement across occlusion conditions. Isaacs and Finch's (1983) findings were consistent with those of Jones and Miles (1978), both confirming differences in the capability of experts and novices to acquire and process advanced information.

Later in the 1980s, Buckolz, Prapavesis, and Fairs (1988) made a more qualitative attempt to examine advanced cue utilisation in the context of predicting the type of an opponent's passing shot as well as how the shot was determined. Two groups of tennis players (intermediate and advanced) watched film presentations of various forehand and backhand passing tennis shots including: down the line, cross-court, and lob shots. Findings indicated that the advanced players were more adept at predicting the type of passing shot than were intermediates. In addition, the advanced players used different and more pertinent cues, as indicated by verbal report. The researchers attributed their findings primarily to the notion that experts were more aware of what the telegraphic cues were for given shots (e.g. forehand or backhand down the line or cross-court). They were also more capable of using these cues for decision making, even when both groups were aware of them.

Direct measurement of visual search: eye movements

Although the capability to measure eye movements has existed since the late 1800s (Ebbinghaus used suction cups on the eyes tethered to strings to diagram scan paths), and interest in applying the use of eye tracking technology to understanding visual perception occurred approximately at the same time, the application of this technology to sport did not occur until almost a century later. In 1989, Goulet, Bard, and Fleury conducted a study on eye movements of tennis players.

Goulet, Bard and Fleury's (1989) is one of the most oft-cited, methodologically sound, and comprehensive studies of visual search techniques and anticipation in tennis. They compared expert and novice tennis players watching a video serve sequence for two purposes: (a) to assess differences in visual search tendencies and (b) to determine how the absence of visual information (through occlusion techniques) influenced information pick-up. Participants were asked to predict the type of serve (flat, topspin, or slice) in two related experiments. In addition, visual search characteristics were examined for different phases of the serve, thus providing a more detailed examination of differences in selection tendencies than would be the case when fixation tendencies are collapsed across an entire serve sequence. In other words, by evaluating visual fixation patterns during individual phases of the tennis serve, it became possible to isolate differences in search patterns that occurred as well as how they were manifested. Such information was unavailable from studies in which eye movement characteristics were accumulated across an entire shot sequence (i.e. Abernethy and Russell, 1987a, 1987b; Isaacs and Finch, 1983; Jones and Miles, 1978).

In their first experiment (Goulet, Bard and Fleury, 1989), expert–novice differences in visual search patterns (eye movement characteristics) were examined with particular attention paid to fixation location, scan path, and search rate variability between groups across three phases of the serve (ritual sequence of movements completed prior to the preparatory stage, and execution stage). For search rate, experts exhibited more fixations than did novices during the ritual phase of the serve. The authors ascribed this new search rate finding to the notion that, because experts process information faster, they are capable of fixating on more areas in a given time period than their novice counterparts. Although search patterns were similar during the preparatory phase, expert–novice differences emerged during the ritual and execution phases. Results showed that during the ritual phase, experts tended to organise their search around the head and shoulder/ trunk complex to obtain information about general body position. During the preparatory phase, scan paths were similar for both experts and novices and centred primarily around the ball in hand, ball toss area, and the server's head. In the execution phase, expert–novice differences again emerged. Experts terminated fixation on the racket sooner than novices, and novices tended to prolong their processing by following the ball's trajectory longer after impact. Goulet, Bard and Fleury (1989) concluded that experts were more in-tune with the body positioning function during the ritual stage to better obtain advanced information for decision making. That is, the elite players were able to use body-positioning cues to minimise decision-making time.

In Experiment 2, Goulet, Bard and Fleury (1989) evaluated the information pick-up of experts and novices during a cue occlusion paradigm in which filmed sequences were edited into five segments of variable duration. The segments included the following situations: (a) preparatory phase (875 ms), (b) preparatory phase and first part of execution phase (1125 ms), (c) preparatory and execution stages until ball/racket impact (1208 ms), (d) beginning of ritual phase until impact (4710 ms), and (e) entire serve without occlusion (5048 ms). These conditions complemented the subdivisions of ritual, preparatory, and execution stages of interest examined in the first experiment. Again, participants determined serve type. A significant interaction of expertise and occlusion situation emerged when the preparatory phase only was shown and response accuracy significantly decreased for experts. This was not the case in any of the occlusion conditions. In contrast, significant improvement in response accuracy did not occur among novice players until the ritual phase was included. Evidently, the experts were more capable of using information presented during the preparatory stage than were novices. Initial analysis of the decision time data indicated an imposed decision bias based on the inclusion of the ritual phase. More specifically, when the duration of the ritual phase was eliminated, expert–novice differences persisted, suggesting that experts were more capable of (a) accessing memory-driven anticipatory information (i.e. perceptual anticipation), and (b) using stimulus-driven sources of information (i.e. receptor anticipation) when the film displayed the preparatory phase only.

Findings from Experiment 2 supported the idea that although eye movements were similar between groups during the preparatory phase, there were differences in decision capabilities during this phase that must be attributed to the use of the information acquired. However, experts were shown to be faster decision-makers, a finding that is primarily based on the influence of the processing during the ritual phase where, once again, there were eye movement differences. Goulet, Bard and Fleury (1989) admitted that the expert–novice differences identified in the search strategy during the ritual and execution stages could explain performance variability. However, they argued in favour of Abernethy's (1988, 1990) contention that eye movement differences may not be indicative of expertise. Although this article is often cited as support for Abernethy's conclusion, it is apparent that eye movement differences were evident, and that these differences could account for a significant portion of the variance in the prediction of accuracy and speed.

Singer *et al.* (1996) conducted an extension to the work of Goulet, Bard and Fleury (1989). Two complementary methodologies were used to assess the visual search, anticipatory behaviour, reaction time, and movement time of expert and novice tennis players in a variety of laboratory contexts. The initial stage of the experiment was designed to examine visual search tendencies while viewing opponents' serves and ground strokes as presented via video presentation. Participants responded as quickly and accurately as possible to the type and location of these shots. Decision speed concerning the type of serves was determined by recording the duration between the initiation of the ball toss to the point at which participants pressed one of two switches mounted on the arm of a chair (using the dominant arm) in which they were seated (the index finger indicated a flat serve and middle finger indicated a spin serve). Directional measures of serve and ground strokes were indexed by the duration of time taken to move a joystick (using the non-dominant arm) in the direction toward which the participant expected the shot to proceed. Results indicated that novices fixated more toward the head than did experts during serves. Furthermore, a gender effect was found: males spent more time fixating the arm and racket than did females, and females spent more time fixating the ball. For ground strokes, expert females exhibited a higher number of fixations on the head and ball than did male experts, who fixated more on the racket. The novice females fixated more on the ball, left shoulder, and hip than did males. Male beginners exhibited more fixations on the racket than did females. Finally, experts were faster and more accurate in their responses for ball direction than were novices for both ground strokes and serves.

Singer *et al.* (1996) also conducted a qualitative analysis by comparing the visual search tendencies of the two best players with two randomly chosen individuals from the novice group. Search patterns were markedly different, with experts exhibiting a very systematic search of the most relevant cues. During the serve, the experts search patterns were clustered around the racket arm and the racket region, and after ball contact they tracked the ball. For ground strokes, search patterns began at the waist region and then progressed distally to the racket and racket–ball contact area before tracking the ball. These tendencies were noticed to be highly consistent across multiple presentations of serves and ground strokes. In contrast, novice search patterns were scattered in a highly variable fashion to various locations and were inconsistent from trial to trial for both tennis serves and ground strokes.

The work of Singer *et al.* (1996) provides direct evidence to support the importance of the mental quickness aspects of tennis. Specifically, although reaction time and movement time are certainly contributors to being in the right place at the right time, Singer *et al.* (1996) demonstrated that the capability to extract critical informational sources from the presented cues accounted for the majority of the performance variability between skill levels. Furthermore, discriminant analysis revealed that the most salient variables for classifying experts and novices were the eye movement characteristics rather than the reaction time or movement time differences.

Visual search on a tennis court (during play)

Despite the encouraging results of these studies in terms of identifying differences in search strategies exhibited by players at different skill levels, methodological limitations induced by the contrived film presentations used in the majority of the work in this area caution against extrapolation to real world contexts. Specifically, the two dimensional displays as well as the simplistic response requirements (e.g. a button press or joystick movement) used in the investigations described thus far, may mask other potential differences that characterise expert search tendencies. Abernethy, Thomas, and Thomas (1993) argued that the contrived laboratory environment may not accurately portray expert advantages due to (a) removal of experience factors that are associated with actually performing the task in an ecologically valid setting, (b) the introduction of potential floor or ceiling effects in measurement variability, and (c) constraining the experts' typical responses to either using different information to create a response or preventing access to information normally available in the performance context. Thus, although slight variations in eye movements and perceived point of gaze were evident in the studies reviewed thus far, possible alterations in those search tendencies that may favour expert performers, as well as response capabilities that compliment these strategies, may not emerge in contrived contexts.

Given the film limitations, Singer *et al.* (1998) sought to more thoroughly describe the eye movements of experts as they returned serve in a live action environment. To negate the inherent limitations of eye-tracking systems, particularly those induced by the inability to collect eye-tracking data in direct sunlight, data collection took place at night under lighted tennis courts. Five expert tennis players returned serves from an opponent, just as if during actual play. Eye movement characteristics and the quality of the return of serve were measured. In addition, the returner was also videotaped and a picture-in-picture splicing of the videotape allowed the gaze behaviour to be interpreted during the three phases (ritual, backswing, and foreswing) of the return. These behaviours could therefore be analyzed during phases of the serve (ritual, ball toss, ball–racket contact to ball bounce, and ball bounce to ball–racket contact by the receiver). The experimental set-up and specific camera views are shown in Figure 3.1 Descriptive analyses revealed particularities in search patterns that were unique to the highest quality male and female players in the study. Intra-expert differences were noticed during the ball toss phase such that the two best players demonstrated 100 per cent pursuit tracking. Furthermore, these players were the only ones to exclusively pursuit track the ball during the entire ball flight sequence. In contrast, the three lesser skilled university team players were more diffuse in fixation locations and search tendencies, favouring a strategy of using an anticipatory saccade to place the point-of-gaze in front of the ball and then letting the ball catch up to the expected point

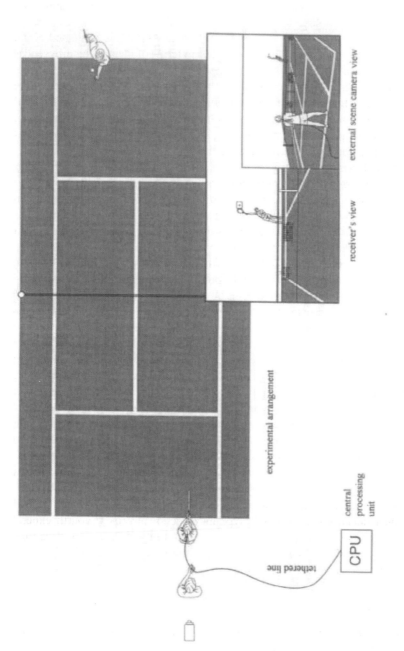

Figure 3.1 An illustration of simultaneous views from the external scene camera and a service receiver's view showing the coupling of the receiver's gaze behaviour to reception and return movements. Adapted from Singer, R.N., Williams, A.M., Frehlich, S., Janelle, C.M., Radlo, S., Barba, D. and Bouchard, L. (1998). New frontiers in visual search: an exploratory study in live tennis situations. *Research Quarterly for Exercise and Sport* **69**, 290–6.

of contact with the racket. Despite the lack of comparison with a group of novice players in the 1998 study, the work of Singer *et al.* (1996, 1998) signifies an important advance in understanding what characterises expert anticipatory tendencies, and one that certainly should be explored in future studies with appropriate control groups.

An additional study by Ward, Williams, and Bennett (2002) investigated visual search patterns while expert and novice tennis participants viewed and physically responded to normal and point light displays of ground strokes. In contrast to the investigations discussed thus far, Ward, Williams and Bennett (2002) approached the role of expertise and anticipation from a perception–action theoretical framework. Questions asked concerned how the relative motion versus background structure information of the opponent influenced the use of various perceptual cues. Generally, results indicated that there were no differences in search rate as a function of skill level, but that both experts and novices demonstrated a greater number of fixations of shorter durations under point light conditions. Group differences were evident in the duration of fixations to particular locations, with experts' search distributed primarily to central regions of the opponent's body and novices search patterns centered around more peripheral locations. A key point about these findings was that experts were more attuned to the minimal essential kinematic information as indicated by the consistent search strategy than novices.

In summary, racket sports (e.g. tennis play) are constrained by spatial and time parameters such that players must be able to visually search the opponent looking for cues to anticipate direction and force of shots. In general, the reviewed visual search studies revealed that expert players follow less variable search patterns and maintain fixations on specific areas for longer times than novice players. An implication drawn from these findings is that players of disparate skill levels pursue visual search and cue utilisation in a different manner. Indeed, superior performers demonstrate efficacious visual search patterns and cue utilisation strategies that yield effective anticipation of opponents' actions (Williams and Grant, 1999).

Collectively, the results from relevant empirical investigations of various racket sports (as summarised in Table 3.1) suggest four conclusions. First, prediction accuracy improves as exposure to the duration of stroke sequence increases. Second, experts are capable of prediction accuracy that is far greater than that of novices at earlier periods in the stroke sequence. Third, the orientation of arm and racket, as well as (but to a lesser extent) the shoulder and trunk area are critical locations for information acquisition concerning the type and direction of strokes. Fourth, experts are more attuned to advanced cues that occur earlier in the stroke sequence than are novices, allowing greater speed and accuracy in predicting stroke type and location.

Training visual search and cue utilisation

Are players able to learn the visual search patterns to recognise or identify the relevant cues for making an accurate prediction about an upcoming stroke? Asked differently, what experiences with visual search patterns would help tennis players

Table 3.1 Summary of racket sport studies

Sport/Author/Participants	Purpose
Badminton Abernethy and Russell (1987a) (Experiment 1) *Participants:* N = 55 (experts = 13 M and 12 F, mean age = 18–32 yrs.; novices = 22 M and 13 F, mean age = 18–29 yrs)	Compared characteristics of anticipatory cues used by expert and novice racket sport players. Temporal occlusion effects on prediction accuracy were tested. Film was occluded at (1) 167 ms prior to shuttle contact, (2) 83 ms prior, (3) at shuttle contact, (4) 83 ms post contact, and then (5) for the full shot.
Badminton Abernethy and Russell (1987a) (Experiment 2) *Participants:* N = 55 (experts = 13 M and 12 F, mean age = 18–32 yrs.; novices = 22 M and 13 F, mean age = 18–29 yrs) (Same as Experiment 1)	Compared characteristics of anticipatory cues used by expert and novice badminton players. In Experiment 2, spatial occlusion effects on prediction accuracy. Elements of the display that were occluded included (1) the racket and arm, (2) the racket, (3) the head, (4) the lower body, and (5) an irrelevant background cue.
Badminton Abernethy and Russell (1987b) *Participants:* N = 31 (experts = 12 M and 3 F, mean age = 18–32 yrs.; novices = 11 M and 5 F, mean age = 18–29 yrs)	Examined the relationship between expertise and visual search strategy through the use of both occlusion paradigms and visual search strategies. Temporal and spatial occlusion conditions were identical to those presented in Abernethy (1987a).
Squash Abernethy (1990) (Experiment 1) *Participants:* N = 32 (experts = 8 M and 7 F, mean age = 23.3 yrs.; novices = 8 M and 9 F, mean age = 20.2 yrs)	Examined visual search activity to see how experts and novices utilize environmental info to guide skilled action in filmed display occluded at five time periods: (160 ms prior to ball contact, 80 ms prior, at contact, 80 ms post contact, and whole shot).
Squash Abernethy (1990) (Experiment 2) *Participants:* N = 8 (experts = 2 M and 2 F, mean age = 19–30 yrs.; novices = 2 M and 2 F, mean age = 19–29 yrs)	Examined if the same general visual search strategy (as was found in Experiment 1) for the film task was comparable in the natural setting.

Measures	Findings
Subjects predicted the landing position of the stroke that was viewed on film. Prediction accuracy was based on radial error, lateral error, and depth error.	The critical period for extraction of visual information appears to be from 83 ms prior to 83 ms post shuttle contact. Advanced cues appear to be most relevant for resolving depth perception, but early flight information is needed to identify direction of the shuttle. Expert/novice differences were evident from 83 ms prior to contact through the entire duration of the serve.
Predicted the landing position of the stroke that was viewed on film. Prediction accuracy was based on radial error, lateral error, and depth error.	Experts were more accurate than novices in serve position identification. The striking implement (the racket) was most important for both novices and experts, but the experts also apparently relied on information from the arm and its relative position with the racket.
Predicted the landing position of the stroke that was viewed on film. Prediction accuracy was based on radial error, lateral error, and depth error. Also, visual search patterns of interest included visual correction time, dwell time, mean fixation duration, and percentage of film trial time per cue.	Experts exhibited lower prediction error from temporal occlusion periods 2 through 5, and were more reliant on the racket and arm regions in the spatial occlusion paradigm. Predominantly similar search patterns characterised experts and novices, although experts were more reliant on the racket and arm regions, while novices typically searched the trunk and head region more than the experts.
While watching a film task participants were required to predict the outcome of an opposing player's stroke (direction and force). Also, eye movements of interest included fixation, location, fixation duration, and order of fixations.	Expert players were more accurate in predicting stroke direction and stroke force at all time periods. Also, experts exhibited a greater fixation duration to the arm and head region, while novices were more reliant on post contact cues.
Participants were required to predict as quickly and accurately as possible the stroke direction and force. Likewise, fixation distribution, order, and duration was of interest with regard to visual search strategies.	In the natural setting, no evidence of expert–novice difference in visual search, in either fixation distribution, order, or duration. For both groups, the preponderance of fixations were to the ball, racket, and arm region.

continued...

Table 3.1 continued

Sport/Author/Participants	Purpose
Tennis Benguigui and Ripoll (1998) *Participants:* $N = 48$ (24 tennis players and 24 novices. Ages: 7, 10, 13, and 23)	Examined the development of perceptuomotor processes involved in coincidence timing tasks according to age and experience.
Tennis Davids, Palmer, and Savelsbergh (1989) *Participants:* $N = 30$ (M tennis players equally divided into three groups: elite, competitive club, and recreational)	Examined forehand volley performance under conditions of full and occluded visual feedback, with specific reference to the role of peripheral vision.
Tennis Farrow, Chivers, Hardingham, and Sachse (1998) *Participants:* $N = 24$ (13 F and 11 M novice tennis players). Assigned and stratified by gender to (1) a video based perception training group, (2) a placebo training group, (3) and a control group.	Measured the effects of video-based perceptual training on the effectiveness of tennis return of a serve.
Tennis Goulet, Bard, and Fleury (1989) (Experiment 1) *Participants:* $N = 29$ (Novice group 8 M and 6 F, mean age = 21.6 yrs. Expert group 7 M and 8 F, mean age = 22.3 yrs)	Identified the type of serve presented (flat, top-spin, and sliced), as well as the visual search patterns involved at different serve phases (ritual, preparation, execution).
Tennis Goulet, Bard, and Fleury (1989) (Experiment 2) *Participants:* $N = 20$ (10 Novices, mean age = 22.1 yrs. 10 Experts, mean age = 21.2 yrs)	Identified the type of serve presented (flat, top-spin, and sliced), and determined the relative importance of serve phase to serve type recognition through temporal occlusion paradigm.

Measures	*Findings*
Tested in a coincidence timing task which estimated the arrival of a stimulated moving object on a target. Constant velocity, constant acceleration, and constant deceleration were analysed.	Timing accuracy improves between 7 and 10 years. Tennis practice accelerates the development of timing accuracy. Acceleration or deceleration of a moving stimulus had no effect on timing accuracy.
Measures of interest included shot placement accuracy (based on court scoring zones) and stroke quality (based on height errors and quality errors) under the conditions of effector visual feedback and at two different ball speeds: 29.06 m/s and 20.12 m/s.	No variations in scores between screen conditions. Difference in performance according to level of expertise and speed of the oncoming projectile. Volleying in slow speed was better than in fast for higher expertise groups (elite and club level players).
Eight training sessions of 15 minutes over four weeks between pre- and post-testing. Measured decision making time and directional accuracy.	Perceptual training group was significantly faster than placebo and control group for deciding appropriate response. No significant difference between training groups with regard to directional accuracy.
Visual search patterns (number of fixations and scan paths/associations between areas). Accuracy of serve type identification.	Experts organized their search around the shoulder/trunk region during the ritual phase while novices searched the head region. In the execution stage, experts search was predominantly on the racket while novice search patterns were more scattered.
Speed (decision time) and accuracy (number of correct serve types identified) of decisional processes.	Experts exhibited significantly faster and more accurate decision making. Within the expert group, there was no difference in decision making accuracy from time periods 2 through 5 (from first part of preparatory phase through the execution of the serve), but including only the preparatory phase was detrimental to decision making capabilities.

continued...

Table 3.1 continued

Sport/Author/Participants	Purpose
Tennis Isaacs and Finch (1983) *Participants:* $N = 50$ (34 beginning and 16 intermediate players)	Examined the differences in expertise as related to the ability to anticipate placement of tennis serves under different viewing conditions as manipulated by occlusion techniques: 10 ms before contact, 0 ms (at contact), 15 ms after contact, and 30 ms after contact during flight.
Lawn Tennis Jones and Miles (1978) *Participants:* $N = 92$ (32 highly experienced professional lawn tennis coaches (age 22–66), and 60 undergrads (age 18–25) with little or no experience)	Compared the relative usefulness of advanced cues through occlusion techniques in which the film was temporally occluded in three conditions: (A) film cut off 336 ms after impact of ball on racket, (B) cut off at 126 ms post contact, and (C) cut off at 42 ms before contact.
Table Tennis Ripoll and Fleurance (1988) *Participants:* $N = 5$ (expert table tennis players between 18 and 28 yrs of age)	Analysed the visuo–motor behaviour of expert table tennis players to determine the predominant visual search behaviors (i.e. image–retina vs. eye–head) exhibited during different strokes.
Tennis Singer, Cauraugh, Chen, Steinberg, Frehlich, and Wang (1994) *Participants:* $N = 34$ (beginner/ intermediate players were randomly assigned to (1) mental quickness group or (2) physical quickness training (control) group)	Assessed the trainability of anticipatory skills for beginning and intermediate tennis players.
Tennis Singer, Cauraugh, Chen, Steinberg, and Frehlich (1996) *Participants:* $N = 60$ (30 highly rated university players and 30 beginner players (15 M and 15 F in each group))	Compared expert–novice differences in visual search characteristics while viewing serves and ground strokes. Also compared the relative contribution of physical skill differences to the attainment of relative expertise.

Measures	Findings
Measures of interest included serve placement accuracy (altitude, longitude, and exact placement).	Longer viewing times improved prediction of ball location for both groups. Likewise, intermediate players were more capable of predicting the latitude of the serve across conditions.
Assessed the frequency of correct responses with regard to the location of service position.	Significant differences were noticed with coaches performing better than undergrads in situation B and C, indicating more effective use of advance cues.
Forehand, forehand with top spin, and backhand drives were analysed for the (1) frequency, total duration, and mean duration of visual pursuit on the ball, (2) ball frequency, total duration, and mean duration of eye head stabilization during ball strike.	Only the first part of the ball flight was tracked and the eye–head coordination strategy dominated in a manner where the eye was stable in the orbit during strike.
Pre- and post-testing one week before and then after a three week training program. Testing conducted on three laboratory tasks (measuring decision time, anticipation time, and accuracy) and three on court tasks (serves, ground strokes, and volleys)	Mental quickness group made faster decisions in reactions to serves and anticipation times, and improvement in predicting serve type and location. They also improved RT and committed fewer errors in filmed match play situations. No improvements in accuracy for the physical quickness group and no differences were found for on-court transfer of training.
Visual search patterns (e.g. number of fixations and fixation duration) while viewing filmed opponent's serve and ground strokes. Response accuracy, as well as the speed and location of serves and placement of ground strokes, were recorded. For the simulated split-step task, RT and MT were collected.	Beginners allocated more search time toward the head region during serves. Experts and novices exhibited similar visual search patterns for ground strokes. Experts faster and more accurate with anticipation measures for the serve and men were faster than women. Finally, experts were faster than novices and men were faster than women on the split step.

continued...

Table 3.1 continued

Sport/Author/Participants	Purpose
Tennis Singer, Williams, Frehlich, Janelle, Radlo, Barba, and Bouchard (1998) *Participants:* $N = 5$ (3 M and 2 F, all highly ranked university tennis players)	Determined whether visual search data could be collected on-line in a live action, outdoor sport situation, and examined intraexpert differences in visual search strategies.
Tennis Ward, Williams, and Bennett (2002) *Participants:* $N = 16$ (8 experienced (mean age = 23.0 yrs, with 11.9 yrs of experience) and 8 inexperienced (mean age = 27.2 yrs, with 3.8 yrs experience) tennis players)	Assessed the relationship between visual search, anticipation, biological motion perception, and expertise in tennis

acquire the necessary components to make quick and accurate decisions and effective anticipatory behaviour? Will directing players to watch task relevant cues or relative motions help them to become more accustomed to informative movement invariances within the continually changing tennis environment (Ward, Williams and Bennett, 2002)? Of course, a related critical issue concerns whether videotape training is positively transferred to match play on the court. These questions have begun to receive empirical attention from researchers interested in applying the principles learned from studies using the expert–novice paradigm.

Training with on-court videotapes for decision making speed and accuracy is a viable candidate for assisting racket sport players with their anticipatory behaviour. Singer *et al*. (1994) investigated the effectiveness of training novice players to use reliable visual cues for developing decision-making ability and anticipatory behaviour. Recreational (beginning) tennis players were randomly assigned to one of two training groups: (a) video observations with verbal cues (mental quickness) and (b) video observations without verbal cues (physical quickness). Both quickness training groups experienced 60 minutes of video-based match play training over three consecutive weeks and 120 minutes of on-the-court training (twice a week for three weeks). The videos portrayed actual match play situations from a baseline camera perspective. The microcomputer stopped the video situations at specific times during serves and ground strokes, and participants

Measures	Findings
Visual search measures of interest included: pursuit tracking, saccades, and fixation location and duration. Also, search patterns and physical actions during the ritual, backswing, foreswing, and follow through phases were analysed relative to each other and with respect to the different temporal phases of the serve.	Findings suggested that the best male and female players of the sample used more pursuit tracking during ball toss and that the majority of fixation duration was in the arm/racket region during the ritual phase of the serve. Also, the best players used exclusively pursuit tracking during initial and final ball flight.
Responses to ground strokes presented using normal and pointlight displays. Anticipation data included: decision time, movement time, total response time, and response accuracy. Visual search measures of interest included search rate, percent viewing time, and search order.	Experienced performers showed superior anticipatory performance than inexperienced players. No group differences were found for search rate. All participants exhibited fewer fixations of longer duration when viewing PLD compared with ND. Group differences were evident in percentage of viewing time per fixation location, with experts using less peripheral , in favor of more central, regions of the body for information pick-up.

made decisions about where to move on the court (left, right or centre) to return the ball. Participants in the mental quickness with verbal cues group were faster and more accurate in predicting type of serve and direction than the physical quickness training group (see Figure 3.2). The mental quickness and verbal cues group's advantage demonstrated the importance of visually searching for cues about an opponent's intended serve (e.g. ball tossing shoulder angle, ball toss over the head or forward, and angle of racket face) and quickly anticipating what will happen. Despite the encouraging laboratory results, the decision-making and anticipatory behaviour benefits for the mental quickness group were not differentiated on the court when rated by two tennis coaches.

A related case study in the dynamic interceptive sport of volleyball was conducted by Adolphe, Vickers and LaPlante (1997). Three expert volleyball receivers were tested before and after six weeks of visual attention training. The training videos were designed to improve tracking ability with extensive practice on four gaze behaviours. Analyses indicated an advantage in the visual attention capabilities in the post-training values. Furthermore, accuracy performance increased in the three players, monitored as they played in international volleyball matches over the next three years. Although this transfer task to the video training programme was interpreted as confirming evidence on the importance of visual

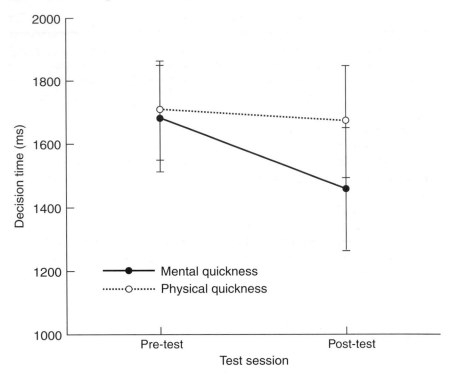

Figure 3.2 Mean service anticipation times (and standard deviation bars) for the mental quickness and physical quickness groups as a function of test session. Adapted from Singer, R.N., Cauraugh, J.H., Chen, D., Steinberg, G., Frehlich, S. and Wang, L. (1994). Training mental quickness in beginning/intermediate tennis players. *The Sport Psychologist* **8**, 305–18.

attention training as well as augmented coaching, methodological complications preclude definitive conclusions.

More recently, Farrow, Chivers, Hardingham and Sachse (1998) conducted a study on video-based perceptual training on novice tennis players. They examined how 24 novice players received tennis serves shown on a videotape, and asked players to respond by swinging at an imaginary ball. The perceptual training group received four weeks of training (twice a week; 15 minutes each) with key visual cues highlighted and feedback provided after every trial. A placebo group watched videotapes of professional tennis matches in the same schedule as the experimental (perceptual) training group. A third group (control) only completed the pre-post laboratory anticipation test. Comparisons indicated faster responses to the serves by the perceptual training group than either of the other two groups. An apparent group by test session interaction was not explored. In fact, both the placebo and control groups displayed slower response times as well as less accuracy across the test sessions.

The efficacy of video-based training programmes shows good potential as a variable to facilitate learning visual search patterns and orienting visual attention.

Ideally, researchers will continue to manipulate environmental variables similar to the methods employed Singer *et al*. (1994) and Adolphe, Vickers and LaPlante (1997). That is, video-based training for improving visual tracking should include more than repetitive match performances. Players should receive verbal instructions and effective cues so that they will be able to use the available visual information to their advantage in making quick and accurate motor responses. When examining training effects, researchers/practitioners should be careful about potential confounds. Laboratory tests of coincidence timing for different skill levels of tennis players revealed that coincidence timing accuracy increases with the amount of tennis practice. Benguigui and Ripoll (1998) argued that expert tennis players may possess superior timing capabilities because of the amount of practice on the courts.

A second word of caution concerning video-based training efficacy was suggested by Greene (1999). His visual search and eye fixations study reported situations that demand manual reactions, which include targets among distractors for real world settings. Incorporating this finding into racket sports research implies that visual search and target fixation evidence must maintain authentic cues on videos or films for training purposes. This approach would allow investigators to compare a direct eye movement index for visual searching. The latency to fixate a target when it appears among a group of distractors is a realistic situation that should be included in video-based training programmes. Further, when developing training tapes, researchers should keep in mind that perceived velocity of an approaching ball is a function of stimulus contrast (Savelsbergh, 1990; Thompson, 1982). Finally, Farrow, Chivers, Hardingham and Sachse (1998) cautioned that even though video-based perceptual training is promising, it should not replace physical practice in racket sports.

Future directions

After critically reviewing racket sports research on visual search patterns and anticipatory behaviour, it is apparent that one limitation across these studies is the lack of an overall theoretical perspective to direct the research. Even though expert vs. novice comparisons have revealed distinct skill level differences, an encompassing theoretical perspective is lacking. Perhaps Milner and Goodale's (1995) model for vision, discussed in the chapter by Keil and Bennett, could provide an appropriate framework and set of hypotheses to direct research on visual search and cue utilisation in various racket sports. Certainly, adding empirical data from racket sports situations would contribute to Milner and Goodale's debate about vision for perception versus vision for action.

Concerning video-based training situations, new technological advances are currently available to turn a desktop computer into an intelligent television and video-editing studio. Video chips and software from Pinnacle systems (Mountain View, CA, USA: pinnaclesys.com) allows an edited video to be stored as a computer file, saved on a compact disk, or transferred back to a video tape. This methodology will allow easy presentation of tennis match situations so as to train players to visually search for relevant cues, to recognise available ones, and make appropriate decisions for action.

Another new technology instrument will allow players to be independent of desktop computers. Olympus eye-trek glasses (Tokyo, Japan) can be used for decision-making and anticipatory behaviour training in tennis. The eye-trek glasses make it appear as though one is watching a video from a TV, VCR, or DVD on a 1.59 m screen from 2 m away, and they do not block peripheral vision. The glasses weigh only 3.8 oz and are portable to the extent that they can be plugged into any video out jack from a TV, VCR, DVD or camcorder. This capability will allow players to watch racket sport matches such as tennis while commuting to their next playing destination. If match play can be extended via detailed videotapes, then players could continue to learn about opponents' cues and tendencies. These off-the-court training programmes may help players to recognise and distinguish specific patterns of play displayed by opponents, but their utility in this respect needs to be empirically demonstrated.

Both of the above technological advances will allow researchers/coaches to present various informational cues to players to assist with visual pattern recognition. However, expecting players to perform better just because they have watched an opponent on video is naive. Additional processing of what the players saw on the videos should be evaluated. In line with this notion, Chi and Bjork (1991) stated that modelling cognitive expertise involves five steps: expert modelling, scaffolding, articulation, reflection, and exploration. As players progress through these steps they will need a knowledgeable coach or researcher with whom to interact and be guided. Chi and Bjork's (1991) cognitive modelling of expertise has been tested in a motor learning experimental situation. Indeed, Cauraugh, Martin and Martin (1999) effectively used Chi and Bjork's (1991) suggestions to assist resident interns with motor learning and control of surgical instruments required for an inguinal hernia operation. The expertise-modelling group demonstrated better skill acquisition and techniques for completing the operation.

This modelling expertise evidence confirms one of the oldest known and most potent manipulations for increasing a subject's memory: elaborative processing (Rock, 1990). When designing new video-based training programmes, players should be required to elaborate on the to-be-remembered material. Further, the content of the videos should be measured by the percentage of information recalled. This would confirm that players are actually processing the appropriate cues in an elaborative manner. Granted, testing the video-based training programs with sound experimental designs and control groups included are prerequisites for establishing and extending a reliable knowledge base.

Closing remarks

In closing, racket sport performers visually search and use cues provided by opponents in an attempt to minimise decision-making delays. Indeed, expert players across three racket sports generally follow different visual search strategies from novice players. Experts are able to read opponents and accumulate enough information to initiate faster and more accurate motor actions than novice players. This integrated review demonstrated that racket sport performers adopt visual search strategies to comply with the limitations imposed by the visual system. A commonality among the above reviewed studies is that participants decouple the line of sight before actual racket contact with the arriving ball while pursuit tracking. Additional visual information appears to arise from peripheral sources. Thus, initiation and execution of the appropriate motor responses in dynamic interceptive situations is a function of visual search strategies and cue utilisation completed early in the process.

References

Abernethy, B. (1988). Visual search in sport and ergonomics: its relationship to selective attention and performer expertise. *Human Performance* **4**, 205–35.

Abernethy, B. (1990). Expertise, visual search, and information pick-up in squash. *Perception* **19**, 63–77.

Abernethy, B. (1993). Searching for the minimal essential information for skilled perception and action. *Psychological Research* **55**, 131–8.

Abernethy, B. and Russell, D.G. (1987a). Expert–novice differences in an applied selective attention task. *Journal of Sport Psychology* **9**, 326–45.

Abernethy, B. and Russell, D.G. (1987b). The relationship between expertise and visual search strategy in a racket sport. *Human Movement Science* **6**, 283–319.

Abernethy, B., Thomas, K. and Thomas, J. (1993). Strategies for improving understanding of motor expertise [or mistakes we have made and things we have learned!]. In J.L. Starkes and F. Allard (eds), *Cognitive Issues in Motor Expertise*. Amsterdam: North Holland Elsevier Science.

Adolphe, R.M., Vickers, J.N. and LaPlante, G. (1997). The effects of training visual attention on gaze behaviour and accuracy: a pilot study. *International Journal of Sports Vision* **4**, 28–33.

Bahill, L.T. and LaRitz, T. (1984). Why can't batters keep their eyes on the ball? *American Scientist* **72**, 249–53.

Bard, C. and Fleury, M. (1976). Analysis of visual search activity in sport problem situations. *Journal of Human Movement Studies* **3**, 214–22.

Bard, C. and Fleury, M. (1981). Considering eye movement as a predictor of attainment. In I.M. Cockerill and W.W. MacGillivary (eds), *Vision and sport*. Cheltenham: Stanley Thornes.

Bard, C., Guezennec, Y. and Papin, J.P. (1980). Fencing: analysis of visual exploration. *Médécine du Sport* **55**, 22–8.

Benguigui, N. and Ripoll, H. (1998). Effects of tennis practice on the coincidence timing accuracy of adults and children. *Research Quarterly for Exercise and Sport* **69**, 217–23.

Buckolz, E., Prapavesis, H. and Fairs, J. (1988). Advance cues and their use in predicting tennis passing shots. *Canadian Journal of Sport Sciences* **13**, 20–30.

Cauraugh, J.H., Martin, M. and Martin, K.K. (1999). Modelling surgical expertise for motor skill acquisition. *The American Journal of Surgery* **177**, 331–6.

Chi, M.T.H. and Bjork, R.A. (1991). Modelling expertise. In D. Druckman and R.A. Bjork (eds), *In the Minds Eye: Enhancing Human Performance*. Washington, DC: National Academy Press.

Davids, K.W., Palmer, D. and Savelsbergh, G.J.P. (1989). Skill level, peripheral vision and tennis volleying performance. *Journal of Human Movement Studies* **16**, 191–202.

Farrow, D., Chivers, P., Hardingham, C. and Sachse, S. (1998). The effect of video-based perceptual training on the tennis return of serve. *International Journal of Sport Psychology* **29**, 231–42.

Goulet, C., Bard, C. and Fleury, M. (1989). Expertise differences in preparing to return a tennis serve: a visual information processing approach. *Journal of Sport & Exercise Psychology* **11**, 382–98.

Greene, H.H. (1999). Temporal relationships between eye fixations and manual reactions in visual search. *Acta Psycholgica* **101**, 105–23.

Helsen, W. and Pauwels J.M. (1990). Analysis of visual search activity in solving tactical game problems. In D. Brogan (ed.), *Visual Search*. London: Taylor and Francis.

Helsen, W. and Pauwels J.M. (1992). A cognitive approach to visual search in sport. In D. Brogan and K. Carr (eds), *Visual Search II*. London: Taylor and Francis.

Helsen, W. and Pauwels, J. (1993). Analysis of visual search activity in solving tactical game problems. In D. Brogan (ed.), *Visual Search II*. London: Taylor and Francis.

Helsen, W. and Starkes, J. (1999). A multidimensional approach to skilled perception and performance in sport. *Applied Cognitive Psychology* **13**, 1–27.

Hubbard, A.W. and Seng, C.N. (1954). Visual movements of batters. *Research Quarterly* **25**, 42–57.

Isaacs, L. and Finch, A. (1983). Anticipatory timing of beginning and intermediate tennis players. *Perceptual and Motor Skills* **57**, 451–4.

James, W. (1890). *The Principles of Psychology* (Vols. 1–2). New York: Holt.

Jones, C. and Miles, J. (1978). Use of advance cues in predicting the flight of a lawn tennis ball. *Journal of Human Movement Studies* **4**, 231–5.

Keele, S.W., Davidson, M. and Hayes, A. (1998). Sequential representation and the neural basis of motor skills. In J. Piek (ed.), *Motor Behaviour and Human Skill: A Multi-disciplinary Approach*. Champaign, IL: Human Kinetics.

Leonard, C.T. (1998). *The Neuroscience of Human Movement*. St. Louis: Mosby.

Milner, A.D. and Goodale, M.A. (1995). *The Visual Brain in Action*. Oxford: Oxford University Press.

Ripoll, H. (1988). Analysis of visual scanning patterns of volleyball players in a problem solving task. *International Journal of Sport Psychology* **19**, 9–25.

Ripoll, H. and Fleurance, P. (1988). What does keeping one's eye on the ball mean? *Ergonomics* **31**, 1647–54.

Ripoll, H., Kerlirzin, Y., Stein, J.F. and Reine, B. (1995). Analysis of information processing, decision making, and visual strategies in complex problem solving sport situations. *Human Movement Science* **14**, 325–49.

Rock, I. (1990). A look back at William James's theory of perception. In M.G. Johnson and T.B Henley (eds), *Reflections on the Principles of Psychology: William James after a Century*. Hillsdale, NJ: Erlbaum.

Sandu, G.S. (1982). Selective attention in competitive volleyball. In J.H. Salmela and T. Orlick (eds), *New Paths of Sport Learning and Excellence*. Ottawa: Sport in Perspective, Inc.

Savelsbergh, G.J.P. (1990). *Catching Behaviour*. Meppel, Netherlands: Krips Repro.

Savelsbergh, G.J.P. and Whiting, H.T.A. (1996). Catching: motor learning and developmental perspective. In H. Heuer and S.W. Keele (eds), *Handbook of Perception and Action*, Volume 2. London: Academic Press.

Shank, M.D. and Haywood, K.M. (1987). Eye movement while viewing a baseball pitch. *Perceptual and Motor Skills* **64**, 1191–7.

Singer, R.N., Cauraugh, J.H., Chen, D., Steinberg, G., Frehlich, S. and Wang, L. (1994). Training mental quickness in beginning/intermediate tennis players. *The Sport Psychologist* **8**, 305–18.

Singer, R.N., Cauraugh, J.H., Chen, D., Steinberg, G.M. and Frehlich, S.G. (1996). Visual search, anticipation, and reactive comparisons between highly skilled and beginning tennis players. *Journal of Applied Sport Psychology* **8**, 9–26.

Singer, R.N., Williams, A.M., Frehlich, S., Janelle, C.M., Radlo, S., Barba, D. and Bouchard, L. (1998). New frontiers in visual search: an exploratory study in live tennis situations. *Research Quarterly for Exercise and Sport* **69**, 290–6.

Starkes, J.L. and Allard, F. (1993). *Cognitive Issues in Motor Control*. Amsterdam: North Holland.

Thompson, P. (1982). Perceived rate of movement depends on contrast. *Vision Research* **22**, 377–80.

Tyldesley, D.A., Bootsma, R.J. and Bomhoff, G.T. (1982). Skill level and eye movement patterns in a sport oriented reaction time task. In H. Reider, K. Bos and K. Reischle (eds), *Motor Learning and Movement Behaviour: Contribution to Learning and Knowledge*. Cologne: Hofmann.

Vickers, J.N. (1988). Knowledge structures of elite–novice gymnasts. *Journal of Human Movement Science* **7**, 4–72.

Vickers, J.N. (1992). Gaze control in putting. *Perception* **21**, 117–32.

Vickers, J.N. (1996). Visual control while aiming at a far target. *Journal of Experimental Psychology: Human Perception and Performance* **22**, 342–54.

Vickers, J.N. and Adolphe, R.M. (1997). Gaze behaviour during a ball tracking and aiming skill. *International Journal of Sports Vision* **4**, 18–27.

Ward, P., Williams, A.M. and Bennett, S. (2002). Visual search and biological perception in tennis. *Research Quarterly for Exercise and Sport* **73**, 107–12.

Williams, A.M., Davids, K., Burwitz, L. and Williams, J.G. (1994). Visual search strategies in experienced and inexperienced soccer players. *Research Quarterly for Exercise and Sport* **65**(2), 127–35.

Williams, A.M. and Davids, K. (1998). Visual search strategy, selective attention, and expertise in soccer. *Research Quarterly for Exercise and Sport* **69**, 111–28.

Williams, A.M. and Elliot, D. (1999). Anxiety, expertise and visual search strategy in karate. *Journal of Sport & Exercise Psychology* **21**, 361–74.

Williams, A.M. and Grant, A. (1999). Training perceptual skill in sport. *International Journal of Sport Psychology* **30**, 194–220.

Williams, A.M., Davids, K. and Williams, J.G. (1999). *Visual Perception and Action in Sport*. London: Spon.

4 Vision and proprioception in interceptive actions

A. Mark Williams and Cornelia Weigelt

Successful performance in many sports requires a ball to be intercepted using a limb or an instrument such as a racket or bat. Although these interceptive actions are routinely performed during the course of a game, many chapters in this book show that successful performance requires an incredible degree of spatial and temporal accuracy. For example, empirical evidence suggests that skilled performers can estimate the time of arrival of an approaching ball to within ±2 to 3 ms, and its instantaneous direction of motion to within 0.1 to 0.2 degree (Regan *et al.*, 1998). An important question for those interested in the acquisition of skill in such tasks is how performers achieve this degree of spatio–temporal accuracy.

Vision plays an integral role in the successful execution of interceptive actions, providing both exteroceptive and proprioceptive information for control of movement. Vision is used exteroceptively in order to extract information regarding ball flight as well as the position and movements of team-mates and/or opponents (e.g. see Singer *et al.*, 1998; Williams and Davids, 1998). This type of visual function, termed 'world vision' by Harris and Jenkin (1998) as outlined in Chapter 1, provides information about the external environment and may contribute to object recognition and movement control. Visual proprioception provides information about the body's orientation and movement (Lee, 1978). It can contribute to action such as in reaching and grasping or to perception by providing knowledge of self-motion and position. Its function may be similar to that of articular receptors such as muscle spindles, joint receptors and Golgi tendon organs and, consequently, these two sources of proprioceptive input are presumed to interact in the control of goal-directed actions (Harris and Jenkin, 1998).

A significant question that has been addressed in the literature concerns the relative importance of visual and articular proprioception during interceptive actions (Whiting, 1969). Are both sources of information necessary for successful performance, highlighting the importance of multisensory convergence, or can either source function independently in the control of action? Does their relative importance vary as a function of the interceptive task (e.g. use of a limb or an implement as an effector) or the performer's skill level? Answers to such questions have implications for skill acquisition and help develop understanding of the complex, bi-directional interactions between vision and action (e.g. see Williams, Davids and Williams, 1999).

In this chapter, we outline current knowledge by providing a critical review of contemporary research on the role of vision and articular proprioception in interceptive actions. We begin by reviewing earlier work on catching and other upper limb interceptive actions. Although the majority of researchers have focused on the upper limbs, a particular emphasis in this review is on lower limb interceptive tasks. Thus far, few researchers have examined the interaction of vision and priprioception using lower limb tasks. This is surprising given the importance of such skills in the various codes of football, particularly Australian rules football, rugby league and union, and soccer. With this in mind, we discuss recent exemplar work that has employed soccer ball control and passing tasks as vehicles to address these theoretical issues. Implications for further research are highlighted throughout the review.

Vision and proprioception in upper limb interceptive actions

Perhaps the earliest study to examine the role of visual and articular proprioception in upper limb interceptive actions was undertaken by Smyth and Marriott (1982). They used a 'screen' paradigm to determine the importance of vision of the effector during a one-handed catching task. Twenty-four participants of an unspecified skill level were required to catch tennis balls under normal viewing conditions (NV) and when vision of the catching hand was occluded using an opaque screen (OS) attached to the head. The screen occluded the final 150–200 ms of ball flight, obscuring the fine orientation and grasp phases of ball catching as outlined by the classical analysis of Alderson, Sully and Sully (1974). Participants received 20 trials in each condition. Results indicated that performance was significantly worse under OS compared with NV conditions. The mean number of successful catches in the NV condition ($M = 17.5$) suggested that the group were competent catchers under normal viewing conditions. In the OS condition, the group mean dropped to 9.21 catches. Catching errors were classified according to whether the hand was accurately positioned in the line of flight (spatial or position error) or due to inadequate grasping of the ball with the fingers (temporal or grasp error). The data showed that participants typically made more position ($M = 7.62$) than grasp ($M = 3.17$) errors in the OS condition.[1] These data were reversed in the NV condition (0.75 position vs. 1.75 grasp errors). As far as the position errors were concerned, participants failed to contact the ball on 52 per cent of trials in the OS condition compared with only 31 per cent in the NV condition. Smyth and Marriott (1982) concluded that the articular proprioceptive system does not provide accurate information for limb positioning during ball catching (see also Diggles, Grabiner and Garhammer, 1987; Smyth, 1982).

Moderating effect of expertise

Fischman and Schneider (1985) replicated part of Smyth and Marriott's design while including the additional variables of alternate catching hand and participant skill level. In one experiment, skilled baseball and softball players were required to catch tennis balls with their dominant and nondominant hand under both NV and OS viewing conditions. Although participants demonstrated a marked improvement in overall catching performance compared with those of Smyth and Marriott (1982), the data confirmed earlier findings, with participants performing better under NV ($M = 19.00$) compared with OS ($M = 16.31$) conditions. No interaction was observed between viewing condition and catching hand. Contrary to Smyth and Marriott, participants made more grasp errors ($M = 8.75\%$) than position errors ($M = 2.99\%$) under all conditions, while there was no significant increase in position errors under OS ($M = 5.55\%$) compared with NV ($M = 0.42\%$). Fischman and Schneider (1985) argued that the participant's skill level mediates the use of articular proprioception in spatially orienting the hand.

To confirm this prediction, Fischman and Schneider (1985) replicated the protocol using participants with no previous experience of baseball and/or softball. As expected, the novice catchers were less successful than the softball/baseball players, particularly in the OS ($M = 12.84$) compared with NV ($M = 15.88$) condition. More importantly, a significant interaction was observed between catching error and viewing condition; a much higher proportion of position errors being reported under OS ($M = 16.41\%$) compared with NV ($M = 4.53\%$). Twenty-four no-contact errors were recorded for the novice catchers under OS compared with only two no-contact errors for the skilled participants.

In combination, these studies suggest that sight of the hand during catching may be important to calibrate or fine-tune the proprioceptive system, particularly with novice catchers. Skilled catchers may have more refined articular proprio-ceptors and consequently, are likely to be less affected by the restricted access to visual proprioception. This delegation of responsibility from vision to proprio-ception enables vision to be used for planning future actions or detecting important environmental events. Theoretically, the assumption is that practice leads to a shift in reliance on different sources of sensory feedback (Fleishman and Rich, 1963; Legge, 1965) or there is a transition from feedback dependent to more open-loop control (Pew, 1966; Keele, 1968; Schmidt and Lee, 1999). Note how this explanation differs from recent arguments (presented in the chapter by Robertson, Tremblay, Anson and Elliott) rejecting the notion of transitions from vision to proprioceptive or from closed to open loop modes of control. Alternatively, skilled performers may develop functional muscle synergies (Newell, 1996), also referred to in the literature as task specific devices (Bingham, 1988) or co-ordinative structures (Fitzpatrick, 1998), to achieve a specific task goal during practice. These functional muscle synergies are soft-assembled to efficiently and effectively achieve specific goals (e.g. reaching to grasp a ball). As learning progresses, functional muscle synergies are more stable and flexible as performers become progressively attuned to all the available and relevant perceptual information sources (e.g. visual, auditory, proprioceptive). This increased attunement to different sources of perceptual information ensures that skilled performers can be guided by a variety of informational constraints during interceptive actions (for a more detailed review, see Williams, Davids and Williams, 1999). When a source of perceptual information is removed (e.g. visual proprioception), skilled performers are able to adapt by making use of other relevant information sources (e.g. articular proprioception).

Potential confounds?

Although conclusions derived from research on upper limb interceptive actions appear logical and intuitive, there is some controversy. With regard to the role of skill in moderating the loss of visual proprioception, follow-up studies by Diggles, Grabiner and Garhammer (1987) and Davids and Stratford (1989) failed to replicate Fischman and Schneider's (1985) observations, whereas support for a skill × viewing condition interaction was reported by Whiting, Savelsbergh and Faber (1988). The apparent controversy may be due to methodological differences in the selection of participants, ball projection velocities, occlusion techniques, achieved occlusion periods and participants' initial start position.

Within-task criterion measures of skill level

Whiting and colleagues (e.g. Whiting, Alderson and Sanderson, 1973; Whiting and Savelsbergh, 1987) suggested that lack of homogeneity in the selection of participants is a significant confound in the literature. They argued that within-task criteria should be employed to distinguish between persistently 'good' and 'poor' performers. The classification of participants into skill groups based on their involvement in a particular sport (e.g. baseball players) is not a direct measure of ability on the task in question (i.e., ball catching). Interestingly, neither Diggles, Grabiner and Garhammer (1987) or Davids and Stratford (1989) employed within-task criteria for the selection of participants. More recent studies employing such criteria have been more successful in highlighting 'good' catchers' increased advantage over 'poor' catchers when sight of the hand is prevented (e.g. Savelsbergh and Whiting, 1988; Whiting, Savelsbergh and Faber, 1988; Whiting and Savelsbergh, 1992).

Variability in occlusion periods

Variability in ball projection velocity and distance as well as the size of the 'screen' used to occlude vision of the hand contribute to the controversy. Ball projection velocity has varied from 6.7 m s^{-1} to 11.64 m s^{-1} over distances between 4.3 m and 9.4 m (see Bennett, Davids and Craig, 1999). This disparity in ball velocity, projection distance and associated ball flight time, has resulted in the ball being occluded for the final 90 ms to 280 ms of its flight. The consistency of the achieved occlusion period also depends on whether the 'screen' is head-mounted (participant-dependent), or suspended from the ceiling or using a floor-mounted stand (participant-independent). The majority of studies have employed the former approach even though there may be increased variability in the occlusion periods as a result of participants' head and/or trunk movements. Few studies have attempted to measure the degree of head and trunk movement or the associated variability in occlusion times. Moreover, researchers may have been more or less stringent in their tolerance of the extent to which they allowed participants to reach forward to the ball or turn their head slightly in the direction of the ball's flight.

Confounding information of hand and ball

A related concern, not often cited in the literature, is that the screen paradigm occludes sight of both the hand and the final portion of ball flight. It is not clear whether the decrement in performance typically observed with this paradigm is due to losing sight of the ball, the effector or both. Previous studies have neglected to control for this issue and consequently, vision of the hand may be less important than currently thought (cf., Fischman and Schneider, 1985). Interestingly, recent work by Milner and Goodale (e.g. Whiting 1993, 1995) suggests that vision may be used to make fine manipulations during movement control far more quickly than the 200 ms latency period initially employed by Whiting and colleagues (e.g. 1968, 1969, Whiting and Sharp, 1974). The implication is that participants may be able to extract useable information from the ball during the final portion of its flight. Since the 'screen' paradigm occludes sight of the hand for the entire period of the ball's flight, another interesting question is whether sight of the hand may only be necessary at specific times during the planning and execution of a catch. For example, if participants could see the hand at varying time periods before or during flight of the ball would this be sufficient for successful performance (Smyth, 1986)? To this end, researchers may wish to consider employing liquid crystal occlusion glasses to examine the potential interaction between occlusion time and viewing period (e.g. see Milgram, 1987).

Variability in performance across studies may be partially due to participants' start position and the experimental instructions provided by the experimenter. In certain studies, participants were required to start in a seated position with the hand by their side (e.g. Diggles, Grabiner and Garhammer, 1987), whereas in others a standing position was adopted with the hand already placed in the general vicinity of the ball's flight path (e.g. Davids and Stratford, 1989). Recent research suggests that catching while standing places different functional constraints on performers relative to catching in a seated position (Davids *et al.*, 1997). Furthermore, employing consistent or variable start positions may increase or decrease access to distance or endpoint location cues as a means of positioning the limb correctly (Keele and Ells, 1972; Laabs, 1973).

Finally, the main effect for viewing condition typically observed in these studies may be confounded by the relatively small number of habituation trials employed. Davids and Stratford (1989) showed that the decrement in performance observed in the occluded screen condition disappeared as the number of trials was increased from 20 to 80. The mean number of balls dropped in the first block of 20 trials under opaque screen conditions was 3.04 compared with 1.37 in the final block. The absence of a suitable habituation period may therefore overestimate the importance of sight of the hand. This ability to rapidly adapt performance following manipulation of viewing conditions has been confirmed in recent studies comparing monocular and binocular vision (see Savelsbergh and Whiting, 1992).

Although these concerns need to be addressed in future research, fortunately the main conclusions from studies using the 'screen paradigm' have been corroborated using an alternative 'catching in the dark' paradigm (e.g. see Rosengren, Pick and von Hofsten, 1988; Whiting, Savelsbergh and Faber, 1988). Whiting, Savelsbergh and Faber (1988) compared groups of both 'good' and 'poor' catchers under conditions where only a luminous ball (UVB) could be seen in an otherwise dark room with similar groups in another condition that involved sight of a luminous ball and hand (UVBH). A significant reduction in catching performance was recorded under UVB compared with UVBH with this decrement in performance being much more pronounced in the 'poor' catchers. Comparable conclusions were reported by Davids (1988) using a novel 'dual-task' catching paradigm.

Moderating effect of task constraints

Another question frequently posed in the literature is whether the relative importance of vision and proprioception interacts with the nature or difficulty of the task. The assumption is that visual proprioception becomes less important as the spatio–temporal accuracy requirements of the task decrease, typically as a result of using an implement with a large surface area such as a racket or baseball glove. The reduction in accuracy requirements ensures that appropriate positioning of the effector occurs without visual proprioception regardless of participants' skill level, overriding any potential interaction between expertise and viewing condition. These assumptions were tested by Davids, Palmer and Savelsbergh (1989) using a task that required expert, intermediate and novice tennis players to play forehand volleys towards defined target areas under opaque, clear and no-screen conditions. Ball velocity was also manipulated as an independent variable. The results supported initial predictions; there were no differences in performance between groups or across viewing conditions. Although performance was better under the slower ball velocity, there was no interaction between ball velocity and viewing condition (for contradictory findings, see Bennett, Davids and Craig, 1999). When intercepting a ball using an implement with a large surface area such as a tennis racket even recreational players can employ articular proprioception to effectively position the effector, requiring less visual monitoring than observed in ball catching. Similarly, Fischman and Mucci (1989) showed that there was no reduction in catching performance using the screen paradigm when the participants employed a baseball glove rather than their bare hand to catch balls. A glove, like the racket in tennis, reduces the degree of positioning and timing accuracy required in simple catching, resulting in a shift in emphasis from visual to articular proprioception.

Although these results illustrated how the relationship between visual and articular proprioception is influenced by the constraints of the task and specific action requirements, several limitations are highlighted. In the tennis study, contrary to the recommendations of Whiting and colleagues, participants were not selected on the basis of within-task performance criteria, making it difficult to determine whether players were 'good' or 'poor' performers on the task. The mean accuracy scores for the three groups of participants under full vision was less than 50 per cent, while even in the slow ball velocity condition only the 'elite' players recorded a mean accuracy score higher than 60 per cent. These percentage accuracy scores are much lower than those typically required for classification as 'good' catchers (e.g. see Whiting, Savelsbergh and Faber, 1988). Moreover, the task employed did not distinguish between intention and action since players could obtain a high score even if the ball was played to a totally different area of the court than intended. The authors themselves highlight this potential lack of sensitivity as an explanation for the absence of a main effect for skill. Requiring players to volley towards a designated area and using concentric circle targets may have improved measurement sensitivity. In the baseball study by Fischman and Mucci (1989), only 'skilled' participants were employed and consequently, the authors ignored the potential interaction between task, viewing condition and skill level. Furthermore, comparison between the two tasks is confounded since in the bare hand condition tennis balls were employed compared with the much larger leather softballs used in gloved catching.

While we have highlighted several concerns with research on upper limb interceptive actions, current understanding suggests that visual proprioception is in certain instances helpful for successful positioning of the effector. This conclusion may be drawn since in studies involving one-handed catching more position errors are recorded when vision of the arm is occluded by an opaque screen or when only the ball is illuminated using the 'catching in the dark' paradigm. The relative importance of visual and articular proprioception appears to interact with the participant's skill level as well as the accuracy requirements of the task (for additional evidence see chapter by Robertson, Tremblay, Anson and Elliott on beam walking). Although the empirical evidence is far from conclusive, skilled performers of interceptive actions do appear to make more effective use of other sources of information to support performance, including tactile information and articular proprioception, thereby enabling visual resources to be employed elsewhere. Finally, it seems that the constraints of the task, particularly its spatio–temporal accuracy requirements, mediate the relative importance of vision and proprioception in dynamic, interceptive tasks involving the upper limbs.

Vision and proprioception in lower limb interceptive actions

Few studies have examined the interaction between vision and proprioception in lower limb interceptive actions. The paucity of research is surprising in view of the qualitative differences between lower and upper limb tasks. In contrast to catching, when performing lower limb tasks such as controlling a ball in soccer, performers have to contend with a bouncing ball, often on an irregular surface. The task is made more difficult by the presence of opposing players and the impending threat of physical challenge. To compound matters, the lower limbs have fewer sensory receptors and are not as well represented in the motor cortex compared with upper limb segments such as the hand or fingers (Pinel, 1997). On a more positive note, the spatio–temporal constraints are less severe when controlling a ball in soccer compared with catching. The surface area of the foot is much greater than the hand and participants are only required to keep the ball within 'playing distance', providing larger error margins for effective action compared with the grasp phase in one-handed catching (see Alderson, Sully and Sully, 1974). Finally, most soccer skills are obviously performed in a dual-task, team game context. Following practice players may learn to position the foot accurately using articular proprioception, enabling the visual system to monitor external events.

The only published study on lower limb interceptive actions was reported by Barfield and Fischman (1990) using a ball control task in soccer. Experienced and novice players were required to control a soccer ball inside a 2.0 m × 1.5 m target area under full vision and in a condition where sight of the foot and the final 125 ms of ball flight were occluded using Kant Peek glasses. The ball was projected at a velocity of 12.96 m s^{-1} from a distance of 10 m. Participants were required to control the ball with the inside surface of their preferred foot using only one touch. Twenty trials were provided in each condition. The results, presented in Table 4.1, revealed a significant main effect for group, indicating that the experienced players executed more trials successfully ($M = 15.20$) compared with their novice counterparts ($M = 7.25$). A significant main effect was also observed for viewing condition, indicating that performance was better with ($M = 13.30$) rather than without ($M = 9.15$) sight of the foot. There was no interaction between group and viewing condition. It appears that vision of the foot is important in a lower limb interceptive task involving soccer ball control, regardless of the participant's skill level. These results are consistent with the earlier work on catching (e.g. Fischman and Schneider, 1985), but contradict those reported by Davids, Palmer and Savelsbergh (1989) for the tennis volley. The relationship between vision and

Table 4.1 Mean and standard deviations for successful trials and the number of position and control errors for experienced and novice participants across the two viewing conditions. Effect sizes (ES) are included to compare the relative decrement in performance under full and occluded viewing conditions (Data from Barfield, B. and Fischman, M. (1990). Control of ground-level ball as a function of skill level and sight foot. *Journal of Human Movement Studies*, **19**, 181–8).

	Group	Full Vision Mean (SD)	Occlusion Mean (SD)	ES
Successful trials	Experienced	17.40 (1.35)	13.00 (3.06)	−2.98
	Novices	9.20 (5.49)	5.30 (3.71)	−0.65
Position errors	Experienced	0.90 (0.88)	1.80 (1.69)	+0.94
	Novices	6.10 (3.78)	6.60 (2.67)	+0.12
Control errors	Experienced	1.70 (1.25)	5.20 (2.66)	+2.56
	Novices	4.70 (3.47)	8.10 (3.81)	+0.89

articular proprioception may therefore be a function of the type of task performed (cf. Davids and Stratford, 1989).

Barfield and Fischman (1990) extended their analysis to consider the mean number of position and control errors (see Table 4.1). Position errors were those in which the ball failed to contact the inside surface of the foot between the base of the first metatarsal and the medial malleolous. Control errors were those in which the ball contacted the foot between these two anatomical landmarks, but failed to stay within the designated control zone. This more discriminating analysis showed that there was no increase in the number of positioning errors when sight of the foot was occluded ($M = 4.2$) compared with the full vision condition ($M = 3.5$). However, a significant increase in the number of control errors was observed under occluded ($M = 6.65$) compared with full viewing ($M = 3.2$) conditions. Rather surprisingly, this increase in the number of control errors was more pronounced in experienced (effect size = 2.56) rather than inexperienced (effect size = 0.89) participants. However, there were no significant interactions between participant skill level, viewing condition and type of error. The disproportionate increase in the number of control compared with positioning errors when sight of the foot was occluded suggested that vision is more important for ball control than for positioning of the foot. Positioning of the foot can be achieved fairly successfully by means of articular proprioception. Vision, however, does appear to be important for the timing of the ball control phase so that the foot 'gives' just before foot/ball contact in order to cushion or absorb the velocity of the ball and maintain it within the control zone.

Several concerns with the methodology and data interpretation make it difficult to draw definitive conclusions from Barfield and Fischman's (1990) study. For example, the authors neglected to employ within-task criteria for participant selection, echoing concerns raised when discussing the literature on one-handed catching (Whiting, 1986). As far as the procedure is concerned, while participants were instructed to keep their head erect during the no-vision condition without flexing more than 10 degrees forward, similar constraints were not imposed during the vision condition. This restriction may have prevented participants from responding 'naturally', negatively affecting performance in the no-vision condition. Also, the authors did not provide any information to explain how the restriction was imposed or whether the extent of participants' head movements were monitored or measured. Variation in head and/or trunk movements can greatly affect the length of the ball's occlusion period prior to foot/ball contact. The absence of kinematic measures to determine the effects of visual manipulation on movement dynamics and the relatively short habituation period in the no-vision condition are additional methodological limitations.

The most significant concern relates to the scheme employed to determine position and control errors. Not surprisingly, given the large surface area of the medial aspect of the foot and the size of a soccer ball, both groups of participants recorded more control errors than positioning errors, regardless of viewing condition. However, the authors did not distinguish between vertical and horizontal positioning errors. It is likely that an unsuccessful trial may have occurred when participants positioned the foot either too high or too low relative to the ball. According to the error classification scheme employed by Barfield and Fischman (1990), such an error would have been incorrectly classified as a control error rather than a vertical positioning error. This potential lack of measurement sensitivity as a result of the error classification scheme employed predisposed the experimenters to record more control rather than positional errors.

In the final section of this review, we briefly outline research that is being carried out to examine the relationship between vision and proprioception in lower limb interceptive actions. In a recent programme of research, we have addressed many of the methodological concerns highlighted in previous literature and attempted to provide a novel theoretical contribution to knowledge in this area. Initially, we attempted to replicate and extend Barfield and Fischman's (1990) study on soccer ball control, whereas in a second study we examined the relative importance of visual and articular proprioception using a soccer-kicking task.

Vision and proprioception in a soccer ball control task

Participants were required to control a soccer ball projected with a velocity of 9.75 m s^{-1} over a distance of 10.75 m inside a 1.5 m × 2.0 m target area. Only one 'touch' was allowed with the inside of the preferred kicking foot. Three viewing conditions were employed; full vision (FV), occlusion of the legs/feet and the final 115 ms of ball flight (OCC_BF) and occlusion of the legs/feet only (OCC_F). When performing under full vision participants wore a head-mounted Perspex face shield, whereas the occlusion conditions were achieved by placing a cloth screen on to the visor at individually fitted heights. The standard fitting procedure required participants to stand with slightly bent knees, to mimic the typical ball control position, and to focus on a stationary ball located either 2 m away from (OCC_BF) or directly in front of their feet (OCC_F). Participants could not see their lower limbs for the duration of each trial. The achieved occlusion period for each trial was obtained by using frame-by-frame video analysis to measure head angle relative to the occlusion screen and the vertical axis at the moment of foot/ball contact.[2] These measures along with ball velocity were employed to calculate the actual occlusion period using simple trigonometry. The distinction was made between the OCC_BF and OCC_F conditions in order to determine the relative importance of seeing the feet/legs as opposed to seeing both the feet/legs and ball in lower limb interceptive actions. A more marked decrement in performance under OCC_BF compared with OCC_F would highlight the importance of seeing the ball over the final 115 ms, while a reduction in percentage success rates in the OCC_F condition relative to FV would signify the importance of visual proprioception. The experimental set up and occlusion helmet are illustrated in Figure 4.1.

As per the recommendations of Whiting (1986), participants were categorised into high or low skill groups based on a within-task criterion. Participants recording accuracy scores higher than 75 per cent on the full vision condition were classified as 'high skill', while those scoring less than 50 per cent were regarded as 'low

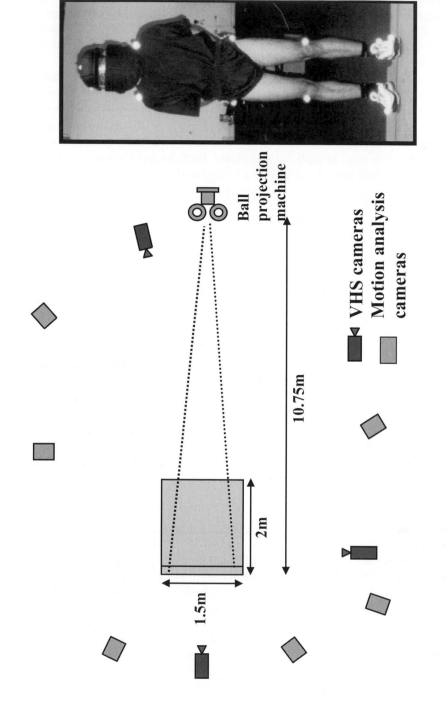

Ball
projection
machine

10.75m

2m

1.5m

VHS cameras

Motion analysis
cameras

Figure 4.1 The experimental set-up and head-mounted occlusion technique (inset) employed in the soccer ball control task.

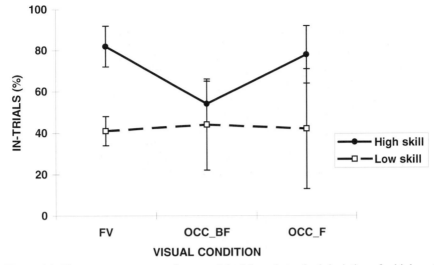

Figure 4.2 The mean percentage of successful trials and standard deviations for high and low skill participants across viewing conditions in the soccer ball control task.

skill'. In an attempt to improve upon the protocol employed by Barfield and Fischman (1990), kinematic measures were recorded for all participants using an optoelectronic system. Qualitative information regarding foot and head orientation at impact was also obtained using three synchronised VHS cameras located lateral and posterior to the participants. Correct foot positioning was noted when the ball made contact with the arch of the foot. An attempt was made to categorise deviations from correct foot position along the vertical (i.e., foot placed too high/low relative to the ball's vertical mid-line) and horizontal axis (i.e., ball did not made contact with the inside surface of the foot between the base of the first metatarsal and the medial malleolous). If a ball did not stay inside the control zone after making contact with any part of the foot other than the arch a positioning error was recorded. Control errors were recorded when the ball did not stay inside the defined control zone after making contact with the arch of the foot. Fifteen trials were presented in each of the three viewing conditions.

The results showed significant main effect for skill level and a skill × viewing condition interaction. The high skill participants recorded a higher success rate when attempting to control the ball inside the control zone under FV and OCC_F than their lesser skilled counterparts, while no between-group differences were apparent under OCC_BF. The most significant finding was the decrement in performance observed for high skill participants under OCC_BF ($M = 53.74\%$; effect size $= -2.42$) compared with FV ($M = 82.43\%$) and OCC_F ($M = 78.37\%$; effect size $= -0.34$). Findings are presented in Figure 4.2. It appears that high skill participants do not require sight of the foot for successful performance on a lower limb control task. The determining factor appears to be the ability to extract meaningful information from the ball over the final portion of its flight. This finding suggests that researchers may have overestimated the importance of being

Table 4.2   Mean and standard deviation for positioning and control errors for high and low skill participants across viewing conditions on the ball control task.

Type of error	Group	FV Mean % (SD)	OCC_BF Mean % (SD)	OCC_F Mean % (SD)
Position	High skill	10.91 (9.23)	4.87 (7.39)	9.42 (6.11)
	Low skill	15.50 (9.05)	10.55 (10.21)	20.50 (17.35)
Control	High skill	12.16 (7.82)	39.49 (11.63)	14.62 (17.82)
	Low skill	42.97 (18.88)	43.13 (22.34)	35.68 (24.12)

able to see the limb during interceptive tasks and highlights the need to explore innovative adaptations to the screen paradigm that do not simultaneously prevent sight of the ball (e.g. see Weigelt and Williams, 1999).

The decrement in performance observed for the high skill participants under OCC_BF compared with FV is accompanied by an increase in control (effect size = 3.49) rather than in position (effect size = –0.34) errors (see Table 4.2). Having sight of the ball during the final portion of its flight helps players to co-ordinate their actions relative to the ball's arrival, ensuring that the foot is used to 'cushion' or absorb the ball's velocity (cf. Barfield and Fischman, 1990). The importance of being able to see the ball during this period was reinforced by the kinematic data which indicated that for high skill participants the foot was withdrawn later under OCC_BF ($M = 19$ ms, $SD = \pm 20$ ms) compared to OCC_F ($M = 37$ ms, $SD = \pm 33$ ms) and FV ($M = 39$ ms, $SD = \pm 29$ ms), respectively. No differences were observed across viewing conditions for less skilled participants in performance outcome or the relative proportion of control and positioning errors. It appears that low skill participants do not effectively employ visual information from the foot or final portion of ball flight. Alternatively, it may suggest a potential ceiling effect on performance for these participants on this particular task.

Another interesting finding is that both groups of participants made more vertical (77.5 per cent) than horizontal (22.5 per cent) position errors, supporting our earlier criticism of the error classification scheme employed by Barfield and Fischman (1990). The height of the foot at impact appears to be one of most important factors underlying successful performance, although this is not visually mediated. Further kinematic analysis indicated that the high skill participants were more consistent in orienting their non-kicking foot relative to the kicking foot at ball contact (as indicated by the standard deviation of the ankle–ankle distance at impact). This latter finding may suggest that high skill participants made more gross postural adjustments based on information arising earlier in the ball's flight than less skilled players. The ability to correctly position the body relative to the ball based on early ball flight information is an important characteristic of successful performance and may be analogues to Alderson, Sully and Sully's (1974) 'transport phase' during one-handed catching.

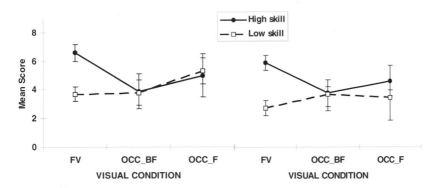

Figure 4.3 The mean score and standard deviations for high and low skill participants across viewing conditions in the low and high spatial uncertainty kicking task.

Vision and proprioception in a soccer passing task

In a second study, the aim was to examine the role of vision and proprioception in a dynamic passing task. Participant skill level and task difficulty were manipulated to determine whether they had any moderating effect on the relative importance of these two sources of information for successful performance. Task difficulty was manipulated by varying the spatial uncertainty of the ball's flight. In one condition, the ball was served within a 'corridor' of 0.7 m (low spatial uncertainty), whereas in the other condition ball service range was increased to 2.0 m (high spatial uncertainty). The same viewing conditions were employed as in the ball control study, namely: FV, OCC_BF and OCC_F. Participants were required to kick an approaching soccer ball with one touch towards a marked target area located 7.4 m to their left at a 15° angle from the ball's trajectory. Soccer balls were projected with a velocity of 9.75 m s^{-1} over a distance of 10.5 m. The target was divided into a central area (worth 10 points) and a number of peripheral areas (worth between 0 and 8 points). High and low skill participants were selected using a within-task criterion (mean score under full vision > 6 and < 3.5, respectively). Qualitative and quantitative measurements were recorded using VHS cameras and an optoelectronic system.

The pattern of results under low spatial uncertainty conditions differed somewhat from that reported for the ball control task with significant main effects being reported for skill level, viewing condition and the interaction of skill level × viewing condition (see Figure 4.3). An interesting discrepancy was that high skill participants performed better under FV (M = 6.6) compared with OCC_F (Mean = 5.0) in the kicking task compared with ball control. Although not statistically significant, possibly due to the small sample size (N = 6) and the high standard deviation under OCC_F, a clear trend was apparent (effect size = –2.02, N = 5), suggesting that vision of the foot may be more important when passing compared with controlling a ball in soccer. This trend was corroborated by an analysis of

Table 4.3   Mean and standard deviation for positioning and control errors for high and low skill participants across viewing conditions on the ball kicking task (low spatial uncertainty condition).

Type of error	Group	FV Mean % (SD)	OCC_BF Mean % (SD)	OCC_F Mean % (SD)
Position	High skill	13.43 (12.93)	29.17 (11.49)	23.91 (22.91)
	Low skill	33.76 (18.09)	40.54 (13.95)	13.23 (13.53)
Control	High skill	19.21 (13.51)	32.18 (13.13)	22.42 (16.04)
	Low skill	25.26 (7.58)	14.72 (15.30)	15.81 (13.67)

position and control errors presented in Table 4.3. A higher percentage of position errors was recorded under OCC_F compared with FV (23.9% vs. 13.4%), whereas the relative proportion of control errors was similar (22.4% vs. 19.2%) across the two conditions. Taken together, these results suggest that visual proprioception may be more important in passing than in control tasks, possibly due to the greater spatio–temporal accuracy requirements involved in passing. In a kicking task, participants have to continually adjust the foot's orientation to ensure that the ball is propelled on the appropriate trajectory towards the target. These adjustments, like the grasp phase in one-handed catching, may be mediated by visual proprioception.

Although these findings suggest that the role of visual proprioception in lower limb interceptive actions is constrained by the accuracy requirements of the task, the greatest decrement in performance for the high skill group was observed under OCC_BF (effect size = –3.55). They recorded lower scores and an increase in the percentage of position and control errors under OCC_BF compared with FV and OCC_F. It appears that, for skilled performers, being able to see the ball over the final portion of its flight is more important than having sight of the feet in a kicking task. Table 4.3 shows that the decrement in performance under OCC_BF compared with OCC_F was accompanied by a slightly greater increase in control (32.18 vs. 22.42 per cent) rather than position (29.17 vs. 23.91 per cent) errors. The implication is that losing sight of the ball affects participants' ability to 'guide' or direct the ball towards the target during foot contact rather than to position the foot beforehand.

An almost identical pattern of results was obtained for both groups of participants in the high spatial uncertainty condition although, as expected, the overall scores were lower than in the low spatial uncertainty condition. There was no interaction between skill level, viewing condition and task difficulty. Interestingly, the low skill participants performed at a similar level across the three viewing conditions ($M = 3.70$), mirroring the findings reported in the ball control task.

Summary and conclusions

So, what can we conclude from current literature on lower limb interceptive actions? First, the relative importance of vision and articular proprioception interacts with the participant's skill level as well as the spatio–temporal accuracy requirements of the task. When controlling a ball in soccer, sight of the foot is less important than the ability to see the ball, possibly in conjunction with the foot, during the final portion of its flight. This information helps players to 'control' the ball rather than to position the foot prior to foot/ball contact. Visual proprioception does appear helpful for skilled players when passing a ball using 'one-touch' in soccer, although, yet again, having sight of the ball during the final portion of its flight is the key factor. Since skilled players are able to use visual information during this 115 ms period, this finding suggests that the visuo–motor delay in such tasks is much lower than predicted based on earlier research outcomes using laboratory-based reaction time paradigms (for a review, see McLeod and Jenkins, 1991). The actual latency period for visual adjustments is likely to be more comparable with those reported in other dynamic tasks involving the upper limbs (e.g. see Bootsma and van Wieringen, 1990; Lee *et al.*, 1983).

The skilled performers' ability to make on-going visual corrections during the final 115 ms raises concerns with the interpretation of findings from previous studies and has clear implications for future research involving the 'screen' paradigm. Another crucial difference between skilled and less skilled players is their ability to perceive early information from the ball's flight for the purposes of gross body orientation. A key question to be addressed is what sources of visual information skilled performers extract from the ball's flight during these early and late time periods. Put differently: what are the important information constraints (e.g. sources of optical information) guiding perception and action in these dynamic lower limb tasks? Recent research involving upper limb interceptive tasks indicates that crucial information may be derived from several different sources of optical information and that their relative importance may vary as a function of task and informational constraints (e.g. see Tresilian, 1994, 1999; Bootsma *et al.*, 1997; Bootsma and Oudejans, 1993). Further research is required to determine whether similar sources of perceptual information underlie successful performance in lower limb interceptive tasks.

Notes

1 Fischman and Schneider (1985) argue that the number of grasp errors may be underestimated since committing a position error could preclude the appearance of a grasp error. Elliott, Zuberec and Milgram (1994) suggest that a more appropriate analysis would be to determine the proportion of grasp errors made only on trials when the hand was correctly positioned.

2 Some variability in achieved occlusion times was observed across participants. In the OCC_BF condition the achieved occlusion times were 115 ms (SD = ± 23) and 114 ms (SD = ± 10) for the high and low skill groups, respectively. Under OCC_F the achieved occlusion periods were 32 ms (SD = ±27) for the high skill participants and 25 ms (SD = ± 29) for the low skill group.

References

Alderson, G.J.K., Sully, D.J. and Sully, H.G. (1974) An operational analysis of one-handed catching task using high speed photography. *Journal of Motor Behavior* **6**, 217–26.

Barfield, B. and Fischman, M. (1990) Control of ground-level ball as a function of skill level and sight foot. *Journal of Human Movement Studies* **19**, 181–8.

Bennett, S., Davids, K. and Craig, T. (1999) The effect of temporal and informational constraints on one-handed catching performance. *Research Quarterly for Exercise and Sport* **70**, 2, 206–11.

Bingham, G.P. (1988) Task-specific devices and the perceptual bottleneck. *Human Movement Science* **7**, 225–64.

Bootsma, R.J. and Oudejans, R.R.D. (1993) Visual information about time-to-collision between two objects. *Journal of Experimental Psychology: Human Perception and Performance* **19**, 1041–52.

Bootsma, R.J. and van Wieringen, P.C.W. (1990) Timing an attacking forehand drive in table tennis. *Journal of Experimental Psychology: Human Perception and Performance* **16**, 21–9.

Bootsma, R.J., Fayt, V., Zaal, F.T.J.M. and Laurent, M. (1997). On the information-based regulation of movement: things Wann (1996) may want to consider. *Journal of Experimental Psychology: Human Perception and Performance* **23**, 1282–9.

Davids, K. (1988) Developmental differences in the use of peripheral vision during catching performance. *Journal of Motor Behavior* **20**, 1, 39–51.

Davids, K. and Stratford, R. (1989) Peripheral vision and simple catching: the screen paradigm revisited. *Journal of Sport Sciences* **7**, 139–52.

Davids, K., Palmer, D.R.P. and Savelsbergh, G.J.P. (1989) Skill level, peripheral vision and tennis volleying peformance. *Journal of Human Movement Studies* **16**, 191–202.

Davids, K., Bennett, S.J., Handford, C.H., Jolley, L. and Beak, S. (1997) Acquiring co-ordination in interceptive actions: an ecological approach. In *Innovations in Sport Psychology: Linking Theory and Practice* (edited by R. Lidor and M. Bar-Eli). Netanya, Israel: International Society of Sport Psychology, Wingate Institute.

Diggles, V.A., Grabiner, M.D. and Garhammer, J. (1987) Skill level and efficacy of effector visual feedback in ball catching. *Perceptual and Motor Skills* **64**, 987–93.

Elliott, D., Zuberec, S. and Milgram, P. (1994) The effects of periodic visual occlusion on ball catching. *Journal of Motor Behavior* **2**, 113–22.

Fischman, M.G. and Mucci, W.G. (1989) The influence of a baseball glove on the nature of errors produced in simple one-handed catching. *Research Quarterly for Exercise and Sport* **60**, 251–55.

Fischman, M. and Schneider, T. (1985) Skill level, vision and proprioception in simple catching. *Journal of Motor Behaviour* **17**, 219–29.

Fitzpatrick, P. (1998) Modelling co-ordination dynamics in development. In *Applications of Nonlinear Dynamics to Developmental Process Modelling* (edited by K.M. Newell and P.C.M. Molenaar). Mahwah, NJ: Lawrence Erlbaum Associates.

Fleishman, E. and Rich, S. (1963) Role of kinesthetic and spatial-visual abilities in perceptual-motor learning. *Journal of Experimental Psychology* **66**, 6–11.

Harris, L.R. and Jenkin, M. (1998) *Vision and Action*. Cambridge: Cambridge University Press.

Keele, S.W. (1968) Movement control in skilled motor performance. *Psychological Bulletin* **70**, 387–403.

Keele, S.W. and Ells, J.G. (1972) Memory characteristics of kinesthetic information. *Journal of Motor Behavior* **4**, 127–34.

Laabs, G.J. (1973) Retention characteristics of different reproduction cues in motor short-term memory. *Journal of Experimental Psychology* **100**, 168–77.

Lee, D.N. (1978) The functions of vision. In *Modes of Perceiving and Processing Information* (edited by H. Pick and E. Saltzman). Hillsdale, NJ: Lawrence Erlbaum Associates.

Lee, D.N., Young, D.S., Reddish, P.E., Lough, S. and Clayton, T.M.H. (1983) Visual timing in hitting an accelerating ball. *Quarterly Journal of Experimental Psychology* **35A**, 333–46.

Legge, D. (1965) Analysis of visual and proprioceptive components of motor skill by means of a drug. *British Journal of Psychology* **56**, 243–54.

McLeod, P. and Jenkins, S. (1991) Timing, accuracy and decision time in high-speed ball games. *International Journal of Sport Psychology* **22**, 279–95.

Milgram, P. (1987) A spectacle-mounted liquid-crystal tachistoscope. *Behavior Research Methods, Instruments and Computers* **19**, 449–56.

Milner, A.D. and Goodale, M.A. (1993) Visual pathways to perception and action. In *The Visually Responsive Neuron: From Basic Neurophysiology to Behaviour.* Progress in Brain Research, vol.95 (edited by T.P. Hicks, S. Molotchnikoff and T. Ono). Amsterdam: Elsevier Publishing.

Milner, D.A. and Goodale, M.A. (1995) *The Visual Brain in Action.* Oxford: Oxford University Press.

Newell, K.M. (1996) Change in movement and skill: learning, retention and transfer. In *Dexterity and its Development* (edited by M.L. Latash and M.T.Turvey). Mahwah, NJ: Lawrence Erlbaum Associates.

Pew, R.W. (1966) Acquisition of hierarchical control over the temporal organization of a skill. *Journal of Experimental Psychology* **71**, 764–71.

Pinel, J.P.J. (1997) *Biopsychology* (3rd edition). London: Allyn and Bacon.

Regan, D., Gray, R., Portfors, C.V., Hamstra, S.J., Vincent, A., Hong, X.H., Kohly, R. and Berverley, K. (1998) Catching, hitting and collision avoidance. In *Vision and Action* (edited by L.R. Harris and M. Jenkin). Cambridge: Cambridge University Press.

Rosengren, K.S., Pick, H.L. and von Hofsten, C. (1988) Role of visual information in ball catching. *Journal of Motor Behaviour* **20**, 150–64.

Savelsbergh, G.J.P. and Whiting, H.T.A. (1988) The effect of skill level, external frame of reference and environmental changes on one-handed catching. *Ergonomics* **31**, 1655–63.

Savelsbergh, G.J.P. and Whiting, H.T.A. (1992) The acquisition of catching under monocular and binocular conditions. *Journal of Motor Behavior* **24**, 320–8.

Schmidt, R.A. and Lee, TD. (1999) *Motor Control and Learning: A Behavioral Emphasis* (3rd edition). Champaign, IL: Human Kinetics.

Singer, R.N., Williams, A.M., Janelle, C., Frehlich, S., Barber, D. and L. Boutchard (1998) Visual search during 'live' on-court situations in tennis. *Research Quarterly for Exercise and Sport* **69**, 3, 109–16.

Smyth, M.M. (1982) Letters to the Editor: sight of the hand in catching. *Journal of Motor Behavior* **14**, 3, 255–6.

Smyth, M.M. (1986) A note: is it a catch or a fumble? *Journal of Motor Behavior* **18**, 492–6.

Smyth, M.M. and Marriott, A.M. (1982) Vision and proprioception in simple catching. *Journal of Motor Behavior* **15**, 237–61.

Tresilian, J.R. (1994) Perceptual and motor processes in interceptive timing. *Human Movement Science* **23**, 1272–81.

Tresilian, J.R. (1999) Visually timed action: time-out for 'tau'? *Trends in Cognitive Sciences* **3**, 301–10.

Weigelt, C. and Williams, A.M. (1999) Vision and proprioception in lower limb interceptive actions: evidence from the soccer field. In *Proceedings of the 4th Annual Congress of the European College of Sport Science, Rome* (edited by B. Paisi, F. Pigozzi and G. Prinzi). Rome: University Institute of Motor Sciences.

Whiting, H.T.A. (1968) Training in a continuous ball-throwing and catching task. *Ergonomics* **11**, 375–82.

Whiting, H.T.A. (1969) *Acquiring Ball Skill: A Psychological Interpretation*. London: Bell.

Whiting, H.T.A. (1986) Isn't there a catch in it somewhere? *Journal of Motor Behaviour* **18**, 486–91.

Whiting, H.T.A. and Savelsbergh, G.J.P. (1987) Catch as catch can. *Perceptual and Motor Skills* **65**, 353–4.

Whiting, H.T.A. and Savelsbergh, G.J.P. (1992) An exception that proves the rule! In *Tutorials in Motor Behavior II* (edited by G.E. Stelmach and J. Requin). Amsterdam: Elsevier Science Publishing.

Whiting, H.T.A. and Sharp, R.H. (1974) Visual occlusion factors in a discrete ball catching task. *Journal of Motor Behaviour* **6**, 1, 11–16.

Whiting, H.T.A, Alderson, G.J.K. and Sanderson, F.H. (1973) Critical time intervals for viewing and individual differences in performance of a ball-catching task. *International Journal of Sport Psychology* **4**, 155–6.

Whiting, H.T.A., Savelsbergh, G.J.P. and Faber, C.M. (1988) Catch questions and incomplete answers. In *Cognition and Action in Skilled Behaviour* (edited by A.M. Colley and J.R. Beech). Amsterdam: Elsevier Science Publishing.

Williams, A.M. and Davids, K. (1998) Visual search strategy, selective attention, and expertise in soccer. *Research Quarterly for Exercise and Sport* **69**, 2, 111–28.

Williams, A.M., Davids, K. and Williams, J.G. (1999) *Visual Perception and Action in Sport*. London: E & FN Spon.

5 Learning to cross a balance beam

Implications for teachers, coaches and therapists

Shannon D. Robertson,
Luc Tremblay, J. Gregory Anson and
Digby Elliott

Maintaining postural stability while performing a gymnastics routine, like walking across a balance beam, requires dynamic balance. Visual, tactile, kinesthetic, vestibular and auditory receptors provide the performer with specific information about the position and motion of the body and various body parts relative to the beam and gravity. Both anticipatory and reactive sensorimotor processes, which depend on these sources of information, allow a skilled gymnast to perform these extremely complex series of movements with tremendous fluency. In this chapter, we examine the role of vision and tactile contact with the beam in the maintenance of postural equilibrium during goal-directed balance beam walking. This task may be studied as an interceptive action because it involves relative approach between a performer and a target location in space. We also review our research concerned with how sensorimotor processes that contribute to dynamic balance, change with practice. Our treatment of beam walking is not exhaustive. However, by examining the learning process, as well as differences in balance beam locomotion between expert and novice gymnasts, we are able to provide a general set of principles that may be useful to teachers, coaches, and therapists.[1]

Specificity of practice

Our initial interest in beam walking was motivated by our desire to extend a series of motor learning studies involving the control of upper limb interceptive movements to a different set of interceptive movements performed in a different performance context. Specifically, work at the University of Montreal (e.g., Proteau, Marteniuk, Girouard and Dugas, 1987; Proteau, Marteniuk and Lévesque, 1992) and McMaster University (e.g., Elliott, Chua, Pollock and Lyons, 1995; Elliott and Jaeger, 1988) on manual aiming has challenged the traditional view that as motor learning and skill development progress, the performer moves from a closed-loop mode of motor control, that is highly dependent on response-produced afferent feedback, to a mode of control that is more centrally-driven (i.e., open-loop control which is not dependent on afferent feedback). This view of skill progression has been associated with the concept of motor programming.

That is, with repeated attempts at the same movement (or class of movements), a specific (or general) efferent representation of the movement develops to control the movement in a feedforward manner without the need for concurrent afferent feedback about the movement while it is in progress (e.g., Schmidt, 1975; Schmidt and McCabe, 1976). Our work, and that of our colleagues, indicates that rather than becoming less dependent on feedback with practice, the learner actually becomes faster and more efficient at using the afferent information available (e.g., Elliott and Lyons, 1998; Proteau, 1992).

A good example of this phenomenon is a study conducted by Proteau, Martiniuk, Girouard and Dugas (1987) in which participants were required to practice a rapid aiming movement to a small target with their non-preferred hand. Some participants practised exactly the same movement for 200 trials (moderate practice), while others completed a total of 2,000 aiming attempts (extensive practice). In each of these two practice groups, half the performers received full visual feedback over the course of their aiming attempts, while the other learners had visual feedback about the movement of their arm eliminated upon movement initiation. After moderate, or extensive, practice in their particular feedback condition, all participants were required to perform the aiming task without concurrent visual feedback. Knowledge of results (KR) was also withdrawn. The absence of KR was an important feature of this transfer phase, because it prevented participants from learning to perform in the no-vision transfer condition (Salmoni, Schmidt and Walter, 1984). As one might expect, the withdrawal of vision and KR had little impact on the people who had trained without vision. They continued to perform as they did during acquisition. Of particular interest was the performance of the participants who had trained with vision and now were required to perform in its absence. The traditional view of skill acquisition holds that after extended practice the importance of feedback, including visual feedback, is diminished. Thus, participants with 2,000 trials performing the same movement would be expected to suffer less than the 200-trial group when vision was withdrawn. However, exactly the opposite result was obtained. That is, target aiming error increased significantly more for the 2,000-trial group than the 200-trial group, and both groups who had trained with vision did more poorly in the no-vision situation than participants who had trained without vision. Thus, practice made the learner more, not less, dependent on the afferent information available during skill acquisition.

Proteau (1992) has suggested that specific 'sensory' representations or internal codes develop with practice. Feedback-based error reduction involves the comparison of on-line afferent information to these internal codes. When sensory feedback no longer takes the same form as the sensory representations (e.g., vision is eliminated), performance deteriorates (negative transfer).

The observation of increased utilisation of afferent information accompanying increased skill is consistent with the Bernstein perspective of co-ordination (Bernstein, 1967; Turvey, 1990). An interpretation of the Bernstein perspective suggests that skill acquisition is associated initially with reducing the many degrees of freedom present in the performer and the environment (see Chapter 1 in this book and Chapter 16 by Lees and Davids, Chapter 15 by Temprado, and Chapter 14 by Tayler; see also Van der Kamp, Savelsbergh and Smeets, 1997). Later, as skill acquisition increases, more of the available degrees of freedom can be utilised. This interpretation of skill performance is analogous to the comparison between strictly serial processing and parallel distributed processing; for the former, too many degrees of freedom are a problem, but in the latter, degrees of freedom become advantageous.

When this interpretation is applied to the utilisation of concurrent afference, the following explanation is tenable. The performance of novices is less automatic and greatly dependent on immediate and specific concurrent feedback for success (termed low level afference). In contrast, the performance of experts does not depend on specific low level afference, but rather the ability to extract and utilise higher order information from the afferent input. Thus, it is not a case of afference or no afference, but the altered capability to extract increasingly relevant information from the rich sensory sources available. For example, the novice walking on a balance beam is likely to exclude all but the essential visual information (reducing the degrees of freedom) whereas the expert gymnast is more likely to select 'personally relevant' visual features. If this were true, it might be predicted that perturbations to visual feedback would also degrade the expert's performance.

In this context, it is interesting that several studies have shown that it is possible to disrupt motor performance by adding a source of information that was not available during practice (Elliott and Jaeger, 1988; Proteau, Martiniuk and Lévesque, 1992). It is certainly the case that changing the relationship between a movement and the expected sensory consequences of the movement is extremely disruptive to performance regardless of how much practice the participant has received (Elliott, Lyons and Dyson, 1997). Our initial work on balance beam walking was designed to determine if the learning specificity principles, developed through laboratory research on manual aiming, applied outside the laboratory to other classes of interceptive tasks (see also Bennett and Davids, 1995; Whiting, Savelsbergh and Pijpers, 1995). In one sense, balance beam walking is similar to manual aiming because each step requires a precise movement of the foot to the beam (target).

Balance beam walking: expert–novice differences in the use of vision

The research strategy employed in most of the specificity of learning work has been to train an unskilled group of participants for a set number of trials on a novel laboratory task, and then, following training, to alter the sensory conditions under which the task must be performed. While this approach allows the experimenter to have tight control over the learning conditions, the amount of practice that can be given in a typical motor learning experiment is modest compared to the training an athlete requires to obtain even moderate expertise in most skill domains (Ericsson and Lehmann, 1996). In our initial study (Robertson, Collins, Elliott and Starkes, 1994), we decided to compare the ability of novice and expert gymnasts to quickly cross a balance beam under a variety of vision conditions. Our primary goal in this study was to examine the relative importance of vision, and by default, other sources of information early and late in the learning process.

Our expert gymnasts were 10 varsity athletes who were competing at the inter-university level and who had been involved in training and competition for at least 15 years. The novice participants were first year physical education students who were required to take an introductory gymnastics course for credit. The task involved locomoting a 5 m regulation beam as quickly as possible without missing the beam (e.g., 10 cm wide target). In order to avoid injury to the participants, the beam was only 21 cm off the floor. Participants were required to cross the beam in eight different vision conditions. We used liquid crystal goggles to manipulate vision of the beam and the rest of the visual surround. In the no-vision condition, the goggles changed from transparent to translucent as the performer left a pressure sensitive mat and stepped onto the beam to begin a walking trial. In the full-vision condition the goggles were transparent for the entire trial. This controlled for nuisance effects of wearing the goggles. The other six conditions involved different intermittent schedules of vision and occlusion. Specifically, the goggle lenses were controlled in such a way that 20 ms samples of vision were provided every 80, 100, 120, 170, 250 and 500 ms (i.e., 12.5, 10, 8.3, 5.9, 4 and 2 Hz).

The purpose of the vision–no vision manipulation was straightforward. That is, if expert gymnasts depend almost exclusively on vision and visual feedback to maintain a high degree of performance then the elimination of vision should disrupt their performance as much or perhaps more than novice performers. The intermittent vision manipulation was designed to extend some work on both manual aiming (Elliott, Calvert, Jaeger and Jones, 1990; Elliott, Chua and Pollock, 1994), and locomotion (Assaiante, Marchand and Amblard, 1989; Laurent and Thomson, 1988). This previous research has demonstrated that the intermittent pickup of visual information may be sufficient for precise motor control if visual samples are available at least every 80 ms (i.e., 10 Hz and above). Our interest was in determining if this sampling frequency for visual continuity is task dependent. For example, because of the various head and body positions that must be maintained during a gymnastics routine, part of an expert's performance may depend on skilled intermittent monitoring of foot and beam position. It was thought that this task constraint would place the experts at an advantage in the intermittent visual situations, particularly at the low sampling frequencies.

The movement time results for this experiment are redrawn in Figure 5.1. The experts outperformed the novice gymnasts in all eight vision conditions, and their performance was not disrupted by either partially or completely eliminating vision. While novice performers did reasonably well in the intermittent visual circumstances, they took almost twice as long to cross the beam when vision was completely eliminated. In this situation, it was also necessary to rerun a number of trials because the novice performer stepped off the beam on approximately 25 per cent of their walking attempts. In all other situations, the discarded trial rate was less than 6 per cent.[2] These findings indicated that skilled gymnasts are not as

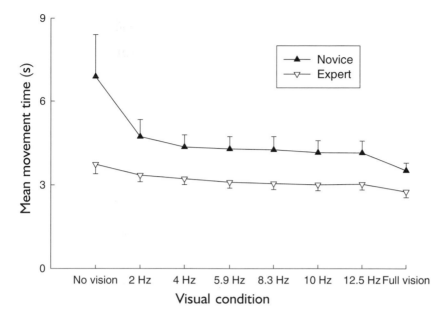

Figure 5.1 Mean movement time as a function of expertise and vision condition (from Robertson *et al.*, 1994, Experiment 1).

dependent on vision for performance as their unskilled counterparts. However, just because skilled gymnasts were able to perform adequately without vision does not mean that visual information is not used when it is available.

In a follow-up study (Robertson, Collins, Elliott and Starkes, 1994, Experiment 2), we decided to take a more detailed look at how experts were able to maintain their performance in the no-vision condition. We did this by asking participants to cross the beam (target) as quickly as possible while maintaining an upright posture. Each performance was filmed. Thus, as well as examining movement time, we were able to count the number of steps each participant took to cross the balance beam. We also developed a reliable procedure for identifying the adjustments made by participants to maintain their posture on the beam. We called these form errors and they included: deviations from an upright posture, arm lifts above the horizontal, lateral leg lifts and bending at the waist or hip. Once again, we had expert and novice gymnasts cross the beam as quickly as possible under different vision conditions. In this study, these included a full-vision condition, a no-vision condition and a condition in which vision was eliminated 8 s before a walking trial began. The last condition was introduced in order to allow any visual–motor representation of the movement environment to decay (see Thomson, 1983) before a walking trial began.

As in the previous study, experts were able to cross the beam just as quickly in the two no-vision conditions as they were in the condition in which full visual information was available (see Figure 5.2a). Interestingly however, experts took more steps and committed four times the number of form errors in the two no-vision situations than in the full-vision condition (see Figure 5.2b for form error information). Although they were able to maintain their speed, they were performing the locomotion task quite differently in the absence of vision. It would seem that although vision was not necessary, it certainly contributed to performance when it was available. As in the first experiment, novice performers were profoundly affected by the elimination of vision in terms of movement time, number of steps to cross the beam and form errors. Presumably for these individuals, vision dominated because they have not had the time or opportunity to develop other afferent strategies to maintain postural stability.

Another way of examining the importance of vision in balance beam walking is to perturb vision and study the impact of the perturbation on performance. Consistent with this research strategy, we had expert and novice gymnasts walk across a balance beam in a full-vision and a no-vision situation and in conditions in which we used a 25 diopter prism spectacle to displace the visual field approximately 15 degrees to the right or the left (Robertson and Elliott, 1996a). These conditions were randomised so as to diminish habituation effects. The rationale for this manipulation was that if expert gymnasts are less dependent on vision for their performance then they should be less disrupted by a visual perturbation than novice performers.

As is apparent in Figure 5.3a, both novice and expert gymnasts crossed the beam much more slowly when their vision was displaced to the right or left by the prism spectacles. These longer movement times coincided with a large number of form errors on successful trials (Figure 5.3b). Even more revealing however was the number of attempts participants had to make in order to obtain 10 successful trials in the two prism conditions (experts = 18.4 trials, novices = 24.0 trials). Thus, it would appear that while both expert and novice gymnasts were able to cross the beam reasonably successfully when vision was not available, they were unable to ignore vision when it was present.

The results of the three expert–novice studies just discussed are somewhat equivocal in terms of distinguishing between a specificity of learning explanation of skill development, and an explanation that posits a progression from closed-loop to open-loop motor control. While experts were not as disrupted as novice performers by the removal of vision, the form error data indicated that neither group was crossing the beam in a programmed/stereotyped manner. The observed postural adjustments suggested that, in the no-vision circumstance, experts were simply more adept at using other afferent information to maintain their equilibrium. Although this finding could indicate that other sources of afferent information, such as proprioception, become dominant over vision after extended practice (e.g., Fleishman and Rich, 1963; Whiting and Savelsbergh, 1992), the prism experiment indicates that when vision is available, both expert and novice performers are affected by it. It appears that expert performers simply have a richer afferent learning history on the beam than novice gymnasts, and thus are able to make use of alternative feedback sources when vision is not available (see Bernstein, 1967; see also Chapter 1 in this book).

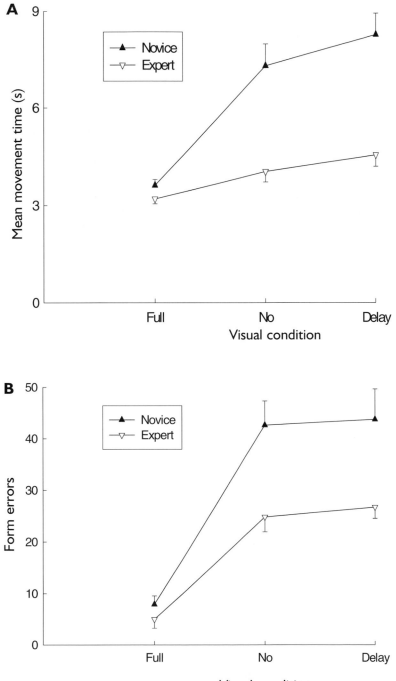

Figure 5.2 Mean movement time (A) and form errors (B) as a function of expertise and vision condition (from Robertson *et al.*, 1994, Experiment 2).

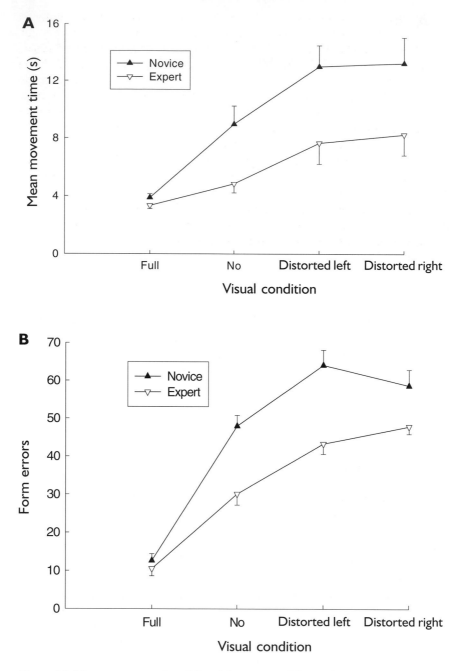

Figure 5.3 Mean movement time (A) and form errors (B) as a function of expertise and vision condition (from Robertson and Elliott, 1996a).

Although the expert–novice paradigm has some advantages, both in terms of the amount of practice afforded an expert and the time needed to conduct an individual study, it has one major shortcoming. Specifically, the researcher has no direct control over the learning history of the participants. In the case of beam walking for example, coaches sometimes ask their already skilled performers to practice walking across the beam with their eyes closed. Presumably this is done in order to have the gymnast focus on other sources of afferent information and/or any internal representation of the movement environment developed over past experiences (e.g., either sensory or motor). In a practical gymnastics coaching environment, this instructional strategy however may not be used with beginning beam performers for safety reasons. Certainly in any study designed to examine the specificity/generality of learning, these potential differences in learning history confound the interpretation of any expert–novice differences related to the sensory circumstances. The experiments reviewed in the next section of this chapter were designed to eliminate this type of learning history confound, albeit at the cost of some external validity.

Learning to cross the beam

In order to exercise complete control over the performers' balance beam history, we recruited 20 physical education students with no beam walking experience and trained them to walk across a secure ground level beam as quickly as possible in two different vision conditions (Robertson and Elliott, 1996b). One group received full visual information while learning to cross the beam, while the second group of participants were required to cross the beam while wearing a blackened ski goggle. In order to provide an adequate degree of practice, the study was conducted over five days. On the first day both groups completed 10 baseline trials in each of the two vision conditions. Thirty trials were then conducted in which each participant practised in their specified learning condition. At the beginning of day two, 10 more trials were conducted in each of the two vision conditions in order to examine the impact of moderate practice (i.e., the 30 trials/ approximately 300 steps; Robertson, Collins, Elliott and Starkes, 1994). This treatment was followed by 100 trials of practice, specific to group assignment on day 2, followed by another 100 trials of specific practice on each of days 3 and 4. On day 5, participants were tested in their own condition as well as the other vision condition (i.e., 10 trials each) in order to examine the impact of extensive practice (approximately 3000 steps) on retention and transfer to the other vision condition. During acquisition, verbal feedback about the movement time for a trial was given following the trial, and participants were encouraged to try to cross the beam more quickly. No feedback was given during transfer trials.

The mean movement time data and the form error data are redrawn in Figures 5.4a and 5.4b respectively. As is apparent in these figures, participants performed exceedingly well when vision was available regardless of training condition. This ceiling effect for performance makes it difficult to adequately evaluate some aspects of the specificity of learning hypothesis. The powerful effect of vision even after

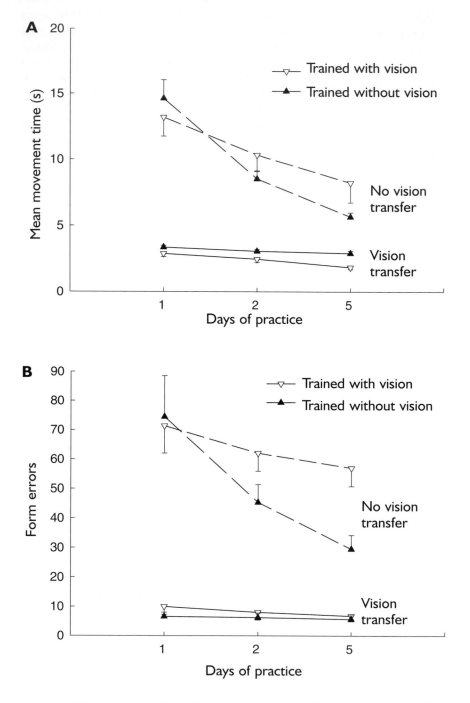

Figure 5.4 Mean movement time (A) and form errors (B) as a function of training condition, transfer condition and days of practice (from Robertson and Elliott, 1996b).

considerable practice creates difficulty for any model of skill acquisition that posits a progression from closed-loop to open-loop control (e.g., Pew, 1966), or a gradual reduction in the importance of vision in favour of some other sensory modality (Fleishman and Rich, 1963). While those who trained without vision performed better than the vision-trained participants under no-vision transfer conditions, there was also a fairly robust transfer between visual training and the no-vision situation. Clearly, participants were learning to use some other afferent sources of information during training as well. Another experiment was designed to determine just what that source of information might be.

In our initial learning study, novice beam-walkers benefited from practice with visual information even in a non-visual circumstance. This finding suggests that, along with vision, they were learning to use some other source of information to maintain equilibrium and quickly navigate the beam. As well, in the expert–novice studies, expert gymnasts were able to maintain their walking speed when vision was eliminated even though they made many more form errors than when full vision was available. Presumably the extra form errors occurred because postural adjustments were being made on the basis of non-visual afferent information. One potentially important source of information that could be mediating performance in all four studies is tactile information from cutaneous receptors on the feet. These sensory organs would provide the performer with feedback about the position of the feet on the beam. Proteau, Tremblay and DeJaeger (1998) conducted a study in which they diminished this source of information by having participants learn to navigate a line on a gymnasium floor. This methodology allowed for the examination specificity of learning in a full vision and no-vision situation under conditions in which meaningful tactile feedback was eliminated.

The locomotor task in this study involved walking a distance of 20 m on a 2.5 cm-wide line painted on the floor (i.e., target). In this study, movement times were constrained by requiring participants to complete a walking attempt in 14 to 16 s. The primary dependent variable was spatial accuracy or the deviation of the participant from the line at the end of each walking attempt. Thirty-two physical education students with no gymnastics experience were randomly assigned to four groups. Half the participants were trained to walk the line with full vision and the other half were trained with no vision (i.e., blindfolded). Half the participants in each group received 20 training trials and the other half received 100 training trials. During acquisition, participants in the full-vision group could continually see their deviation from the line, and thus made no walking errors. The participants trained without vision were instructed to lift their mask at the end of each walking trial in order to see how far they had deviated from the line.

Although the participants who trained with vision were error free during acquisition, what is most important for evaluating the specificity of learning hypothesis is how participants performed in the 20 no-vision transfer trials following the training phase of the study. As is apparent in Figure 5.5, while there was not a great deal of difference between the two no-vision groups and the group that practised 20 trials with full vision, participants in the full vision-100 trial group had difficulty performing the blind walking task. Consistent with the

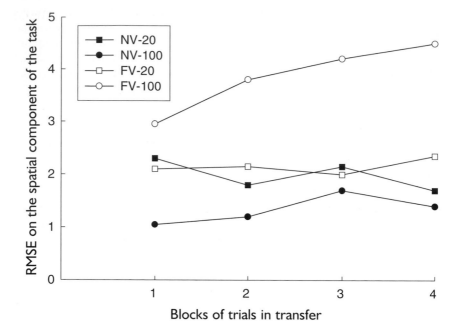

Figure 5.5 Root mean square error as a function of training condition, number of training trials and transfer block (from Proteau, Tremblay and DeJaeger, 1998).

specificity of learning hypothesis, this result may reflect the development of an over-reliance on vision during acquisition phase of the study. Presumably the impact of vision-specific learning was more pronounced in this study than in the Robertson and Elliott study (1996b), because tactile information about the position of the feet on the beam was not available to guide locomotion during the blind transfer situation. By default, this study reinforces the importance of tactile information for error-free beam walking.

In summary, our empirical work on beam walking and locomoting along a target line on the floor indicates that visual information, including response-produced visual feedback, is important to both expert and novice gymnast faced with the task of quickly navigating a balance beam. Visual pickup however does not need to be continuous, since both beginning and expert gymnasts can successfully navigate the balance beam with only intermittent samples of the visual surround. While a certain amount of learning appears to be specific to the visual circumstances the performer is exposed to during skill acquisition, other sources of information contribute to maintaining equilibrium when vision is not available. For example, tactile feedback about the movement of the feet on the beam appears to be important to expert performers. Because tactile and vestibular information are utilised more in beam walking it can be considered a more multisensory activity than manual aiming (cf. Elliott and Lyons, 1998). The multisensory nature of beam walking becomes even more pronounced as skill develops and the performer is able to take advantage of the additional perceptual degrees of freedom afforded by the task environment.

Implications of this research for teaching and coaching

Clearly vision is an extremely important source of information for both beginning and skilled beam performers. Thus, a teaching strategy that directs the performer to the relevant sources of visual information in the performance environment seems appropriate. Because learning appears to be at least somewhat specific to the sensory information available during skill acquisition, it is probably important to concentrate on visual cues that will be consistently available across all performance environments. For example, it would not be advantageous to have a gymnast concentrate on specific features of the floor or ceiling of the home gymnasium while learning a routine, because those visual cues will not be available to the performer when the routine must be performed elsewhere. However the position of the beam, and hopefully the body, will be consistent across different performance venues.

Adding a visual guide during practice that will not be available during competition should be avoided. This recommendation is supported by a powerlifting experiment in which a laser beam was used as a guide to leg position during skill acquisition. In this study, Tremblay and Proteau (1998) demonstrated that, although the laser guide facilitated positioning accuracy during acquisition, performance was disrupted compared to control conditions when the guide was later removed. Presumably the athletes had become dependent on a source of information that was no longer available, and thus were unable to use more intrinsic sources of afferent feedback.

The specificity of learning principles outlined above can probably be generalised to other modalities as well (Coull and Elliott, 1999). For example, coaches often 'talk a gymnast through a routine' during practice (e.g., 'point your toes, breathe, stick'). However, during competition a coach is not allowed to say anything to the gymnast during a routine. If the gymnast has relied on this auditory guidance, and it is taken away, performance will be adversely affected. Especially in the latter stages of skill acquisition, the practice conditions should mirror the competition conditions as closely as possible.

Although vision will always be available during competition, it does dominate the other sensory modalities when it is available (Posner, Nissen and Klein, 1976; Robertson and Elliott, 1996a). Early in learning it may be beneficial to provide the performer with some no-vision training in order draw attention to other afferent sources of information. For example, in their manual aiming work, Soucy and Proteau (2001) have shown that varying sensory conditions during practice provides the learner with at least some resistance to the negative transfer effects associated with eliminating vision. In terms of Proteau's model of specificity (1992), this finding may occur because the performer has the opportunity to develop a visual as well as a kinesthetic representation of movement consequences. Thus, providing some variability in the afferent conditions may help the learner use non-visual sources of information more effectively. This would allow the gymnast to maintain performance when vision of the beam and various body parts are temporarily eliminated or degraded by a particular stance or posture (e.g., during reversing movements such as a back flip). Once again, this instructional strategy would be used to promote greater multisensory use of information as practice progresses.

The selective elimination of specific afferent information in order to focus attention on other sources of feedback is an instructional strategy that can be applied to other sporting activities as well. For example, in basketball, a shot is prepared and later evaluated on the basis of visual information. However, while making the shot it may be important to pay attention to kinesthetic and feedforward information specifying joint angles and the timing of muscular contractions. By practising without vision on some occasions, the learner will be more likely to pay attention to these other sources of information, and perhaps improve his or her performance. If nothing else, it will prepare the player for those situations in which vision of the basket may be blocked by a defender part way through the shot.

In summary, at least one goal of a teacher or coach is to determine which sources of information are important for success at a particular motor skill. Practice then should emphasise the use of this sensory information under conditions similar to those normally present. Additional sensory cues that will not be available during competition should be avoided.

Implications for rehabilitation

The research reviewed in this chapter, particularly some of the specificity of learning principles, also has implications for therapists dealing with people having movement problems. If, for example, a physical therapist is viewed as a 'teacher of motor skills' (Shumway-Cook and Woollacott, 1995), rehabilitation efforts should emphasise functional, goal-directed activities rather than isolated muscle actions. In this context, it is important for the therapist to understand the sensory and motor conditions under which a patient will be required to perform at task, so that the rehabilitation environment can reflect those conditions. Clients who are experiencing specific sensory problems due to age or injury may need to relearn various afferent–motor relations, and this is best done in the sensory and motor context they will be faced with on a day to day basis.

As an example, Lichtenstein, Shields, Shiavi and Burger (1989) had elderly participants perform various activities (e.g., stretching, standing on one leg, walking) in hopes of improving their balance. The trained group did not exhibit any reliable improvement in either one- or two-legged balancing with their eyes opened or closed. This is not surprising given the specificity of learning principles reviewed here. In contrast, Hu and Woollacott (1994) used a training protocol that incorporated different sensory inputs. A training group practised balancing standing on either a firm or foam surface with their eyes open and closed, and their heads neutral or extended. After 16 weeks of training, the trained group demonstrated increased balance stability when tested on these tasks. Four weeks later, the participants were tested in a one-legged balance task with their eyes open and closed. The results revealed that training using different sensory situations improved balance under altered sensory conditions. The training also transferred to other balance tasks.

In summary then, physical therapy should involve determining what afferent information is specific to the task the client needs to accomplish, as well as which sources of information the individual has intact and can rely on. Practice, or rehabilitation, should focus on the sensory information that will be required to successfully complete the task. Depending on the client's movement problem, it may be necessary to focus on the use of different sensory information in various settings or environments.

Summary and conclusions

Dynamic balance is a fundamental part of every day life and is especially important in sports like gymnastics. As we grow older, impaired dynamic balance can lead to problems with locomotion, and restrict our range of daily activity. In this chapter, we have reviewed some of our work on specificity of practice as it relates to dynamic balance during locomotion. Like many of the studies conducted with laboratory tasks (see Elliott and Lyons, 1998 and Proteau, 1992 for a review), research on beam walking indicates that motor learning is highly dependent on the sensory conditions the learner is exposed to during skill acquisition. One goal of a teacher, coach or therapist should be to determine what sensory information is most important for success at an activity, and then to structure a practice environment that emphasises that information. Practice should always be transfer-appropriate (Lee, 1988). That is, it should focus the learner on the sensory cues that will be available when the activity must actually be performed.

Author note

The beam walking and precision walking experiments reviewed in this chapter were funded through grants from the Natural Sciences and Engineering Research Council of Canada. The chapter was prepared while Digby Elliott was a visiting William Evans Fellow at the University of Otago, New Zealand.

Notes

1 Most of the behavioural and physiological principles that govern locomotion in general apply to beam walking. Treatment of this vast literature however is beyond the scope of this chapter. For an excellent review of more general research on vision and locomotion see the edited volume by Patla (1991).
2 This actually created a situation in which the novice performers had more practice in the no-vision circumstance that the experts.

References

Assaiante, C., Marchand, A.R. and Amblard, B. (1989). Discrete visual samples may control locomotor equilibrium and foot positioning in man. *Journal of Motor Behavior* **21**, 72–91.

Bennett, S.J. and Davids, K. (1995). The manipulation of vision during the powerlift squat: exploring the boundaries of the specificity of learning hypothesis. *Research Quarterly for Exercise and Sport* **66**, 210–18.

Bernstein, N. (1967). *The Co-ordination and Regulation of Movement*. Oxford: Pergamon.

Coull, J. and Elliott, D. (1999). Evidence for learning specificity using visual and auditory sources of information. Paper presented at the Canadian Society for Psychomotor Learning and Sport Psychology Conference, Edmonton, Alberta.

Elliott, D. and Jaeger, M. (1988). Practice and the visual control of manual aiming movement. *Journal of Human Movement Studies* **14**, 279–91.

Elliott, D. and Lyons, J. (1998). Optimizing the use of vision in skill acquisition. In J. Piek (ed.), *Motor Control and Human Skill: A Multidisciplinary Perspective*. Champaign, IL: Human Kinetics.

Elliott, D., Chua, R. and Pollock, B.J. (1994). The influence of intermittent vision on manual aiming. *Acta Psychologica* **85**, 1–13.

Elliott, D., Lyons, J. and Dyson, K. (1997). Rescaling an acquired discrete aiming movement: specific or general motor learning? *Human Movement Science* **16**, 81–96.

Elliott, D., Calvert, R., Jaeger, M. and Jones, R. (1990). A visual representation and the control of manual aiming movements. *Journal of Motor Behavior* **22**, 327–46.

Elliott, D., Chua, R., Pollock, B.J. and Lyons, J. (1995). Optimizing the use of vision in manual aiming: the role of practice. *Quarterly Journal of Experimental Psychology* **48A**, 72–83.

Ericsson, K.A. and Lehmann, A.C. (1996). Expert and exceptional performance: evidence of maximal adaptation and task constraints. *Annual Review of Psychology* **47**, 273–305.

Fleishman, E.A. and Rich, S. (1963). Role of kinesthetic and spatial–visual abilities in perceptual–motor learning. *Journal of Experimental Psychology* **66**, 6–11.

Hu, M.H. and Woollacott, M.H. (1994). Multisensory training of standing balance in older adults. I. Postural stability and one-leg stance balance. *Journals of Gerontology* **49**, M52–M61.

Laurent, M. and Thomson, J.A. (1988). The role of visual information in the control of a constrained motor task. *Journal of Motor Behavior* **20**, 17–37.

Lee, T.D. (1988). Transfer-appropriate processing: a framework for conceptualizing practice effects in motor learning. In O.G. Meijer and K. Roth (eds), *Complex Movement Behaviour: 'The' Motor–Action Controversy*. Amsterdam: Elsevier.

Lichtenstein, M.J., Shields, S.L., Shiavi, R.G. and Burger, C. (1989). Exercise and balance in aged women: a pilot controlled clinical trial. *Archives of Physical Medicine and Rehabilitation* **70**, 138–43.

Patla, A.E. (ed.) (1991). *Adaptability of Human Gait*. Advances in Psychology Series 78. Amsterdam: Elsevier.

Pew, R.W. (1966). Acquisition of hierarchical control over the temporal organization of a skill. *Journal of Experimental Psychology* **71**, 764–71.

Posner, M.I., Nissen, M.J. and Klein, R.M. (1976). Visual dominance: an information-processing account of its origins and significance. *Psychological Review* **83**, 157–71.

Proteau, L. (1992). On the specificity of learning and the role of visual information for movement control. In L. Proteau and D. Elliott (eds), *Vision and Motor Control*. Amsterdam: North Holland.

Proteau, L., Marteniuk, R.G. and Lévesque, L. (1992). A sensorimotor basis for motor learning: evidence indicating specificity of practice. *Quarterly Journal of Experimental Psychology* **44A**, 557–5.

Proteau, L., Tremblay, L. and DeJaeger, D. (1998). Practice does not diminish the role of visual information in on-line control of a precision walking task: support for the specificity of practice hypothesis. *Journal of Motor Behavior* **30**, 143–50.

Proteau, L., Marteniuk, R.G., Girouard, Y. and Dugas, C. (1987) On the type of information used to control and learn an aiming movement after moderate and extensive training. *Human Movement Science* **6**, 181–99.

Robertson, S. and Elliott, D. (1996a). The influence of skill in gymnastics and vision on dynamic balance. *International Journal of Sport Psychology* **27**, 361–8.

Robertson, S. and Elliott, D. (1996b). Specificity of learning and dynamic balance. *Research Quarterly for Exercise and Sport* **67**(1), 69–75.

Robertson, S., Collins, J., Elliott, D. and Starkes, J. (1994). The influence of skill and intermittent vision on dynamic balance. *Journal of Motor Behavior* **26**(4), 333–9.

Salmoni, A.W., Schmidt, R.A. and Walter, C.B. (1984). Knowledge of results and motor learning: a review and critical reappraisal. *Psychological Bulletin* **95**, 355–86.

Schmidt, R.A. (1975). A schema theory of discrete motor skill learning. *Psychological Review* **82**, 225–60.

Schmidt, R.A. and McCabe, J.F. (1976). Motor program utilization over extended practice. *Journal of Human Movement Studies* **2**, 239–47.

Shumway-Cook, A. and Woolacott, M.H. (1995). *Motor Control: Theory and Practical Applications.* Baltimore: Williams and Wilkins.

Soucy, M.-C. and Proteau, L. (2001). Development of multiple movement representations with practice: specificity vs. flexibility. *Journal of Motor Behavior* **33**, 243–54.

Thomson, J.A. (1983). Is continuous visual monitoring necessary in visually guided locomotion? *Journal of Experimental Psychology: Human Perception and Performance* **12**, 427–43.

Tremblay, L. and Proteau, L. (1998). Specificity of practice: the case of powerlifting. *Research Quarterly for Exercise and Sport* **69**, 284–9.

Turvey, M.T. (1990). Co-ordination. *American Psychologist* **45**, 938–53.

Van der Kamp, J., Savelsbergh, G. and Smeets, J. (1997). Multiple information sources in interceptive timing. *Human Movement Science* **16**, 787–821.

Whiting, H.T.A. and Savelsbergh, G.J.P. (1992). An exception that proves the rule! In G.E. Stelmach and J. Requin (eds), *Tutorials in Motor Behavior II.* Amsterdam: North Holland.

Whiting, H.T.A., Savelsbergh, G.J.P. and Pijpers, J.R. (1995). Specificity of learning does not deny flexibility. *Applied Psychology: An International Review* **44**, 315–322.

6 Implicit and explicit learning in interceptive actions

Richard Masters, Jon Law and Jon Maxwell

The act of striking a putt in golf involves manipulation of an implement, known as the putter, in order that it will intercept a ball (stationary though that ball is) with both sufficient accuracy and effort to enter a hole some distance removed. The maximum velocity the ball can have upon reaching the hole, if it is to drop, has been calculated at 4.3 feet per second (Biddulph, 1980). Few greens are flat, environmental conditions are seldom constant and the mental state of the performer can often be less than optimal, so a satisfactory interception is not a 'given'. Where performers are highly motivated to perform near the upper limits of their ability dynamic interceptive actions are, in fact, subject to much psychological interference.

For most performers the intention to become expert is realised only through many hours (at least 10 years according to Ericsson, Krampe and Tesch-Römer, 1993) of verbal instruction, coaching, self-analysis and so on. This highly explicit mode of learning is the default mode in most skill acquisition environs. In the golfer, expert putting may entail the processing of vast amounts of information and rules. Faldo (1986) recommends a neutral grip with the left hand a little weak and the right a shade strong. He states that 'the aim is to set up the classic "Y" position at address, so that the arms, firm wrists and putter form the letter "Y" down to the ball, but keeping the hands slightly ahead of the ball. Then ... make a smooth, controlled rocking of the shoulders to produce a good roll across the green ... although the head must stay still throughout the stroke to maintain the delicate balance putting requires' (p. 128–9).

This information does not provide sufficient elucidation of the putting stroke for Faldo, however. He deems further enlightenment necessary if 'a reliable action' is to be achieved. To paraphrase Faldo's words, the performer should adopt a comfortable position over the ball at the address, not overreaching or becoming cramped. The ball should be about two inches from directly under the eyes, with both eyes focused equally on the ball. The stance should be reasonably wide to allow a smooth balanced rocking of the top half of the body. The arms should be relaxed, with no sign of tension, and the right elbow tucked into the side of the body. The left hand should be set in position throughout the stroke. The takeaway needs a triggered action such as a forward press, letting the hands go forward a half-inch. Maintaining the 'Y' formed by the arms and putter itself, just allow the shoulders to rock to bring the blade back smoothly and as squarely as possible. The club head is kept low throughout the stroke; scraping the grass helps.

Just before impact, the address position is regained and with the hands still slightly in front, and the locked left wrist set at an angle allowing every component to move at the same speed. Concentration should be on making a dead square contact. The ball is simply *intercepted* on the way through and powered forward naturally. There should be no leg movement throughout the stroke. The follow through should keep the club blade square to the line and the head should be held down until the ball is well on the way. On the longer putts wait until the ball is out of vision of the left eye before looking up.

This supply of rules and information on how to go about making a successful interceptive action in golf is enough to keep any performer bogged down for much of the 10 years it requires to achieve expertise (Ericsson, Krampe and Tesch-Römer). Ironically, once Faldo has provided this long list of dos and don'ts in the mechanics of the putting stroke he follows up by implying that too much thought can be detrimental to performance, claiming that 'you can look too long and hard in deciding the line of a difficult putt. The more you look, the more you can become confused. First impressions are often the best' (p. 130).

The clash of thinking evident in the above dialogue highlights a continuum of, in lay terms, thinking to non-thinking, which is evident in much of the motor learning literature. Traditional theories postulate that motor skills are initially acquired explicitly via cognitive processing which is verbally based and become automated or implicit as learning proceeds. That is, the verbal rules used to perform the skill are 'forgotten' and task-relevant information processing becomes unconscious (Anderson, 1983; Fitts and Posner, 1967).

Despite the traditional beliefs of the motor learning literature the practice of providing copious amounts of verbal instruction during the initial stages of motor learning may well be misguided. Numerous studies have concluded that verbal instructions do not optimise skill acquisition and, in some cases, may degrade performance and transfer (Hardy, Mullen and Jones, 1996; Hodges and Lee, 1999; Masters, 1992; Wulf and Weigelt, 1997). Instructions may act to increase awareness of an action, a process that has been linked to performance deficits during practice (Green and Flowers, 1991; Singer, Lidor and Cauraugh, 1993; Wulf and Weigelt, 1997) and under psychologically stressful conditions (Baumeister, 1984; Masters, Polman and Hammond, 1993).

Wulf and Weigelt (1997) showed this to be the case in two studies of slalom learning on a ski-simulator. These studies showed that neither providing instructions about a critical feature of the movement nor directing attention to the timing of force production in the movement facilitated learning. Rather, disruptions in overall performance were seen. Additionally, less effective performance was seen in the instructed groups under pressure to perform well.

In a series of other studies Wulf and her colleagues have also shown that an external rather than an internal focus of attention benefits the learning of tasks. Wulf, Höß and Prinz (1998) showed this on the ski-simulator, while Wulf, Lauterbach and Toole (1999) showed this to be the case in golf skills. Directing attention to the 'motion of the club' resulted in better learning than directing attention to the swing of the arms. In essence, it is the focusing on the effects of the action rather than production of the actions which is important (Wulf, McNevin, Fuchs, Ritter and Toole, 2000). This distinction is not dissimilar from the process-oriented versus outcome-oriented distinction made in the goal-setting literature (Orlick and Partington, 1988; Hardy and Nelson, 1988). In contrast, however, process goals, which direct attention to technical aspects of movement production, have generally been regarded as more effective than outcome or performance-related goals, because they help the performer to remain focused during performance (Kingston and Hardy, 1994).

Additional evidence that over-awareness of one's actions can be problematic for effective performance can be gained indirectly from work examining attentional patterns in golf putting performance. Crews (1994) describes a study which utilised EEG measures of alpha and beta activity as indicators of general cortical activation. The best performers primarily used sensory cues and showed reduced cortical activity over time, whereas the worst performers used primarily biomechanical cues, and showed increased cortical activity. Crews concluded that the worst performers were attempting to direct information to the muscles, while the best performers fall in to an attentive state conducive to the reception of sensory feedback. These findings suggest that in this case poorer performance is indicated by internalisation of attention and more active processing.

In another study Weinberg and Hunt (1976) showed that high-anxious individuals use more neuromuscular energy than their low-anxious counterparts before, during and after a throw in a ball-throwing task. They argued that this increased use of neuromuscular energy by high-anxious participants is caused by increased cortical control, or 'cortical steering'. They suggested that the primary control in high-anxious participants is through motor areas of the cerebral cortex, whereas, in low-anxious participants it is more reflexive, originating from the spinal cord and midbrain levels. An alternative explanation for Weinberg and Hunt's (1976) findings, of course, is that increased worry in high-anxious individuals raises general arousal, which is reflected in augmented muscle tension (Van Loon, Masters, Ring and McIntyre, 2001).

Conscious control

The idea that disruption to an interceptive action (or indeed any motor action) can occur if the performer attempts any sort of conscious processing to control the movement is by no means a new one. Numerous authors have shown that anxiety can lead to self-focus (e.g. Carver and Scheier, 1978; Wegner and Giuliano, 1980), and that self-focus can lead to skill failure (Baumeister, 1984; Masters, Polman and Hammond, 1993). Baumeister (1984) argued that 'under pressure, a person realises consciously that it is important to execute the behavior correctly. Consciousness attempts to ensure the correctness of this execution by monitoring the process of performance (e.g. the co-ordination and precision of muscle movements); but consciousness does not contain the knowledge of these skills, so that it ironically reduces the reliability and success of the performance when it attempts to control it' (p. 610).

Models of attention and action, such as that proposed by Norman and Shallice (1986), see conscious control as functional and propose a 'supervisory attentional system' (SAS) which can override automatic actions. Norman and Shallice argue that the SAS has a limited resource capacity and so, like any override system, is used only in specific situations where the automatic mode is deemed inappropriate or unable to cope (e.g. decision making, planning, habitual responses to be avoided). Situations which bring about a high motivation to perform the motor task successfully (i.e. pressure) are amongst this collection, although, often it would seem preferable that the SAS does not override the automaticity of the actions, because of the concomitant negative effect on performance.

The disruption to movement patterns which occurs when attention is dedicated to controlling the movement has variously been described as deautomatisation (Deikman, 1969), the conscious processing hypothesis (Hardy, Mullen and Jones, 1996) and reinvestment (Masters, Polman and Hammond, 1993). Masters, Polman and Hammond described reinvestment as a predisposition to turn one's attention to the mechanics of one's actions and designed a 20-item scale (the Reinvestment Scale) to assess this. It is comprised of items from a series of previously validated scales, including the Cognitive Failures Questionnaire (Broadbent, Cooper, Fitzgerald and Parkes, 1982), the Emotion Control Questionnaire (Roger and Nesshoever, 1987) and the Self-Consciousness Scale (Fenigstein, Scheier and Buss, 1975). Both internal reliability (coefficient alpha = 0.80) and test–retest reliability ($r = 0.74$) are high and the scale has been shown to predict skill failure under pressure, with high reinvesters being more likely to exhibit disrupted performance.

In addition, Maxwell, Masters and Eves (2000) found a positive correlation between reinvestment score and amount of rules and information accumulated in a 3,000-trial discovery learning period ($r = 0.59$), yet a negative correlation with mean performance over the 3,000 trials ($r = -0.73$). This finding provides further evidence that an inward focus of attention can be disruptive to performance, but extends previous findings by suggesting that individuals may be predisposed to focussing on the mechanics of their movements.

If one assumes that reinvestment is an enduring predisposition to turn one's attention to the mechanics of one's movements and that this is most likely under conditions of high motivation or anxiety then it follows that high reinvesters have great difficulty in preventing themselves from paying attention to their movements. Anecdotally, this is a common problem for many performers and can manifest as pseudo-clinical problems such as the 'yips' and 'dartitis' (Lees, 1998).

A means of preventing 'reinvestment' has been proposed by Masters (1992), who suggested turning to the concept of implicit learning, 'the acquisition of knowledge that takes place largely independently of conscious attempts to learn and largely in the absence of explicit knowledge about what was acquired' (Reber, 1993, p. 5). Masters argued that if *motor* skills are acquired implicitly the learner will be unable to reinvest because he or she will have no verbal knowledge of the parameters of the movement, with which to consciously interfere with the hierarchical sequencing and organisation of the motor commands as the skill is executed.

Lack of explicit, verbalisable access to knowledge in the face of improved performance has been taken as the primary indication of implicitly held knowledge (Berry and Broadbent, 1984; Berry and Dienes, 1993; Seger, 1994; Reber, 1993). The general logic behind this characteristic is that reportable introspective knowledge that influences performance is mediated by conscious processes, whereas knowledge that cannot be reported via introspection but, nevertheless, influences performance, is subserved by unconscious processes (Kellogg, 1982).

Implicit motor learning

The investigation of implicit mechanisms in motor learning has taken two slightly divergent routes. Although sharing a common departure point, which sees implicit motor learning as the acquisition of a motor skill without concurrent acquisition of explicit knowledge about the skill, one route has as its agenda 'the acquisition of knowledge about environmental regulatory features that guide the selection and execution of movements involved in performing open motor skills' (Magill, 1998, p. 104), whereas the other has as its agenda the acquisition of knowledge about the movement itself (Masters, 1992; Maxwell, Masters and Eves, 2000). The aim in this chapter is to present the case for implicit learning of specific movements and relate this to interceptive actions. The interested reader is directed to the work of Magill (1998) for a review of implicit learning of regulatory features in the environment.

In an ongoing programme of work Masters and his colleagues have now been investigating methods of implicit motor learning since the early nineties. Gradually, a bank of empirical data regarding the phenomenon of implicit motor learning has developed which demonstrates that complex motor skills can be acquired without a concomitant increase in verbalisable knowledge about the mechanics of the skill.

Early work

During skill acquisition the process of acquiring verbal rules concerning a motor skill develops through conscious hypothesis testing (Allen and Reber, 1980, Hayes and Broadbent, 1988). This process concerns the production of verbal proposals, which are tested and if found to be correct (i.e. improve performance) then stored for future reference. Alternatively, the proposal is discarded if found to be incorrect (i.e. performance fails to improve).

In particular, the initial stages of learning are characterised by this conscious processing of task-relevant information. Typically, the learner adopts a problem-solving approach (Glencross, 1992), using available feedback to compare task outcome with intention and develop alternative strategies as required (Anderson, 1995; Salmoni, 1989).

In the early efforts to explore implicit motor learning dual task paradigms were used to prevent novice learners from testing hypotheses about the motor movements they were making. Masters (1992) showed that novices generating random letters (Baddeley, 1966) throughout a 400-trial period of golf putting (implicit learning) accumulated little or no explicit knowledge of their putting skill compared to both a discovery learning and an explicitly instructed condition. The Masters work also showed the performance of the implicit learners to remain robust under psychological stress, induced by a combination of evaluation apprehension and financial enticement. Robustness is a reported characteristic of implicit functions. Rathus, Reber, Manza and Kushner (1994), for example, found that high-anxious subjects took longer to explicitly learn artificial grammar sequences than low-anxious subjects, but, when their implicit knowledge of the sequences was tested using a well-formedness test they were equally effective at distinguishing correct from incorrect sequences.

Several weaknesses are apparent in the early Masters work. For example, Hardy, Mullen and Jones (1996) pointed out that participants in the implicit group may have shown robust performance because they were no longer required to carry out the secondary task during the stress phase. In examining this they replicated the original study but added a condition in which the implicit group continued with the random letter generation task during the stress phase. Robustness was maintained, providing support for the implicit motor learning argument. Bright and Freedman (1998) asked this question also. Using the same design they failed to find robustness under stress. Numerous problems exist, however, in the Bright and Freedman study. They claimed, for example, to replicate the earlier work, yet their learning phase consisted of 160 trials as opposed to the 400 used by both Masters and Hardy *et al*. Additionally, their putting task was easier in that the target was 200 cm away on a flat surface. In the earlier studies the target was 150 cm away, but on a 1:4 incline. Finally, Bright and Freedman claimed to use naive golfers in the study, but the criterion they used was that each participant had not played a round of golf within the last 12 months. It is very likely that participants were included in the study who had previous experience of the game, but had not played for 12 months. Some support for this seems evident from the amount of explicit knowledge reported by participants in the implicit conditions. Almost four rules were reported by these participants, despite the small number of learning trials (160). In stark contrast, Maxwell, Masters and Eves (2000) found that implicit learners reported an average of 1.5 rules after as many as 3,000 trials. In addition, verbal protocols generally provide a difficult medium through which to assess the amount of information accumulated by an implicit learner. The distinction between rules a learner actually becomes of aware of during learning and those generated retrospectively can be blurred, so, typically, at least two independent raters are asked to assess verbal protocols blindly (Hardy, Mullen and Jones, 1996; MacMahon and Masters, in press; Masters, 1992; Maxwell, Masters and Eves, 2000). The Bright and Freedman work fails to assess the verbal protocols in this way, so it is difficult to be confident in their findings.

In a second study Bright and Freedman attempted to substantiate their findings by proposing that the difficulty of the secondary task used to bring about implicit learning will mediate the degree to which performance improves under stress when the secondary task is removed. They argued that release from an undemanding task would yield smaller performance increases than release from a demanding task. Indeed, they claimed to find less improvement following release from an easy task (random letter generation every three seconds) compared to a difficult task (random letter generation every second). Disappointingly, the study they describe again exhibits flaws which make it difficult to be confident in the findings. The same doubt lingers about the naivety of the participants to the putting task. Further, no data is presented to support a differential effect of easy versus difficult secondary task on acquisition of rules during learning. This rather undermines any claims regarding implicit learning of the putting skill. In addition, the assumptions Bright and Freedman make regarding the difficulty of the two tasks are less than rigorous; the sum total of evidence being 'a couple of volunteers who tried both dual tasks reported that the tasks differed in the demands placed upon the individuals' (p. 259). The credibility of this evidence is further undermined by the fact that the difficult secondary task condition resulted in a higher level of performance than the easy task throughout most of the acquisition trials.

While the contrast in findings between the Hardy, Mullen and Jones work and that of Bright and Freedman serves to highlight uncertainties about the interpretation of dual-task effects in implicit motor learning, an added problem is that performance of the motor task tends to be held down during such learning. Inconsistencies exist in the cognitive implicit learning literature regarding this. Hayes and Broadbent (1988), for example, found no negative effects of random letter generation on a human–computer interaction task, whereas, Dienes, Broadbent and Berry (1991) did. Even if we accept that an interceptive action can be learned implicitly by concurrent performance of a secondary task it is not an ideal way to learn. Not only can concurrent performance of the two tasks be tiring and dull for the learner, but, the continual impairment to performance can undermine levels of perceived competence (Weiss and Chaumeton, 1992).

In the Masters (1992) work there was a hint that after 400 trials the putting skill of the implicit learning group was catching up to that of the explicit learning group. On the grounds that passive aggregation of task-relevant information is a tedious business in implicit learning (Berry and Broadbent, 1984, 1988; Gentile, 1998) Maxwell, Masters and Eves (2000) investigated whether performance may catch up over as many as 3,000 trials. In the implicit motor learning task (again golf putting) participants carried out a tone-counting task, which required them to monitor and report the number of high and low pitched tones presented during each block of 50 trials. Throughout the 3,000 trials this tone-counting group performed at a lower level than an explicit (discovery) learning group.

The demise of the secondary task

In an attempt to cause implicit learning, but avoid the negative impact on performance, MacMahon and Masters (in press) turned to the concept of working memory (Baddeley and Hitch, 1974) believing that the problem lay with the type of secondary tasks employed in the previous implicit motor learning studies. Logie (1999) describes working memory as the 'desktop of the brain' (p. 174). That is, it provides an interactive workspace that allows us to keep track of where we are, and what we are doing and provides the capacity to hold information long enough to make a decision, write down a telephone number or test a hypothesis. Working memory is comprised of a collection of distinct systems involved in cognitive functioning. The main tool is the central executive, which processes, stores and regulates the flow of information in the working memory system, retrieves information from alternative memory systems (e.g. long-term memory) and co-ordinates its slave systems – the visuo–spatial sketchpad and the phonological loop (Baddeley, 1992). The former is linked to short-term storage and manipulation of material of a visual or spatial nature, whereas, the latter provides temporary storage and manipulation of verbal material, while the central executive is occupied with alternative processing (Logie, 1999). The process of conscious hypothesis testing utilises the resources of working memory because it requires the generation and testing of verbal propositions and the organisation and eventual storage of the resulting information in a verbalisable form. It is likely that the phonological loop allows maintenance of task-related information which can be processed, via the central executive, into explicit rules and knowledge of the motor skill. This forms the basis of 'Flint's conjecture' (Broadbent, 1984; Flint, 1979) which proposed that working memory is involved in the development of verbalisable associations and cognitive structure.

MacMahon and Masters (in press) argued that the random letter generation task employed by both Masters (1992) and Hardy, Mullen and Jones (1996) is a central executive task, in that, it is the job of the central executive to monitor and maintain the randomness of each letter which is generated (Logie, Gilhooly and Wynn, 1994). The requirement for such supervision disrupts hypothesis testing (minimising the likelihood that the learner will become aware of many aspects of their motor output), but exceeds the capacity of the central executive to carry out the motor task effectively. MacMahon and Masters hypothesised that for implicit motor learning to occur at a performance level comparable with that of explicit learning, a secondary task was required that would interfere with the build up of information from hypothesis testing without exceeding the capacity of the central executive to carry out the motor task.

They proposed that such a task might be one that dominates the articulatory control process, disrupting its storage and rehearsal properties, but does not require supervision from the central executive (Baddeley, Lewis and Vallar, 1984). Two such tasks are articulatory suppression, the repetitive articulation of an irrelevant word (e.g. 'the, the, the…'), and presentation of unattended speech, which has been shown to gain direct entry into the phonological store and cause the same kind of disruption (Salame and Baddeley, 1982, 1987, 1989).

In two studies MacMahon and Masters (in press) investigated the effect of these phonological loop tasks on 400 trials of the customary golf putting task, comparing the performance and the amount of explicit knowledge acquired by these learners with that of two central executive tasks (random letter generation and counting backwards in sevens). As predicted by MacMahon and Masters, the tasks which interfered with phonological loop functioning did not compromise performance on the putting task. Accumulation of explicit knowledge about the putting task was not restricted by the phonological tasks, however. MacMahon and Masters concluded that 'the practical use of concurrent secondary tasks in [implicit] motor learning is limited. Even if it is possible to balance the difficulty of the secondary task so that it does not prove significantly detrimental to performance (and this point is likely to differ for each individual) the problem of central executive secondary tasks losing their effectiveness over time still remains. Continued practice at a secondary task, such as random letter generation, is likely to result in greater automaticity and a consequent reduction in the effectiveness of the task in blocking the accumulation of explicit knowledge. Secondary tasks, such as articulatory suppression, do not suffer from this problem but, unfortunately, do not prevent the accumulation of explicit knowledge' (p. 21).

The comparative failure of dual-task paradigms of any type to bring about satisfactory implicit motor learning has resulted in a search for less intrusive ways of disrupting explicit hypothesis testing during motor learning. Two techniques have been developed. The first technique surmises that a learner will not test hypotheses if they make no errors – why change a movement pattern which always achieves the desired goal? The second technique surmises that a learner will be unable to test hypotheses if no information is available to show whether the hypothesis is correct or incorrect.

Errorless learning

Minimisation of errors, through guided learning, such as, visual cueing (e.g. Singer and Pease, 1976), ongoing knowledge of results (e.g. Schmidt and Wulf, 1997) and, of course, physical guidance (e.g. Hagman, 1983; Wulf, Shea and Whitacre, 1998) has been considered in numerous studies. Historically, guided learning, although effective during the learning phase, shows little transfer when the guidance system is removed. One explanation of this is that such techniques are disadvantaged because they prevent information processing activities critical for learning (Wulf, Shea and Whitacre, 1998). Wulf, Shea and Whitacre showed some benefit of guided learning (via the use of ski poles) on a ski simulator task requiring slalom movements when the poles were removed, and speculated that rather than reducing processing activity the poles 'may have allowed the performer to explore earlier and more fully what Newell (1991) called the *perceptual–motor work-space*...[providing] the performer an opportunity for richer processing because of the increased freedom of movement afforded by the poles' (p. 378).

This conclusion contrasts with the observation of Prather (1971) that errorless learners tend to acquire skills in a passive manner, reminiscent of implicit processes. In fact, Baddeley and Wilson (1994) suggested that explicit processes can detect and eliminate errors during learning, whereas implicit processes are unable to eliminate errors because they encode frequency information, regardless of whether it is correct or incorrect. Baddeley (1992) and Baddeley and Wilson (1994) argued that this may explain poorer performance in implicit learners, as they are unable to avoid repetition of errors. This, of course, provides an alternative explanation of the poorer performance seen in the previous implicit motor learning work (Hardy, Mullen and Jones, 1996; Masters, 1992; Maxwell, Masters and Eves, 2000).

Maxwell, Masters, Kerr and Weedon (2001) considered it plausible that the presence of errors in performance will result in explicit motor learning due to efforts by the learner to actively test hypotheses which will eliminate the errors, but, the absence of errors will result in implicit motor learning due to it being unnecessary for the learner to test hypotheses.

The studies carried out by Maxwell, Masters, Kerr and Weedon introduced a new test of implicitness to the implicit motor learning literature. Ironically, the new test uses secondary task loading as a way of distinguishing between implicit versus explicit processes. Its use is based on the fact that explicit processes require mediation by abstract working memory, whereas implicit processes do not. This distinction has been shown in a variety of recent studies (Cohen, Ivry and Keele, 1990; Frensch, Wenke and Rünger, 1999; Hayes and Broadbent, 1988; Jiminéz and Méndez, 1999; Mulligan 1997; Wolters and Prinsen, 1997). Performance of a concurrent secondary task requires input from abstract working memory, which, in explicitly learned tasks, is also needed to manipulate the verbal knowledge underpinning performance of the task. Working memory capacity tends to be exceeded in these situations, with a consequent disruption to performance. In implicitly learned tasks, however, working memory capacity is not exceeded because verbal knowledge does not underpin task performance. The tasks can therefore be carried out concurrently without disruption.

In Study 1 Maxwell, Masters, Kerr and Weedon produced errorless, errorful or random (control) conditions by varying the distance from which learners practised their golf-putting skill. In the errorless condition they initially began 25 cm from the hole and gradually moved away in increments of 25 cm (up to 200 cm). This resulted in relatively error free learning compared with an errorful condition which carried out the same number of trials from the same distances but in the reverse order, beginning at 200 cm and ending at 25 cm from the hole. A control condition also performed the same number of trials from the same distances, but in a pseudo-random order, producing similar overall results to the errorful condition. Following learning the imposition of a secondary task load (tone counting) was found to have no detrimental effect on performance in the errorless learning condition, but a significant reduction in performance was seen in the errorful conditions, commensurate with implicit and explicit processes respectively. Unfortunately, no differences were found in the level of explicit, task-related knowledge accumulated. If errorless conditions do result in implicit learning participants should develop fewer verbalisable rules than in errorful conditions.

A closer look at the learning phase data in this first study indicated that the errorless learning condition was not technically errorless. Few, if any, errors were made from 25, 50 and 75 cm, but, as the distances became greater (100, 125, 150, 175 and 200 cm) errors increased. Maxwell, Masters, Kerr and Weedon hypothesised that in order to eliminate these errors performers began to actively test hypotheses about their actions. Consequently, the explicit knowledge base increased in line with errorful conditions.

A second study was designed to test this hypothesis, utilising a similar experimental design, but reducing the overall frequency of errors committed in the errorless condition by using only the three shortest distances (25, 50 and 75 cm). A matching errorful condition performed from the three greatest distances (175, 150 and 125 cm). Again, following learning the imposition of a secondary task load (tone counting) was found to cause no disruption in the errorless condition, but significant disruption in the errorful condition. In contrast to Study 1, however, verbal protocols differentiated errorless from errorful learning on the basis of a strict 'hypothesis testing' criterion, with errorless learners articulating significantly fewer hypotheses (e.g. I changed my grip when the ball went to the left). Additionally, video analysis was used to observe the number of visible modifications to technique during learning. The errorless learners were seen to make significantly fewer modifications, suggesting a more passive, less active hypothesis testing approach to the task.

No-feedback learning

The second technique developed as an alternative to secondary task learning again relies on restriction of hypothesis testing. No-feedback learning uses the simple expedient of, rather than removing the motivation to test hypotheses, removing information with which to test hypotheses.

In a series of studies Maxwell, Masters and Eves (1999) have attempted to induce implicit motor learning by manipulating the sensory feedback available to the performer. By suppressing the availability of visual and auditory feedback regarding the outcome of each putt Maxwell, Masters and Eves argued that learners would be unable to appraise the outcome of their actions and so unable to test hypotheses about the best way to perform. Subjects wore liquid crystal glasses, which permitted vision before striking the ball, but which then prevented visual feedback of the outcome. Curtains, which occluded the room and the putting surface, provided little or no encouragement to the subject to align or target their movements. Moreover, cushioning of the area behind the curtain removed any auditory feedback. In the first study learners completed 750 trials in this environment and then transferred to a normal, full feedback environment where they completed two 50-trial retention tests interspersed with a 50-trial transfer test (secondary task loading, as used in the errorless learning studies discussed previously). Implicit motor learning was not found. Not only was robustness of performance under secondary task loading not found, but collection of verbal protocols following the learning phase indicated that, in the absence of visual and auditory feedback, proprioceptive (and to a lesser extent tactile) feedback was used as a basis for hypothesis testing. Paradoxically, the absence of visual and auditory forms of information to process left learners in a position to pay attention to this, perhaps less salient, form of information.

In a second study, no-feedback learners were therefore asked to carry out a visual search task after striking the ball. The task consisted of locating the position of a specific item presented in one of five random positions on a monitor (top, bottom, left, right or middle). It was hypothesised that attention to the proprioceptive (and tactile) information available during the movement would be minimised by giving participants in the no-feedback condition a similar visual search task to that which they would normally perform (i.e. searching for, and processing, visual and auditory feedback regarding the whereabouts of the ball in relation to the target (top, bottom, left, right or middle)). On this occasion verbal protocols indicated that the no feedback learners, relative to the full-feedback back learners, accumulated significantly fewer rules. Moreover, the no-feedback learners also exhibited robustness of performance under secondary task loading. On the face of it this alteration to the paradigm appeared to bring about implicit motor learning. One problem with this conclusion, however, was that learning was inferred from the change in performance seen in the retention tests following the 750 no-feedback trials. This change (or accelerated attunement) may, however, have resulted from increases in motivation once participants found themselves in the normal full-feedback environment of the retention tests. Taking part in 750 trials in which one aimlessly putts a golf ball under a curtain is surprisingly tedious. As a check on learning, kinematic analysis was carried out in a third study, which showed that over 750 trials the no-feedback and full-feedback conditions resulted in almost identical decreases in root mean square (RMS) jerk and increases in smoothness in the putting stroke (the interceptive action in this case). The kinematic data also reinforced the findings of the second study regarding robustness in the no-feedback condition under secondary task loading. Both RMS jerk and smoothness in the no-feedback condition were unaffected by the imposition of the secondary task, whereas, in the full-feedback condition significant deficits in both smoothness and RMS jerk were seen.

On the basis of these findings Maxwell, Masters and Eves concluded that the removal of outcome feedback resulted in the acquisition of task-relevant information in an implicit manner, demonstrated by limited verbalisable knowledge and robust performance under secondary task loading.

Discussion

The search for ecologically valid methods of implicit motor learning continues. Techniques, for example, which require a youngster to carry out a secondary task during training, not only suffer from the theoretical flaws previously described, but they also lack practicality. 'Street cred' is not easy for a youngster to maintain (despite the advent of designer sportswear) if they are running around a tennis court shouting random letters in time with a metronome. Moreover, swimmers may find themselves in 'deep water' if asked to carry out such a task while doing the 100 m freestyle. In the same breath, manipulation of outcome feedback is hardly a practical approach to the problem. Prevention of feedback is not easily achieved in the sporting environment.

Having said that, the NEC World Championship golf tournament, held in Akron, Ohio in 2000 saw Tiger Woods play his best shot of the tournament on the final hole in darkness. After he tapped it in for a 'birdie' he admitted that as a child he used to practice at night with his father on a US Navy course in Southern California. One might argue that this is taking no-feedback learning a bit far, but, on the other hand, his winning margin was 11 shots.

Errorless learning techniques may be more applicable. For example, one or two British Football Association coaches who are familiar with this technique currently coach youngsters their passing techniques with great success by starting the passing off from very close quarters so that mistakes are impossible. For sure, these coaches now have budding David Beckhams and Ronald Koemans flighting perfectly weighted passes 70 yards across the pitch when under the greatest of pressure. Even errorless techniques have their drawbacks though. Not only are they likely to prove demotivating due to their repetitive nature, but, inevitably, they will become obsolete as the performer attains a skill level which allows him or her to enter competition. Stephen Hendry is unlikely to be allowed to put the black over the corner pocket during a match, in order to keep his errors down. Additionally, performers are likely to become more and more active in their hypothesis testing as the pressure to win drives them in search of improvements in their performance.

The chances of maintaining implicit motor learning over the many years that it takes to become an expert seem remote, so it is of particular importance in the errorless learning studies of Maxwell, Masters, Kerr and Weedon (2001) that robustness under secondary task loading was evident even after verbal knowledge had begun to accumulate (Study 1). That is, although learners began to accumulate a pool of explicit knowledge (via hypothesis testing) once their performance became errorful (e.g. more than 75 cm from the hole) their putting was seen to retain implicit characteristics in the post-learning retention tests (e.g. robustness under secondary task loading). This hints at a durability of implicit motor learning, which is, in fact, another characteristic of implicit functions. Allen and Reber (1980), for example, found that the accuracy at distinguishing between grammatically correct and incorrect sequences generated by an artificial grammar remained high two years after having implicitly learned the grammar, even though the learners had considerable difficulty in explaining (explicitly) their classification decisions. This phenomenon, of course, can be seen in motor learning. A person may not drive a car for many years, and even begin to doubt that they still can, yet, upon sliding behind the wheel, handbrake turns and reverse parking immediately are possible.

Analogy learning is a recent candidate for implicit motor learning. Work by Liao and Masters (2001) has shown that using an analogy to teach beginners a topspin forehand shot in table tennis results in characteristics of implicit motor learning, including robustness to both stress and secondary task loading. Liao and Masters argue that the function of the analogy is to integrate the complex rule structure of the to-be-learned skill in a simple biomechanical metaphor which can be reproduced by the learner without reference to, or manipulation of, large amounts of explicit knowledge.

Another possibility is the use of goal setting principles to encourage a passive, less explicit hypothesis testing approach to motor learning. Huber (1985) argues that specific, difficult goals can provoke anxiety in the performer, because they require action and are not necessarily achievable. In such circumstances it is likely that such goals will motivate performers to actively test hypotheses and ideas about their performance in order to match up to the demands of the task. For the learner, in particular, most goals are challenging and difficult, and it may be that goals for the learner need to be carefully constructed so that they are achieved without default to explicit hypothesis testing modes of performance. This suggestion flies in the face of the commonly held, empirically supported, belief that specific, challenging goals provide a more effective learning tool than vague, easy goals (Locke, Shaw, Saari and Latham, 1981). It should be noted though, that much of the literature on which this belief is based emanates from examination of industrial settings where attention to motivational effects on performance overrides attention to motor skill learning *per se*. If we accept that specific, challenging goals hold a greater motivational charge than vague, easy goals, a compromise may be needed in early learning where the motivational charge is maintained by setting highly specific goals, but explicit hypothesis testing is minimised by making them very easily achieved.

While it is clear that, given time, most of us develop interceptive actions which are highly efficient, the way in which we acquire these actions plays a major role in our ability to maintain efficiency under conditions of high motivation. In sports where the interceptive actions called for are exceedingly complex, requiring the co-ordination of many degrees of freedom, athletes, almost without exception, default to an explicit mode of learning and action, feeling that this gives them more control over their movement repertoires (Masters and Polman, 1996). It is clear that explicit modes of action carry with them the ingredients for skill failure, and a strong case exists for arguing that the robustness and durability of implicitly acquired movement repertoires is a distinct advantage in many sporting environments. It is likely that over the next decade a raft of empirical evidence will emerge to keep afloat the case for implicit motor learning.

References

Allen, R. and Reber, A.S. (1980). Very long term memory for tacit knowledge. *Cognition* **8**, 175–85.

Anderson, J.R. (1983). *The Architecture of Cognition*. Cambridge, MA: Harvard University Press.

Anderson, J.R. (1995). *Learning and Memory: An Integrated Approach*. New York: Wiley.

Baddeley, A.D. (1966). The capacity for generating information by randomisation. *Quarterly Journal of Experimental Psycholog*, **18**, 119–29.

Baddeley, A.D. (1992). Implicit memory and errorless learning: a link between cognitive theory and neuropsychological rehabilitation? In L.R. Squire and N. Butters (eds), *Neuropsychology of Memory*. New York: Guilford Press.

Baddeley, A.D. and Hitch, G. (1974). Working memory. In G.A. Bower (ed.), *Recent Advances in Learning and Motivation*, Vol. 8. New York: Academic Press.

Baddeley, A. and Wilson, B.A. (1994). When implicit learning fails: amnesia and the problem of error elimination. *Neuropsychologia* **32**(1), 53–68.

Baddeley, A.D., Lewis, V.J. and Vallar, G. (1984). Exploring the articulatory loop. *Quarterly Journal of Experimental Psychology* **36**, 233–52.

Baumeister, R.F. (1984). Choking under pressure: self-consciousness and paradoxical effects of incentives on skilful performance. *Journal of Personality and Social Psychology* **46**, 610–20.

Berry, D.C. and Broadbent, D.E. (1984). On the relationship between task performance and associated verbalizable knowledge. *Quarterly Journal of Experimental Psychology* **36A**, 209–31.

Berry, D.C. and Broadbent, D.E. (1988). Interactive tasks and the implicit explicit distinction. *British Journal of Psychology* **79**, 251–72.

Berry, D.C. and Dienes, Z. (1993). *Implicit Learning: Theoretical and Empirical Issues.* Hove: Lawrence Erlbaum Associates, Inc.

Biddulph, M.W. (1980). *The Golf Shot.* London: Heineman.

Bright, J.E.H. and Freedman, O. (1998). Differences between implicit and explicit acquisition of a complex motor skill under pressure: an examination of some evidence. *British Journal of Psychology* **89**, 249–63.

Broadbent, D.E. (1984). Mental models: a critical notice. *Quarterly Journal of Experimental Psychology* **36**, 673–81.

Broadbent, D.E., Cooper, P.F., Fitzgerald, P. and Parkes, K.R. (1982). The Cognitive Failures Questionnaire (CFQ) and its correlates. *British Journal of Clinical Psychology* **21**, 1–16.

Carver, C.S. and Scheier, M.F. (1978). Self-focusing effects of dispositional self-consciousness, mirror presence, and audience presence. *Journal of Personality and Social Psychology* **36**, 324–32.

Cohen, A., Ivry, R. and Keele, S. (1990). Attention and structure in sequence learning. *Journal of Experimental Psychology: Learning, Memory and Cognition* **16**, 17–30.

Crews. D.J. (1994). Research based golf: from the laboratory to the course. In A.J. Cochran, A.J. and M.R. Farrally (eds), *Science and Golf II.* London: Spon.

Deikman, A.J. (1969). Deautomatization and the mystic experience. In C.T. Tart (ed.), *Altered States of Consciousness.* New York: Wiley.

Dienes, Z., Broadbent, D. and Berry, D. (1991). Implicit and explicit knowledge bases in artificial grammar learning. *Journal of Experimental Psychology: Learning, Memory and Cognition* **17**, 875–87.

Ericsson, K.A., Krampe, R.T. and Tesch-Römer, C. (1993). The role of deliberate practice in the acquisition of expert performance. *Psychological Review* **100**, 363–406.

Faldo, N. (1986). Putting: you must rock and roll on the greens. In M. Wilson (ed.), *The PGA European Tour Guide to Better Golf.* London: Pan Books.

Fenigstein, A., Scheier, M.F. and Buss, A.H. (1975). Public and private self-consciousness: assessment and theory. *Journal of Consulting and Clinical Psychology* **43**, 522–7.

Fitts, P.M. and Posner, M.I. (1967). *Human Performance.* Belmont, CA: Brooks/Cole.

Flint, C.R. (1979). The role of consciousness in memory. Unpublished D.Phil thesis, University of Oxford.

Frensch, P.A., Wenke, D. and Rünger, D. (1999). A secondary tone-counting task suppresses expression of knowledge in the serial reaction task. *Journal of Experimental Psychology: Learning, Memory and Cognition* **25**, 260–74.

Gentile, A.M. (1998). Implicit and explicit processes during acquisition of functional skills. *Scandinavian Journal of Occupational Therapy* **5**, 7–16.

Glencross, D.J. (1992). Human skill and motor learning: a critical review. *Sport Science Review* **1**, 65–78.

Green, T.D. and Flowers, J.H. (1991). Implicit versus explicit learning processes in a probabilistic, continuous fine-motor catching task. *Journal of Motor Behavior* **23**, 293–300.

Hagman, J.D. (1983). Presentation- and test-trial effects on acquisition and retention of distance and location. *Journal of Experimental Psychology: Learning, Memory and Cognition* **9**, 334–45.

Hardy, L. and Nelson, D. (1988). Self control training in sport and work. *Ergonomics* **31**, 1573–85.

Hardy, L., Mullen, R. and Jones, G. (1996). Knowledge and conscious control of motor actions under stress. *British Journal of Psychology* **87**, 621–36.

Hayes, N.A. and Broadbent, D.E. (1988). Two modes of learning for interactive tasks. *Cognition* **28**, 249–76.

Hodges, N.J. and Lee, T.D. (1999). The role of augmented information prior to learning a bimanual visual-motor co-ordination task: do instructions of the movement pattern facilitate learning relative to discovery learning? *British Journal of Psychology* **90**, 389–403.

Huber, V.L. (1985). Effects of task difficulty, goal setting, and strategy on performance of a heuristic task. *Journal of Applied Psychology* **64**, 434–45.

Jiminéz, L. and Méndez, C. (1999). Which attention is needed for implicit sequence learning? *Journal of Experimental Psychology: Learning, Memory and Cognition* **25**, 236–59.

Kellogg, R.T. (1982). When can we introspect accurately about mental processes? *Memory and Cognition* **10**, 141–4.

Kingston, K. and Hardy, L. (1994). When some goals are more beneficial than others? *Journal of Sport Sciences* **10**, 610–11.

Lees, A.J. (1998). Abnormal movement disorders. In B.D. Jordan (ed.), *Sports Neurology* (2nd edn). Philadelphia: Lippincott-Raven.

Liao, C. and Masters, R.S.W. (2001). Analogy learning:a means to implicit motor learning. *Journal of Sports Sciences* **19** 307–19.

Locke, E.A., Shaw, K.N., Saari, L.M. and Latham, G.P. (1981). Goal setting and task performance: 1969–1980. *Psychological Bulletin* **90**, 125–52.

Logie, R.H. (1999). Working Memory. *The Psychologist* **12**, 4, 174–8.

Logie, R.H., Gilhooly, K.J. and Wynn, V. (1994). Counting on working memory in artithmetic problem solving. *Memory and Cognition* **22**(4), 395–410.

MacMahon, K.M.A and Masters, R.S.W. (in press). The effects of secondary tasks on implicit motor skill performance. *International Journal of Sport Psychology.*

Magill, R.A. (1998). Knowledge is more than we can talk about: implicit learning in motor skill acquisition. *Research Quarterly for Exercise and Sport* **69**, 104–10.

Masters, R.S.W. (1992). Knowledge, knerves and know-how: the role of explicit versus implicit knowledge in the breakdown of a complex motor skill under pressure. *British Journal of Psychology* **83**, 343–58.

Masters, R.S.W and Polman, R.C.J (1996). What are 'normal movements' in *any* population? *Behavioral and Brain Sciences* **19**, 81–2.

Masters, R.S.W., Polman, R.C.J. and Hammond, N.V. (1993). 'Reinvestment': a dimension of personality implicated in skill breakdown under pressure. *Personality and Individual Differences* **14**, 655–66.

Maxwell, J.P., Masters, R.S.W. and Eves, F. (1999). Explicit versus implicit motor learning: dissociating selective and unselective modes of skill acquisition via feedback manipulation *Journal of Sports Sciences* **6**, 559.

Maxwell, J.P., Masters, R.S.W. and Eves, F. (2000). From novice to no know-how: a longitudinal study of implicit motor learning. *Journal of Sport Sciences* **18**, 1–10.

Maxwell, J.P., Masters, R., Kerr, E. and Weedon, E. (2001). The implicit benefit of learning without errors. *Quarterly Journal of Experimental Psychology* **54A**, 1049–68.

Mulligan, N.W. (1997). Attention and implicit memory tests: the affects of varying attentional load on conceptual priming. *Memory and Cognition* **25**, 11–17.

Newell, K. (1991). Motor skill acquisition. *Annual Review of Psychology* **42**, 213–37.

Norman, D.A. and Shallice, T. (1986). Attention to action: willed and automatic control of behaviour. In R.J. Davidson, G.E. Schwarts and D. Shapiro (eds), *Consciousness and Self-regulation*. Advances in Research and Theory, Vol 4. New York: Plenum Press.

Orlick, T. and Partington, J. (1988). Mental links to excellence. *The Sport Psychologist* **2**, 105–30.

Prather, D.C. (1971). Trial-and-error versus errorless learning: training, transfer and stress. *American Journal of Psychology* **84**, 377–86.

Rathus, J.H., Reber, A.S., Manza, L. and Kushner, M. (1994). Implicit and explicit learning: differential effects of affective states. *Perceptual and Motor Skills* **79**, 163–84.

Reber, A.S. (1993). *Implicit Learning and Tacit Knowledge: An Essay on the Cognitive Unconscious*. New York: Clarendon Press.

Reber, A.S., Kassin, S.M., Lewis, S. and Cantor, G. (1980). On the relationship between implicit and explicit modes of learning a complex rule structure. *Journal of Experimental Psychology: Human Learning and Memory* **5**, 492–502.

Roger, D. and Nesshoever, W. (1987). The construction and preliminary validation of a scale for measuring emotional control. *Personality and Individual Differences* **8**, 527–34.

Salame, P. and Baddeley, A.D. (1982). Disruption of short term memory by unattended speech. *Journal of Verbal Learning and Verbal Behaviour* **21**, 150–64.

Salame, P. and Baddeley, A.D. (1987). Noise, unattended speech and short-term memory. *Ergonomics* **30**, 1185–93.

Salame, P. and Baddeley, A.D. (1989). Effects of background noise on phonological short-term memory. *Quarterly Journal of Experimental Psychology* **41A**, 107–22.

Salmoni, A.W. (1989). Motor skill learning. In D.H. Holding (ed.), *Human Skills*. London: John Wiley and Sons Ltd.

Schmidt, R.A. and Wulf, G. (1997). Continuous concurrent feedback degrades skill learning: implications for training and simulation. *Human Factors* **39**, 509–25.

Singer, R.N., Lidor, R. and Cauraugh, J.H. (1993). To be aware or not aware? What to think about while learning and performing a motor skill. *The Sport Psychologist* **7**, 19–30.

Singer, R.N. and Pease, D. (1976). A comparison of discovery learning and guided instructional strategies on motor skill learning, retention and transfer. *Research Quarterly* **47**, 788–96

Seger, C.A. (1994). Implicit learning. *Psychological Bulletin* **115**, 163–96.

Van Loon, E.M., Masters, R.S.W., Ring, C. and McIntyre, D.B. (2001). Changes in limb stiffness under conditions of mental stress. *Journal of Motor Behavior* **33** 153–64.

Wegner, D.M. and Giuliano, T. (1980). Arousal-induced attention to self. *Journal of Personality and Social Psychology* **38**, 719–26.

Weinberg, R.S. and Hunt, V. (1976). The interrelationships between anxiety, motor performance, and electromyography. *Journal of Motor Behavior* **8**, 219–24.

Weiss, M.R. and Chaumeton, N. (1992). Motivational orientations in sport. In T.S. Horn (ed.), *Advances in Sport Psychology*. Champaign, IL: Human Kinetics.

Wolters, G. and Prinsen, A. (1997). Full versus divided attention and implicit memory performance. *Memory and Cognition* **25**, 764–71.

Wulf, G. and Weigelt, C. (1997). Instructions about physical principles in learning a complex motor skill: to tell or not to tell… *Research Quarterly for Exercise and Sport* **68**, 362–7.

Wulf, G., Höß, M. and Prinz, W. (1998). Instructions for motor learning: differential effects of internal versus external focus of attention. *Journal of Motor Behavior* **30**, 169–79.

Wulf, G., Lauterbach, B. and Toole, T. (1999). Learning advantages of an external focus of attention in golf. *Research Quarterly for Exercise and Sport* **70**, 120–6.

Wulf, G., Shea, C.H. and Whitacre, C.A. (1998). Physical-guidance benefits in a complex motor skill. *Journal of Motor Behavior* **30**, 367–80.

Wulf, G., McNevin, N.H., Fuchs, T., Ritter, F. and Toole, T. (2000). Attentional focus in complex motor skill learning. *Research Quarterly for Exercise and Sport* **71**, 229–39.

7 Visual information for one-handed catching

Gilles Montagne and Michel Laurent

As far back as the late 1960s, John Whiting (e.g. Whiting, 1968) instigated and became the principal leader of a line of experimental research aimed at studying the effects of critical viewing time intervals on one-handed ball catching. These studies (e.g. Whiting, Gill and Stephenson, 1970; Whiting, Alderson and Sanderson, 1973) were solidly anchored in the information-processing framework, and information was assumed to be processed discretely within 'perceptual moments' (Shallice, 1964), which had to be identified and quantified. Initial work led to a second research trend in which a special device was used to precisely control the portions of trajectory where the ball was visible (Whiting and Sharp, 1974, Sharp and Whiting, 1974, 1975; Sharp, 1975). The idea was to analyse performance in relation to (i) the joint effect of the visible and non-visible portions of ball flight trajectory (Whiting and Sharp, 1974), and (ii) the impact of critical time intervals and the so-called movement detector systems (i.e. image–retina and eye–head) (e.g. Sharp and Whiting, 1975). This work was essentially concerned with the amount of information required for successful catching performance, and the time required to process this information.

A change in emphasis

Publications on this issue started dwindling in the mid 1970s and remained scarce until Smyth and Marriott (1982) brought new impetus into the field by raising some interesting new questions. Their idea was to study ball-catching tasks by looking at the respective functions of proprioceptive and visual feedback from the effector segment, as well as the potential impact of the participant's level of expertise (e.g. Savelsbergh and Whiting, 1988; Davids and Stratford, 1989). Although the theoretical basis remained the same, Smyth and Marriott's (1982) work marked a turning point in the way the problem was approached. The goal now became to find out *what*, rather than *how much*, information was needed for successful performance (for a thorough review of this topic, see Savelsbergh, Whiting and Pijpers, 1992). This new outlook gave rise to many studies on ball-catching tasks aimed at determining what information is drawn from the environment (e.g. Rosengren, Pick and von Hofsten, 1988), what is obtained from the effector segment (e.g. Smyth and Marriott, 1982), and what comes from the moving object itself (e.g. Savelsbergh, Whiting and Bootsma, 1991). This chapter looks solely at the information available in the moving object's trajectory.

The ecological approach to perception and movement

When an object, like a ball, is moving towards a stationary observer, it produces a local optical flow at the observation point that is specific to the type of movement produced (Gibson, 1958). In other words, the local flow conveys optical information that describes the movements of the object with respect to the observation point. The optical information in question allows the observer to gain access to the state of the performer–environment system via the property (spatial, temporal or spatio–temporal) it specifies. In illustration, take the example of a non-deforming object moving straight towards the observation point. In the local flow, the contours of the moving object expand symmetrically. The optical information conveyed by the relative rate of expansion of these contours (i.e. *tau*) informs the participant about how much time is left until contact, via the first-order temporal relation (Lee, 1976). The existence of this 'higher-order' information in the optical flow suggests that there are some extremely sophisticated and parsimonious control mechanisms, or laws of control, that relay optical information to movement parameters (Warren, 1988).

State of the art

Most research conducted to date has focused on certain aspects of the theoretical framework presented above. Some studies have attempted to formally analyse the local optical flow generated by a moving object in order to determine what information is available (e.g. Lee, 1976; Bootsma and Peper, 1992; Laurent, Montagne and Durey, 1996). Others have tried to identify the relevant property in the performer–environment system (hereafter called the PES) that the performer uses to reach his/her goal (e.g. Lee, Young, Reddish, Lough and Clayton, 1983; Wann, 1996). Still others have been devoted to finding out what information is actually used by the performer, based on experimental protocols specifically designed to (i) limit the available information (e.g. Rosengren, Pick and von Hofsten, 1988; Lenoir, Mush and La Grange, 1999) or (ii) de-correlate[1] it (e.g. Judge and Bradford, 1988; Savelsbergh, Whiting and Bootsma, 1991; Bennett, Van der Kamp, Savelsbergh and Davids, 1999).

Although these studies offer a number of highly interesting findings on the perceptual mechanisms underlying interception actions, there are no conclusive results on the use of any one specific kind of optical information (e.g. Michaels and Beek, 1995; Wann, 1996; Tresilian, 1999). This state of affairs appears to be due to the fragmented nature of the experimental methods used by the large majority of the authors. In our opinion, it is quite unrealistic to attempt to determine what information is used in ball catching or any other interception task, without having a clear conception of (i) the links between optical information and the properties of the PES, and (ii) the mechanisms responsible for integrating that information in view of movement control (i.e. what law of control is implemented).

Understanding information–property relationships

There are a number of arguments available today, both theoretical (e.g. Cutting, 1986; Laurent, Montagne and Durey, 1996) and experimental (e.g. Heuer, 1993; Van der Kamp, Savelsbergh and Smeets, 1997), which suggest that access to the relevant PES property requires several types of optical information. Each piece of optical information points directly to one and only one property of the PES, but the particular conditions under which the task is being carried out determine what information will in fact get used by the performer (Tresilian, 1999). As outlined in Chapter 1, there is only one model proposed so far, Rushton and Wann's (1999) dipole model, which accounts for how one particular property (e.g. the first-order temporal relation between a performer and an approaching ball) is accessed by combining two distinct kinds of optical information: disparity and optical size. In the dipole model, optical information is automatically weighted according to the physical size of the moving object. This model can handle cases where one of these pieces of information is missing. It can also cope with situations where the two are conflicting, in which case priority is given to the one that specifies the earliest time-to-contact with the target.

The dipole model is obviously only valid for this particular property (the first-order temporal relation), and it only takes into account a limited amount of the available optical information. One of its merits, however, is that it proposes a testable conception of the relationship between optical information and PES properties. It seems to us that only models like this can benefit progression in research on interception actions. In a recent study (De Rugy, Montagne, Buekers and Laurent, 2001), we used a locomotor foot-pointing task (i.e. the participant was asked to walk and put their foot on a target) to test the dipole model. We hypothesised that participants used information about the first-order time remaining before they passed the target. As discussed in Chapter 1, several sources of information are thus available, including the relative rate of target expansion. We were able to show that de-correlating expansion information (i.e. manipulating target expansion while keeping the other information unchanged) had no effect on behaviour when the physical size of the target is reduced during the approach.

Lacking a theoretical understanding of the relationships between the different types of optical information and the properties of the PES, one might conclude from this finding that expansion information does not enter into goal-oriented locomotor movement control. Rushton and Wann's (1999) model allows us to go beyond this first level of analysis: the fact that behaviour is not affected when the physical size is reduced can be ascribed to the priority granted by the performer to another information source that predicts the shortest time-to-contact with the target (i.e. see De Rugy, Montagne, Buekers and Laurent, 2000, for details on this information). The results obtained in the second part of our study (De Rugy et al., 2001) support this idea. If, on the other hand, the de-correlation is produced by increasing the physical size of the target during the approach, the expansion information is taken into account, while the other information becomes less important.

Understanding information–movement relationships

Despite the numerous types of optical information identified so far, very few laws of control that formalise the mechanisms responsible for integrating that information in view of movement control have been proposed (e.g. Bootsma, Fayt, Zaal and Laurent, 1997; Bootsma, Montagne and Laurent, 1998; Montagne, Laurent and Durey, 1998). It seems well-established (e.g. Bootsma, Fayt, Zaal and Laurent, 1997) nonetheless that without some kind of conception of the links between optical information and movement, any behavioural prediction is risky, even if the information tested does in fact correspond to the information used by the participants.

In order to discuss this issue further, we can refer to the chapters by Benguigui, Ripoll and Broderick, and by Michaels and Zaal on perception of information from accelerating projectiles. In those chapters it is outlined how various studies on movement control in catching fly balls have shown, for example, that the only thing a performer has to do to catch a ball is make the vertical optical acceleration null (e.g. McLeod and Dienes, 1993) or make the ball's optical displacement linear (e.g. McBeath, Schaffer and Kaiser, 1995). An interesting question raised by these chapters is whether the mere cancellation of the ball's optical acceleration or the linearisation of its optical displacement actually proves that these strategies are, in fact, used by performers. We argue that without a theoretical understanding of the mechanisms that integrate this optical information, it is virtually impossible to answer this question. When a performer initiates a movement, the optical acceleration is not null and the optical displacement is not linear. One can nevertheless assume that the same control mechanism takes effect before the movement is initiated, during its initiation, and throughout its occurrence. This control mechanism could start by bringing the performer towards the required value (i.e. zero acceleration or a linear optical displacement) and then later contribute to stabilising it. Moreover, the rapidity of access to the required value may depend on task-related constraints (e.g. available time, type of ball contact required, etc.). Clearly a mere formalisation of the information is not very useful unless it is integrated into a law of control.

An important attempt to formalise the relationship between perception and movement in ball-catching tasks has been made by Bootsma and Peper (Peper, Bootsma, Mestre and Bakker, 1994; Bootsma, Fayt, Zaal and Laurent, 1997; Bootsma, 1998) (but see also Schöner, 1994). According to their required velocity model, a performer engaged in a ball-catching task only has to control the hand's acceleration based on an optically-specified velocity differential (Equation 7.1). Current velocity is the hand's movement velocity at a given instant t. Required velocity is the current theoretical velocity needed to catch the ball. The required velocity can be expressed as the ratio of the current lateral distance (distance between the hand and the ball's projection onto the hand–movement axis; see Figure 7.1) to the first-order temporal relation between the ball and the hand–movement axis (Equation 7.2). Note that the velocity differential (right side of Equation 7.1) includes the relevant PES properties, but it has an optical equivalent,

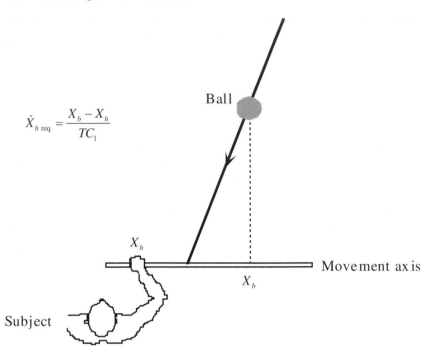

$$\dot{X}_{h\,req} = \frac{X_b - X_h}{TC_1}$$

Ball

X_h

X_b

Movement axis

Subject

Figure 7.1 Diagram showing the current lateral distance. The current lateral distance is the distance between the hand's current position and the current projection of the ball onto the hand–movement axis. In the trial shown here, the hand is placed to the left of the interception point and the ball is approaching along an inward trajectory.

i.e. monocular *and* binocular information capable of specifying it (Laurent, Montagne and Durey, 1996).

$$\ddot{X}_h = \alpha \dot{X}_{h\,req} - \beta \dot{X}_h \qquad (7.1)$$

$$\text{with} \quad \dot{X}_{h\,req} = \frac{X_b - X_h}{TC_1} \qquad (7.2)$$

where $\ddot{X}_h, \dot{X}_{h\,req}$ and $\dot{X}_h$ and are the hand's current acceleration, current required velocity, and current velocity, respectively, and α and β are constants, and where X_h, X_b and TC_1 are the hand's current position, the projection of the ball's current position on the hand-movement axis, and the first-order time-to-contact between the ball and the hand-movement axis, respectively.

According to this model, the performer engaged in a ball-catching task positions his/her hand in the right place at the right time simply by modulating its acceleration on the basis of optical information. Access to the spatiotemporal properties of the interception point with the moving object is never necessary. In the two studies presented below, we describe how the required velocity model was tested experimentally by manipulating two PES properties: the current lateral distance between the hand and the ball, and the first-order temporal relation.

Experimental data

Manipulating the current lateral distance (Montagne, Laurent, Durey and Bootsma, 1999)

The required velocity model predicts that for a given ball approach duration, different current lateral distances will influence hand acceleration and consequently will give rise to movements with different kinematic properties. The hand is thought to move in 'an object-related frame of reference' (Zaal, Bootsma and van Wieringen, 1999), as if there was a spring connecting the hand to the ball that attracted the hand towards the ball with a force that varied with the distance to travel. In an earlier experiment (Montagne, Laurent, Durey and Bootsma, 1999), participants had to catch balls moving at a constant speed on a rectilinear trajectory, with their hand movements constrained along the transverse axis. The hand was positioned to the right of, to the left of, or at the interception point (Figure 7.1), without the participant knowing which. The ball could reach the interception point along a trajectory that was outward or inward with respect to the participant, or perpendicular to the hand's movement axis (Figure 7.1).

As predicted, there were as many kinematic profiles as there were experimental conditions. Following this descriptive analysis which provided some initial support for the model, we looked at each individual experimental condition. With the hand initially positioned at the interception point, different angles of approach were expected to give rise to different behaviours. For outward and inward angles, participants were expected to start by moving their hand to fill in the lateral distance (to the left for an outward angle, to the right for an inward angle) and then change direction in order to catch the ball (causing a movement reversal). With a perpendicular angle of approach, participants were not expected to move their hand at all.

The results showed that there were indeed many more movement reversals for outward and inward angles than for the perpendicular trajectory. This finding is in line with our predictions. However, not all outward and inward approach angles gave rise to movement reversals (approximately 40 per cent did not), and some participants even produced movement reversals when the trajectory was perpendicular. The presence of movement reversals in the perpendicular condition (exhibited by eight participants out of nine) suggests that participants have trouble carrying out this perceptual activity outside of the perception–movement cycle. The task constraints of having to produce a movement may activate the perception–movement cycle based on the lateral hand-to-ball distance created. In this light, the lack of movement reversals on an outward or inward angle is difficult to interpret.

In the last part of the analysis, we tested the model directly. We were interested in how the difference between the lateral distance to travel, and the distance that would be travelled based on the current velocity, evolved between movement onset

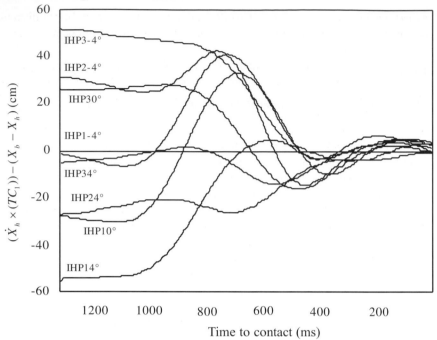

Figure 7.2 Time course (between movement onset and contact) of the difference between the lateral distance to travel and the distance that would be travelled on the basis of the current velocity (i.e. $(\dot{X}_h \times (TC_1)) - (X_b - X_h)$) on a trial performed by the same participant in the different experimental conditions. The difference stabilized around 0 at an average of 300 ms before contact, regardless of the experimental condition. The hand was placed to the left of the interception point (IHP1), at the interception point (IHP2), or to the right of the interception point (IHP3). The ball was approaching along an outward (–4°), perpendicular (0°), or inward (4°) trajectory (from Montagne, Laurent, Durey and Bootsma,

and contact. The results showed that, on the average, this difference stabilised around zero at approximately 300 ms before contact (Figure 7.2). In other words, the participants started moving their hand at the required velocity approximately 300 ms before they caught the ball. This allowed them to put their hand in the right place at the right time, without knowing the spatiotemporal characteristics of the interception point with the ball.

Manipulating the first-order temporal relation (Montagne, Fraisse, Ripoll and Laurent, 2000)

One of the limitations of the required velocity model is that the movement must start as soon as the required velocity is greater than zero. If this were, in fact, the case, then the performer would have to begin moving at extremely small required velocity values, even if the task constraints do not require doing so (for example, if a moving object 10 m away is approaching at a slow speed and the lateral hand-to-ball distance is 10 cm). This led us to add a required velocity threshold to the model (0.5 m/s^{-1}), beyond which the movement begins (see also Peper, Bootsma, Mestre and Bakker, 1994).

The available literature contains a number of contradictory results regarding the role of variables such as the moving object's approach duration, movement speed, and distance travelled (e.g. Payne, 1986; Li and Laurent, 1994; Fayt, Bootsma, Marteniuk, MacKenzie and Laurent, 1997). In the required velocity model, the first-order temporal relation (TC_1), and more specifically, its time course, is an input variable. The movement velocity and the distance travelled are not important in themselves; only the relationship between them, TC_1. If TC_1 is indeed an input variable, then different combinations of travelled distances and movement velocities that give rise to the same TC_1 pattern over time should have no effect on the participants' behaviour. Inversely, different TC_1 patterns should give rise to specific adaptations that can be predicted by way of simulations. In this study (Montagne, Fraisse, Ripoll and Laurent, 2000), we manipulated both the distance travelled by the moving object (4 m and 2 m) and its approach duration (1.6 s, 1.25, and 1 s). Taking all combinations of these two variables gave us six experimental conditions in which the moving object's speed varied across conditions (but was held constant within a given trial) (Table 7.1).

The participants had to move a cart along a 0.65 m long runway (situated on a transverse axis) so as to 'hit' the object in the target zone. The object's motion (perpendicular to the hand–movement axis) was simulated by the successive lighting up of a row of 200 diodes. The model predicts an effect on response latency while the movement should remain unchanged. These predictions, though counter intuitive, are illustrated in Figure 7.3. If, as we hypothesised, the movement is initiated at a required velocity threshold, i.e. when TC_1 reaches a threshold value, then manipulating TC_1 should affect latency time (i.e. longer latency time for longer TC_1), but not the movement kinematics, since from movement onset to object arrival, the time course of TC_1 is the same whatever the experimental constraints.

The data showed that the distance travelled had no impact on the variables recorded, whereas the manipulation of TC_1 gave rise to different behaviours (Figure 7.3).

Table 7.1 Independent variables used in the experiment. The first-order time-to-contact (TC_1) had three levels and the distance performer had two levels. The six experimental conditions were obtained by taking all combinations of these two performers and varying the moving object's speed (within-condition speed was held constant).

TC_1 / Distance	*1s*	*1.25 s*	*1.6 s*
2 m	2 ms^{-1}	1.6 m s^{-1}	1.25 m s^{-1}
4 m	4 ms^{-1}	3.2 m s^{-1}	2.50 m s^{-1}

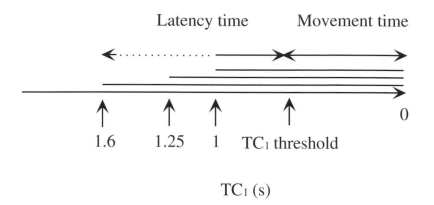

Figure 7.3 Time course of TC_1 (s) in the three experimental conditions.

These results confirmed the specific role of TC_1 relative to the moving object's speed and distance travelled. Contrary to our predictions, though, variations in TC_1 resulted in different movement kinematics (i.e. movement duration, maximal velocity, and moment of maximal velocity; see Figure 7.4). It is also worth noting that the required velocity at movement onset was affected by TC_1; the required velocity at movement onset increased as the object's approach duration decreased. We can thus reject the hypothesis according to which movement initiation is initiated at an invariant required velocity threshold. In view of these findings, we replaced the invariant required velocity threshold with a required velocity calibrated to the moving target's presentation time (by relating the threshold value to the initial value of presentation time) and we ran new simulations. All the results obtained were replicated in the simulations: reducing the moving object's approach duration shortens the response latency, decreases the duration of the movement, and increases its maximal velocity. These results helped us to further refine and validate the model, in addition to showing how it is used.

Conclusions and perspectives

The dipole model (Rushton and Wann, 1999) and the required velocity model (Peper, Bootsma, Mestre and Bakker, 1994; Bootsma, Fayt, Zaal and Laurent, 1997) are consistent with the conceptual framework presented in the first part of this paper. The former describes the relationships between optical information and PES properties, and the latter, between perception and movement. Testing these two models requires experimentally manipulating the informational and/or physical variables they involve. In the first phase of our experimental research, we manipulated the two physical variables (the properties) in the required velocity model: the current lateral distance (Montagne, Laurent, Durey and Bootsma, 1999) and TC_1 (Montagne, Fraisse, Ripoll and Laurent, 2000). The results obtained in both experiments support the model.

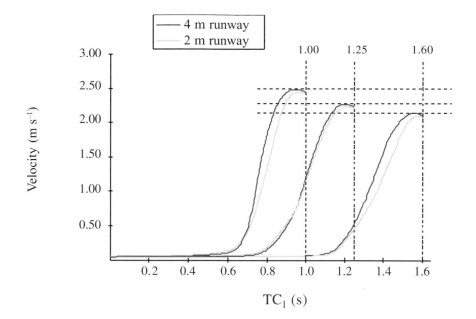

Figure 7.4 Typical velocity curves obtained during a trial by the same participant in each of the six experimental conditions. Increasing the approach duration gave rise to (i) a decrease in response latency, (ii) an earlier maximal velocity, and (iii) a higher maximal velocity. In contrast, for a given approach duration manipulating the distance travelled by the object (2 m vs. 4 m) did not change the kinematics of the movement (from Montagne, Fraisse, Ripoll and Laurent, 2000).

Of course, certain aspects of these results call for some additional remarks. The irregular occurrence of movement reversals in the first experiment is worth further examination. In our second experiment, we showed that the velocity required for movement onset depends on the object's approach duration. One can assume that different participants start to move at different required velocities, causing some to produce movement reversals where others do not. Alternatively, the irregular occurrence of movement reversals may simply illustrate that the laws of control guide rather than determine the catcher's movement (Warren, 1988). The second experiment also showed via multiple linear regressions on Equation 7.1 that hand acceleration did depend upon the velocity differential, but that the law of control (in its current form) accounted for 'only' 60 per cent of the total variance. This result obviously suggests that the law of control, as it stands, does not provide a complete explanatory account of movement timing and must be improved. Now that we have accumulated this body of experimental findings, one of our goals in the near future will be to propose a new formula for the law of control, one that better accounts for the data obtained so far. We will then be in a position to manipulate the different information variables in order to identify the information used (see Rushton and Wann, 1999).

The required velocity model was proposed and tested using a highly specific paradigm in which the movements of the hand and the ball were severely restricted. One can wonder whether and to what extent the same type of mechanism plays a role in controlling less constrained ball-catching actions. Let us look for a moment at the problem facing a team games player who wants to catch or intercept a ball travelling along a parabolic trajectory. If we project the sequence of positions occupied by the ball onto the horizontal plane of the head, the required velocity model can solve the problem. If the player is capable of aligning laterally with the ball (i.e. of keeping the direction of the horizontal head–ball axis constant; Chapman, 1968) then all he/she has left to do is control his/her acceleration along the current horizontal head–ball axis. The required velocity is equal to the ratio of the distance between the head and the ball's projection onto the ground, to the time the ball takes to cross the head plane (i.e. time-to-contact). The current velocity corresponds to the current velocity of the player along the horizontal head-ball axis. A particularly interesting question in our minds is whether a given control mechanism (here, the required velocity model) can be generalised to a class of tasks.

Once these control mechanisms are uncovered, it will be possible to address the issue of training in such skills. A question worth raising is whether expertise in ball-catching tasks consists of optimising perception–movement relationships, or whether experts and novices use totally different control mechanisms. In our conceptual framework, information is always available in the optical flow, regardless of the participant's age or level of expertise. How could access to this information be facilitated? Could setting up richer learning environments promote access to useful information? Finally, the control mechanisms described in our model are sensorimotor ones, so another question one might ask concerns the cognitive permeability of these mechanisms. Would it be possible through specific instructions, or by directing attention to particular aspects of the optical flow, to make learners more attuned to this information and thereby instill functional relationships between the optical flow and the movement forces? Or, would it be better to construct learning environments which facilitated emergence and use of appropriate sensorimotor control processes for interception, with less emphasis on prescriptive verbal instructions ? These unanswered questions provide the incentive for designing and implementing a number of specific research programmes.

Note

1   The de-correlation method is designed to manipulate selectively a given information source (e.g. Savelsbergh, Whiting and Bootsma, 1991) in order to assess its function in the perceptual process.

References

Bennett, S., Van der Kamp, J., Savelsbergh, G.J.P. and Davids, K. (1999). Timing a one-handed catch. I. Effects of telestereoscopic viewing. *Experimental Brain Research* **129**, 362–8.

Bootsma, R.J. and Peper, C.E. (1992). Predictive visual information sources for the regulation of action with special emphasis on catching and hitting. In L. Proteau and D. Elliott (eds), *Vision and Motor Control*. Amsterdam: Elsevier Science Publishers.

Bootsma, R.J., Fayt, V., Zaal, F.T.J.M. and Laurent, M. (1997). On the information-based regulation of movement: things Wann (1996) may want to consider. *Journal of Experimental Psychology: Human Perception and Performance* **23**, 1282–9.

Bootsma, R.J., Montagne, G. and Laurent, M. (1998). Testing the use of information: what and how. In B. Bril, A. Ledebt, G. Dietrich and A. Roby-Brami (eds), *Advances in perception–action coupling*. Paris: EDK Editions.

Bootsma, R.J. (1998). Ecological movement principles and how much information matters. In A.A. Post, J.R. Pijpers, P. Bosch and M.S.J. Boschker (eds), *Models in Human Movement Science*. Enschede: Print Partners Ipskamp.

Chapman, S. (1968). Catching a baseball. *American Journal of Physics* **36**, 868–70.

Cutting, J.E. (1986). *Perception with an Eye for Motion*. Cambridge: Bradford Books/ MIT Press.

Davids, K. and Stratford, R. (1989). Peripheral vision and simple catching: the screen paradigm revisited. *Journal of Sport Sciences* **7**, 139–52.

De Rugy, A., Montagne, G., Buekers, M.J. and Laurent, G. (2000). The control of human locomotor pointing under restricted informational conditions. *Neuroscience Letters* **281**, 87–90.

De Rugy, A., Montagne, G., Buekers, M.J. and Laurent, G. (2001) Spatially constrained locomotion under informational conflict. *Behavioral and Brain Research* **23** 11–25.

Fayt, V., Bootsma, R.J., Marteniuk, R.G., MacKenzie, C. and Laurent, M. (1997). The effects of task constraints on the organization of interception movements. *Journal of Sport Sciences* **15**, 581–6.

Gibson, J.J. (1958). Visually controlled locomotion and visual orientation in animals. *British Journal of Psychology* **49**, 182–94.

Heuer, H. (1993). Estimates of time to contact based on changing size and changing target vergence. *Perception* **22**, 549–63.

Judge, S.J. and Bradford, C.M. (1988). Adaptation to telestereoscopic viewing measured by one-handed catching performance. *Perception* **17**, 783–802.

Laurent, M., Montagne, G. and Durey, A. (1996). Binocular invariants in interceptive tasks: a directed perception approach. *Perception* **25**, 1437–50.

Lee, D.N. (1976). A theory of visual control of braking based on information about time-to-collision. *Perception* **5**, 437–59.

Lee, D.N., Young, D.S., Reddish, D.E., Lough, S. and Clayton, T.M.H. (1983). Visual timing in hitting an accelerating ball. *Quarterly Journal of Experimental Psychology* **35a**, 333–46.

Lenoir, M., Mush, E. and La Grange, N. (1999). Ecological relevance of stereopsis in one-handed ball-catching. *Perceptual and Motor Skills* **89**, 495–508.

Li, F.-X. and Laurent, M. (1994). Effect of practice on intensity coupling and economy of avoidance skill. *Journal of Human Movement Studies* **27**, 189–200.

McBeath, M.K., Shaffer, D.M. and Kaiser, M.K. (1995). How baseball outfielders determine where to run to catch fly balls. *Science* **268**, 569–72.

McLeod, P. and Dienes, Z. (1993). Running to catch the ball. *Nature* **362**, 23.

Michaels, C.F. and Beek, P. (1995). The state of ecological psychology. *Ecological Psychology* **7**, 259–78.

Montagne, G., Laurent, M. and Durey, A. (1998). Visual guidance of goal-oriented locomotor displacements: the example of ball interception tasks. *Ecological Psychology* **10**, 25–37.

Montagne, G., Fraisse, F., Ripoll, H. and Laurent, M. (2000). Perception–action coupling in interceptive task: first order temporal relation as an input variable. *Human Movement Science* **19**, 59–72.

Montagne, G., Laurent, M., Durey, A. and Bootsma, R.J. (1999). Movement reversals in ball catching. *Experimental Brain Research* **129**, 87–92.

Payne, V.G. (1986). The effects of stimulus runway length on coincidence-anticipation timing performance. *Journal of Human Movement Studies* **12**, 289–95.

Peper, C.E., Bootsma, R.J., Mestre, D.R. and Bakker, F.C. (1994). Catching balls: how to get the hand to the right place at the right time. *Journal of Experimental Psychology: Human Perception and Performance* **20**, 3, 591–612.

Rosengren, K.S., Pick, H.L. and Von Hofsten, C. (1988). Role of vision in ball-catching. *Journal of Motor Behavior* **20**, 150–64.

Rushton, S.K. and Wann, J.P. (1999). Weighted combination of size and disparity: a computational model for timing a ball catch. *Nature Neuroscience* **2**, 186–90.

Savelsbergh, G.J.P. and Whiting, H.T.A. (1988). The effect of skill level, external frame of reference and environmental changes on one-handed catching. *Ergonomics* **31**, 1655–63.

Savelsbergh, G.J.P., Whiting, H.T.A. and Bootsma, R.J. (1991). 'Grasping' tau. *Journal of Experimental Psychology: Human Perception and Performance* **31**, 1655–63.

Savelsbergh, G.J.P., Whiting, H.T.A. and Pijpers, J.R. (1992). The control of catching. In J.J. Summers (ed.), *Approaches to the study of motor control and learning*. Amsterdam: North Holland.

Schöner, G. (1994). Dynamic theory of action–perception patterns: The time before contact paradigm. *Human Movement Science* **13**, 415–39.

Shallice, T. (1964). The detection of change and the perceptual moment hypothesis. *British Journal of Statistical Psychology* **17**, 113–35.

Sharp, R.H. (1975). Skill in fast ball games: some input considerations. Unpublished Ph.D. Thesis, Department of Physical Education, Leeds University.

Sharp, R.H. and Whiting, H.T.A. (1974). Exposure and occluded duration effects in a ball-catching skill. *Journal of Motor Behavior* **6**, 139–47.

Sharp, R.H. and Whiting, H.T.A. (1975). Information-processing and eye movement behaviour in a ball catching skill. *Journal of Human Movement Studies* **1**, 124–31.

Smyth, M.M. and Marriott, A.M. (1982). Vision and proprioception in simple catching. *Journal of Motor Behavior* **14**, 143–52.

Tresilian, J.R. (1999). Visually timed action: time-out for 'tau'? *Trends in Cognitive Sciences* **3**, 301–10.

Van der Kamp, J., Savelsbergh, G.J.P. and Smeets, J. (1997). Multiple information sources in interceptive timing. *Human Movement Science* **16**, 787–821.

Wann, J.P. (1996). Anticipating arrival: is the tau margin a specious theory? *Journal of Experimental Psychology: Human Perception and Performance* **22**, 1031–48.

Warren, W.H. (1988). Action mode and laws of control for the visual guidance of action. In O. Meijer and K. Roth (eds), *Complex Movement Behavior: 'The' Motor–Action Controversy*. Amsterdam: North Holland.

Whiting, H.T.A. (1968). Training in a continuous ball throwing and catching task. *Ergonomics* **13**, 445–54.

Whiting, H.T.A. and Sharp, R.H. (1974). Visual occlusion performers in a discrete ball-catching task. *Journal of Motor Behavior* **6**, 11–16.

Whiting, H.T.A., Alderson, G.J.K. and Sanderson, F.H. (1973). Critical time intervals for viewing and individual differences in performance in a ball-catching task. *International Journal of Sport Psychology* **4**, 155–64.

Whiting, H.T.A., Gill, E.B. and Stephenson, J.M. (1970). Critical time intervals for taking in flight information in a ball-catching task. *Ergonomics* **13**, 265–72.

Zaal, F.T.J.M., Bootsma, R.J. and van Wieringen, P.C.W. (1999). Dynamics of reaching for stationary and moving objects: data and model. *Journal of Experimental Psychology: Human Perception and Performance* **25**, 149–61.

8 Intercepting accelerating projectiles

Nicolas Benguigui, Hubert Ripoll and Michael P. Broderick

For actions involving interception and, more generally, for any action requiring tracking of moving projectiles, the performer's essential problem consists of co-ordinating his/her actions with the movements of the projectile. One of the unanswered questions in this domain concerns how humans adapt their actions to accord with the accelerating or decelerating trajectories of projectiles. This question is essential since one can easily observe that, in dynamic sport environments, the velocity of projectiles that need to be intercepted is rarely uniform. For example, in sports such as cricket and tennis, the trajectories of approaching balls are influenced either by decelerations due to air resistance, gravity, surface resistance, or accelerations due to muscular or mechanical impulsion or gravity. One can conceive, as did Rosenbaum (1975), that individuals adapted to the environment are capable of using strategies that allow them to cope with variations in velocity of moving projectiles.

In examining the work on perception of movements of non-constant velocity, one finds apparently rather contradictory results. One of the first scientists to address this problem was Gottsdanker (1952). The results of his study, obtained using a visual–manual pursuit task, requiring extrapolation of the displacement of a moving target after its disappearance, showed that the participants were more precise in their extrapolations for movements at constant velocity than for accelerated movements. This observation led Gottsdanker to speculate that human beings are incapable of regulating their actions in accordance with an accelerating projectile.

This conclusion was later questioned by Rosenbaum (1975) in his analysis of the nature of Gottsdanker's experimental task. According to Rosenbaum, it is conceivable that the incapacity of the participants to pursue the accelerating projectile was due to the complexity of the task itself, rather than to a general incapacity to perceive (and act on) a projectile's accelerating movements. To eliminate this ambiguity, Rosenbaum sought to diminish the motor response component by using a prediction–motion task in which the participant only had to press a switch to indicate his/her estimation of the moment of arrival of a ball at a target after the occlusion of the final part of the ball's trajectory. In the second experiment reported, three constant velocities (0.19, 0.43, and 0.73 m/s) and three accelerations (0.23, 0.39, and 0.44 m/s^2) were used. The participants were as precise in their estimates of constant velocities as for accelerations, suggesting that people are able to follow and estimate arrival of an accelerating projectile. Nevertheless, there are still some remaining questions about the generality of the results, since the lack of difference between the two conditions could have been due to the relatively low rates of acceleration used.

Other work on perception and action with respect to non-constant velocity includes an experiment by Jagacinski, Johnson, and Miller (1983). Projectile displacement, simulated by an oscilloscope, was at first visible right to left, then occluded on its return from left to right. The results demonstrated that the participants were apparently capable of taking account of a projectile's accelerations when the time required for extrapolation was less than 500 ms, but apparently, when greater than this, it was no longer possible.

Thus, the results of early studies left many questions unanswered about perception of variations in velocity. More recent studies have provided some clarity, without, it is clear, providing an unequivocal answer.

Perception and identification of acceleration

One way to examine the problem consists of determining a human being's capacities for detection of acceleration. A number of studies have addressed this specific question by testing people's sensitivity to accelerating and decelerating trajectories (Babler and Dannemiller, 1993; Calderone and Kaiser, 1989; Mateeff, Dimitrov and Hohnsbein, 1995; Regan, Kaufman and Lincoln, 1986; Werkhoven, Snippe and Toet, 1992). In these studies, the task consisted of determining whether there was a variation in the velocity of a projectile. The main objective was finding a detection threshold under the form of Weber's Law corresponding to the difference between final and initial velocity with respect to mean velocity (e.g. Calderone and Kaiser, 1989; Regan, Kaufman and Lincoln, 1986). This quantity, known as the velocity ratio (v_{ratio}), corresponds exactly to a percentage of the variation of velocity (e.g. Babler and Dannemiller, 1993). Even though the results are somewhat different in each studies of this body of work, it emerges that a human being is capable of detecting a projectile's changes in velocity when the v_{ratio} exceeds 20 per cent (e.g. Werkhoven, Snippe and Toet, 1992; Babler and Dannemiller, 1993).

Nevertheless, it is one thing to find in such studies that people are capable of perceiving and identifying acceleration or deceleration of a projectile when they are sufficiently obvious, and another to show that such variations of velocity can be grasped and utilised in the regulation of an interceptive action. Indeed, the detection of acceleration demonstrated in these experiments does not imply that people can necessarily use the information available in the quantitative change of velocity of a projectile to precisely regulate an interceptive action.

To better understand this problem, one may refer to the work of Werkhoven, Snippe and Toet (1992) suggesting that human beings are not equipped with a visual receptor that would permit them to directly perceive acceleration. Instead, the detection of acceleration might be connected to a second-order process consisting of comparing at different instants the velocity of a projectile. As a consequence, it appears difficult to imagine that the mechanisms implicated in the identification of acceleration are equally implicated in interceptive tasks.

Making reference to the two visual streams identified at the neuro–functional level (e.g. Goodale and Milner, 1992), Dubrowski and Carnahan (2000) suggested that the characteristics of a moving projectile can be treated either in the ventral (cognitive) visual stream or in the dorsal (motor) visual stream as a function of the response to be produced (for discussions see Chapter 12 by Keil and Bennett; Keil, Holmes, Bennett, Davids and Smith, 2000; Michaels, 2000; Tresilian, 1995, 1999b). As Keil and Bennett indicate in their chapter, for verbal responses requiring the identification of acceleration, the cognitive stream may be sufficient, whereas for actual interceptive actions the motor stream would be implicated. As Tresilian (1999b) emphasised, the function of the motor stream is largely automatic and non-conscious. If accepted, this argument means that perception in the sense of utilisation of information (including acceleration information) for interception actions must be viewed differently from tasks of perceptual discrimination (see Chapter 1).

Perception and utilisation of acceleration information in interceptive actions

In the case of interceptive actions, the perception and utilisation of acceleration information can be considered at two different levels (Michaels and Oudejans, 1992). Such information can be used by the performer both for regulating locomotion into a zone permitting catching or hitting a ball in flight, and for regulating the catching or hitting movements themselves.

Locomotor displacement and catching: optical acceleration cancellation (OAC)

As Michaels and Zaal point out in their chapter, since the initial work of Chapman (1968), a number of studies have hypothesised that the locomotor displacements necessary to catch a ball in flight depend directly on the perception of acceleration of the ball (e.g. see Babler and Dannemiller, 1993; Michaels and Oudejans, 1992; McLeod and Dienes, 1993). According to these studies, the performer's strategy for catching a ball consists of seeking, by his/her own appropriate movements, the vertical optical acceleration cancellation (OAC strategy). The optical acceleration is specifically determine by the relation $d^2(y)/dt^2$, with y corresponding to the height of the ball (Michaels and Oudejans, 1992), or in other form, $d^2(\tan \alpha)/dt^2$ with α corresponding to the angle formed at the point of observation with the ball and a point on the ground directly under the ball (e.g. McLeod and Dienes, 1993). Theoretically, the OAC strategy can explain all displacements of the performer when the ball moves in a plane that includes the performer himself/herself. A positive optical acceleration means that the catcher is situated behind the landing point, and a negative optical acceleration indicates that the catcher is in front of the landing point, while a zero optical acceleration indicates that the catcher is standing at the landing point. The optical acceleration indicates, therefore, the action necessary (advance, reverse, do not move) for moving to catch the ball. By searching to keep the optical acceleration at zero, the performer can regulate his/her displacement to place himself/herself at the right place and time for performing the catch (Michaels and Oudejans, 1992; McLeod and Dienes, 1993).

It is worth remarking that the data on this concept are at the present time somewhat tentative for at least three reasons. The first problem is linked to the fact that the data that seem compatible with the model do not permit effective testing of the utilisation of information concerning a projectile's vertical variation in velocity. The reason for this is that there has been no experimentation to specifically manipulate the optical quantity $d^2(\tan \alpha)/dt^2$ to examine whether the performer's behaviour is completely determined by this variable. The second difficulty is linked to the fact that this strategy necessitates in the performer a rather extreme sensitivity to the variations in velocity of a projectile since it requires a kind of 'online' cancelling of optical acceleration. However, some previous studies have suggested that the visual system has very little sensitivity to this type of information (see e.g. Calderone and Kaiser, 1989; Werkhoven, Snippe and Toet, 1992). Finally, the concept of OAC only allows explanation of the displacement of a performer in situations where the performer is, at the beginning of the task, aligned in the vertical plane of a projectile's trajectory. In other words, its explanatory power currently lies in very narrow task constraints, and it does not account for constraints under which lateral displacements of a performer are necessary for catching a ball in flight. Other more general models that do not include the perception of vertical acceleration have since been proposed to explain this type of displacement (McBeath, Schaffer and Kaiser, 1995). In light of these questions, further research is necessary to validate or reject the OAC hypothesis. One recent study has suggested the possibility of a type of extra-retinal perception of vertical acceleration (see Oudejans, Michaels, Bakker and Davids, 1999). In this experiment, Oudejans, Michaels, Bakker and Davids (1999) showed that it was possible to run and catch a luminescent ball in the dark. This finding suggested that a visual background was not necessary to succeed in catching; rather, information from the vestibular system could be used to detect the vertical acceleration of the ball. Without background visual information, the data imply that another functional strategy consists of moving the head in order to maintain a stationary image of the ball on the retina. The information from the semicircular canals of the vestibular system can be used for detecting the acceleration of the head in fixating the ball.

Timing of the effector: estimating time to contact

With respect to time, it is generally believed that effector control in interceptive action necessitates estimation of time to contact (TC) information, that is, to the time remaining before the arrival of the projectile at the performer or a point in space adjacent to the performer (e.g. Lee, 1976; Peper, Bootsma, Mestre and Bakker, 1994). Estimation of TC requires the perception and utilisation of information relative to the displacement of a projectile. An interesting question concerns how the performer takes into account the relevant kinematic properties of the projectile for timing interceptive actions.

Hypotheses for regulating interception of projectiles travelling at non-constant velocity

For interceptive actions, two hypotheses can be proffered for explaining the mechanisms of regulating interception of accelerating and decelerating projectiles: (i) the performer is capable of accessing information to account for variations in projectile velocity utilising second-order TC (TC2); and (ii) the performer does not have this capacity and continually regulates action on the basis of first-order TC (TC1).

The latter hypothesis comes from the initial work of Lee (1976), based on the principle that perception and action can be coupled by utilisation of a first-order optic variable called tau (τ). This optic variable, as defined initially by Lee (1976), in situations of radial approach, corresponds, from the point of view of the observer, to the inverse of the rate of dilation of the optical contour of the approaching projectile. This optical quantity is expressed mathematically by $\tau(t) = \varphi / \dot{\varphi}$, in which φ corresponds to the angle formed by the point of observation and the approaching projectile and $\dot{\varphi}$ corresponds to the variation of this angle with respect to time. This optical quantity is directly available on the retina of the performer and necessitates no additional cognitive treatment as it is not necessary to engage in computations of the distance and the velocity of the approaching projectile. The essence of this quantity is that it directly provides information on the temporal relation between the performer and the approaching projectile. More precisely, it allows the performer to access a temporal variable that Lee and Young (1985) called the 'tau-margin' that permits the performer to regulate interceptive actions. More recently, Bootsma, Fayt, Zaal and Laurent (1997) proposed to denote this variable as the first-order time to contact (TC1) suggesting that this variable corresponds to a first-order temporal relation between the performer and the moving projectile. Indeed, it appears that this variable is equal to TC solely when the projectile moves at constant velocity.[1] For non-constant velocities, this relation does not exist, since TC1 does not take into account variations in projectile velocity. It was this point that led Tresilian (1994a, 1995) to define this variable as a first-order approximation of TC.

It must be noted, however, that this approximation of the temporal relation between the projectile and the performer does not prevent the performer from producing appropriate actions, since, according to the hypothesis, the utilisation of TC1 implies a continuous coupling between the perceptual system and the motor system. This coupling permits 'on-line' adjustment of movement characteristics as a function of the evolution of the value of TC1 (e.g. see Chapter 7 by Montagne and Laurent; Montagne, Fraisse, Ripoll and Laurent, 2000). This conceptualisation is strengthened by the fact that the value of TC1 more closely approximates the value of TC2 as the projectile approaches the point of contact (Figure 8.1).

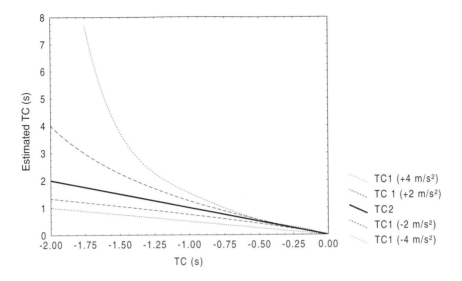

Figure 8.1 Representation of the evolution of TC1 and TC2 for accelerating and decelerating trajectories as a function of time to contact (TC) for four trajectories having different accelerations (+4, +2, −2, −4 m/s², with initial velocities respectively of 0, 2, 6, 8 m/s and final velocities respectively of 8, 6, 2, 0 m/s). As TC diminishes, the difference between TC1 and TC2 diminishes.

With this perspective, Lee, Young, Reddish, Lough and Clayton (1983) were interested in the timing of action using a task of hitting an accelerating ball. The task consisted of jumping up to hit a ball dropped from different heights above the participant. The analysis of Lee, Young, Reddish, Lough and Clayton (1983), who measured the angular variations of the ankle and the knee during the extension phase, showed that the temporal regulation of the action could be described independently from the height of the drop by a function relying on the performer's utilisation of TC1.[2]

Generalising this hypothesis to non-radial approaches of projectiles, Bootsma, Fayt, Zaal and Laurent (1997, note 1), after Bootsma and Oudejans (1993, p. 1043, equation 9), defined an information source combining the relative velocity of the expansion of the optical contour of the projectile with the relative velocity of the constriction of the optical angle formed at the point of observation by the projectile and the point of interception. This information variable, permitting specification of TC1 at any point in space, is formalised by:

$$\frac{1}{\text{tau margin}} = \frac{\dot{\varphi}}{\sin \varphi} - \frac{\dot{\theta}}{\sin \theta} = -\frac{1}{\text{TC1}},$$

where $\dot{\varphi}/\sin \varphi$ can be assimilated to the inverse of the optical variable tau as it is defined by Lee (1976) when φ is small (when $\varphi \leq 10°$, $\sin \varphi \approx \varphi$), θ corresponds to the angle formed at the point of observation by the projectile and

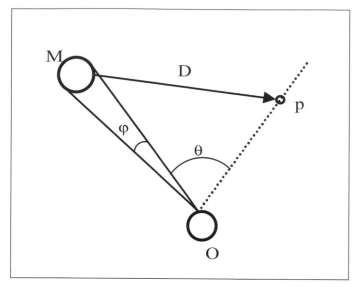

Figure 8.2 Geometrical relations between an observer O and a projectile
M that moves distance D toward point p.

the point of interception, and $\dot{\theta}$ corresponds to the variable of this angle as a function of time (Figure 8.2).[3]

On the basis of this relation, Bootsma and Oudejans (1993) designed a forced-choice task in which the participants had to predict as quickly as possible the order of arrival of two projectiles moving toward the same target. They demonstrated that neither acceleration nor deceleration were accurately judged. Participants committed more errors when one of the projectiles or both projectiles moved at a non-constant velocity.

These results were partially confirmed by Kaiser and Hecht (1995, experiment 1) in a prediction–motion task. In their experiment, the participants were required to estimate the arrival time of a simulated approaching target star which was presented in a flow field of constant-sized stars. The approach of the star was either accelerating, decelerating, or at constant velocity. The utilisation of these different conditions should have induced overestimates of arrival time in the case of accelerating approaches and underestimates in the case of decelerating approaches. The results of this experiment confirmed the hypotheses in the deceleration condition but not in the acceleration condition. In order to explain this absence of overestimation in the former condition, Kaiser and Hecht (1995) suggested that the values of accelerations and the durations of occlusion utilised in the experiment were not sufficiently great to produce the expected results.

In a study using a virtual interception task, Port, Lee, Dassonville and Georgopoulos (1997) addressed the question of the use of information from a projectile's acceleration or deceleration. The task consisted of intercepting a projectile on a computer screen using a cursor controlled by a manipulandum with movement in two dimensions. The projectile moved either with acceleration (six different trajectories from 5.84 to 129.41 cm/s²), constant velocity (six trajectories from 8.84 to 35.35 cm/s), or deceleration (six trajectories from 5.84 to 129.41 cm/s²). A trial was considered successful if the cursor entered the interception zone (0.6 cm radius) within ± 100 ms of the arrival of the projectile within the interception zone. Trials in which the cursor arrived more than 100 ms before the projectile were considered early errors, and trials in which the cursor arrived more than 100 ms after the projectile were considered late errors. Only 41.3 per cent of the trials were successful under these criteria. The large majority of the early errors were produced for decelerating trajectories while the large majority of late errors were produced for accelerating trajectories. These results, which have been confirmed by Ripoll and Latiri (1997) in a coincidence-timing task using a simple button press, reveal difficulty in dealing with variations in velocity when co-ordinating responses to projectile movement. The results also suggest that, in this task, the participants were unable to compensate completely for the effect of acceleration by means of a continuous regulation mechanism.

In another study using the same task, Lee, Port and Georgopoulos (1997) looked at the kinematic characteristics of the cursor displacement and observed different velocity peaks, notably in response to slow accelerations and decelerations. The authors suggest that the different peaks result from the production of sub-movements whose goal was to adjust to the characteristics of the target specifically adjusting to the first-order estimate of target position and velocity. It can be speculated that no information concerning the variation in velocity of the target is truly perceived as part of the production of interception movements.

The only research evidence that supports the possibility of humans being able to adequately pick up and use acceleration or deceleration information of a moving projectile during interception, was provided by Lacquaniti, Carozzo and Borghese (1993). In their experiment, the timing precision observed in participants when asked to catch balls falling from a height less than or equal to 1.5 m had to be due, the authors argued, to the participants' use of acceleration information. Nevertheless, it is also possible to explain this result by maintaining that the visual system does not permit the direct perception of acceleration information (Regan, Kaufman and Lincoln, 1986; Werkhoven, Snippe and Toet, 1992). Tresilian (e.g. 1993, 1997, 1999b) suggested that in free-fall situations where projectile acceleration is produced uniquely by the force of gravity (g), it is possible for a person to learn to integrate this value and to use it from the moment the height of the drop is known in order to produce and/or adjust the interception movement on the basis of a temporal variable of the type: $TC = \sqrt{2 \cdot h / g}$, in which h corresponds to the height of the drop and g to gravitational acceleration.

Some recent relevant experiments

Even with the particularly interesting results reported in the study above, it is worth noting that the data were collected under rather specific task constraints that allow little generalisation to many typical situations requiring timing of action with the movement of a projectile. More generally, it appears that many actions can be correctly regulated, even if accelerations are ignored, by using a first-order estimate of TC. Nevertheless, it must be cautioned that this hypothesis is supported by very little direct empirical data and demands rigorous empirical testing (Tresilian, 1999).

It is precisely for this reason that two experiments were performed using two tasks allowing relative predictions for utilisation or non-utilisation of information about a projectile's variation in velocity (Benguigui and Ripoll, 2000). The goal of these experiments was to collect quantitative data about the nature of perception of temporal variation when projectile trajectory was accelerated or decelerated.

In the first experiment, the apparatus consisted of a ramp of lights (4 m length) that simulated projectile movement toward a target situated at the end of the ramp. The participants were required to estimate time of arrival by pressing a button at the moment the moving stimulus arrived at the target, but with the stimulus occluded during the final part of the trajectory. This prediction–motion task was used to measure prediction-estimation responses of an occluded moving projectile since it allowed quantitative predictions of estimation errors in cases where participants could not perceive information relative to a projectile's variation in velocity. The goal of this experiment was also to re-examine the contradictory findings of Rosenbaum (1975) and Kaiser and Hecht (1995) by using longer occlusion times and administering greater accelerations. Eight values for accelerations (range: − 2.45 to +2.45 m/s²) and eight values for occlusion times (range: 300 to 1110 ms) were applied.

To validate the hypothesis of the utilisation of TC1, the theoretical errors were calculated for each trajectory from the difference between TC1 and the real TC (i.e. TC2) of the projectile at the moment of occlusion. These theoretical errors were then compared by regression analysis to the errors committed by the participants.

The results of this analysis indicated an R^2 of 0.66 and a regression-line slope of 0.96 (Figure 8.3). These statistical analyses signify a direct relation between the errors committed by the participants and the predicted errors. The results confirm the most recent hypotheses of Bootsma, Fayt, Zaal and Laurent (1997) and Tresilian (1999a) that, in a prediction–motion task, humans cannot use information about the acceleration or deceleration of a projectile to estimate the time of arrival of the projectile based on TC1 perceived at the moment of occlusion.

A second recent experiment followed the same principle as the first but used an indirect interception task. This task consisted of projecting a ball a distance of 2 m in order to intercept a moving target. The purpose of this task was to require, as in the prediction–motion task, a response produced on the basis of predictive information picked up before the projectile's arrival at the interception point. In this type of action, contrary to classic interception actions (catching or hitting a ball), it is not possible to control the effector movement at the moment preceding contact. One can, therefore, predict that if the participants produced their action on the basis of TC1, they will commit the error of attempting to intercept the ball too soon for decelerated trajectories and too late for accelerated trajectories.

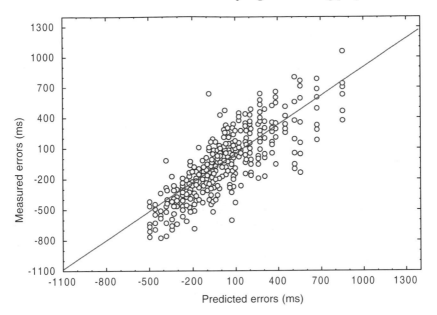

Figure 8.3 Errors committed (measured errors) as a function of predicted errors. The equation of the line of regression is: Measured Error = 44 + 0.96 × Predicted Error, with R^2 = 0.66.

In this experiment, nine values for accelerations/decelerations (range : –2.4 to +2.4 m/s^2) were used for a total of 54 trials. To validate the predictions relative to the utilisation of TC1, TC and TC1 of the projectile with respect to the point of interception at the instant of ball release were calculated. These calculations allowed a prediction of error for each trial conforming to the TC1 hypothesis. These theoretical errors were then compared with the participants' errors by regression analysis.

The results show an R^2 of 0.65 with a regression-line slope of 1.72 (Figure 8.4). The errors committed by the participants confirmed that information relative to the projectile's acceleration was not used. The participants committed some errors with over- and under-estimations higher than the model predicted. This finding could mean that, under these task constraints, the information used to produce action could be picked up at a pre-motor stage, the moment before release of the ball. Indeed, in this type of task, if the participants used information uniquely specifying the projectile's velocity (i.e. TC1), then the earlier the information was perceived, the greater the magnitude of errors.

In the course of these two experiments, it was shown that, the participants made temporal estimates (in the prediction–motion task) and produced action (in the indirect-interception task) on the basis of TC1. The results of our two experiments, considered in relation to the most relevant work in this domain (Bootsma and Oudejans, 1993; Kaiser and Hecht, 1995; Lee, Young, Reddish,

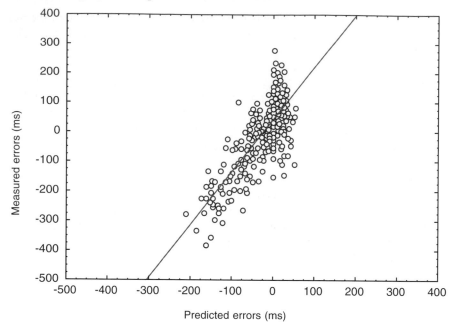

Figure 8.4 Errors committed as a function of predicted errors. The regression equation is:
Measured Error = 39 + 1.72 × Predicted Error, with $R^2 = 0.65$.

Lough and Clayton, 1983; Lee, Port and Georgopoulos, 1997; Port, Lee,
Dassonville and Georgpoulos, 1997; Tresilian, 1999a), served to underscore the
validity of their quantitative predictions and confirmed the effective utilisation of
TC1. On the perceptual side, the results clearly indicated that people perform
poorly in tasks requiring accurate perception of information about a projectile's
acceleration or deceleration. The results also confirm the observations of
Werkhoven *et al.* (1993) that the visual system is not equipped to directly detect
acceleration.

Conclusions

Some experimental findings have indicated that people are capable of identifying
variations in velocity (e.g. Babler and Dannemiller, 1993; Calderone and Kaiser,
1989; Mateeff, Dimitrov and Hohnsbein, 1995; Regan, Kaufman and Lincoln,
1986; Werkhoven, Snippe and Toet, 1992). Moreover, the experiment of Lacquaniti,
Carozzo and Borghese (1993) suggested the possibility that performers could take
into account the vertical acceleration in a ball-catching task. Nevertheless, it appears
that for most interception tasks, people do not use information relative to
acceleration or deceleration. The optical quantity defined by Bootsma, Fayt, Zaal
and Laurent (1997, equation 2) is a good candidate for explaining how interceptive
actions are produced and regulated. This optical quantity permits a person to specify
TC1 in any situation. It is, nevertheless, not currently possible to draw more

definitive conclusions since there has not been a direct demonstration of the use of this variable. New experiments are therefore necessary to evaluate the effective use of this source of information.

A last point to be discussed concerns the errors produced in the final two experiments presented, where the magnitude of variations in velocity increases were as high as 800 ms (Benguigui and Ripoll, 2000). This means that TC1 is approximate as soon as the participant is unable to pick up and use information to support an interceptive action right up until the point of arrival of a projectile. One can nevertheless say that these situations are extremely rare and that, in most interceptive actions, the regulation of the action is possible up until time of contact with an approaching object. It is not necessary to have information relative to the variation in velocity of the projectile. It seems that the human visual system does not need to quickly and accurately measure accelerations, since such an ability would not confer a significant survival advantage (Tresilian, 1999a). The on-line systems of regulation based on the perception of first-order information suffice in the production of motor acts adapted to dynamic environments in which projectiles typically move at non-constant velocities.

Notes

1   Lee (1976, pp. 440, 441, equations 5, 6, 7, and 8) demonstrated that for a rectilinear displacement at constant velocity, $\tau(t) = \varphi / \dot{\varphi} = Z / \dot{Z} = TC$, with Z corresponding to the distance between the observer and $\dot{Z}$ at the velocity at which this distance diminishes. Note here that tau margin corresponds to the relation $Z / \dot{Z}$.

2   Michaels, Zeinstra and Oudejans (2000) found a number of failures in this experiment and criticised the conclusions made by Lee, Young, Reddish, Lough and Clayton (1983) (see also Tresilian, 1993 and Wann, 1996, for criticisms of this study). They attempted to rectify these problems by examining elbow extension only in seated punchers. The results of this experiment suggest that different kind of variables could be used to control action. The flexion of the elbow appeared to be initiated and regulated by the expansion velocity of the ball, rather than by the tau-margin (i.e. TC1). For the extension movement, it was not possible to clearly identify the variable utilised. Finally, Michaels, Zeinstra and Oudejans (2000) concluded that different variables could be used depending on availability of information and depending on the organisation of action. However, no suggestions were offered for the possible use of information regarding the variation of velocity of the ball.

3   It appears that this formalisation combines a function of radial tau $(\varphi / \dot{\varphi})$ and a function of tangential tau $(\theta / \dot{\theta})$ when φ and θ are small (less than 10°).

References

Babler, T.G. and Dannemiller, J.L. (1993). Role of image acceleration in judging landing location of free-falling projectiles. *Journal of Experimental Psychology: Human Perception and Performance* 19, 15–31.

Benguigui, N. and Ripoll, H. (2000). Perception and use of information about acceleration in a prediction motion task and in an indirect interception task. In P. Fleurance (ed.) *Proceedings of the French Society of Sport Psychology Conference.* Paris: INSEP.

Bootsma, R.J. and Oudejans, R.R.D. (1993). Visual information about time to collision between two projectiles. *Journal of Experimental Psychology: Human Perception and Performance* **19**, 1041–52.

Bootsma, R.J., Fayt, V., Zaal, F.T.J.M. and Laurent, M. (1997). On the information-based regulation of movement. *Journal of Experimental Psychology: Human Perception and Performance* **23**, 1282–9.

Calderone, J.B. and Kaiser, M.K. (1989). Visual acceleration detection: effect of sign and motion orientation. *Perception and Psychophysics* **45**, 4, 391–4.

Chapman, S. (1968). Catching a baseball. *American Journal of Physics* **36**, 868–70.

Dubrowski, A. and Carnahan, H. (2000). Task dependent processing of visual information about target acceleration. *Brain and Cognition* **43**, 172–7.

Goodale, M.A. and Milner, A.D., (1992). Separate visual pathways for perception and action. *Trends in Neurosciences* **15**, 20–5.

Gottsdanker, R.M. (1952). The accuracy of prediction–motion. *Journal of Experimental Psychology* **43**, 26–36.

Jagacinski, R.J., Johnson, W.W. and Miller, R.A. (1983). Quantifying the cognitive trajectories of extrapolated movements. *Journal of Experimental Psychology: Human Perception and Performance* **9**, 43–57.

Kaiser, M.K. and Hecht, H. (1995). Time-to-passage judgments in nonconstant optical flow fields. *Perception & Psychophysics* **57**, 817–25.

Keil, D., Holmes, P., Bennett, S., Davids, K. and Smith, N. (2000). Theory and practice in sport psychology and motor behaviour needs to be constrained by integrative modelling of brain and behaviour. *Journal of Sport Sciences* **18**, 433–43.

Lacquaniti, F., Carozzo, M. and Borghese, N. (1993). The role of vision in tuning anticipatory motor responses of the limbs. In A. Berthoz (ed.), *Multisensory Control of Mouvement*. Oxford: Oxford University Press.

Lee, D.N. (1976). A theory of visual control of braking based on information about time-to-collision. *Perception* **5**, 437–59.

Lee, D.N. and Young, D.S. (1985). Visual timing in interceptive actions. In D.J. Ingle, M. Jeannerod and D.N. Lee (eds). *Brain Mechanisms and Spatial Vision*. Dortrecht: Martinus Nijhoff.

Lee, D., Port, N.L. and Georgopoulos A.P. (1997). Manual interception of moving targets. II. On-line control of overlapping submovements. *Experimental Brain Research* **116**, 3, 421–33.

Lee, D.N., Young, D.S., Reddish, P.E., Lough, S. and Clayton, T.M.H. (1983). Visual timing in hitting an accelerating ball. *Quarterly Journal of Experimental Psychology* **35A**, 333–46.

Mateeff, S., Dimitrov, G. and Hohnsbein, J. (1995). Temporal thresholds and reaction time to changes in velocity of visual motion. *Vision Research* **35**, 3, 355–63.

McBeath, M.K., Schaffer, D.M. and Kaiser, M.K. (1995). How baseball outfielders determine where to run to catch fly balls. *Science* **268**, 569–73.

McLeod, P. and Dienes, Z. (1993). Running to catch the ball. *Nature* **362**, 23.

Michaels, C.F. (2000). Information, perception, and action: what should ecological psychologists learn from Milner and Goodale (1995)? *Ecological Psychology* **12**, 3, 241–58.

Michaels, C.F. and Oudejans, R.R.D. (1992). The optics and actions of catching fly balls: zeroing out optical acceleration. *Ecological Psychology* **4**, 199–222.

Michaels, C.F., Zeinstra, E.B. and Oudejans, R.R.D. (2000). Information and action in punching a falling ball. *The Quarterly Journal of Experimental Psychology* **54**, 1, 69–93.

Montagne, G., Fraisse, F., Ripoll, H. and Laurent, M. (2000). Perception–action coupling in an interceptive task: first order time-to-contact as an input variable. *Human Movement Science* **19**, 59–72.

Oudejans, R.R.D., Michaels, C.F., Bakker, F.C. and Davids, K. (1999). Shedding some light on catching in the dark: perceptual mechanisms for catching fly balls. *Journal of Experimental Psychology: Human Perception and Performance* **25**, 531–42.

Peper, C.E, Bootsma, R.J., Mestre, D.R. and Bakker, F.C. (1994). Catching balls: how to get the hand in the right place at the right time. *Journal of Experimental Pyschology: Human Perception and Performance* **20**, 591–612.

Port, N.L., Lee, D., Dassonville, P. and Georgopoulos, A.P. (1997). Manual interception of moving targets. I. Performance and movement initiation. *Experimental Brain Research* **116**, 3, 406–20.

Regan, D.M., Kaufman, L. and Lincoln, J. (1986). Motion in depth and visual acceleration. In K.R. Boff, L. Kaufman and J.P. Thomas (eds), *Handbook of Human Perception and Human Performance*. New York: Wiley.

Ripoll, H. and Latiri, I. (1997). Effect of expertise in a fast ball game on coincident-timing accuracy. *Journal of Sport Sciences* **15**, 6, 573–80.

Rosenbaum, D.A. (1975). Perception and extrapolation of velocity and acceleration. *Journal of Experimental Psychology: Human Perception and Performance* **1**, 395–403.

Tresilian, J.R. (1993). Four questions of time to contact: a critical examination of research on interceptive timing. *Perception* **22**, 653–80.

Tresilian, J.R. (1994). Approximate information sources and perceptual variables in interceptive timing. *Journal of Experimental Psychology: Human Perception and Performance* **20**, 154–73.

Tresilian, J.R. (1995). Perceptual and cognitive processes in time-to-contact estimation: analysis of prediction motion and relative judgment tasks. *Perception & Psychophysics* **57**, 231–45.

Tresilian, J.R. (1997). A revised tau hypothesis: consideration of Wann's analysis. *Journal of Experimental Psychology: Human Perception and Performance* **23**, 1272–81.

Tresilian, J.R. (1999a). Analysis of recent empirical challenges to an account of interceptive timing. *Perception & Psychophysics* **61**, 3, 515–28.

Tresilian, J.R. (1999b). Visually timed action: time-outfor 'tau'? *Trends in Cognitive Sciences* **3**, 8, 301–10.

Wann, J.P. (1996). Anticipating arrival: is the tau-margin a specious theory? *Journal of Experimental Psychology: Human Perception and Performance* **22**, 1031–48

Werkhoven, P., Snippe, H. and Toet, A. (1992). Visual processing of optic acceleration. *Vision research* **32**, 2313–29.

9   Catching fly balls

Claire F. Michaels and
Frank T.J.M. Zaal

In sports such as soccer, cricket and baseball, players need to intercept balls travelling long distances in the air from the point of contact with a foot or a bat. As outlined in the chapter by Montagne and Laurent, these interceptive actions can be difficult because players often need to run a long way to make the interceptions. In cricket and baseball, such trajectories are known as fly balls. The goal of our chapter is to provide an overview of theory and research on how people catch fly balls. More particularly, we address the issue of locomotion in interception: how do people control their movement so that they are at the right place at the right time to intercept a ball?.

A psychological account of locomotion in catching must comprise two elements. First, as discussed by Montagne and Laurent, researchers need to identify an optical variable or collection of optical variables that can be used by the catcher in getting to the right place at the right time. Second, researchers must identify the strategies employed by catchers for using that variable (or collection of variables) in the control of locomotion. As Montagne and Laurent noted, such strategies are termed control laws (Kugler and Turvey, 1987; Warren, 1988). Control laws describe how an energy pattern available to the senses (e.g. an optical pattern) is used to guide the creation of forces by the motor system. In our chapter we discuss the various candidate optical variables and candidate control laws that have been presented in the literature on catching.

The physics and optics of ball flight

On the moon, where there is no atmosphere, a projectile follows a parabolic path. As long as its initial velocity and launch angle are known, one can determine where the projectile will be at any time, and where it will land and when. Only one force, gravity, affects the trajectory. The parabolic path, which is a reasonably good approximation for ball sports on earth, served as the starting point for the first scientific theory explaining how people catch balls.

The first theory of the catching of fly balls was published in 1968 in an article by Seville Chapman and that explanation has come to be known as the Chapman Strategy. The strategy deals with the case in which the ball flies in the catcher's sagittal plane, which is usually considered the most difficult of fly balls to catch,

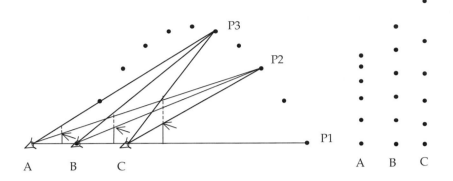

Figure 9.1 A ball flies on a parabolic path from right to left: its position is shown at equal
temporal intervals. The ball can be viewed from three positions, A, B, and C,
where B is the ball's landing point. Lines connect three ball positions (P1, P2,
and P3) to the three viewing positions. To the right of each viewing position is a
line segment that starts on the line to P1 and ends on the line to P3, comprising
a solid and a dashed segment. The line segments represent an image plane.
Notice where the line to P2 intersects the segments (indicated by the arrows).
At position A, the smaller segment is above the arrow (dashed); at Position B,
the segments above and below the arrow are equal; at C the segment below the
arrow is smaller than that above the arrow. This means that viewed from position
A, the ball is decelerating on the image plane; at B, the ball has a constant
velocity, and at C, the ball is accelerating on the image plane. In short, the ball
will arrive at the eye if its image on the plane moves at a constant velocity. The
right panels show a succession of images that schematise the successive ball
locations viewed from positions A, B, and C.

but the strategy is easily generalisable to other trajectories. The optical information
it exploits is vertical optical acceleration (also sometimes known as 'acceleration
of the tangent' or AT). The optics behind the strategy are presented in Figure 9.1.

Chapman (1968) proposed one way that the optical relations captured in Figure
9.1 might be used to guide locomotion in catching. The gist of the strategy is
obvious from Figure 9.1: if outfielders detect deceleration, they must run forward;
if they detect acceleration, they must run backward; and if they detect neither
acceleration nor deceleration, they must stay put. The Chapman Strategy can be
used throughout the trajectory; as long as would-be catchers run in such a way
that the image velocity of the ball is constant, they will be at the right place at the
right time to catch the ball. Whether they are stationary, running forward, or running
backward, the strategy works. For example, if a catcher is running forward too
fast, the increasing image velocity specifies that the ball will land behind them if
they keep running at their current speed.

Notice that the catcher does not need to be able to predict the place that the ball
will land, nor the time that it will land there. All that needs to be done is to maintain
the constant vertical optical velocity. Getting to the right place at the right time is
solved not by prediction, but by continuously adapting the action to information.
That means, incidentally, that some other information source is required to lay a

basis for timing the interception itself (e.g. when to jump to head a soccer ball or when to start to close a baseball glove around the ball).

Some authors imply that the use of optical acceleration is equivalent to the Chapman Strategy, but there could be any number of strategies – control laws – exploiting optical acceleration. The first experiments related to optical acceleration did not, in fact, test catching actions at all, but only the perception of where a projectile would land. Todd (1981) asked observers to judge whether an object approaching on a parabolic path and simulated on a computer screen would land at or in front of the observation point. Todd's participants were not very good at this, so he concluded that optical acceleration was not used to judge future landing direction. One can argue however, that the information might have been easier to exploit if accelerating patterns had also been used instead of only constant-velocity and decelerating patterns. Thus, Todd's test may not have been sensitive enough.

Later, Michaels and Oudejans (1992) tested three predictions related to the use of optical acceleration and the Chapman Strategy: a) that people attempting to catch balls would run in such a way that the optical acceleration is cancelled, b) that because optical acceleration is a monocular variable, running to catch should be the same for monocular and binocular viewing, and 3) that, contrary to Todd's (1981) finding, with accelerating, decelerating, and constant velocity simulations, observers would accurately report where a ball would land. All three predictions were supported. Catchers tended to linearise optical velocity (though not perfectly, as illustrated in Figure 9.2; see also McLeod and Dienes, 1993). Binocular viewing conditions led to the same movement patterns as monocular viewing (up to just before the catch, at least). Observers were able to judge the landing position of simulated balls much better than Todd (1981) had found. However, it should be noted that the support mustered for the Chapman Strategy by Michaels and Oudejans (1992) was not unequivocal. The computer-generated displays showed that not only acceleration, but also velocity, appeared to affect some observers' judgements.

In spite of a promising start, and analyses showing that the strategy could work from a control-theory perspective (Tresilian, 1995), the Chapman Strategy and the use of vertical optical acceleration, in general, have been criticised on two primary grounds. One criticism questions human sensitivity to optical acceleration and the other points out how unrealistic the assumption of a parabolic flight path is. Let us consider these two criticisms in turn.

Detecting acceleration

As discussed in Chapter 8 by Benguigui and colleagues, several psychophysical studies have failed to find that humans are sensitive to optical acceleration (e.g. Calderone and Kaiser, 1989; Gottsdanker, Frick and Lockard, 1961; Runeson, 1974). These observations led McBeath, Shaffer and Kaiser (1995) to the conclusion that optical acceleration could not be used to guide locomotion during catching. Babler and Dannemiller (1993) explicitly tested sensitivity to vertical optical acceleration of the sort required for the Chapman Strategy – that would-be

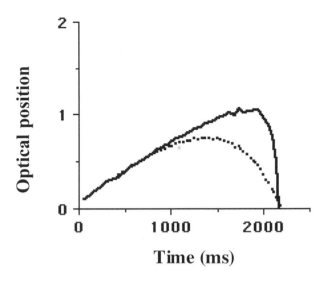

Figure 9.2 Two optical positions given as a function of time, one (dotted) is the optical position of the ball with respect to the catcher's initial observation point; the solid line is the optical position of the ball with respect to the catcher's (moving) eye. Notice that the solid line is straighter for longer than the dotted line. A perfectly straight solid line would indicate a constant optical velocity (i.e. that the catcher was completely successful in cancelling optical acceleration). From Michaels and Oudejans (1992).

catchers detect the presence of acceleration and deceleration. (Perceivers need not be able to discriminate one acceleration from another to use this strategy). Babler and Dannemiller indeed found that perceivers' sensitivity to the presence of acceleration and deceleration was good enough to permit the use of optical acceleration for catching. It is interesting to note, however, that it was not optical acceleration *per se* that was sufficient, but a variable they termed the *velocity ratio*, the change in velocity divided by the average velocity. Perceivers could detect optical velocities that increased or decreased by about 20 per cent over about one second. Thus, it seems that perceivers are sensitive to a relative change in velocity, rather than to pure acceleration. (This finding may also explain why velocity was a significant predictor in the Michaels and Oudejans study.)

Given their conviction that sensitivity to acceleration was not sufficient, McBeath, Schaffer and Kaiser (1995) sought an explanation of catching fly balls in other variables that did not require sensitivity to acceleration (or, in fact, sensitivity to any changes over time). The model they developed is applicable only to the case where the ball has some horizontal velocity with respect to the catcher, that is, the case in which the ball does not stay in the sagittal plane connecting the catcher and ball's initial position. McBeath, Schaffer and Kaiser (1995) claimed that outfielders run so as to keep the ball travelling in an optically straight line. That is, catchers are proposed to run so as to linearise optical trajectory (the LOT model). In other words, if a correctly-running catcher wore a head-mounted camera with the shutter open, the theory predicts that the ball would leave a straight streak on the film. For this to happen, the tangents of the vertical and horizontal angles must change proportionally. Figure 9.3 illustrates how the LOT model works.

Dannemiller, Babler and Babler (1996) raised a problem for the LOT model by claiming that the strategy leaves the would-be catcher underconstrained and it permits some running paths that simply would not work. When two angles get larger and *then smaller* in proportion, a linear optical trajectory is still created, but the ball cannot be caught. Only if the vertical optical acceleration is also cancelled, Dannemiller, Babler and Babler (1996) claimed, will the LOT strategy work. A second problem with the LOT model is that it cannot explain the catching of balls flying in the sagittal plane, where angle β stays at 0°. A separate theory would be required to explain catching under these task constraints. Most devastating to the LOT theory are recent demonstrations that the locomotion patterns of catchers simply do not correspond to those that the model predicts (McLeod, Reed and Dienes, 2001).

The consequences of drag

Projectile trajectories get much more complicated than parabolas when drag (friction between ball and air) comes into play. Among the variables that affect drag are the mass, size, and shape of the projectile, and various characteristics of the air, such as temperature, humidity, pressure, and currents. Even the nature of the surface and the spin on the projectile can influence its trajectory, which is why, for example, major-league pitchers and professional cricketers 'rough up' a ball or try to spin it when pitching and bowling. The consequences of drag on ball trajectories are not trivial, especially when the ball is very light or when high speeds are involved. For example, the drag force on a baseball thrown at 43 m/s, the speed of a well-pitched fastball, is equal to the gravitational force. Also, a ball batted at an angle of 35° from the horizontal at a velocity of 62 m/s will go only about half as far in Shea Stadium (sea level) as it would in a vacuum (Adair,[1] 1990).

Brancazio (1985) was the first scientist to claim that the trajectories of baseballs are so non-parabolic as to threaten the Chapman Strategy. To take the example given above, if one ran with a constant velocity that had cancelled optical acceleration when the ball was first hit at an angle of 35° and a velocity of 62 m/s, one would end up more than 100 m from where the ball landed. Of course, the Chapman Strategy is not a ballistic strategy; running is presumed to be continuously coupled to the ball's optical acceleration. In that regard, the Chapman Strategy is self-correcting and would eventually bring the would-be catcher to the right place at the right time, even though running speed and direction might change. Two empirical lines of evidence favour a continuous-coupling view over a predict-landing-then-run theory. First, stationary observers cannot accurately judge whether they could run to catch a ball that will not land at their position. The 'catchableness'

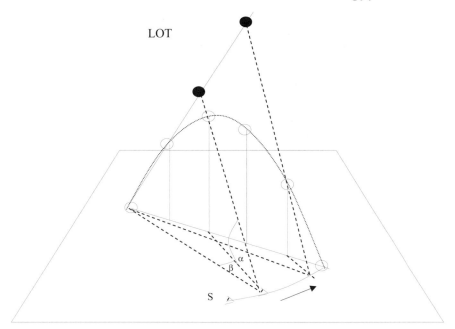

Figure 9.3 The LOT model applies when the ball does not fly in the catcher's sagittal plane. The catcher must go from the starting point, S, to where the ball comes down. According to McBeath, Schaffer and Kaiser (1995), one will get linear optical trajectories when the tangents of angles a and b change proportionally. Angle a is the vertical angle of the ball; b is the horizontal angle. The LOT model predicts curvilinear running paths and non-constant running velocities. After McBeath, Schaffer and Kaiser (1995).

of a ball only becomes apparent when the catcher is running (Oudejans, Michaels, Bakker and Dolné, 1996). As outlined in Chapter 1, this finding fits neatly with the Gibsonian idea of 'acting to perceive and perceiving to act'. Second, it has been shown that people have difficulty predicting where the ball will land in a computerised ball-catching game (Saxberg, 1987).

Brancazio (1985) claimed that not only did drag pose a threat to the Chapman Strategy, but also that the optical acceleration hypothesis is flawed by the fact that it deals with the tangents of optical angles, rather than optical angles themselves (see also McBeath, Schaffer and Kaiser, 1995). The underlying idea is that the visual system picks up optical angles, rather than the tangents of optical angles. However, it seems to us that this argument confuses optical patterns with the mechanisms that might pick them up. If one shows that a catcher's locomotion strategy is consistent with cancelling the acceleration of the tangent of the elevation angle, then it is up to neuroscientists to figure out the nature of the mechanism (cf. the integrative modelling approach to studying interceptive actions proposed in the chapter by Keil and Bennett). One should not presuppose that the visual system cannot (learn to) trade in the tangents of optical angles. Nevertheless, it is interesting to ask whether a strategy related to rates of change of optical angles, rather than their tangents, might provide the basis for locomoting to catch. Such a strategy was presented by Brancazio (1985).

Angular optical acceleration

For small angles, an optical angle is essentially equal to its tangent,[2] so a strategy of cancelling the acceleration of the tangent hardly differs from cancelling the acceleration of an optical angle itself. As the angle gets larger and larger, however, the two strategies depart more and more from each other and the latter strategy ultimately fails. Obviously, a projectile moving at a constant angular velocity will *always* eventually sail over the would-be catcher's head. To maintain a theory that angular acceleration, rather than acceleration of the tangent, is cancelled, Brancazio (1985) had to suggest a two-part strategy: cancel angular acceleration at small angles, then shift over to a strategy of cancelling angular velocity (i.e., hold the angle of the ball constant). McLeod and Dienes (1996; see also Dienes and McLeod, 1993) pointed out some problems with the constant-velocity strategy and suggested an alternative – that one should let the optical angle continue to rise, but not let it get above 90°.

Brancazio (1985) also points out that if the task is to cancel angular acceleration, rather than acceleration of the tangent, the problems of detecting angular acceleration could be solved by using vestibular, rather than retinal, mechanisms of detection. We do know that, at least under normal illumination, catchers track the ball with eye and head movements (Oudejans, Michaels, Bakker and Davids, 1999). This means that the image of the ball is more or less stationary on the retina, except for retinal slip. If retinal mechanisms were involved in detecting optical acceleration, then they would have to detect the acceleration of background motion (e.g. images of the stadium or clouds). The alternative is that the detection depends on non-retinal mechanisms. To determine whether pickup is by retinal or extra-retinal mechanisms, Oudejans, Michaels, Bakker and Davids (1999) had people try to catch luminous balls in the dark. Assuming that people also track the luminous ball in the dark (and that is to be expected because there is nothing else in the dark to fixate on), there would be no motion at all on the retina. It was reasoned that if people could not catch the balls in the dark, retinal mechanisms would be implicated, and if they could catch the balls, extra-retinal mechanisms would be implicated. It was found that people could run and catch the balls in the dark! As Brancazio (1985) pointed out, the vestibular system is a good candidate because it has a well-understood mechanism – the semicircular canals – for detecting (changing) angular velocities in the sagittal plane. Oudejans, Michaels, Bakker and Davids (1999) concluded that optical acceleration seems to be picked up by mechanisms that are not normally considered as part of the visual system.

Catching in a CAVE

The empirical research laid out above involved either psychophysical studies in which participants had to judge the landing of balls simulated on rather small computer screens or the tracking of real catchers catching real balls. The former has the disadvantage that the successive illumination of several pixels on a computer screen may not optimally stimulate visual systems and making judgements about landing positions certainly does not approximate running. Studying real catching of real balls by tracking the catcher's movements and relating these to the ball paths would ultimately provide the answers on the use of an optical acceleration strategy or not. However, studying catching in the field is very labour-intensive, which usually leads to a rather limited set of conditions and limited numbers of trials. Furthermore, one has to live with the physical constraints of real life. One cannot easily manipulate ball paths, speeds, and so on, to give us a set of conditions to differentiate among different candidate variables and strategies. However, such manipulations are possible using virtual reality simulations.

In virtual reality, ball trajectories, optics, and much more can easily be changed from trial to trial. Thus, we recently started to study ball catching in a CAVE (Cave Automated Virtual Environment). The CAVE is a 3 m by 3 m by 3 m space, on the three walls and the floor of which a computer-created world can be projected. The projections are updated with respect to the position of a freely moving observer in the CAVE. This outcome is achieved by having the observer wear a marker that is tracked by a motion-registration system, and by updating the display to the new registered position. In our first experiments (Zaal and Michaels, 1999), participants had to try to intercept virtual balls in one condition; in another condition, they stood in one place and indicated whether the ball would land in front of or behind them by pushing one of two buttons. It turned out that our participants were not very successful at intercepting the virtual balls with a hand-held joystick. However, the next experiment suggested that they were able to intercept balls with their heads, as if heading a ball in soccer (Zaal and Michaels, 2001). The same participants were also able to indicate where the ball would land (in front or behind). One interesting finding was that the timing of participants' judgements could be predicted from the optical acceleration profiles. Different ball trajectories gave rise to different optical accelerations and decelerations. Assuming that there exists some threshold for detecting a change in velocity, one would expect earlier judgements on the balls accelerating or decelerating more rapidly than on balls accelerating or decelerating more slowly. Figure 9.4 shows that this is essentially what we found in the experiments.

Comparisons of the head movements of our participants in the catching and judging tasks revealed a surprising difference between the tasks (see Figure 9.5). When asked to *catch* a virtual ball, catchers tracked the ball with their heads (we did not monitor eye movements, but presumably they track the ball with their eyes as well), as had been seen before in the Oudejans, Michaels, Bakker and Davids (1999) study. In contrast, however, when asked to *judge* whether the ball will land in front or behind, participants tended to look straight ahead; they did not track

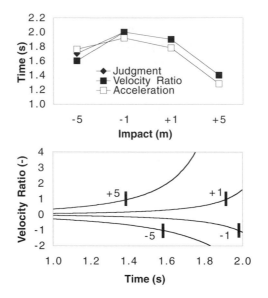

Figure 9.4 Balls that landed far from a (stationary) observer had higher optical accelerations (and velocity ratios) than balls that landed close to the observer (impact distance is in metres: 5 m is far and 1 m is close by; positive numbers are balls landing behind the observer, negative number are balls landing in front of the observer). Assuming a threshold of 1 (optical velocity ratio does not have a dimension), observers should identify most quickly where balls would land if balls would land 5 m behind them, a little later if balls would land 5 m in front of them, notably later if balls would land 1 m behind them, and latest if balls would land 1 m in front of them. This is exactly what we see in the data (upper panel).

the ball. Notice from Figure 9.4 that the judgements occurred well after the 240 ms that Sharp and Whiting (1975) have associated with the use of the eye/head system (vs. the image/retina system), so the effect is not an artefact of not having enough time to initiate tracking. Might these findings be interpreted as showing that judging and catching are different tasks, which shows up in the different head movements in the two situations? This possible difference in detection strategy raises concerns about the generality of all simulation studies done in the optical-acceleration paradigm (and perhaps in more paradigms). Our findings that people use optical acceleration for their judgements of where a ball will land, then, may have little to say about what information they would use in a real catching situation. However, before leaping too far in our conclusions, the difference in looking behaviour may be due to the fact that catchers need to see the ball for longer to make a catch, compared to task constraints under which perceivers need to make a perceptual judgement about landing location.

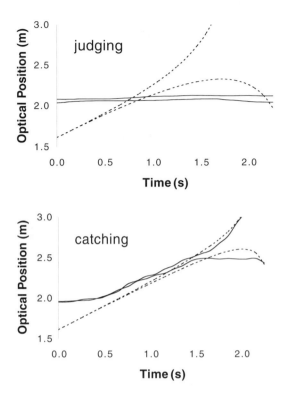

Figure 9.5 People tend to track the ball with head rotations if they are trying to catch it, but not if they are judging where it will land. The dashed lines in the two figures are the projections of the ball on the CAVE front wall in two situations, one of a ball landing in front of the observer and one of a ball landing behind the observer. The solid lines are the projections on the same wall of the participant's head orientation. There are flat lines in the judging conditions and tracking in the catching conditions.

Other variables?

Thus far we have looked at several possible bases to inform locomotion for catching balls: the presence of acceleration or deceleration on the image plane, the presence of angular acceleration or deceleration, the presence of angular velocity, and the optical pattern associated with the LOT model. Are there other possibilities? If one considers only the case of balls in the sagittal plane, there are not many possibilities left, especially if we think about baseball, where the outfielder can be 100 m from where the ball is hit. Such distances are too far for binocular disparity and rate of change of binocular disparity (Regan, 1997). Similarly, optical expansion rate, whatever that might offer (see, for example, Todd, 1981), would be well below threshold. Sound is sometimes suggested as a possible basis for helping the catcher (see Chapter 10 by Button), but it could take 0.3 s or so for the sound of bat–ball contact to reach the outfield. Add reaction time to that and it becomes apparent that catchers would not have enough time to rely on auditory information to successfully catch fly balls.

The angular velocity at which the ball rises is another variable that might support catching. On average a ball with a higher velocity will go higher than a ball with a lower velocity. However, height is not all that interesting to a player confined to the ground. Height may be interesting as a metric of time – how long before the ball hits the ground, but not as a metric of distance – how far the ball will go before it hits the ground. In fact, for any given initial ball velocity, there is a non-monotonic relation between vertical optical velocity and distance travelled. A ball with a low vertical velocity will not go far because it does not stay in the air long enough to travel far. A ball with a high vertical velocity (a pop-up) will also not go far. The intermediate values will go the farthest.

What about a combination of variables? It may be that professional outfielders are so tuned to all the regularities of the game that they perceive kinetic energies of the ball and bat before bat–ball contact, the angle of the bat swing, the location of the collision on the bat relative to the centre of percussion, the sound of bat–ball contact, and the horizontal and vertical impact angles. But even a physicist having all that information, plus knowledge of the spin on the ball, atmospheric pressure, and humidity cannot accurately predict where the ball will land (Adair, 1990). Given that level of understanding, we think the current best bets are a self-correcting strategy based on vertical optical acceleration or a combination of angular acceleration + zeroing velocity, with the acceleration perhaps being detected by non-retinal mechanisms.

Notes

1   Robert Adair was Physicist to the National League, 1987–1989. His book *The Physics of Baseball* is an informative and delightful book for any baseball fan.
2   At an angle of 10°, an angle and its tangent differ by about 1 per cent; at 20°, 4 per cent; and 30°, 10 per cent. These correspond to angles in radians of 0.18, 0.36, and 0.58, which can be compared to Figure 9.2.

References

Adair, R.K. (1990). *The Physics of Baseball*. New York: Harper and Row.
Babler, T.G. and Dannemiller, J.L. (1993). Role of image acceleration in judging landing location of free-falling projectiles. *Journal of Experimental Psychology: Human Perception and Performance* **19**, 15–31.
Brancazio, P.J. (1985). Looking into Chapman's homer: the physics of judging a fly ball. *American Journal of Physics* **53**, 849–55.
Calderone, J.B. and Kaiser, M.K. (1989). Visual acceleration detection: effect of sign and motion orientation. *Perception and Psychophysics* **45**, 391–4.
Chapman, S. (1968). Catching a baseball. *American Journal of Physics* **36**, 868–70.
Dannemiller, J.L., Babler, T.G. and Babler, B.L. (1996). On catching fly balls, 'Technical Comments', *Science* **273**, 256–7.

Dienes, Z. and McLeod, P. (1993). How to catch a cricket ball. *Perception* 22, 1427–39.

Gottsdanker, R., Frick, J.W. and Lockard, R.B. (1961). Identifying the acceleration of visual targets. *British Journal of Psychology* 52, 31–42.

Kugler, P.N. and Turvey, M.T. (1987). *Information, Natural Law, and the Self-Assembly of Rhythmic Movement*. Hillsdale, NJ: Erlbaum.

McBeath, M.K., Shaffer, D.M. and Kaiser, M.K. (1995). How baseball outfielders determine where to run to catch fly balls. *Science* 268, 569–73.

McLeod, P. and Dienes, Z. (1993). Running to catch the ball. *Nature* 362, 23.

McLeod, P. and Dienes, Z. (1996). Do catchers know where to go to catch the ball or only how to get there? *Journal of Experimental Psychology: Human Perception and Performance* 22, 531–43.

McLeod, P., Reed, N. and Dienes, Z. (2001). Towards a unified fielder theory: what we do not yet know about how people run to catch a ball. *Journal of Experimental Psychology: Human Perception and Performance* 27, 1347–55.

Michaels, C.F. and Oudejans, R.R.D. (1992). The optics and actions of catching fly balls: zeroing out optical acceleration. *Ecological Psychology* 4, 199–222.

Oudejans, R.R.D., Michaels, C.F., Bakker, F.C. and Davids, K. (1999). Shedding some light on catching in the dark: perceptual mechanisms for catching fly balls. *Journal of Experimental Psychology: Human Perception and Performance* 25, 531–42.

Oudejans, R.R.D., Michaels, C.F., Bakker, F.C. and Dolné, M. (1996). The relevance of action in perceiving affordances: perception of catchableness of fly balls. *Journal of Experimental Psychology: Human Perception and Performance* 23, 879–91.

Regan, D. (1997). Visual factors in hitting and catching. *Journal of Sport Sciences* 15, 533–58.

Runeson, S. (1974). Constant velocity – not perceived as such. *Psychological Research* 37, 3–23.

Saxberg, B.V.H. (1987). Projected free fall trajectories: II. Human Experiments. *Biological Cybernetics* 56, 177–84.

Sharp, R.H. and Whiting, H.T.A. (1975). Information-processing and eye movement behaviour in a ball catching skill. *Journal of Human Movement Studies* 1, 124–31.

Todd, J.T. (1981). Visual information about moving objects. *Journal of Experimental Psychology: Human Perception and Performance* 7, 795–810.

Tresilian, J.R. (1995). Study of a servo-control strategy for projectile interception. *The Quarterly Journal of Experimental Psychology* 48A, 688–715.

Warren, W.H., Jr. (1988). Action modes and laws of control for the visual guidance of action. In O.G. Meijer and K. Roth (eds), *Complex Movement Behaviour: 'The' Motor Action Controversy*. Amsterdam: North Holland.

Zaal, F.T.J.M. and Michaels, C.F. (1999). Catching and judging fly balls in a CAVE™. In M.A. Grealy and J.A. Thomson (eds), S*tudies in Perception and Action V.* Mahwah, NJ: Erlbaum.

Zaal, F.T.J.M. and Michaels, C.F. (2001). The information for catching fly balls: judging and intercepting virtual balls in a CAVE. Submitted for publication.

10 Auditory information and the co-ordination of one-handed catching

Chris Button

Understanding the relationship between key informational constraints, provided by the visual, auditory and proprioceptive perceptual sytems, and human goal-directed behaviour remains a major goal of researchers working from an ecological perspective on perception and action. Many of the other chapters in this book show that the majority of previous research on perception–action couplings during ball catching has tended to focus on the role of visual information as a constraint on co-ordination (e.g. see Bennett, Davids and Woodcock, 1999; Savelsbergh, Whiting and Bootsma, 1991; Smyth and Mariott, 1982). However, Keele and Summers (1976) suggested many years ago that the auditory perceptual system may actually be superior to the visual system in supporting the temporal patterning of movements. This may be the case particularly in ball games where the time constraints for performing hitting or striking actions dictate the need to initiate movement prior to, or at least by the initiation of ball flight (Land and McLeod, 2000; Williams, Davids and Williams, 1999).

The role of auditory information in sport: some examples

Clear anecdotal evidence exists to support the important role of auditory information in sport. For example, in volleyball, the sound of the setter's fingers contacting the ball can give additional information to blockers about whether a short, shoot or long set is being played. Volleyball coaches have long understood this point and have designed practices to occlude vision of the setter's hands, forcing blockers to seek other sources of perceptual support for their decision-making and timing. Similarly, in table tennis, and other racket sports, the sound of bat–ball contact at the serve can give the experienced player important anticipatory information about the type of spin being imparted onto the ball. For this reason, some table-tennis coaches advocate that servers stamp their foot during the serving action in order to disguise the sound of bat–ball contact for the receiver.

Theoretical observations

In contemporary motor control literature, there is currently an increasing amount of empirical support for the view that haptic, proprioceptive and auditory information may act as important constraints on the emergence of co-ordination in movement systems (Beak, Davids and Bennett, 2002; Collins and DeLuca, 1993, 1995; Riley, Wong, Mitra and Turvey, 1997). For example, Warren, Kim and Husney (1987) showed that the auditory perception of elastic properties of a bouncing ball can inform a performer about its rebound height. It has been demonstrated that auditory information can play an important role in informing a performer about environmental events and properties, such as when an approaching object will pass close by for interception.

Some studies have shown that when visual information from ball flight is occluded, successful catchers can engage in 'perceptual and motor substitution' to intercept the ball (Lacquiniti and Maioli, 1989a, 1989b). The implication is that when visual information from ball flight is perturbed, other sources of perceptual information can be used to constrain the timing of the grasp action as catchers successfully adapt their behaviour to achieve the task goal. The co-ordination pattern used by good catchers is different when visual and non-visual sources of information constrain the timing of interceptive actions. An interesting question to arise from the suggestion of 'perceptual and motor substitution' is whether the removal of auditory informational constraints at the point of ball projection has similar effects on the nature of the emergent co-ordination patterns used by catchers.

Some previous work on auditory information constraints has looked at how hearing-impaired individuals cope with timing interceptive actions, compared to age-related hearing individuals. Savelsbergh, Netelenbos and Whiting (1991) examined differences in catching ability between deaf and hearing children aged between ten and twelve years. In deaf children, auditory perception of information from ball release cannot occur and cannot, therefore, aid co-ordination of hand transport and prehension phases of catching. The authors found that deaf children could satisfy the task constraints of one-handed catching as successfully as hearing children, although they had problems with balls approaching them from the periphery or outside the field of view. However, it was found that deaf children showed later initiation times after ball release from a ball machine, although no differences were found in overall movement times between the deaf and hearing children. It seems likely that there was a compensation in the co-ordination of the hand transport and grasp phases, for the deaf children, due to the lack of auditory information about projectile release. Unfortunately this study did not provide a detailed kinematic analysis of the temporal co-ordination of the catching action to help understanding on whether co-ordination differs when auditory information from projection was available.

To summarise the previous literature, much work examining ball catching has focused on the role of visual information as a constraint on co-ordination. There have been some previous suggestions that auditory information could also act a significant constraint on co-ordinating interceptive tasks. The existing evidence for this statement is mainly anecdotal, and the small amount of empirical support is based on outcome measures such as accuracy and error scores, or has involved congenitally deaf children. There has been no previous work looking at processes of perceptual and motor substitution in hearing participants when auditory informational constraints have been systematically manipulated.

Experimental work to examine auditory information as a constraint on one-handed catching

In the remainder of this chapter, an experiment to examine the effects of removal of auditory information prior to ball release in a one-handed catching task in hearing participants is described. Since auditory information from ball release was being removed rather than ongoing trajectory or velocity-related information concerning the ball-path, it was expected that the influence of this type of informational constraint would only be observed at the beginning of the action (i.e., at movement initiation). In the experiment, it was decided to use skilled catchers as participants to ascertain what effect (if any) perturbing auditory information might have on the co-ordination of well established perception–action couplings. If unskilled catchers were used in the experiment, there was a possibility that they had not yet discovered the utility of auditory information for timing the initiation of catching movements. A specific question of interest was: if alterations to motor patterns were observed in non-auditory conditions, what particular effects would be noted on the coupling of the grasp and transport phases of the one-handed catch?

In the study, eight participants (four males, four females, mean age = 27.6 years) volunteered to take part. All participants were right-hand dominant with normal vision. A pre-test ($n = 20$ trials) conducted on a within-task criterion (i.e. the one-handed catching task) confirmed that all participants could be considered skilled catchers with at least a 75 per cent success rate. This is an important method for sampling an appropriate skill level for the study. Typically in ball-catching studies, a ball-projection machine has been used in order that the location and speed of ball feed can be experimentally controlled (e.g. Bennett, Davids and Woodcock, 1999; Tayler and Davids, 1997; Savelsbergh, Netelenbos and Whiting, 1991b). Such machines (e.g. the Bola Ball Trainer, Stuart and Williams, Bristol, UK) generally emit a low-pitched clicking noise as the ball is mechanically fed into the machine giving participants an advance 'warning' approximately 100 ms before actual ball release. During pilot work in other studies, participants have revealed qualitative perceptions that auditory information from the ball machine seemed helpful for timing the initiation of their movements. In the study described here, a repeated-measures experimental design was employed, with all participants tested in experimental and control conditions. Auditory information from the ball-machine was present in the control condition but was eliminated in the experimental (non-auditory) condition. To remove auditory information, participants wore foam ear plugs and head phones which emitted white noise. Manipulation checks were made prior to testing, usually by calling out the participant's name from behind. Testing began when participants reported being unable to hear any noise from the ball machine or ball whilst wearing the head phones. The presentation of the two conditions was counterbalanced across participants (i.e. half the participants performed the auditory condition first, the other half had the non-auditory condition first). There were 20 trials to be performed in each condition and each testing session took approximately one hour.

In the study, participants were required to perform one-handed catches whilst sitting upright in a chair.[1] Pressurised tennis balls (Donnay) were projected to the participant at an initial velocity of approximately 8 m s^{-1} with a tennis ball projection machine (Bola Ball Trainer, Stuart and Williams, Bristol, UK) placed 5.5 m away. The flight time of the ball for each trial was approximately 750 ms. The ball machine was located such that each ball flew to the right hand side of the seated participant at knee height. Pilot work had shown that the ball trajectory was accurate within a circular area of approximately 30 cm^2. The loading of the ball machine was hidden from the participant behind a black curtain, so that they had no visual information concerning when the ball was about to be released through a hole in the curtain.

Located on the right hand side of the participant was an on-line motion analysis system (Elite system, Italy) which allowed the analysis of kinematic variables. Two cameras with a sampling frequency of 100 Hz, were placed 3.5 m from the participant at a 40 degree intra-camera angle. Reflective markers (10 mm) were placed on the anterior aspect of the wrist, elbow and gleno-humeral joints of the right arm and also on the medial surfaces of the thumb and index finger. The resulting x, y and z axis displacement data were then smoothed using a digital filter with a variable cut-off frequency (D'Amico and Ferrigno, 1992). Whilst the majority of the movement typically took place in the anterior–posterior plane, the lateral variability of ball-path necessitated a three-dimensional kinematic analysis. Hence the dependent variables reported in this chapter are resultant values calculated from the anterior-posterior, lateral and vertical planes.

The maximum velocity of the wrist (MWV) was derived from the movement of the wrist joint centre marker. Several temporal variables were also calculated for each trial. Initiation time (IT) was defined as the moment at which movement began following ball release. Movement time (MT) was calculated from the time at which the maximal closing velocity of the hand was zero (i.e. when the ball was caught) minus the time at which the movement started (IT). The displacement of the wrist from the starting position (MWD) was measured at the end of each trial as an indication of where the termination of the movement took place. Only the last six caught balls of both testing sessions were included in the kinematic analysis. By using the last few trials the participants had enough time to familiarise themselves with the task before kinematic data were collected. Dependent t-tests were carried out on the raw data of the dependent variables.

A comparison between the two conditions for all participants revealed that 12 out of 160 trials in total (7.5 per cent) were dropped in the auditory condition whilst only six trials (3.25 per cent) were dropped in the non-auditory condition. When compared with a dependent t-test, this difference in catching performance was not significant, $t(7) = 1.00$, $p = 0.351$. So, clearly the skilled catchers were able to adapt to differing informational constraints. The question is: did they adapt their co-ordination patterns to ensure successful catching?

Table 10.1   Descriptive group statistics for selected kinematic variables in the auditory and non-auditory conditions. Group means are in bold type, between-subject standard deviations are below in normal type font.

Kinematic variables	Auditory	Non-auditory
Initiation time	**276**	**310**
(ms)	66	52
MOV	**250**	**340**
(mm s^{-1})	80	130
Time of MOV	**319**	**371**
(ms prior to catch)	59	69
MCV	**−270**	**−367**
(mm s^{-1})	100	115
Time of MCV	**123**	**165**
(ms prior to catch)	57	39
MWD	**767**	**792**
(mm)	58	107

The means and standard deviations for the selected kinematics variables are illustrated in Table 10.1. Pooled group data demonstrated a significant effect in MOV, t (7) = 8.16, p < 0.03. For the non-auditory condition, MOV was generally increased (345 mm s^{-1}) compared to the auditory condition (260 mm s^{-1}). Another group effect concerning the co-ordination of grasp was an increased MCV, also observed in the non-auditory condition compared to the auditory condition (366 mm s^{-1} vs. 269 mm s^{-1}), t (7) = 5.77, p < 0.05. The times at which maximum opening and closing velocity of the hand were attained prior to ball contact were also compared in both conditions. Pooling across all participants, MCV occurred earlier in the non-auditory condition (0.17 s prior to hand–ball contact, compared to 0.12 s), t (7) = 7.05, p < 0.03. None of the other dependent variables, such as initiation time or MWD, differed significantly between conditions.

An even more interesting picture emerges when the data were analysed at an individual level. In this type of analysis it was observed that the increase in MOV and MCV in the non-auditory condition rarely reached conventional levels of statistical significance (0.05 level) (only for MOV of Participant 8 in the study). This finding might be attributed to the high levels of variance across trials that most participants exhibited.[2] Group comparisons of the standard deviations of these variables revealed no significant effects between conditions. In order to examine the way in which each participant attempted to satisfy the task constraints of the different conditions, profiling of the co-ordination patterns assembled by each individual was undertaken. This is an important requirement in studies of co-ordination of interceptive actions because of evidence that common optimal movement patterns do not exist, particularly in highly skilled performers (see Bauer and Schöllhorn, 1997; Brisson and Alain, 1996; Button and Davids, 1999;

and Chapter 16 by Lees and Davids). For these analyses, mixed model Anova (2 conditions × 6 trials) were carried out on each dependent variable. In this chapter, to exemplify these analyses, the results of three participants are detailed below.

Participants 3 and 5

These participants typified those who showed an increased initiation time in the non-auditory condition and also increased wrist velocities. Sample trials of participant 5 (see Figure 10.1a) reflect the general trend of increased movement time in the non-auditory condition. Furthermore, the time of MOV was earlier for both of these participants relative to the point of contact with the ball in the non-auditory condition (see Figure 10.1b). This finding indicates that these participants were able to flexibly co-ordinate and re-arrange hand and transport kinematics depending on whether auditory information was available or not.

Participant 8

Initiation time was also increased for this participant in the non-auditory condition, as was movement time. The opening velocity of the hand was greater and the timing of MOV was also earlier when auditory information was not available. Spatial plots of hand position in sample trials can be observed in Figure 10.2. This participant tended to catch the ball nearer the body when auditory information was not available.

So, what can be learned from the experiment described in this chapter? To start with, one striking feature of the data was the similarity of the outcome scores under both conditions. Results indicated that very few balls were dropped even when auditory information of ball release was not present. These data on the performance of skilled catchers suggest that the information used to assemble the catching action can, at least in part, be specified by auditory information. In line with previous investigators (e.g. Lacquiniti and Maioli, 1989a, 1989b; Van der Kamp, Vereijken and Savelsbergh, 1996) it appears that a multiple source strategy may be used for catching. Skilled participants can make use of different types of information (e.g. visual, auditory, proprioceptive, haptic) to support catching behaviour, as performance conditions change. The notion of flexible re-assembly of perception–action couplings under differing informational constraints is supported by observing the kinematic data on the actual co-ordination patterns used to achieve the task goal. While catching performance, as indexed by gross outcome measures, seemed unaffected by the auditory manipulation, fine-grained analysis of the co-ordination of the movement patterns showed a clear effect. At the level of group comparisons between conditions, the timing of MCV and MOV generally occurred earlier without auditory information of ball projection.

In previous work by Savelsbergh, Whiting and Bootsma (1991), it was argued that the timing of MCV relative to hand–ball contact was geared to changes in visual information (even when these changes were made during the last 200 ms of ball flight). The observed re-organisation of motor patterns by participants in the

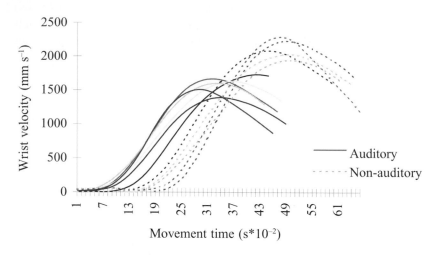

Figure 10.1a   Sample trials taken from participant 5. Wrist velocity is plotted against time.

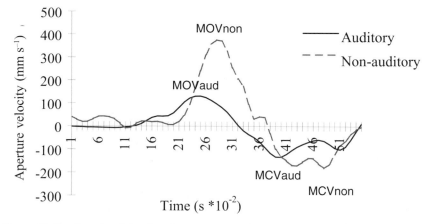

Figure 10.1b   Sample trials taken from participant 5. Aperture velocity is plotted against time.

non-auditory condition of the study described in this chapter confirmed that relevant sources of auditory information (the noise of the ball being fed into the ball machine) may also contribute to perception of time-to-contact information (in conjunction with visual information from the ball). In the study described, the auditory information providing potential time-to-contact information occurred about 100 ms *before* ball flight. The adjustments in both MCV and MOV under non-auditory informational constraints seem to have occurred as a direct result of

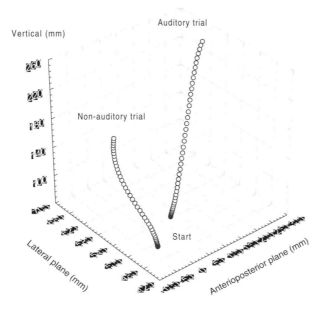

Figure 10.2   3-D space plots of wrist displacement during sample trials taken from participant 8. The location of ball-contact is represented relative to the start position of the hand. Note that this participant implemented a strategy of varying the location of the catch.

the delay in movement initiation time for several participants. Since auditory information at release was the only constraint manipulated in the experimental setting, it is feasible that these participants were using it to time the initiation of movement. Furthermore, it became apparent that participants generally exhibited a large degree of variability in MOV and MCV from trial-to-trial. It seems likely that the co-ordination of grasp and transport phases exhibits functional inter-trial variability in order to adapt to small, unexpected variations in ball flight (Button, Davids, Bennett and Tayler, 2000).

The most consistent observation highlighted in this chapter was that participants generally initiated movements later in the non-auditory condition. In order to intercept the ball after this delayed initiation, some participants (three out of eight) used a strategy of moving the catching hand more quickly toward the approaching ball (increased wrist velocity). An example from one of the individual kinematic profiles illustrates this point (see Figure 10.1a). Increased wrist velocity can be observed in the non-auditory condition for participant 5. However, in order to compensate for the later initiation time in this condition, this participant altered not only the transport phase of the action but also the grasping component (see Figure 10.1b). The increased opening velocity of the hand was also necessary in the auditory condition to maintain the coupling of transport and grasp phases, and achieve the task goal.

It is evident from the individual co-ordination profiles that any adjustments to the action were idiosyncratic, reflecting how each individual obtained different solutions to the constraints imposed by the experimental manipulation. For example, another strategy employed, if the overall movement time was increased in either condition, was to catch the ball nearer to the body. Sample trials depicting the displacement of the wrist during the catching action show this strategy clearly (see Figure 10.2). These findings support the arguments proposed by many theorists that perceptual and motor substitution is a hallmark of skilled behaviour (Lacquiniti and Maioli, 1989a, 1989b: Schmidt and Fitzpatrick, 1996; Fitzpatrick, 1998; Beek and Bingham, 1991). That is, in order to achieve an intended outcome goal, skilled performers have become flexibly attuned to the various sources of information available in specific performance contexts to support actions. The data showing such high levels of on-line variability are difficult to reconcile with the idea that catching movements may be pre-programmed in advance. As constraints on performance change, perhaps through unforeseen occlusion of typically available information, skilled performers are able to immediately re-assemble a perception–action coupling by substituting other available sources of information to achieve the same task goals. That is, through experience, they might become better attuned to multiple information sources that can be used to guide the co-ordination of the arm and hand in catching (Van der Kamp, Vereijken and Savelsbergh, 1996).

To conclude, taken as whole, data from the previous literature reviewed in this chapter indicate that auditory information provided prior to the perception of visual information from ball flight, can also be used by skilled performers to time the initiation of an interceptive action. The data fit with other previous work on the role of audition in regulating ongoing movement behaviours such as postural control and rhythmical actions (Collins and DeLuca, 1993; 1995; Davids, Button and Bennett, 1999). The role of auditory information in successful interceptive actions can be described as non-essential, but nevertheless contributory in skilled performers, especially if objects approach from within the field of view (see also Savelsbergh, Netelenbos and Whiting, 1991b). Generally, movement initiation time was later when auditory information was removed. This key finding suggests that some individuals are better than others in adopting a multi-source strategy to exploit auditory information to support action.

Finally, the individual nature of the catching responses that were exhibited lends further support to the use of participant-specific kinematic analyses in future studies of movement co-ordination (Beek, Rikkert and van Wieringen, 1996). Further work is needed to examine whether perturbing informational constraints during interceptive actions could be a useful strategy in allowing learners to acquire skill in perceptual and motor substitutions. In particular, it would be interesting to investigate how individuals develop perception–action couplings based on the interaction of various sources of (visual and non-visual) information under a variety of task constraints (Newell and Slifkin, 1998).

Notes

1 The participants were seated to ensure that any changes in co-ordination was limited to the catching arm. Had they been standing (the typical posture adopted in catching experiments) they might have compensated for the lack of auditory information by stepping forward or backward, introducing more possible confounding variables.

2 Note that for the majority of participants there were often high levels of standard deviation for MOV and MCV. I believe that inter-trial variance masked individual effects. However the pooled group analysis does not reflect this variance as it was based on mean averages.

References

Bauer, H.U. and Schöllhorn, W. (1997). Self-organizing maps for the analysis of complex movement patterns. *Neural Processing Letters* **5**, 193–9.

Beak, S., Davids, K. and Bennett, S.J. (2002). Child's play: children's sensitivity to haptic information in perceiving affordances of rackets for striking a ball. In J.E. Clark and J. Humphreys (eds), *Motor Development: Research and Reviews, V.2*. Reston, VA: NASPE.

Beek, P.J. and Bingham, G.P. (1991). Task-specific dynamics and the study of perception and action: a reaction to von Hofsten (1989). *Ecological Psychology* **3**, 35–54.

Beek, P.J., Rikkert, W.E.I. and van Wieringen, P.C.W. (1996). Limit cycle properties of rhythmic forearm movements. *Journal of Experimental Psychology: Human Perception and Performance* **22**, 1077–93.

Bennett, S.J., Davids, K. and Woodcock, J. (1999). The structural organisation of practice: the effects of practicing under different informational constraints on the acquisition of one-handed catching skill. *Journal of Motor Behaviour* **31**, 3–9.

Brisson, T.A. and Alain, C. (1996). Should common optimal movement patterns be identified as the criterion to be achieved? *Journal of Motor Behavior* **28**, 211–23.

Button, C., Davids, K., Bennett, S.J. and Tayler, M. (2001). Mechanical perturbation of the wrist during one-handed catching. *Acta Psychologica* **105**, 1, 9–30.

Button, C. and Davids, K. (1999). Interacting intrinsic dynamics and intentionality requires co-ordination profiling of movement systems. In J. Thomson, D.N. Lee and M. Grealy (eds), *Studies in Perception and Action*, Vol. 10. Mahwah, NJ: Erlbaum Associates.

Collins, J.J. and De Luca, C.J. (1993). Open-loop and closed-loop control of posture: a random-walk analysis of center of pressure trajectories. *Experimental Brain Research* **103**, 308–18.

Collins, J.J. and De Luca, C.J. (1995). The effect of visual input on open-loop and closed-loop postural control mechanisms. *Experimental Brain Research* **103**, 151–63.

D'Amico, M. and Ferrigno, G. (1992). Comparison between the more recent techniques for smoothing and derivative assessment in biomechanics. *Medical and Biological Engineering and Computing* **30**, 193–204.

Davids, K., Button, C. and Bennett, S.J. (1999) Modeling human motor systems in nonlinear dynamics: intentionality and discrete movement behaviours. *Nonlinear Dynamics, Psychology and Life Sciences* **3**, 3–30.

Fitzpatrick, P. (1998). Modeling co-ordination dynamics in development. In K.M. Newell and P.C.M. Molenaar (eds), *Applications of Nonlinear Dynamics to Developmental Process Modeling*. Mahwah, NJ: Lawrence Erlbaum Associates.

Keele, S.W. and Summers J.J. (1976). The structure of motor programs. In G.E. Stelmach (ed.), *Motor Control: Issues and Trends*. New York: Grune and Stratton.

Lacquiniti, F. and Maioli, C. (1989a). The role of preparation in tuning anticipatory and reflex responses during catching. *Journal of Neuroscience* **9**, 134–48.

Lacquiniti, F. and Maioli, C. (1989b). Adaptation to suppression of visual information during catching. *Journal of Neuroscience* **9**, 149–59.

Land, M.F. and McLeod, P. (2000). From eye movements to actions: how batsmen hit the ball. *Nature Neuroscience* **3**, 1340–5

Newell, K.M. and Slifkin, A.B. (1998). The nature of movement variability. In J.P. Piek (ed.), *Motor Behaviour and Human Skill: A Multidisciplinary Perspective*. Champaign, IL: Human Kinetics.

Riley, M.A., Wong, S., Mitra, S. and Turvey, M.T. (1997). Common effects of touch and vision on postural parameters. *Experimental Brain Research* **117**, 165–70.

Savelsbergh, G.J.P., Netelenbos, J.B. and Whiting, H.T.A. (1991). Auditory perception and the control of spatially coordinated action in deaf and hearing children. *Journal of Child Psychology and Psychiatry* **32**, 489–500.

Savelsbergh, G.J.P., Whiting, H.T.A. and Bootsma, R.J. (1991). Grasping tau. *Journal of Experimental Psychology: Human Perception and Performance* **17**, 315–22.

Schmidt, R.C. and Fitzpatrick, P. (1996). Dynamical perspective on motor learning. In H.N. Zelaznik (ed.), *Advances in Motor Learning and Control*. Champaign, IL: Human Kinetics.

Smyth, M.M. and Marriott, A.M. (1982). Vision and proprioception in simple catching. *Journal of Motor Behaviour* **14**, 143–52.

Tayler, M.A. and Davids, K. (1997). Catching with both hands: an evaluation of neural cross-talk and coordinative structure models of bimanual co-ordination. *Journal of Motor Behaviour* **29**, 254–62.

Van der Kamp, J., Vereijken, B. and Savelsbergh, G.J.P. (1996). Physical and informational constraints in the co-ordination and control of human movement. *Corpus, Psyche et Societas: An International Review of Physical Activity, Health and Movement Science* **2**, 102–18.

Warren, W.H, Kim, E.E. and Husney, R. (1987). The way the ball bounces: visual and auditory perception of elasticity and control of the bounce pass. *Perception* **16**, 309–36.

Williams, A.M., Davids, K. and Williams, J.G. (1999). *Visual Perception and Action in Sport*. London: Routledge.

11 Sensitivity of children and adults to haptic information in wielding tennis rackets

Keith Davids, Simon J. Bennett and Sam Beak

Many of the chapters in this book examine theoretical literature on the role of visual information in co-ordinating and controlling interceptive actions such as those involved in racket sports. In addition, other chapters, such as Chapter 10 by Button, Chapter 5 by Robertson, Trembley, Anson and Elliott, Chapter 18 by Li and Turrell and Chapter 19 by Glazier, Davids and Bartlett, emphasise the multimodal nature of the information used to successfully perform interceptive actions in sport (see also Tresilian, 1999). When performing in racket sports like tennis it has been pointed out by Cauraugh and Janelle, in their chapter, that the search for important sources of visual information by the performer may be enhanced by use of proprioceptive and auditory information from wielding the racket and the sound of bat–ball contact during a rally. This chapter examines previous research which shows how well humans perceive the haptic information provided when an implement is held in the hand. In addition, we discuss the findings from research investigating the sensitivity of adults and children of different levels of ability in tennis learn to use haptic information, provided by holding and swinging tennis rackets, for the selection of implements for striking balls. In this chapter, tennis racket wielding is used as a task vehicle to highlight data in support of theoretical ideas. However, there is no reason to believe that the findings from the research studies discussed cannot be generalised to other sports in which implements may be wielded for intercepting projectiles, including other racket sports, cricket, baseball, field- and ice-hockey and lacrosse. We begin by reviewing theoretical work highlighting the importance of haptic information for perceiving the utility of implements interceptive actions in racket sports.

Dynamic touch

Recently in the human movement sciences, there has been a growing interest in the haptic information from implements and and objects afforded by grasping, wielding, hefting and other manipulatory activities (e.g. see Bingham, Schmidt and Rosenblum, 1989; Solomon and Turvey, 1988; Turvey, 1996; Turvey, Burton, Amazeen, Butwill and Carello, 1998; Beak, Davids and Bennett, 2002; Carello, Thuot and Turvey, 2000). This research thrust has been inspired by early ideas in ecological psychology. Gibson (1966, 1979) believed that the significant perceptual contribution of the haptic system during manipulative skills was often overlooked because of the theoretical emphasis on information from movements of the body and body parts, rather than from what is felt.

Turvey and colleagues have since explored the relevance of these Gibsonian ideas by attempting to highlight how dynamic touch supports many common manipulative movements in everyday life activities (for a review see Turvey, 1996). In fact, the prevalence of manipulative movements in everyday life led Turvey, Burton, Amazeen, Butwill and Carello (1998) to argue that 'the role of dynamic touch in the control of manipulatory activity may be both more continuous and fundamental than that of vision' (p. 35). In the context of interceptive actions in racket sports, dynamic touch refers to the haptic information provided when muscles, ligaments and tendons are stretched, compressed and extended during wielding, hefting, and grasping objects and implements such as balls, rackets and bats. The information provided by the muscular effort of exerting when wielding a racket can be picked up by the nervous system and perceived in terms of the affordances of the racket for specific movements such as striking a ball.

The role of haptic information in racket sports

What source of haptic information is the human central nervous system sensitive to when wielding an implement such as a racket for the purposes of striking a projectile? Anecdotally, racket players tend to talk about a racket's 'feel'. In fact, a racket's 'feel' can be measured as a variable. So, what information may be gained about a racket's 'feel'? When statically holding a striking implement, information regarding its shape, size, texture and structure may be obtained by a performer. Information about its resistance to being displaced (i.e. its mass) can also be acquired. However, typically humans do not hold an implement such as a racket in a static manner, but tend to wield it. Wielding is a process where an implement is twisted and turned in alternate directions, not necessarily in a systematic way. The impression a racket games player gets through wielding a racket is more accurately described as one of how easy or hard it is to rotate in different directions. A racket's resistance to rotation is defined by the term moment of inertia. As we outline in this chapter, biomechanical analysis allows us to measure moment of inertia information from rackets as well as limb segments involved in wielding activities.

Work by Solomon and Turvey (1988) implied that differences in the haptic invariant moment of inertia from each wielded racket, actually provides the performer with key information regarding a racket's 'feel'. In an extensive programme of work, Solomon and Turvey (1988) demonstrated that, when rod-wielding, humans are sensitive to haptic information provided by the invariant moment of inertia. Moment of inertia is an object's resistance to being turned and/or rotated and can be picked up during wielding or hefting activities.

For example, in their programme of nine experiments, Solomon and Turvey (1988) examined how adults perceived the spatial characteristics of hand-held rods. The participants could not see the rods, but could wield them only by movements about the wrist. Typically, there was a linear relation observed between perceived and actual reaching distances with the rods held at one end. The data from these experiments indicated that this relationship was unaffected by the density of the rods, the direction of wielding relative to body co-ordinates, and the rate of wielding. It was also found that perceived reaching distance was determined by the principal moments of inertia of the hand–rod system about the axis of rotation. Interestingly, studies of dynamic touch (e.g. see also Pagano and Turvey, 1995) have typically tended to examine the performance of younger and older adults in perceiving the spatial orientation of an occluded arm and/or implement. That is, during nonvisual perception tasks including rod-wielding or reaching with tennis rackets, adults have been required to perceive key characteristics such as length and centre of percussion of the implement (Bingham, Schmidt and Rosenblum, 1989; Solomon and Turvey, 1988; Carello, Thuot and Turvey, 2000).

Haptic information for wielding rackets: how sensitive are adults and children?

An interesting question, in the context of this book on interceptive actions, is whether these findings can generalise to natural settings where adults and children need to perceive affordances for action rather than an implement's spatial characteristics. Racket sports provide such a natural context in which to study the perception of haptic invariants for interceptive actions. Racket games always involve wielding of rackets for goal-directed actions such as serving and striking a ball. For example, when selecting implements for practising in tennis, squash and badminton, wielding is an integral part of the decision-making process.

Experiments on adult sensitivity to perception of haptic information from tennis rackets

Racket sports are popular with many adults and it is interesting to note what factors contribute to performance decline, during the ageing process. As well as more obvious factors such as flexibility, speed on court and strength, perceptual factors are important. The task of ensuring an intersecting trajectory of ball and racket is regulated by both visual and haptic information. This is because rackets are large and the ball needs to contact the racket's centre of percussion or sweet spot. Although the previous research in ecological psychology has demonstrated the sensitivity of adults to the moment of inertia of wielded implements (see Turvey, 1996), there have actually been few attempts to examine adult perception of haptic information from tennis rackets. One exception is a programme of work by Carello and colleagues comparing the ability of expert adult tennis players to novice adults in perceiving the length of a tennis racket as well as its centre of percussion (e.g. Carello, Thuot, Andersen and Turvey, 1999).

Force control and contact of a ball on a racket's centre of percussion

The quality of the hand and racket interface ensures the control of the stroke in tennis. As Li and Turrell, and Glazier, Davids and Bartlett point out, when a ball hits the surface of the racket it causes a load force, which allied to other causes, for example, due to acceleration of the racket when swinging, force of gravity and inertial forces, can cause a racket to slip in the hand during contact. Consequently, tennis players have to exert a grip force to ensure enough friction to maintain a stable contact to control ball placement during the stroke. One way to maintain stability of racket grip is to increase grip force at the expense of energy conservation. This is an unskillful and impractical way, given the length of competitive tennis matches.

Another way is to ensure that the ball is struck on the racket's centre of percussion. Striking a ball on the centre of percussion of a racket ensures that a player does not have to constantly exert muscular forces in maintaining an adequate grip on the racket. A performer can get feedback about a racket's centre of percussion from a post-contact impulse produced by the ball hitting the racket. The chapters by Li and Turrell and by Glazier, Davids and Bartlett suggest that a tight coupling develops between grip and load forces during the production of a collision of bat and ball during cricket and tennis. Direct collisions between the centre of percussion of the striking implement and the pendulum would result in minimal or no increase in load force during impact, providing excellent feedback on contacting the centre of percussion of a striking implement. The experiments discussed in the chapter by Li and Turrell indicate that visual information was not essential for anticipating collision between bat and ball, under the static task constraints of their experimental set-up where uncertainty about spatio–temporal constraints of the target was low. Li and Turrell suggest that this could be due to participants's use of proprioceptive information, including haptic sources.

Perception of haptic information on a racket's centre of percussion

The experiments in the programme of work by Carello and colleagues were concerned with the perception of the centre of percussion without bat–ball contact occurring, and their data confirm the arguments proposed by Li and Turrell. It seems that adults are quite good at suggesting where on a racket they would prefer to contact a ball, when they cannot see the racket.

For example, Carello, Thuot, Andersen and Turvey (1999) actually found no differences in non-visual spatial perception of a racket's centre of percussion in skilled and unskilled adult racket games players. Using visual manipulations, they found that novices were as adept as experts in perceiving the location of a racket's sweet spot and key spatial characteristics, such as length, and that these perceptions were constrained by the inertial properties of the racket.

One implication of these results is that extensive task-specific attunement to haptic information from tennis rackets is not necessary for successful spatial perception of an implement's characteristics. The perceptual success of the unskilled adult group may have been based on the exploitation of an initial sensitivity to haptic information from manipulated objects through evolutionary design of the human nervous system (see Beak, Davids and Bennett, 2002). This suggestion receives some support from a study which examined perception of haptic information in older adults (age range: 62–89 years) (Carello, Thuot and Turvey, 2000). Like the younger adults in the study by Carello, Thuot, Andersen and Turvey (1999) they were asked to distinguish a racket's length from its centre of percussion. Data fitted with previous findings. Younger adults' perceptions predicted those of the older group, a finding interpreted as support for the idea of a common underlying perceptual mechanism as an indication of sensitivity, although there seems some deterioration in the sensitivity to perception of haptic information in the seventh and eighth decade of life.

However, it is also possible that, by early adulthood, previous *general* experience in wielding objects and implements by the unskilled adults, in non-sport contexts, may have helped them to become quickly attuned to the haptic information from the tennis rackets. General experience in manipulating objects is part of most normal development throughout life, and it is possible that these experiences may have allowed the novice adults in the studies by Carello and colleagues (e.g. 1999, 2000) to spatially perceive centre of percussion and endpoint information from wielding the rackets.

Perception of haptic information from tennis rackets in children

Such questions have been examined in other work attempting to dissociate the effects of sensitivity and general experience of wielding objects in the study of the pick-up of haptic information. In regard to specific context of interceptive actions in racket sports, the lack of expert–novice differences in previous work poses the question whether humans have an innate sensitivity to moment of inertia information, which can be exploited for selecting appropriate tennis rackets for practice. For example, in tennis, a major difficulty for junior players is that, during development, as the properties of the learner change, the perceptual information relevant for assembling movement task solutions also changes. During development, organismic constraints (growth, strength, postural control etc.) change, along with the individual's action capabilities. Despite the huge amount of individual variability, typically during practice there is a very limited range of rackets available for learners to choose from. This problem in teaching and coaching classes is compounded by the fact that racket companies only manufacture junior rackets with uniform moments of inertia (Beak, Davids and Bennett, 2000). In the next section we review ideas from ecological psychology and the motor development literature on the relationship between sensitivity and attunement to information as affordances for action. We follow that by examining some research on the issue whether children are indeed sensitive to haptic information and discuss the implications for practical applications.

Children's sensitivity to moment of inertia information from rackets

To summarise so far, the haptic information available when wielding a racket, is picked up by the nervous system through contortion of biological material such as muscle, tendon and ligament, and perceived in terms of appropriateness for specific actions such as striking a ball. Haptic perception of object properties is only possible through active and intentional exploration (i.e. through dynamic touch). Previous research poses some specific questions of a developmental nature for those interested in how learners select rackets for playing tennis. Theoretically, these questions can be framed in the following way: how sensitive are children to moment of inertia information from wielded rackets as affordances for action? With increased exploration (i.e. with task-specific experience) does the nonvisual perception of haptic information become better attuned?

Although there has been extensive theoretical and empirical work on the roles of development and maturation as constraints on action (e.g. Thelen and Fisher, 1983; Kugler, 1986; Newell, 1986; Konczak, 1990), the effects of task-specific experience on action have not been subjected to the same amount of scrutiny. This is an important issue for understanding the acquisition of skill in perception and movement co-ordination, highlighted by Michaels and Beek (1995). They suggested that 'we must look not only at what expert perceivers and actors exploit in the way of information, but at how they come to be expert, both in their manner of exploration and in the information they detect' (Michaels and Beek, p. 274).

Affordances

The lack of previous work on sensitivity to haptic information in children raises questions about changes in affordances over time and the design of striking implements for children's ball sports. Affordances of an object for action are determined by the information perceived by the performer with an intrinsic reference to their own action capabilities (Konczak, 1990). For example, although a racket affords an objective function to an individual in sport (i.e. striking a ball), the invariant information gained from wielding a racket determines the perceived affordance for each particular individual. This perceptual judgement is shaped by the organismic constraints (e.g. strength and limb length) of the perceiver. Thus, for a given individual two tennis rackets may not necessarily have the same perceived affordance for striking a ball over a long distance, although objectively they do. Clearly, through changes in organismic constraints (i.e. growth and development) it is predicted that the observer's perception of the affordances of a striking implement can vary over time. This instability, brought on by growth and development, highlights the need for understanding how well children can perceive haptic information for assembling task specific devices for action.

Newell (1986) highlighted prolific growth periods during infancy and early childhood and the strong impact these changes can have on the biomechanical constraints on perception and action. For example, Jensen (1981) observed the effect of a 12-month growth period on the whole body moments of inertia of children ranging from four to 12 years old. He reported an average increase for whole body moment of inertia of 27.7 per cent over the 12-month time span. Not only do growth spurts affect biomechanical constraints, but they also have a great effect upon the perceptions of an individual interacting with the immediate environment. Newell's (1986) model of interacting constraints predicts that as organismic constraints change and interact with other constraints from the task and environment, the emergent behaviour will alter the perceptual judgement of the individual in each specific setting. Over an extended period of time, all children demonstrate some changes in organismic constraints through growth and development. How prolific these changes are will determine the size of the effect upon a child's perceived affordances for action. In summary, despite the lack of empirical work, ecological theory predicts that changes due to development can have a direct effect on an individual's perception of affordances (Konczak, 1990). Changes in organismic constraints have implications for the acquisition of ball skills within children, and particularly for equipment design and teaching and coaching practices.

With respect to the perception of environmental properties to support action, according to Michaels and Beek (1995), learners face a similar 'degrees of freedom' problem similar to that identified by Bernstein (1967) in relation to the movement system. Learners are confronted with a large number of potential information sources, within and across modalities, which may be exploited to support action (see also Van der Kamp, Savelsbergh and Smeets, 1997). In the pick-up of information for action, early in learning and development there is potential for ambiguity between different ambient energy arrays (e.g. vision and haptics from rackets for striking a tennis ball) in specification of environmental properties (Stoffregen and Bardy, 2001). In light of previous work suggesting that vision may conflict with perception of haptic information (e.g. Rock and Harris, 1967; Marks, 1978; Warren and Rossano, 1991), an interesting question concerns how wielding in visual and non-visual conditions by children and adults is influenced by sensitivity and attunement to moment of inertia information from implements.

Experimental work comparing pick-up and use of haptic information from rackets by children and adults

The rest of this chapter is devoted to describing research comparing choices of rackets for striking a ball in groups differing in developmental status and task-specific experience. We conducted a programme of work to examine the relationship between sensitivity and attunement to haptic information as a constraint on the perception of an affordance of an implement to strike a ball, in children and adults. To exemplify the main findings, in this chapter we present some findings from one study in our programme (e.g. see Beak, Davids and Bennett, 2000). In that study our aim was to examine differences in ability to perceive haptic information across two different age groups, varying in task-specific experience, under two conditions where visual information of a tennis racket was manipulated. The latter condition allowed the investigation of Turvey and colleagues' (1998) statement that dynamic touch (e.g. haptic wielding) was more fundamental than that of vision during manipulatory activities. It was predicted that any differences in the perception–action systems of the participants, due to experience and development, would be observed through changes in perceived affordances of the racket for striking a ball. Any effect of condition would also be seen through changes in perceptual judgements on each racket.

Manipulating moments of inertia in tennis rackets

The study required six identical rackets with equal moments of inertia. The rackets employed in the study were from the junior 'Rad' range (Prince, Inc.), which are marketed as purpose-designed rackets for use by children aged six to 12. To coincide with the age range of the youngest participant group and to meet the age criteria of the 'Rad' range, the racket used throughout the study was a Rad Ten. By using this same racket for all groups, it was possible to examine the effects of development and task experience on the perception of a racket's affordance for a specific action. Each racket was constructed of aluminium with length 63.5 cm and mass 0.252 kg.

It is interesting to note that each Rad Ten racket had the same moment of inertia, despite the fact that there are large individual differences in moments of inertia of limb segments among 10-year-old children. This baseline moment of inertia was manipulated to produce different overall moments of inertia for each racket. In order to precisely control this experimental manipulation, a mass of 0.05 kg was added to the longitudinal axis of each of the six rackets at intervals of 10 cm. The mass was covered in black tape to secure it to the racket and to prevent any biasing through knowledge of its value. The calculations for moment of inertia of the six racket systems (I_{RS}, where a racket system constitutes the racket and additional weight) were based upon the formula:

$$I_{RS} = I_{butt} + m\,r^2$$

where I_{butt} = moment of inertia of the racket about its butt end, m = mass of attached weight (kg) and r = position of weight from butt. The moments of inertia for the six new racket systems were then calculated to be 0.0334, 0.0349, 0.0375, 0.0410, 0.0456 and 0.0512 kg m^2 for rackets 1–6 respectively (see Figure 11.1). For the purposes of that experiment, the racket with the lowest moment of inertia (0.0334 kg m^2) was closest to the racket marketed as appropriate for 10-year-olds, and the highest value (0.0512 kg m^2) was closer to rackets in Prince's adult range.

The values chosen for moments of inertia were kept within this limited range to be suitable for both children and adults. For example, larger increments in moment of inertia would have resulted in racket dimensions falling outside marketed adult ranges, thus resulting in inappropriate, over-sized implements. The limited range also prohibited any clustering of choices that would have been attributable to the use of an inordinately wide selection range. Therefore, any evidence of the clustering of perceived affordances would provide more meaningful support for the notion of sensitivity to haptic information.

The adult and children groups

Three groups participated in the study: an inexperienced child group, an inexperienced adult group and an experienced adult group. The inexperienced child group consisted of ten children (mean age = 10 years) from a local school. All participants were selected because they had had no previous coaching in any racket sports and had very limited experience in wielding a racket. The second

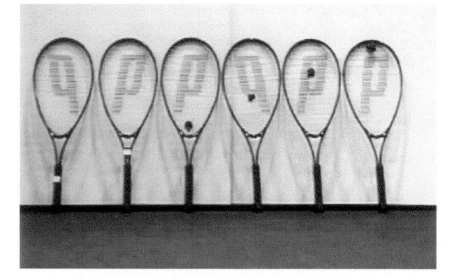

Figure 11.1 The Rad ten rackets provided by Prince Inc., in which moment of inertia was manipulated by adding a mass of 50 g. The position of the individual weight increases with each racket by 10 cm. All the rackets were identical in weight, size and design but altered only in their moment of inertia values. Prince Inc. calculated that the basic Rad ten racket was 0.0328 kg m² for each racket. With the addition of 0.05 kg at different positions along the longitudinal axis of the rackets, new moment of inertia values were calculated. Using the formula above, values were calculated in the following way: $I_{butt} = 0.0328$ kg m², $m = 0.05$ kg and $r = 0.106$ m, 0.206 m, 0.306 m, 0.406 m, 0.506 m and 0.606 m respectively for rackets 1–6. Subsequently, the moment of inertia values for the six new rackets were calculated to be 0.0334, 0.0349, 0.0375, 0.0410, 0.0456 and 0.0512 kg m² for rackets 1–6 respectively.

group (inexperienced adults) was composed of eight male and two female right-handed adults (mean age = 28 years). Once again the criteria for selecting these participants required that they had limited or no experience with racket sports or any other task involving the wielding of an implement. The third group consisted of 10 experienced, adult tennis players (mean age = 22 years; nine male and one female). All were right-handed players playing competitively at varsity level. To be classified as an experienced player, all participants in this group were required to be University first team standard or above and have at least five years competitive experience.

The task

In the experiment by Beak *et al.* (2000), each participant was asked to wield the rackets during an individual testing session lasting approximately 10 minutes. There were two randomly-ordered wielding conditions: visual and non-visual. The participants were required to wield each of the six rackets separately, and were asked to judge each racket for its affordance to strike a ball to a maximum distance. After wielding, participants indicated their preferred three rackets that optimally afforded such an action, in a forced-choice paradigm. Participants were allowed to wield each racket as many times as required. The rackets were presented in a random order to counterbalance any possible sequence effects. Grip position was standardised throughout, with the participants holding the racket at the very end of its handle. Participants were not instructed how to wield, nor given a specific length of time in which to complete the procedure. In the visual condition, the participants were able to see the rackets. In the non-visual condition, vision of the rackets was occluded by the use of a large screen. The screen was designed with a hole in the middle to allow the participants unrestricted wielding. A black sheet draped over the screen provided adequate deprivation of any visual information of the rackets.

Reliability data

During a pilot study, the reliability of the children's and the inexperienced adults' perceived affordances for each racket, was tested. Both groups repeated the above procedure at two separate data collection periods, one week apart under two different conditions. A 2 × 2 (Condition by Time) repeated measures analysis of variance found no significant differences across time for either the child group, or the adult group. These results confirmed the reliability of the data across a one-week period, indicating that the perceived choices of both groups were consistent and not randomly selected. Based on this evidence of reliability, there were no obvious reasons to suspect that the preferences of the experienced adults would also not be reliable.

How we measured selection of rackets

For each participant, a mean preferred moment of inertia was calculated using a method employed by Bingham, Schmidt and Rosenblum (1989). They suggested the use of weighted scores to provide a more sensitive approach to data analysis of perceptual judgements. The method involved multiplying the moment of inertia value of the first preferred racket by three, the second by two and the third preference value by one, thus weighting the scores according to preference. The sum of the weighted scores was then divided by six to obtain the mean weighted score. The data in our study were then subjected to analysis of variance.

Significant main effects of condition and group were found. Although no condition by group interaction was found, a simple effects analysis was carried out on the data to clarify the statistical outcomes (see Howell, 1993, for justification of the use of such analysis in the absence of an interaction). The simple effects analysis revealed significant differences between the visual and non-visual conditions for the child group. Significant differences were also found between the groups in both the visual and the non-visual conditions. Our experiment also found significant differences in the visual condition, between the child group and

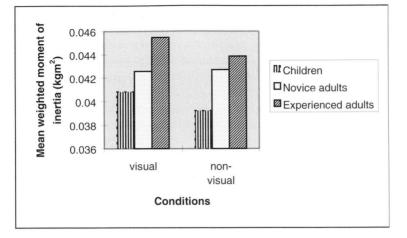

Figure 11.2 Mean moment of inertia values for the rackets selected within each subject group during the visual and non-visual conditions.

the experienced adult group, and between the inexperienced adult group and the experienced adult group. Under the non-visual condition, significant differences were reported between the child and inexperienced adult groups, and between the child and experienced adult groups. Figure 11.2 illustrates these findings.

In Figure 11.2, there is an apparent trend in the data with the two adult groups preferring those rackets with a higher moment of inertia value (i.e. those rackets which are similar to adult rackets and hence perceived to be 'heavier'). The children demonstrated a preference for values at the lower end of the inertia scale. This finding concurs with the dimensions of the manipulated rackets and the age range that similar rackets are marketed towards. This trend is also clearly observed in Figures 11.3 (a–c). Both adult groups showed a distinct preference towards the top end of the inertia scale.

A further point of interest represented in Figures 11.3a–c, is the tight clustering of perceived choices. The child group (Figure 11.3a) shows a greater degree of intra-individual variability in the choice of rackets compared to choices made by the adult groups (Figures 11.3b–c). The experienced adult group (Figure 11.3c) demonstrated the lowest levels of intra-individual variability of all groups by picking consecutive rackets along the inertia scale, resulting in a very tight clustering of choices. This trend was evident under both conditions, although the visual condition did yield a tighter degree of clustering.

Levels of inter-individual variability was found to be highest within the child group, although there was also some variability evident in both adult groups (see for example Participant 9 in the experienced adult group (see Figure 11.3c). Inter-individual levels of variability increased under the non-visual condition for both the adult groups, but appeared to decrease slightly in the child group (i.e. the children's perceived choices became increasingly clustered when vision was occluded).

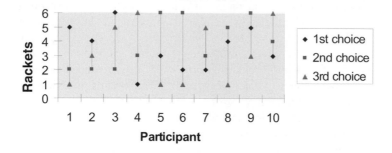

Figure 11.3a   The data illustrate the children's individual choice of rackets under the visual condition.

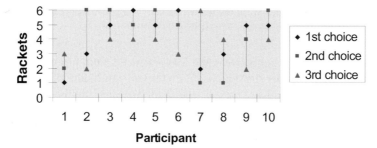

Figure 11.3b   The data illustrate the inexperienced adults' individual choice of rackets under the visual condition.

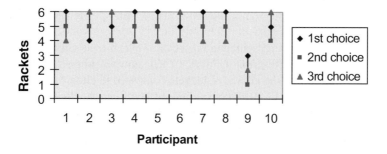

Figure 11.3c   The data illustrate the experienced adults' individual choice of rackets under the visual condition.

So what conclusions can we draw from the experiment described in this chapter? It seems that all three groups displayed a sensitivity to small changes in the physical properties of the wielded rackets, signifying their ability to detect and perceive haptic information in the invariant form, moment of inertia. In this respect, our data confirmed the previous findings of Solomon and Turvey (1988) and Bingham,

Schmidt and Rosenblum (1989) on the significance of haptic information for perceiving characteristics of implements and objects during manipulatory activities, such as hefting and wielding. In addition, there was evidence of significant differences between the three groups, in the perception of affordances of the six different rackets in relation to the specific action of striking a ball. There was a clear difference in the preferred choice of rackets by participants in each group. The children demonstrated greater variability in their choices, whilst both adult groups showed a trend towards those rackets with greater moment of inertia values (i.e. those rackets with values approximating 'normal' adult rackets).

It is interesting to comment on a further difference that we noted across the child group and the experienced adults under the two different conditions. Indeed, it seems that the sensitivity of each group to haptic information clearly altered as a function of age and experience (see Figures 11.3a–c). Although clustered choices were made by all three groups, the clustering became progressively tighter and less variable in the adult groups, particularly in the experienced adults. In the child group it appeared that when both visual and haptic information were present, there was a conflict in the informational constraints, creating greater variability in choices made. Without any prior experience in wielding rackets for striking, the children seemed unable to integrate both the visual and the haptic information gained from the manipulation of the rackets. When vision was occluded, the pick-up of affordances seemed to become easier, resulting in a greater clustering effect in the children's choices.

The higher degree of variability observed in the children's data may be consistent with the instability frequently associated with developing perception-action systems (e.g. Beak, Davids and Bennett, 2002). Children, particularly, are subject to prolific changes in the movement system because of a number of different factors associated with growth and maturation. These changes constantly perturb the dynamic movement system causing instability in the perceptual and action subsystems.

In addition to developmental perturbations, task experience appears to be another major constraint. The participants in the child group were all selected for their lack of previous experience in wielding tennis rackets. This experimental manipulation meant that the task was relatively novel and the children had no specific prior experience on which to base their preferences. Hence, more intra- and inter-individual variability was predicted, and observed, in the choices made by the children. The aim of the task was to perceive which three rackets afforded striking a ball to a maximum distance. In order to detect an affordance, the information specifying the particular affordance must be picked up (Michaels and Carello, 1981). It is possible that the children were sensitive to moment of inertia information on the basis of haptic experiences during early infancy and childhood. However, without the specific experience of striking a ball with a racket, they might have been unable to map the haptic information gained through wielding onto the movement dynamics of each racket, and hence detect the affordances that each racket offered. In this respect, their lack of experience and understanding about the movement information of the rackets constrained the perception–action system, and thus the detection of affordances.

Implications for skill acquisition

Taking advantage of sensitivity to haptic information

The research discussed in this chapter raises several implications for skill acquisition in racket sports in children and adult learners. First, it seems that humans are able to detect important sources of haptic information, such as a racket's centre of percussion, quite successfully. This capacity stands them in good stead when they are faced with learning to play racket sports. During learning, if new affordances are to be discovered and new appropriate modes of action acquired, then there must be continuous opportunities for active search and exploration during practice. This strategy allows learners to become more sensitive and attuned to relevant information to guide their actions by coupling the information to movements (Savelsbergh *et al.*, 2000). If learners are to become skilled at picking up the affordances of one racket over another, they need to have experience in actively searching and exploring different possible solutions to a given task problem. This means that learners must be provided with a variety of rackets to choose from in order to learn to use haptic information for selecting optimal implements.

By the time children reach adulthood they have typically had many opportunities for wielding and striking with implements (e.g. through picking up and throwing sticks and stones and playing bat and ball). Although these experiences may not be considered task-specific, they provide vital opportunities for search and exploration of non-visual properties of implements and objects. From Figure 11.3b in this chapter, it can be seen that inexperienced adults showed a trend towards rackets with the larger moment of inertia values. While this group may not have understood the concept of moment of inertia, they appear to have had a good idea, based on past experience, that implements which feel 'top-heavy' can often produce greater power, in relative terms, than those implements whose mass distribution is nearer the handle (Sol, 1995). As a result, the inexperienced adults demonstrated a general preference towards those rackets where the mass distribution was greater towards the head of the racket. This finding has implications for the design and manufacture of rackets for the non-specialist market.

It can be inferred from the extant literature that previous task-specific experience in wielding rackets permits experienced adults to show more certainty in their choice of rackets for performance. When able to see rackets, inexperienced adults show a tighter clustering of choices than children, but not as much as an adult group experienced in tennis (see Figures 11.3a–c). This developmental difference may be explained through the greater opportunities that adults have had for general wielding experiences. The non-specific experience of wielding and perceiving for action that the inexperienced adults have gained throughout their lifetime may have allowed their perceptual systems to have become more attuned to the availability of haptic information from implements. Visual information is no longer the dominant source of information attended to as in infancy and childhood (Gallahue, 1993). So, when only haptic information is available to inexperienced adults, they can simply rely on more general previous experiences to guide their actions and choices.

The consistent finding from previous research is that lack of specific experience in tennis does not inhibit learners from perceiving the centre of percussion of a racket or from making reliable choices in selecting preferred rackets for striking a ball (see Figure 11.3b). These results support previous proposals that haptic information is more important than visual information during dynamic touch (see Turvey, Burton, Amazeen, Butwill and Carello, 1998).

Summary and conclusions

Future work also needs to examine some of the other issues raised in this chapter. For example, moment of inertia has been identified as a key source of information to which performers, differing in development and experience, are sensitive during wielding and hefting actions. However, moment of inertia is made up of two components, m (mass) and r^2 (distance of m from the point of rotation). During manipulatory events, it is currently not clear whether the performer is sensitive to moment of inertia as a whole, or to one of the components that make up this haptic invariant. Michaels and Beek (1995) described this issue as one of sensitivity to the peception of higher or lower order variables. After Runeson (1977), they argued that smart perceptual devices are developed through the exploitation of lower order variables which guide the search for, or come to be selected as intergral parts of, a higher order informational complex or both. This proposal leads to the question of identifying the lower and higher order variables available for perception of haptic information during wielding. More specifically, an interesting question is: is moment of inertia, in the global sense, the higher order variable to which experienced wielders are attuned, therefore resulting in its components being perceived as lower order variables?

Another relevant issue is whether a performer with greater levels of task-specific experience would show greater sensitivity to changes in one of the components of moment of inertia, compared to less experienced performers. The implications that these questions raise are of relevance to the design and manufacture of rackets and other implements which require wielding or hefting. Finally, the data that children and adults are sensitive to moment of inertia information from specific implements in sport suggest that coaches and teachers need to provide a broad range of implements to match the range of organismic constraints in groups of learners during skill acquisition.

References

Beak, S., Davids, K. and Bennett, S.J. (2000). One size fits all? Sensitivity to moment of inertia information from tennis rackets in children and adults. In S.J. Haake and A. Coe (eds), *Tennis Science and Technology*. London: Blackwell.

Beak, S., Davids, K. and Bennett, S. (2002). Children's sensitivity to haptic information in perceiving affordances of rackets for striking a ball. In J.E. Clark and J. Humpreys (eds.), *Motor Development: Research and Reviews*, Vol. 2. Reston, VA: NASPE.

Bernstein N.A. (1967). *The Coordination and Regulation of Movements*. Oxford: Pergamon Press.

Bingham, G., Schmidt, R.C. and Rosenblum, L. (1989). Hefting for a maximum distance throw: a smart perceptual mechanism. *Journal of Experimental Psychology: Human Perception and Performance* **15**, 507–28.

Carello, C., Thuot, S. and Turvey, M.T. (2000). Aging and the perception of a racket's sweet spot. *Human Movement Science* **19**, 1–20.

Carello, C., Thuot, S., Andersen, K.L. and Turvey, M.T. (1999). Perceiving the sweet spot. *Perception* **28**, 1128–41.

Gallahue, D.L. (1993). *Developmental Physical Education for Today's Children*. Dubuque, IA: Brown and Benchmark.

Gibson, J.J. (1966). *The Senses Considered as Perceptual Systems*. Boston: Houghton Mifflin.

Gibson, J.J. (1979). *The Ecological Approach to Visual Perception*. Boston: Houghton Mifflin.

Jensen, R.K. (1981). The effect of a 12-month growth period on the body moments of inertia of children. *Medicine and Science in Sports and Exercise* **13**, 238–42.

Konczak, J. (1990). Toward an ecological theory of motor development: the relevance of the Gibsonian approach to vision for motor development research. In J. Clark and J. Humphrey (eds), *Advances in Motor Development Research 3*. New York: AMS Press.

Kugler, P.N. (1986). A morphological perspective on the origin and evolution of movement patterns. In M. Wade and H.T.A. Whiting (eds), *Motor Development in Children: Aspects of Co-ordination and Control*. Dordrecht: Nijhoff.

Marks, L.E. (1978). *The Unity of the Senses: Interrelations Between the Modalities*. New York: Academic Press.

Michaels, C. and Beek, P. (1995). The state of ecological psychology. *Ecological Psychology* **74**, 259–78.

Michaels, C.F. and Carello, C.C. (1981). *Direct Perception*. Englewood Cliffs, NJ: Prentice Hall Inc.

Newell, K.M. (1986). Constraints on the development of co-ordination. In M.G. Wade and H.T.A. Whiting (eds), *Motor Development in Children: Aspects of Co-ordination and Control*. Dordrecht: Nijhoff.

Pagano, C.C. and Turvey, M.T. (1995). The inertia tensor as a basis for the perception of limb orientation. *Journal of Experimental Psychology: Human Perception and Performance* **21**, 1070–87

Rock, I. and Harris, C.S. (1967). Vision and touch. *Scientific American* **216**, 96–104.

Runeson, S. (1977). On the possibility of 'smart' perceptual mechanisms. *Scandinavian Journal of Psychology* **18**, 172–9.

Savelsbergh, G., Wimmers, R., Van der Kamp, J. and Davids, K. (2000). The development of movement control and co-ordination. In M.L. Genta, B. Hopkins and A.F. Kalverboer (eds.), *Basic Issues in Developmental Biopsychology*. Dordrecht: Kluwer Academic Publishers.

Sol, H. (1995). Computer aided design of rackets. In T. Reilly, M. Hughes and A. Lees (eds), *Science and Racket Sports*. London: E & FN Spon.

Solomon, H.Y. and Turvey, M.T. (1988). Haptically perceiving the distances reachable with hand-held objects. *Journal of Experimental Psychology: Human Perception and Performance* **14**, 404–27.

Stoffregen, T.A. and Bardy, B.G. (2001). On specification and the senses. *Behavioral and Brain Sciences* **24**, 195–241.

Thelen, E. and Fisher, D. (1983). The organization of spontaneous leg movements in newborn infants. *Journal of Motor Behavior* **15**, 353–77.

Tresilian, J.R. (1999). Analysis of recent empirical challenges to an account of interceptive timing. *Perception and Psychodynamics* **21**, 515–28.

Turvey, M.T. (1996). Dynamic touch. *American Psychologist* **51**, 1134–52.

Turvey, M.T., Burton, G., Amazeen, E.L., Butwill, M. and Carello, C. (1998). Perceiving the width and height of a hand-held object by dynamic touch. *Journal of Experimental Psychology: Human Perception and Performance* **24**, 35–48.

Van der Kamp, J., Savelsbergh, G.J.P. and Smeets, J.B. (1997). Multiple information sources in interceptive timing. *Human Movement Science* **16**, 787–822.

Warren, D.H. and Rossano, M.J. (1991). Intermodality relations: vision and touch. In M.A. Heller and W. Schiff (eds) *The Psychology of Touch*. Hillsdale, NJ: Lawrence Erlbaum Associates.

12 Perception and action during interceptive tasks

An integrative modelling perspective

Damian Keil and Simon J. Bennett

Throughout the course of this book, the reader has had the opportunity to digest a range of chapters on interceptive actions, focused on processes of perception and action, and typically involving psychological modelling, such as cognitive science or ecological psychology. It is the purpose of this chapter to adopt an integrative modelling approach to the study of interceptive actions. By adopting an integrative modelling approach, we hope to place the study of human movements such as interceptive actions within a multi-dimensional framework that may be more insightful than a uni-dimensional, psychological perspective. We present an integrative modelling approach because it is argued that functional, goal-oriented behaviour, exemplified in this book by interceptive actions, cannot be understood completely through kinematic variables or psychophysiological variables alone, for instance. While these measures of human movement behaviour may help to describe motor patterns or perceptual processes in answering specific questions, human beings are not that simple. Integrative modelling, as well as recognising the multi-faceted nature of human behaviour, also adds depth and constraints to psychological theorising (see Keil *et al.*, 2000 for discussion).

Why develop an integrative modelling perspective on interceptive actions?

What exactly do we mean by integrated modelling? An integrated modelling approach to the study of brain processes and movement behaviours, such as interceptive actions, is predicated on the idea that the provision of an adequate theoretical account must be constrained by neuroscientific knowledge of the central nervous system (CNS) and enriched by phenomenological modelling of the human movement system (see Bruce *et al.*, 1996). Arbib *et al.* (1998) proposed that such an integrated, multi-level analysis is required to help interpret the structure, function, and dynamics of brain and behaviour. An integrative modelling view proposed by some theorists is that the brain should be viewed as 'embodied' (e.g. Thelen and Smith, 1994; Varela *et al.*, 1991). For example, Edelman (1992) employed the term 'biological epistemology', highlighting the need to integrate understanding of the neurophysiological basis of brain activity and morphology of the body as major constraints on human behaviour. From this perspective, although the brain is most accurately described as a physiological organ, its bi-directional interaction with numerous body modalities (Kutas and Federmeier, 1998) places it at the heart of human behaviour. In fact, this idea has a rich history in the movement sciences literature. As Bernstein argued in the 1940s, and re-emphasised by Sporns and Edelman (1998) more recently, attempts to understand brain function should be 'rooted in the evolution of morphology and behavior, dominated by the action of large populations of neurons acting as collectives, and regulated by modulatory systems' (p. 283).

Parallel to the increasing acknowledgement that the brain is located within the human movement system, in the last two decades there has been a huge growth in neuroscience knowledge providing a sound platform to develop theoretical under-standing of human behaviours such as interceptive actions. Neuroscience work is no longer limited to reductionist approaches such as tissue staining and cellular recording or to primate studies with their comparative limitations to human neural physiology.[1] By combining our understanding of neural organisation with modern imaging techniques such as functional Magnetic Resonance Imaging (fMRI), we have been exposed to significant insights into human cognition and behaviour (for example see Freeman, 1999; Greenfield, 1997). The sheer numbers of neuroscience articles published in recent years have made these advances in our understanding possible. For example, Wagemans *et al.* (2001) have drawn attention to the fact that key textbooks on neuroscience, such as the seminal handbook by Gazzaniga (1995, 2000), have been virtually re-written in the space of five years. Moreover, with approximately 35,000 neuroscience articles published every year (between 1991 and 1994) and this figure increasing by 10 per cent every year (Seemungal *et al.*, 1999), it is understandable why the American Congress declared the 1990s as the 'decade of the brain'.

However, the position that we are advocating in this chapter should not be misinterpreted as a suggestion to dismiss attempts to psychologically model interceptive actions, and to accept uncritically the offerings of neuroscience. Rather the position that we advocate is that psychological modelling needs to be constrained by as well as inform neuroscientific research. In the extant literature, there are some very limited indications that investigators are beginning to recognise that the goal of mapping mental processes to specific brain structures in the neurosciences needs to be supplemented with the provision of a theoretical framework for understanding how such processes are achieved by humans during goal-directed behaviour (for compelling arguments see Kelso, 1995; McCrone, 1999). For example, Wagemans *et al.* (2001) have argued that 'there is more to understanding behaviour and cognition than tracing the neural activities alone.' (p. 1), and influential neuroscience texts argue that the specific goal of neuro-scientists is to 'understand the mind – how we perceive, move, think and remember.' (Kandel, Schwartz and Jessell, 2000, p. xxxv).

One of the more eloquent criticisms has been made by Freeman (1997) who criticised much neuroscience work for the lack of contact with theoretical modelling. He argued that 'most researchers still try to find memories in the temporal lobe, emotions in the amygdala, cognitive maps in the hippocampus, linguistic operations in Broca's and Wernicke's areas, holistic thinking in the right hemisphere..and so on' (p. 292). This form of neuro-reductionism is detrimental to the development of a coherent theoretical framework for explaining the processes involved in movement behaviours such as interceptive actions. Further recognition of the need for contact between theoreticians and neuroscientists was advocated by Michaels (2000), while discussing the merits of a neuroscientific model of two cortical visual systems. She stated that 'many psychologists persist in behaving like the poor cousins of neuroscience, waiting for and overvaluing its handouts and ignoring the extent to which neuroscientific research itself can rest on very poor, if tacit, folk psychology.' (p. 246).

In this chapter we make a similar argument about the implicit assumption made by many neuropsychologists that an information-processing paradigm provides the only adequate framework for guiding integrative modelling research on movement learning and control (see Davids *et al.* 2001). We develop this argument by discussing the implication that psychological and neuroscientific modelling of behaviours, such as interceptive actions, should proceed in a mutually-constraining and cooperative fashion, without the implementation of a priori tacit and uncritical assumptions about the underpinning theoretical frameworks. In the following section we aim to stimulate this process by examining the relevance of an integrated modelling approach and by critically evaluating data and theory from recent models of perception and action processes in interceptive movements.

The two-visual system and its implications for integrative modelling

It is a primary assumption in much traditional research that the only role of the eyes, and the associated cortical areas, is to build a representation of the world around us (e.g. Gregory, 1998). For example, in cognitive science explanations of processes of perception and action, the nature of the representation in the CNS implies a 'copy theory of knowledge' in which information about the world can be symbolically represented and stored (see Willingham, 1998). More recently, there has been growing criticism against such a uni-dimensional view of the functional role of the visual system. As outlined in Chapter 1, some have blamed the prevalence of this view on the traditional 'psychophysical' paradigm, which has dominated vision research since the last century (e.g. Harris and Jenkin, 1998). Indeed, the idea that we are able to process sensory information from the eyes and commit it to a unified representation of the world stored in the CNS has been called 'the grand illusion' (Harris and Jenkin, 1998).

Implicit assumptions in the neuroscience literature on perception and action

It is evident in much of the visual neuroscience literature that many authors have implicitly developed their ideas from within the traditional psychophysical paradigm. The implicit nature of the psychological framework behind much traditional research on processes of perception and action is revealed by examination of the extant literature. For example, De Angelis (2000) has posed the question 'How is binocular disparity initially *encoded* [our italics] by V1 neurons, and what implications does this *encoding scheme* [our italics] have for stereoscopic perception?' (p. 82). The concern from an integrated modelling perspective is that there are many implicit and underlying assumptions accepted in using such terminology. As Eggermont (1998) argued, 'The existence of a code assumes neural elements that do the *encoding* and other neural elements that do the *decoding*' (p. 358). The result is an air of simplistic assumption, in which it is to use terminology that cover gaps in theorising, rather than trying to elucidate them, referred to elsewhere as an approach based on 'boxology' (see Williams *et al.*, 1999). However, at some point there is a need for explicit conceptual definitions and the relation to neural mechanisms. Without an integrative modelling approach, definitions of hypothetical constructs require more constructs to clarify and qualify the function of the original term, thereby perpetuating the need for additional system sub-levels.

A good example of such terminology is observed within the two-visual system literature. The terms 'egocentric coding' and 'allocentric coding' offer the reader an easy way of conceptualising the way we use information during perceptual tasks. If we egocentrically code an object, it is 'represented' relative to ourselves, which generally means we are going to act upon it. If, however, it is allocentrically coded, it is coded relative to other objects in the environment, therefore allowing us to perform judgements on its size or shape for instance. But again we face the same problem as before. What precisely is doing the coding, how is the object coded/represented, what decodes it and how? The key issue is the lack of contact between advanced localisation imaging technology and traditional theoretical modelling, recognised by Kandel *et al.* (2000) who proposed that 'neuroimaging techniques like PET and fMRI are quite limited in supporting inferences about computations and representations in the brain' (p. 6).

As discussed in Chapter 1, Harris and Jenkin (1998) have emphasised that vision is made up of a 'bundle of processes' which all serve disparate behavioural goals. Since different types of visual information need to be extracted from the environment to support the rich diversity of tasks performed by humans, it makes sense that the visual system is composed of numerous functional divisions. Probably the most widely known of these functional divisions is that of the 'two-visual system', where the functional division is between perception for action and perception for recognition (Milner and Goodale, 1995). This system highlights how the brain utilises information depending on the aim of the task to be performed.

Over the years research into these two divisions has proliferated. For example, Ungerleider and Mishkin (1982) have utilised electrophysiological techniques, identifying two discrete visual processing streams in the macaque monkey. They considered that information was divided between the two streams. The ventral stream picks up information regarding the identification of an object, and the dorsal stream is dedicated to information about the object's spatial location with respect to the movement system. These functions were interpreted as the 'what'

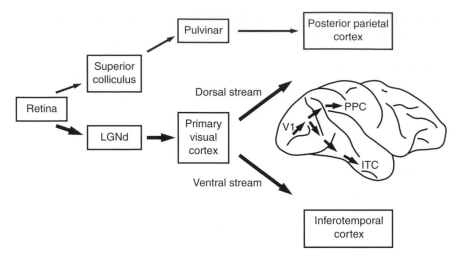

Figure 12.1   Representation of the two visual pathways within the right hemisphere of the macaque brain. LGNd, lateral geniculate nucleus, pars dorsalis; V1, primary visual cortex; PPC, posterior parietal cortex; ITC, inferotemporal cortex. Adapted from Milner and Goodale (1995).

and 'where' classification of objects by the CNS. Information is carried via the lateral geniculate nucleus to the primary visual cortex (V1), from which the ventral stream projects to the inferotemporal cortex and the dorsal stream projects to the posterior parietal cortex. A further connection to the posterior parietal cortex has been identified from the pulvinar via the superior colliculus (see Figure 12.1).

The work of Goodale, Milner and colleagues

Goodale and Milner (1992) however, offered another interpretation for the findings described above. Rather than the type of information being important, they suggested it was the cortical associations that differentiated the two streams. For instance, the dorsal stream connecting to motor areas of the brain more frequently, allows for online control of actions, while the ventral stream, connected to higher processing areas such as memory, is used for recognition of objects. As such, Goodale and Milner's (1992) alternative interpretation is for distinguishing between the visual system functions is 'what' vs. 'how' rather than 'what' vs. 'where'

In clarifying this distinction, Milner and Goodale (1995) have drawn from various research sources (include work on lower order vertebrates, primates, brain-damaged patients and pictorial illusion studies) to produce a comprehensive argument for a more diverse role of the visual system. Evidence for cortical associations have been found (in the primate brain) between the posterior parietal cortex and the premotor cortex (involved in movement selection) and striatum (a combination of two nuclei within the basal ganglia which is a major subcortical motor structure; Sakata *et al.*, 1995; Wise *et al.*, 1997). The ventral stream, ending in the inferotemporal cortex, has been found to associate with the prefrontal cortex (involved in volition), perirhinal cortex, amygdala (suggested to be involved in the acquisition of long-term memories), along with others (Tanaka, 1996).

Adding to the evidence for the two visual systems, Goodale *et al.* (1991) and Milner *et al.* (1991) described the case of a human patient (DF) who suffered brain damage (as a result of carbon monoxide poisoning) predominantly to the occipital area, specifically V2, V3 and V4. It was noted that DF had many deficits in visual perception, including discrimination between geometric shapes and recognition of letters and numbers. Disorders such as these have been described as 'visual form agnosia' or 'blindsight'. The interesting feature with patients with visual form agnosia is the apparent paradox between their obvious limitations in recognition tasks and their ability to perform visuomotor actions such as grasping. Milner *et al.* (1991) examined this distinction by asking DF to orientate her hand or a disk and insert it into a slot that was randomly set at different angles. Although DF was unable to verbalise or manually represent the orientation of the slot, she had no problem in reaching forward and inserting the disk or her hand from a starting point at arm's length away. By accepting the interpretation by Milner and Goodale, this apparent paradox is removed – while one of the pathways has been damaged (the ventral) information for action can still be utilised via the dorsal stream.

Although this somewhat simplistic review fits the purpose of this chapter in aiding the description of neural processes, unfortunately human neural evolution has not granted us the same luxury of simplicity in the way that the brain regulates perception and action processes. Detailed examination of the cortex reveals a labyrinth of connections between many areas (see Felleman and van Essen, 1991 for a comprehensive review of the primate visual areas). In fact, any particular neuron, for which there are 10,000 per mm^3, may synapse with 80,000 other neurons (Basar, 1998). Interestingly, not only are there cortico–cortical connections between the dorsal and ventral streams and the rostral superior temporal sulcus, but there are also direct connections between the posterior parietal cortex and inferotemporal cortex. These connections permit 'crosstalk' between the two pathways (Milner and Goodale, 1995).

Consequently, the two visual pathways are unlikely to act completely independently of each other. They are likely to be activated simultaneously during most visuomotor acts. Indeed, Goodale and Milner (1992) state, 'We do not, however, wish to claim that the division of labour we are proposing is an absolute one' (p. 24). Further, they suggest that the 'crosstalk' may aid the production of a cohesive perceptual experience. Evidence for simultaneous activation of both pathways, has been reported by Dobbins *et al.*, (1998). They found that both pathways were activated when primates were required to analyse depth information. Recent work by Decety and Grèzes (1999) has suggested that it is the aim or intention behind a particular perceptual task that governs which brain areas are active during behaviour. That is, the functional separation tends not to be observed (i.e. both areas are active) when there are no constraints on the perceptual task (as in some psychophysical work). However, when there are clear task constraints (e.g. perception for action or perception for recognition) the separation becomes more apparent. This interaction also makes itself obvious when considering the

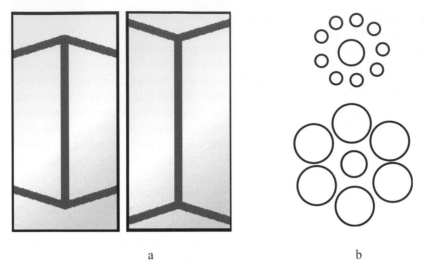

a   b

Figure 12.2 Both illusions show how the surrounding environment can impinge upon our
perceptions. However, when acting upon the illusions, our action system is
not fooled. **a).** The Müller–Lyer illusion: the vertical line on the left looks
smaller than the one on the right. In fact they are the same size. **b).** The
Ebbinghaus illusion: although the inner circle on the left looks smaller than
the one on the right, in fact they are the same size.

task constraints of intercepting a hard or a soft projectile. It appears that how we
choose to intercept an object is intricately bound up with our intentions for a hard
or soft contact, as well our perception of the fragility or robustness of the projectile.
This evolutionary capacity of the CNS, allows us to use the cortical pathways to
perceive information about the characteristics of an object to be intercepted at the
same time as (different) information sources to regulate the interceptive action. In
this way, we can flexibly adapt our interceptive movements to produce hard and
soft contacts with a projectile in a safe and functional manner.

An interesting question that still remains concerns the validity of Goodale and
colleagues' hypotheses for generalising the findings to normal human participants
under natural task constraints. The generality issue has only been partially addressed
in research that has utilised pictorial illusions such as the Ebbinghaus illusion (for
example Aglioti *et al.*, 1995) and the Müller–Lyer illusion (e.g. Gentilucci *et al.*,
1996; Figure 12.2a). Studies such as those by Aglioti *et al.* (1995; see also
Haffenden and Goodale, 1998), presented participants with two adjacent
Ebbinghaus illusions (Figure 12.2b) and by manipulating the size of the annulus,
participants either perceived the two inner disks as the same size, when in fact
they are physically different. Or, the perception can be of two different-sized disks
when in fact they were the same size. Depending on the nature of the disk
perception, participants were asked to reach out and grasp the inner disk. That is,
with equal size perception, participants were required to pick up the left-hand
disk. With unequal size perception the right-hand disk was chosen. By their choice

of disks, participants indicated that were susceptible to the illusion throughout the experiment. However, while their perceptual selection processes did not pick up the appropriate information to distinguish between characteristic features of the disks (e.g. picking up the left-hand disk when in fact the disks were the same size), participants' grip aperture remained scaled to the actual size of the disk. In other words, the perceptual system controlling perception for recognition was deceived by the illusion, while the system controlling perception for action was not as susceptible to the illusion.

Practical implications

To summarise the implications of the two-visual system model, it would seem that information is perceived in conjunction with the constraint of individual intentionality, that is, what performers intend to do with the information they pick up. If the performer's aim is to engage in a perceptual recognition task, then the information from the ventral stream is most important. If, however, co-ordinated movement, coupled to an optical information source, is required e.g. during an interceptive action in sport, then it seems that information from the dorsal stream is most important. This interpretation of the data is well illustrated by some of the research discussed in Chapter 9 by Michaels and Zaal. They refer to the observation of different behavioural responses produced when experimental task constraints have required participants to judge the landing position of a ball compared to when they have been required to 'catch' a virtual ball. In other words, under two distinct task constraints, participants have two different types of perceptual task to perform. The first is perception for recognition and the second is perception for action. Based on their findings, Michaels and Zaal suggest that the generalisability of data from simulation studies used in the optical acceleration paradigm may be limited, since the behavioural outcomes are different from those task constraints where object-directed action takes place. The argument proposed in this chapter is that, by considering Milner and Goodale's (1992) model, the conclusions of Michaels and Zaal may also have a neurological basis. The ventral stream may be utilised for perception of information in judgement tasks and the dorsal stream may be used for task constraints emphasising movement production. So, simulation studies may not only produce different behavioural outcomes, but they also could have different neural substrates adding further weight to their lack of generalisability to tasks beyond perceptual discrimination.

Does the dorsal stream support perception during interceptive movements?

A concept that is crucial to interceptive actions is that of perception-action coupling (Gibson, 1966; see also Chapter 8 by Benguigui, Ripoll and Broderick, Chapter 7 by Montagne and Laurent, Chapter 17 by Handford, Chapter 20 by Scott and Chapter 21 by Maraj). It is fundamental to discussions of the nature of 'online control' where perceptual information is intricately linked to movement, producing a circular causal relationship. It has been suggested (Goodale and Humphrey, 1998; see also Keil *et al.*, 2000) that the neural foundations of perception–action coupling may lie within the dorsal stream. This neural pathway seems well suited to support this role, with its evident influence in performing online control of actions such as reaching and grasping (see the discussions on patient DF and on the illusions studies above). Previous Gibsonian-inspired work on perception–action coupling and online control, has produced fascinating, elaborate, even ground-breaking, theorising. It has, however, tended to lack any substantial neural explanation (see Summers, 1998), although Gibson himself did make an attempt to rectify this weakness in his 1966 book (Warren, 1998). With the accumulated neuroscience evidence that has become available in recent years, and the improvements in technology, we now have the ability to make predictions and test the neural correlates of various psychological frameworks for modelling processes of perception and action. There is little need to rely on implicit assumptions, now that it is becoming possible to directly test conceptualisations. Furthermore, as discussed in the chapters by Handford, Scott and by Maraj, knowledge of the functional divisions of the visual system, allied to theorising on perception–action coupling in ecological psychology, may form a sound basis for deciding how to organise practice of multi-component interceptive actions such as self-paced extrinsic timing tasks and running to locate a target in space.

Integration of modelling in cognitive science and ecological psychology

Goodale and Humphrey (1998) have recently suggested that the ventral stream with its links to higher brain areas such as memory, could be analogous with the idea of information-processing from cognitive theories. In other words the neural substrate of a representational approach may be best described through the qualities of the ventral stream. Patient DF with her inability to name objects, express their orientation or express their relation to other objects best illustrates this. By utilising the two-visual system model, it is possible to offer a pathway that integrates concepts and ideas from dynamical systems theory and cognitive science (Davids *et al.*, 2001).

In fact, this idea of integrating paradigms is not new. Colley (1989) produced a model that proposed three different processing routes for perception and action. The first route was considered to be mediated by working memory and is used in instances such as learning and intentional behaviour. The second route, which is more automatic, was proposed to be used during well-rehearsed or automated ontogenetic tasks. The final route has direct links from the perceptual systems to the action systems and was proposed to be most appropriate for understanding control of phylogenetic skills such as locomotion and postural control.

Davids *et al.* (1994) argued that this model could provide a possible basis for the integration of ideas from the dynamical systems and cognitive science approaches to the study of human behaviour. The premise of their argument for the possible reconciliation between the two paradigms is the obvious involvement of intentional, goal directed behaviour in many human movements. To support their arguments, they used an example of the strategic actions of a spin bowler in cricket. In order to create a 'mental set' in which a batsman's perception of information is heavily constrained by expectations based on past probabilities, the bowler may deliver four consecutive leg breaks followed by a flipper.[2] The authors suggested 'such tactical behaviour may require an element of top-down interpretation which non-linear dynamical approaches have yet to account for' (p. 517). The use of the model developed by Colley (1989) to highlight a possible avenue for the integration of the two paradigms (cognitive and dynamical systems) in highlighting how intentionality and dynamics may be integrated in goal-directed behaviour, is an interesting theoretical suggestion (see also Chapter 13 by Button and Summers). However, as Davids *et al*. (1994) argued at the time, further empirical work was needed to justify such a proposition. There is a strong possibility that by utilising Milner and Goodale's (e.g. 1995) model, we now have another avenue for integration, one which has a significantly stronger empirical evidence base.

Conclusion

The purpose of this chapter was to explore how, with the present wealth in neuroscience evidence, we could utilise research to substantiate theoretical frameworks for understanding perception and action processes for interceptive movement tasks. With current technological advances and data from a wide range of behavioural research studies, we have the opportunity to describe far more about goal-directed human behaviours, such as interceptive actions, than ever before. Consequently, there may be little need to over-rely on hypothetical constructs to complete our theorising. By integrating ideas and theory from multiple disciplines, including cognitive science, ecological psychology, dynamical systems theory and the neurosciences, it is hoped that understanding of perception and action processes can be progressed from its current level. Of course, a critical stance has always to be maintained, as suggested by Michaels (2000), in order to address any 'thorny' philosophical issues raised by mixing metaphors (Keil and Davids, 2000). Nevertheless, the next few years may represent an exciting time to be investigating within the field of interceptive actions, due to the potential of an integrative modelling approach.

Notes

1 Obviously, evidence from primates has to be considered with caution. Anatomical features and connectivity may not necessarily be the same as in the human CNS, although many homologues have been found in previous research.

2 For readers unfamiliar with the vagaries of cricket, spin bowlers learn how to bowl leg breaks and flippers using apparently similar movement patterns. However, highly refined differences in placement of fingers on the ball and release characteristics from the hand, result in the ball deviating from the turf with completely different trajectories, leaving an unsuspecting batsman waving the bat in thin air. Leg breaks move suddenly away from a right-handed batsman after hitting the ground, whereas flippers 'squirt' unexpectedly straight towards the stumps.

References

Aglioti, S., DeSouza, J.F.X. and Goodale, M.A. (1995). Size-contrast illusions deceive the eye but not the hand. *Current Biology* **5**, 679–85.

Arbib, M.A., Érdi, P. and Szentágothai, J. (1998). *Neural Organization: Structure, Function and Dynamics.* Cambridge, MA: MIT Press.

Basar, E. (1998). *Brain Function and Oscillations I: Brain Oscillations. Principles and Approaches.* New York: Springer.

Bruce, V., Green, P.R. and Georgeson, M. (1996). *Visual Perception: Physiology, Psychology and Ecology* (3rd edn). London: Lawrence Erlbaum Associates.

Colley, A. (1989). Learning motor skills: integrating cognition and action. In *Acquisition and Performance of Cognitive Skills* (edited by A. Colley and J. Beech). Chichester: John Wiley.

Davids, K., Handford, C. and Williams, M. (1994). The natural physical alternative to cognitive theories of motor behaviour: an invitation for interdisciplinary research in sports science? *Journal of Sports Science* **12**, 495–528.

Davids, K., Williams, A.M., Button, C. and Court, M. (2001). An integrative modeling approach to the study of intentional movement behavior. In *Handbook of Sport Psychology* (2nd edn.) (edited by R.N. Singer, H. Hausenblas and C. Jannelle). New York: John Wiley and Sons.

De Angelis, G.C. (2000). Seeing in three dimensions: the neurophysiology of stereopsis. *Trends in Cognitive Sciences* **4**, 80–90.

Decety, J. and Grèzes, J. (1999). Neural mechanisms subserving the perception of human actions. *Trends in Cognitive Sciences* **3**, 172–8.

Dobbins, A.C., Jeo, R.M., Fiser, J. and Allman, J.M. (1998). Distance modulation of neural activity in the visual cortex. *Science* **281**, 552–5.

Edelman, G. (1992). *Bright Air, Brilliant Fire: On the Matter of Mind.* New York: Penguin.

Eggermont, J.J. (1998). Is there a neural code? *Neuroscience and Behavioural Reviews* **22**, 355–70.

Felleman, D.J. and van Essen, D.C. (1991). Distributed hierarchical processing in the primate cerebral cortex. *Cerebral Cortex* **1**, 1–47.

Freeman, W.J. (1997). Nonlinear neurodynamics of intentionality. *Journal of Mind and Behavior*, **18**, 291–304.

Freeman, W.J. (1999). *How Brains Make up their Mind.* London: Weidenfeld & Nicolson.

Gazzaniga, M.S. (1995). *The Cognitive Neurosciences.* Cambridge, MA: MIT Press.

Gazzaniga, M.S. (2000). The New Cognitive Neurosciences (2nd edn). Cambridge, MA: MIT Press.

Gentilucci, M., Chieffi, S., Daprati, E., Saetti, C.M. and Toni, I. (1996). Visual illusion and action. *Neuropsychologia* **34**, 369–76.

Gibson, J.J. (1966). *The Senses Considered as Perceptual Systems.* Boston: Houghton Mifflin.

Goodale, M.A. and Humphrey, K.G. (1998). The objects of action and perception. *Cognition* **67**, 181–207.

Goodale, M.A. and Milner, A.D. (1992). Separate visual pathways for perception and action. *Trends in Neurosciences* **15**, 20–5.

Goodale, M.A., Milner, A.D., Jackobson, L.S. and Carey, D.P. (1991). A neurological dissociation between perceiving objects and grasping them. *Nature* **349**, 154–6.

Greenfield, S. (1997). *The Human Brain: A Guided Tour.* London: Phoenix.

Gregory, R. (1998). *Eye and Brain. The Psychology of Seeing.* Oxford: Oxford University Press.

Haffenden, A.M. and Goodale, M.A. (1998). The effects of pictorial illusion on prehension and perception. *Journal of Cognitive Neuroscience* **10**, 122–36.

Harris, L.R. and Jenkin, M. (1998). *Vision and Action*. Cambridge: Cambridge University Press.

Kandel, E.R., Schwartz, J.H. and Jessell, T.M. (2000). *Essentials of Neural Science and Behavior*. London: Prentice Hall International.

Keil, D. and Davids, K. (2000). Lifting the screen on neural organization: is computational functional modelling necessary? *Behavioural and Brain Sciences* **23**, 102–3.

Keil, D., Holmes, P., Bennett, S., Davids, K. and Smith, N. (2000). Theory and practice in sport psychology and motor behaviour needs to be constrained by integrative modelling of brain and behaviour. *Journal of Sports Sciences* **18**, 433–43.

Kelso, J.A.S. (1995). *Dynamic Patterns: The Self-Organization of Brain and Behavior*. Cambridge, MA: MIT Press.

Kutas, M. and Federmeier, K.D. (1998). Minding the body. *Psychophysiology* **35**, 135–50.

McCrone, J. (1999). *Going Inside*. London: Faber & Faber.

Michaels, C.F. (2000). Information, perception and action: what should ecological psychologists learn from Milner and Goodale (1995)? *Ecological Psychology* **12**, 241–58.

Milner, A.D. and Goodale, M.A. (1995). *The Visual Brain in Action*. Oxford: Oxford University Press.

Milner, A.D., Perrett, D.I., Johnston, R.S., Benson, P.J., Jordan, T.R., Heeley, D.W., Bettucci, D., Mortara, F., Mutani, R., Terazzi, E. and Davidson, D.L.W. (1991). Perception and action in 'visual form agnosia'. *Brain* **114**, 39–49.

Sakata, H., Taira, M., Murata, A. and Mine, S. (1995). Neural mechanisms of the visual guidance of hand action in the parietal cortex of the monkey. *Cerebral Cortex* **5**, 429–38.

Seemungal, D., Ginns, S. Dixon, D. and Ewart, W. (1999). *Neuroscience: An Audit of Research Activity*. London: Wellcome Trust.

Sporns, O. and Edelman, G.M. (1998). Bernstein's dynamic view of the brain: the current problems of modern neurophysiology (1945). *Motor Control* **2**, 283–305.

Summers, J. (1998). Has ecological psychology delivered what it promised? In J.P. Piek (ed.), *Motor Behavior and Human Skill: A Multidisciplinary Approach*. Champaign, IL: Human Kinetics.

Tanaka, K. (1996). Inferotemporal cortex and object vision. *Annual Review of Neuroscience* **19**, 109–39.

Thelen, E. and Smith, L.B. (1994). *A Dynamic Systems Approach to the Development of Cognition and Action*. Cambridge, MA: MIT Press.

Ungerleider, L.G. and Mishkin, M. (1982). Two cortical visual system. In *Analysis of Visual Behavior* (edited by D.J. Ingle, M.A. Goodale and R.J.W. Mansfield). Cambridge MA: MIT Press.

Varela, F., Thompson, E. and Rosch, E. (1991). *The Embodied Mind*. Cambridge, MA: MIT Press.

Wagemans, J., Verstraten, F.A.J. and He, S. (2001). Beyond the decade of the brain: towards a functional neuroanatomy of the mind. *Acta Psychologica* **107**, 1–7.

Warren, W.H. (1998). The state of flow. In *High-Level Motion Processing: Computational, Neurobiological, and Psychophysical Perspectives* (edited by T. Watanabe). Cambridge MA: MIT Press.

Williams, A.M., Davids, K. and Williams, J.G. (1999). *Visual Perception and Action in Sport*. London: Routledge.

Willingham, D.B. (1998). A neuropsychological theory of motor skill learning. *Psychological Review* **105**, 558–84.

Wise, S.P., Boussaoud, D., Johnson, P.B. and Caminiti, R. (1997) Premotor and parietal cortex: corticocortical connectivity and combinatorial computations. *Annual Review of Neuroscience* **20**, 25–42.

13 Co-ordination dynamics of interceptive actions

Chris Button and Jeffrey Summers

An interceptive action can be defined as an externally-directed movement, the trajectory of which is intended to coincide with that of a desired target, which may or not be in motion. In order to successfully intercept an object, perceptual information from the environment needs to be picked up to place the appropriate limb/s at the right place and time, usually while imparting the appropriate amount of force in relation to the object. A wide variety of interceptive actions form essential features of our everyday lives, from pressing a key on a computer, to shaking someone's hand or hitting a ball in a game of squash. Accordingly, researchers working in the field of human movement behaviour have been intrigued by the co-ordination of interceptive actions for some time (e.g. Hubbard and Seng, 1954; Fitts and Posner, 1967; Alderson, Sully and Sully, 1974; Tyldesley and Whiting, 1975; Lee, 1976; Whiting, 1986; Bootsma, 1989). Undoubtedly, interceptive tasks provide a good opportunity to study the complex interaction between human motor control processes and the dynamic environment in which we live (Tresilian, 1999). They provide researchers with an opportunity to investigate how we co-ordinate our movements with the external environment (Turvey, 1990). However, despite the rich source of literature that has considered this group of movements, a complete understanding of the co-ordination processes underpinning interceptive actions remains elusive.

It is widely believed that a detailed knowledge of the dynamics of the movement system could help us to identify some of the physical, perceptual and mental processes underlying its behaviour (see Chapter 10 by Button; Kelso, 1995; Williams *et al.*, 1999; Chapter 2 by Williams and Starkes). Accordingly, the application of dynamical systems theory to the study of movement co-ordination emphasises an abstract, mathematical description of the kinematics (space–time displacements of limb segments) of movement behaviour (Beek *et al.*, 1995). Researchers studying this approach have focussed attention on the stability and adaptability in the kinematic patterns which emerge from the movement system (e.g. Schöner, 1990; Kelso, 1995). With a background rooted in the tools and applications of nonlinear oscillations, it is not surprising that the main research vehicle of dynamical systems theorists has been rhythmical movements (e.g. Haken, 1983; Schöner and Kelso, 1988; Wallace, 1996). However, due to the lack of empirical evidence utilising other forms of movement, Summers (1998) recently questioned the capacity of a dynamical systems framework to account for discrete movements such as interceptive actions (see also Walter, 1998).

The aim of this chapter is to describe some recent studies on interceptive actions using the dynamical systems approach to movement co-ordination (e.g. Button *et al.*, 2001; Guiard, 1997; Peper *et al.*, 1994; Temprado, Chapter 15 of this volume; Zaal *et al.*, 1999). In the first section, we provide a brief overview of the dynamical systems approach and some of its theoretical predictions in relation to general movement behaviour. An early attempt to formalise a mathematical model of discrete movement (Schöner, 1990) will be described in the following section. We will relate predictions from this theoretical model, in the third section, to behavioural data gained from a range of interceptive actions such as prehension and ball catching.[1] Also, where appropriate, we highlight some of the shortcomings of alternative theoretical models in relation to interceptive actions. Finally, we discuss some of the implications for the dynamical systems approach in explaining the co-ordination and control of interceptive actions.

The dynamical systems approach to the co-ordination of movement behaviour

Traditionally, motor control theorising on interceptive actions has emphasised the role of movement planning in which the trajectory of the intercepting limb is determined by the performer in advance of the movement itself (e.g. Bullock and Grossberg, 1989; Latash, 1993). However, this theoretical approach seems less feasible when the object to be intercepted is moving due to the increase in demands on the performer in terms of processing ongoing feedback and modulation (Zaal *et al.*, 1999). It seems that a theoretical perspective that places a greater emphasis on the close coupling of perceptual information with the co-ordination dynamics of the performer is required for the study of interceptive actions. This type of control requires a model of the movement system in which the co-ordination dynamics are emergent depending on the specific task constraints at any one moment (Peper *et al.*, 1994; Saltzman and Kelso, 1987).

Over the last couple of decades the dynamical systems approach has been increasingly applied to the study of human movement behaviour. It has been proposed that the self-organising tendencies of the movement system can lead to ordered patterns of co-ordinated behaviour emerging from a myriad of possible alternatives (Williams *et al.*, 1999). The fundamental problem for dynamical systems theorists is to identify general laws with which to model the behaviour of complex systems tending towards instability (Kelso, 1995). More specifically, it is important to discover what sources of order exist within movement systems and also whether these stable movement tendencies can be associated or coupled with particular forms of environmental information (for an ecological psychology explanation see Bootsma *et al.*, 1997; Michaels and Beek, 1995; Chapter 7 by Montagne and Laurent).

In a classical model proposed by Haken, Kelso and Bunz (1985), it was formally demonstrated how complex co-ordination patterns can be characterised by just a few key variables, termed collective variables. These authors conceptualised collective variables as properties that describe the relationship between individual micro-components in a system and which can also distinguish between different stable patterns of co-ordination. A relatively common example is the relative phase of two oscillating limbs (i.e. the legs during walking), which is the phase lag in one component's cycle of movement compared to the other component (Clark, 1995). Gait dynamics are based on different phase lag relations between the oscillating limbs. If human locomotion were restricted to only one stable relative phase, life would be very difficult indeed! In order to achieve the flexibility required to meet different circumstances, such as the transition from walking to running (at around 2.0 m s^{-1} for a man of average height) to catch a cricket-ball in the outfield, control parameters guide the system into different states of co-ordination. In this example, the control parameters are the intentions of the performer and the frequency of his/her leg movement. The point is that pattern formation in the movement system occurs spontaneously when one or more control parameters change and guide the system through various stable states.

The stable states that the movement system is drawn towards are known as attractors. In a physical system (e.g. the flow of water in a bathtub), an attractor is a region of state space where the resultant force vector converges to zero (Kugler *et al.*, 1990). For a biological system, on the other hand, attractors represent co-ordination pattern tendencies that may not necessarily be the most energy-efficient patterns, although there is often a strong pull towards these tendencies (e.g. Van Dieen *et al.*, 1998; Sparrow, 2000). For example, Beek and van Santvoord (1992) showed that, if required, skilled jugglers can intentionally revert from a more stable to a less stable phase locking of hand movements to ball flight characteristics in order to 'juggle with flair', despite the additional energy cost to the movement system. A movement system temporarily residing in an attractor is identifiable by several key features: i) localised stability close to the attractor; ii) a resistance to perturbation; iii) enhanced variability leading to fluctuations and sudden transitions when a control parameter is changed; and iv) rapid reversion back to a more stable state (enhanced relaxation time) after a perturbation. There are numerous examples within the dynamical systems literature where attractors have been identified in rhythmical tasks. Such tasks include: finger-tapping (Scholz and Kelso, 1989); wrist and elbow oscillatory actions (Kelso *et al.*, 1991); hand circling (Carson *et al.*, 1996); upper and lower limb movements (Kelso and Jeka, 1992); speech production (Tuller and Kelso, 1990); walking (Whitall and Clark, 1994), and even between-people coupling! (Schmidt *et al.*, 1990).

An important question to answer in the study of interceptive actions is: how does the movement system adapt to the changing task characteristics of a dynamic environment? In order to explain how goal-directed movements are achieved, Schöner and Kelso (1988) introduced the concept of behavioural information. It was proposed that behavioural information (such as memories, intentions, environmental information sources) contributes to the unfolding co-ordination dynamics by 'pulling' the movement system in a particular direction. This should not be construed as a 'one-way' process, however. Whilst behavioural information constrains the co-ordination dynamics to some degree, the performer's existing organisation also constrains what can actually be intended. An example of this subtle relationship is that no matter what movement pattern is utilised, jumping a distance of over nine metres unaided is a very difficult task for humans to achieve! Hence, behavioural information is best expressed as an inherent part of the underlying co-ordination dynamics which is required to achieve a specific goal or aim (Kelso, 1995). This view represents a radically different approach to traditional theoretical approaches in that intentionality is seen as one of a number of important constraints that contribute to the self-organising properties of the human movement system (i.e. heterarchical organisation rather than hierarchical control; see Davids and Button, 2000; Turvey, 1990).

In summary, we have outlined the key concepts of the dynamical systems approach to movement co-ordination. In order to meet the aims of this chapter, it will also be necessary to relate these theoretical principles to empirical data from interceptive actions. But first, we shall describe a dynamical model of discrete movement (Schöner, 1990) which has been formulated from the principles laid down in this section. Using this model it should be possible to construct more specific theoretical predictions with regards to the co-ordination of interceptive actions.

Intentional dynamics of discrete movements (Schöner, 1990)

The work of Schöner (1990) represents one of the few attempts to model discrete, interceptive movements from the dynamical systems approach (see also Saltzman and Kelso, 1987). By mathematically simulating bimanual reaching, Schöner (1990) showed that the components of a discrete action drift in and out of co-ordinated states (attractors) as a result of the interplay between intentional information and the intrinsic dynamics of the movement system (see Figure 13.1). In the model, sufficient scaling of the strength of one parameter (e.g. intentional information) gives rise to movement from an initial stable posture toward a desired target. In order to produce *synchronised* movement from two arms reaching out to intercept targets (fixed-point attractors) the movement system is stabilised by a limit cycle attractor. This effect was described as the discrete analagon of in-phase co-ordination with rhythmical movements (Kelso and Schöner, 1988; Schöner, 1990).

Schöner (1990) also made an interesting observation regarding the co-ordination of bimanual reaching movements when the movement system received an external perturbation. It was argued that the coupling of the two arms generally led to a tendency to synchronise the movement times of the individual limbs. However, if one arm was perturbed relative to the other arm this synchronising effect changed to a tendency to move sequentially (depending on the strength of the perturbation). It was shown that the breakdown of synchronisation was gradual as the two end positions of the arms were made more dissimilar. Moving the arms sequentially was compared to anti-phase co-ordination in rhythmical movement where homologous muscle groups contract in an alternating fashion (Kelso and Schöner,

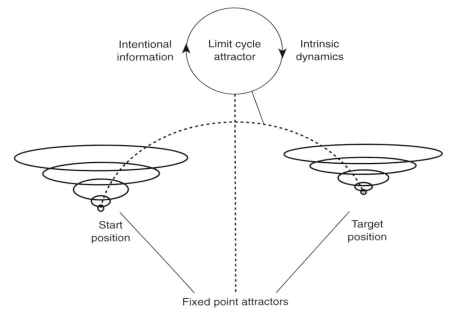

Figure 13.1 Pictorial representation of Schöner's (1990) model of discrete movement.

1988). Therefore, an implication from Schöner's (1990) model is that if the strength of perturbation during an interceptive action, such as prehension, is sufficiently strong, the coupling between components could break down to form separate components (e.g. sequential transport and grasp phases, see Button *et al.*, 2001 for preliminary evidence).

In a subsequent article, Schöner (1994) elaborated on his model to describe how discrete actions can be coupled to environmental sources of information and need not be pre-programmed in advance. The role of behavioural information in the model may be best understood by considering the task of moving the hand from the side of the body to a target (e.g. a stationary ball) located nearby in the environment. He proposed that a movement transition and stabilisation of the target point attractor is only achieved when a critical expansion rate of the object to be intercepted is reached. In other words, with eyes fixed on the ball, visual information received on the retina contributes to the dynamic stabilisation of the initial posture for low expansion rates and to transition to, and stabilisation of, the target posture for sufficiently large expansion rates. With this addition to the model, a target posture need not be specified (planned) in advance of the interceptive movement, instead it is continuously coupled to the perceptual dynamics of the task. Schöner (1994) successfully related his model to a body of work examining a range of discrete movements from the time-to-contact paradigm (e.g. see Lee and Young, 1986) as evidence for the mutuality of perception and action in such tasks (for more recent examples of continuous online regulation of movements by perceptual information see Chapter 1).

In summary, Schöner (1990, 1994) argued that a discrete movement can be modelled as intentional information temporarily shifting the stability of a postural state in order to favour an oscillatory state. The end-point of this oscillation is specified directly by perceptual information (i.e. visual, auditory, proprioceptive information) in a continuous manner until a transition occurs and the system relaxes into the final target postural state. In the following section, we will relate Schöner's work (1990, 1994) to behavioural data taken from some common interceptive tasks, such as reaching, grasping, catching, and striking.

Empirical support for the dynamical systems approach to interceptive actions

Whilst Schöner's (1990) paper represents an encouraging attempt to model discrete movement there has, as yet, been very little effort expended on applying the model's predictions to actual discrete movements. One possible explanation for this state of affairs is that the model was originally conceived for bimanual reaching movements (interlimb co-ordination) to a static target and therefore may not have been considered suitable for describing interceptive actions under a broader range of task constraints. Below, we consider empirical support for the model from a range of task constraints involving reaching, grasping and hitting in static and dynamic task conditions.

Reaching tasks

One recent attempt to make progress was exemplified in a study by Zaal *et al.* (1999) who sought to examine the dynamics of unimanual reaching (intralimb co-ordination) using Schöner's (1990) model as a framework. In this study it was revealed that the dynamics of reaching for both stationary and moving objects can be predicted if the motion of performer and object are considered relative to each other. This theoretical emphasis is different from traditional movement-planning models in which the estimated movements of performer and object are considered independently (e.g. Hoff, 1994; Rosenbaum *et al.*, 1995). In other words, 'movement-planning models thus require that the future interception location and the time remaining until the object will arrive at this location need to be estimated prior to movement execution.' (Zaal *et al.*, 1999: p. 150).

Zaal *et al.* (1999) asked ten healthy adults to reach to targets placed between 20 and 40 cm away. In roughly a third of the trials, the object was moving away from the participant at constant speeds (25, 35 or 45 cm s^{-1}). On the basis of previous work (e.g. Bootsma *et al.*, 1994; Gentilucci *et al.*, 1991; Jakobsen and Goodale, 1991) it has been shown that the behaviour of three key kinematic variables: movement amplitude, movement time and peak velocity, are highly interrelated when reaching for stationary objects. Indeed, Zaal *et al.* (1999) found that as required movement amplitude increased so did the peak velocity and movement time of the arm in a roughly linear fashion (respectively, $R^2 = 0.987, p < 0.001$ and $R^2 = 0.984, p < 0.001$). However, when the object to be grasped was moving, target motion determined the relationship between these variables. With these types of reaches an increase in peak movement velocity accompanied an increase in object speed, whereas movement time only varied slightly.[2]

Zaal *et al.* (1999) implied from their results that the co-ordination of reaching movements unfolds in a continuous manner, as suggested by Schöner (1990), rather than being planned in advance of the movement. It was also proposed that the same underlying dynamic can explain interceptions to both stationary and moving targets. The authors state that, 'the hand can then be best described as moving in an object-related frame of reference (i.e. as if the hand is attached to the object by a springlike device)' (p. 156). Such findings support the principles of the dynamical systems approach and hence the generalisation of Schöner's (1990) model in which a tight coupling is set up between the dynamics of the performer and the target object. However, what do we know about reaching under different task constraints, for example during rhythmical and discrete modes of reaching towards static targets?

Reaching under rhythmical and discrete task constraints

The behavioural study of Guiard (1997) represents one of the few attempts to directly compare rhythmical and discrete modes of movement using a reaching task. Two hypotheses were offered to describe the relation between rhythmical and discrete movements. Either rhythmical movements were concatenations of discrete movements (a chain of discontinuous elements linked together) or discrete movements were a special kind of rhythmical movement in which the number of consecutive cycles is just half. In order to test these hypotheses, Guiard (1997) asked participants to slide a small carriage between two targets. A classical Fitts' law paradigm was used to examine the nature of energy transfer at different indices of difficulty, by changing the size of the targets. It was shown that the acceleration profiles of rhythmical movements exhibited qualitative differences compared to discrete movements, but only above a certain index of difficulty (four to five bits in information processing terms). Therefore, Guiard (1997) concluded that, provided the accuracy requirements are not too stringent, rhythmical movements are not simply a concatenation of discrete movements. In fact, the findings were taken as support for a dynamical systems explanation of reaching movements, in that 'the cyclical case should be considered the general case, and the discrete case a special case' (p. 128).

Summarising so far, the work of Schöner (1990, 1994), Zaal *et al.* (1999) and Guiard (1997) are among the first attempts to adopt a dynamical systems approach to model the control of discrete reaching movements. In these studies, the co-ordination dynamics of reaching movements were analysed and shown to exhibit several identifiable features. For example, where the movement involves more than one moving component (i.e. bimanual reaching) the two components tend towards synchronisation (see Chapter 14 by Tayler). Furthermore, if one component is perturbed relative to the other, this tendency could change so that the components are decoupled to move sequentially (Schöner, 1990). Guiard (1997) showed that the co-ordination dynamics underpinning rhythmical and discrete reaching movements were similar (provided the accuracy requirements of the task were not too demanding). Finally, the relationship shared by key kinematic variables, such as peak velocity and movement time during reaching depends on the initial conditions presented to the performer. Regardless of whether the object to be intercepted is moving or not, the co-ordination of the movement system takes place in an object-related frame of reference. The implication is that a continuous pursuit-tracking, rather than an *a priori* movement-planning, type of control is used (Zaal *et al.*, 1999).

Prehension tasks

Having considered how reaching movements have been used as a task vehicle for studying motor system dynamics, it could also be instructive to consider whether prehension (or reaching and grasping) is amenable to such an analysis. Button *et al.* (2001) addressed this issue by comparing the co-ordination dynamics of prehension when performed in rhythmical and discrete modes. In their study, six adults performed a unimanual, prehension task whilst movement time was systematically increased via an auditory metronome. In a rhythmical condition,[3] participants moved between two plastic dowels in a continuous manner to correspond with six different frequencies: 0.5, 0.75, 1.0, 1.25, 1.5, and 1.75 Hz respectively. However, for the discrete condition only, the movement time from the first dowel to the second dowel was specified by the metronome (participants could return to the first dowel whenever they wanted). Co-ordination of grasp and transport phases was characterised by the relative time of final hand closure (T_{rfc}) which previous work had highlighted as a potential collective variable for this task (Wallace *et al.*, 1994; Button *et al.*, 1998).

Button *et al.* (2001) examined the assumption that the Schöner (1990) model could be generalised to the study of intralimb co-ordination of a unimanual movement, where the two related components are the reach and grasp phases (see also Zaal *et al.*, 1999). In line with the predictions of Schöner (1990), the reach and grasp components tended toward synchrony, with the final grasp beginning at roughly 85 per cent of the overall movement time. Button *et al.* (2001) also found that there were no differences in T_{rfc} between the rhythmical and discrete conditions. This finding has important implications for the dynamical systems approach as it indicates that rhythmical and discrete movements could have similar control principles underlying them (see also Guiard, 1997).

During the scaling technique, the slowest step (0.5 Hz) seemed to have the greatest effect on the subject's co-ordination, in that T_{rfc} was often earlier at this step than at any other (see Table 13.1). This effect was perhaps due to the availability of a greater amount of time which afforded a different movement strategy to that available at the other frequencies. Notably, during testing, several subjects moved to the dowel at a comfortable speed then waited with finger and thumb by the dowel for the auditory signal. In effect, this strategy resulted in a comparatively earlier maximum aperture in the transport phase, and hence a decreased T_{rfc} during

Table 13.1 Summary data taken from Button *et al.* (2001a). Mean T_{rfc} is shown at each step of the scaling trials for the rhythmical and discrete conditions. The moment of final closure is expressed as a ratio of overall movement time and converted to degrees (multiplied by 180°). Note that there were significant differences between steps 1 and 3, and steps 1 and 5 in the rhythmical condition ($p < 0.05$).

Step	1	2	3	4	5	6
Rhythmic T_{rfc}	145.3	154.5	157.3	155.4	160.4	153.6
Degrees	(21)	(24)	(21)	(26)	(18)	(26)
Discrete T_{rfc}	144.0	154.6	158.0	160.5	158.2	158.1
Degrees	(29)	(20)	(20)	(18)	(21)	(23)

the lowest frequency. At other speeds this reactionary-response strategy was not functional due to increased time constraints. A similar breakdown of synchronous to sequential behaviour was also predicted by Schöner (1990). He argued that a sufficiently large perturbation to the co-ordination dynamics (brought about here by the changing task constraints of increased movement time) would tend to result in sequential behaviour from the individual components of the system.

Catching tasks

Another interceptive action that has intrigued movement scientists for some time is ball-catching (e.g. Smyth and Marriott, 1982; Whiting, 1986; Savelsbergh *et al.*, 1991; Peper *et al.*, 1994; Laurent *et al.*, 1994; Bennett *et al.*, 1999). This body of literature has been mainly concerned with identifying what forms of perceptual information that are used by the catcher to guide his/her movements (see Chapter 7 by Montagne and Laurent and Chapter 2 by Williams and Starkes). For example, it has been argued that proprioceptive information from the catching limb can be used to help the catcher move the hand to the right 'ball-park spatial location' for catching (Smyth and Marriott, 1982; Bennett *et al.*, 1999). However, the predominant source of perceptual information used by catchers regardless of skill level is vision (Bootsma and Peper, 1992).

Peper *et al.* (1994) were intrigued by whether the control of ball catching is regulated by predictive, visual information about where and when the ball would pass the catcher or alternatively by the kind of pursuit-tracking type of online control advocated by the dynamical systems approach. A series of experiments was conducted in which a ball was swung from a pendulum to the catcher at various angles of approach relative to the performer. As the movement patterns were shown to vary considerably for the different angles of approach, the authors concluded that subjects were not engaged in the strategy of estimating future passing distance and then programming a movement response. Interestingly, it was apparent that the moment of final hand closure was unaffected by the angle of ball approach providing further indication that this movement parameter acts as an attractor during these types of interceptive movements. In line with the work of Schöner (1990) and Zaal *et al.* (1999), the reach component of the hand toward the target seemed continuously geared to perceptually specified information about the required velocity (e.g. the tau margin, or the inverse of the relative rate of dilation of the approaching object). This model seems intuitively appealing as it explains how the skilled catcher can take advantage of the visually perceived relationship between the hand and the approaching ball to make fine-tuned adjustments to hand position relatively close to hand–ball contact if necessary.

One important prediction of the dynamical systems approach to movement behaviour is that stable movement patterns (attractors) are resistant to the effects of an external perturbation. Button et al. (2000) studied this issue with a ball-catching task by examining the co-ordination of reach and grasp components in response to an unexpected perturbation applied to the wrist. Six skilled catchers (mean age = 27.5 years) performed 64 trials in which tennis balls were projected at approximately 8 m s⁻¹. The trial blocks consisted of ten non-perturbed trials (baseline), and a block of 54 trials of which 20 trials were perturbed. The perturbation was in the form of a resistive force (12 N) applied via a piece of cord attached to a computer-controlled mechanical brake. Button et al. (2000) employed a detailed individual analysis of the catching kinematics to ascertain whether T_{rfc} was generally resistant to the sudden perturbation to the movement.

In perturbed trials, the catchers tended to achieve maximal wrist velocity earlier in relation to the time of hand–ball contact (309 ms before contact ± 61) than in the baseline condition (237 ms ± 68). Furthermore, the wrist velocity profile of five out of six participants generally exhibited a double peak immediately after a perturbation. However, aperture variables such as the T_{rfc} (approximately 70 per cent of overall movement time) were not typically affected. Such data support the view that the relative time of final hand closure could be a stable parameter, which is linked to a critical expansion rate of the ball as it approaches the hand (Schöner, 1994). Button et al. (2000) argued that, in order to compensate for the perturbation, the relative stability of grasp and transport coupling was varied from trial to trial. This finding shows how 'dynamic stability' (Kelso, 1981), rather than stability per se, is a characteristic of skilled performers. Skilled catchers were able to exploit redundant degrees of freedom in the motor system to adapt their movements when faced with sudden, unexpected changes in task constraints.

To summarise, several behavioural studies have emerged recently in which the findings support the dynamical systems approach to co-ordination and control of interceptive actions. The fine-grained movement patterns associated with tasks such as reaching, prehension and ball-catching, have been described in relation to the principles of the dynamical systems approach. Furthermore, some of the key sources of information that are used to guide such actions are beginning to be identified (see also Schöner, 1994). In the final section, we shall consider some of the important implications that are emerging for future work to consider.

Implications of the dynamical systems approach for future work interceptive actions

The modelling of discrete, interceptive actions is an important challenge for dynamical systems theorists. In this chapter we have described how recent studies examining interceptive actions can be interpreted from this theoretical perspective. Several implications can be drawn as a consequence of this process that should be considered in future work.

First, an important methodological consideration for research on interceptive actions is that the level of analysis adopted must be carefully considered in order to verify theoretical predictions. It could be argued that our understanding of interceptive actions in the past has been previously limited by a tendency to focus on outcome scores or error-based measures (Williams *et al.*, 1999). However, it is only with a detailed knowledge of the kinematics of the movement system that we may start to identify potential collective variables and relevant parametric influences. In order to achieve this goal, researchers investigating interceptive actions must have access to sensitive measuring instruments such as high-speed video or virtual reality environments (de Rugy *et al.*, 2000). Such equipment will allow us to examine in much greater detail how movement patterns emerge and are adapted to specific task constraints.

It is also becoming apparent that the statistical tools used to analyse movement data must be appropriate to account for individual variation and subtle changes over time (Bauer and Schöllhorn, 1997; Button and Davids, 1999). For example, more theorists are now advocating individual analysis of movement via the frequency domain (Newell and Slifkin, 1998) or phase-plane plots (Beek *et al.*, 1995) rather than group-based averages and standard deviations which can often be uninformative with regard to system changes over time. Indeed, subtle changes in timing are often a key characteristic for success in interceptive actions and, therefore, the way in which we measure and analyse such movements must begin to reflect this.

The second implication that can be drawn from this chapter concerns how the theoretical modelling of interceptive actions should proceed. One issue in need of further attention is the specific nature of the attractor layout underpinning discrete movements. Previously rhythmical movements were demonstrated to possess a bistable regime (which could be altered through learning, see Zanone and Kelso, 1992). Indeed the collective variable, relative phase, was identified via transitions from one stable regime to another. However, there is considerably less evidence from the research discussed in this chapter that interceptive actions possess a similar potential landscape (see also Sternad *et al.*, 1999). For example, whilst the time of final hand closure appears to exhibit stability when the movement system receives a perturbation (Button *et al.*, 2000), the lack of observable transitional behaviour means that this parameter should remain a collective variable by conjecture for the time being. It is arguable that the kinematics of such movements need to be probed further under more extreme task constraints to unravel whether a multistable regime exists or not.

Another important theoretical issue concerns the type of control used during interceptive actions (i.e. predictive vs. prospective). Traditionally, predictive strategies have been adopted in information-processing models of the performer, in which the future location of the target and the required kinematics of the limb/s are both estimated in advance (e.g. Jeannerod, 1981). However, some recent evidence was discussed suggesting that a prospective control strategy can adequately explain actions such as reaching and ball catching (Peper *et al.*, 1994; Chapter 7 by Montagne and Laurent; Zaal *et al.*, 1999). An important characteristic of this type of control is that timing is regulated directly on the basis of sensory information about the time remaining until hand–target contact. A further possibility not discussed in this chapter is a combination of the two types of control, such as that advocated by the minimum jerk principle (Flash and Hogan, 1985). Here an approximate prediction of final interception location is used (ballistic phase) and once the limb is in the correct 'ball-park', information from the target is used to continually fine-tune the final position of the limb (see also Hoff and Arbib, 1993). Whilst the 'jury is still out' on which theory of control is most appropriate,[4] it seems fair to argue that more common ground exists in regard to a prospective mode during dynamic interceptive actions. For tasks such as catching a ball or playing a shot in tennis, it would seem more functional to the performer to continually couple perception with action to adapt to subtle, unexpected changes inherent in such environments.

A final concern with the theoretical modelling of interceptions is how the description of behavioural information, such as intentionality, should proceed. As Summers (1998) argued, 'all the ingredients now appear to be in place for the modelling of cognition [such as intentionality] as a subset of dynamics. The success of this enterprise is vital for the future development of the dynamical systems approach' (p. 395). In this chapter it has been argued that intentionality should be modelled as a specific parametric influence on the co-ordination dynamics of the movement system. An intention is therefore measurable by the amount of disruption of the intrinsic dynamics in achieving a desired movement goal. In order to comprehensively embed intentionality within the dynamical systems framework, researchers must now seek ways in which the measurement of movement dynamics can be related to neural dynamics in the brain during the unfolding of an interceptive act (for an interesting discourse on dynamics in the brain see Freeman, 2000). This goal represents a difficult challenge and will undoubtedly require some advances in existing technological resources (e.g. functional magnetic resonance imaging, electro-encephalography, etc.), and will also emphasise the interdisciplinary skills of the researcher.

Finally, the present chapter confirms the view that we should no longer consider perception and action as separate systems. The tight coupling between our environment and the way in which our limbs are co-ordinated is unlikely to exist in unrealistically constrained, laboratory-based tasks or those in which perceptual judgements are made in the absence of movement (Bootsma, 1989; Peper *et al.*, 1994). Rather, the important role for movement scientists is to determine the specific information sources (e.g. perceptual invariants) that constrain movement dynamics (Davids *et al.*, 2001a). In fact Chapter 12 by Keil and Bennett shows how there is exciting empirical support emerging from neurophysiology (e.g. Milner and Goodale, 1995) about the way in which the brain receives information to achieve this coupling. Milner and Goodale (1995), amongst others, have argued that there are two separate pathways connecting visual and motor centres in the cerebral cortex (Goodale and Humphrey, 1998; Young, 1992). These pathways consist of a ventral stream, which is critical for the perception and identification of objects, and a dorsal stream, which acts as a dedicated visuomotor pathway suitable for the direct mapping of visual information onto action. An intriguing challenge for future work would be to examine how the co-ordination of interceptive actions is influenced by changes in perceptual information that are mainly picked up via the dorsal stream.

In summary, we have discussed the co-ordination dynamics of interceptive actions and highlighted some relevant implications from key recent experiments in this area. It has been demonstrated that the dynamical systems approach is evolving into a suitable theoretical framework with which to explain the co-ordination of these types of movement. Further modelling is still required, however, to demonstrate how the potential landscape which underlies rhythmical, interlimb movements is altered in comparison to discrete, interceptive movements (Sternad *et al.*, 1999). A body of empirical evidence is also accumulating that is supportive of an emergent, type of control which is continually fine-tuned to perceptual information. The level of analysis chosen for interceptive actions throughout this chapter has been focused on the movement kinematics of the performer. It is likely that future research will seek an integrated application of dynamical systems principles simultaneously at the levels of movement kinematics, kinetics, and the neurophysiology of the motor system, in order to uncover some of the control principles underpinning interceptive actions.

Notes

1 Note also the dynamical systems interpretation adopted in the study of intralimb co-ordination of striking actions such as the volleyball serve (see chapters by Handford and Temprado in this book).

2 Interestingly, Zaal *et al.* (1999) instructed participants to move as quickly and as accurately as possible. However, movement accuracy was not formally measured in this study. In other words, it is possible that participants may have sacrificed the accuracy of their reaching movements by maintaining a constant movement time at different movement amplitudes.

3 Note that, although the prehension has been studied under rhythmical constraints previously by Wallace *et al.* (1994), they did not also consider the co-ordination of this task in its more common discrete mode.

4 The findings of MacLeod and Jenkins (1991) could be interpreted as contradictory evidence to the notion of prospective control. They showed that elite batsmen in cricket could not modify their shots in less 190 ms from the ball bouncing off an unpredictable surface, indicating that, in this task, subjects could not track visual information beyond this time. It should be noted, however, that in the cricket-batting task, a greater inertial force must be generated in order to produce any required corrections. Furthermore, as Lee *et al.* (1983) point out, the time taken to modify an action on the basis of continuously available and changing information is likely to be less than that required to initiate a novel action following a sudden change in visual information.

References

Alderson, G.J.K., Sully, D.J. and Sully, H.G. (1974). An operational analysis of a one-handed catching task using high speed photography. *Journal of Motor Behavior* **6**, 217–26.

Bauer, H.U. and Schöllhorn, W. (1997). Self-organizing maps for the analysis of complex movement patterns. *Neural Processing Letters* **5**, 193–9.

Beek, P.J., Peper, C.E. and Stegeman, D.F. (1995). Dynamical models of movement co-ordination. *Human Movement Science* **14**, 573–608.

Beek, P.J. and van Santvoord, A.A. (1992). Learning the cascade juggle: a dynamical systems analysis. *Journal of Motor Behaviour* **24**, 85–94.

Bennett, S.J., Button, C., Kingsbury, D. and Davids, K. (1999). One-handed catching behavior in children: the effects of practicing in conditions of different informational constraints. *Research Quarterly in Exercise Science* **70**, 220–32.

Bootsma, R.J. (1989). Accuracy of perceptual processes subserving different perception–action systems. *Quarterly Journal of Experimental Psychology* **41A**, 489–500.

Bootsma, R.J. and Peper, C.E. (1992). Predictive visual information sources for the regulation of action with special emphasis on catching and hitting. In L. Proteau and D. Elliott (eds) *Vision and Motor Control*. Amsterdam: Elsevier Science Publishers.

Bootsma, R.J., Fayt, V., Zaal, F.T.J.M. and Laurent, M. (1997). On the information-based regulation of movement. *Journal of Experimental Psychology: Human Perception and Performance* **23**, 1282–9.

Bootsma, R.J., Marteniuk, R.G., MacKenzie, C.L. and Zaal, F.T.J.M. (1994). The speed–accuracy trade-off in manual prehension: effects of movement amplitude object size and object width on kinematic characteristics. *Experimental Brain Research* **98**, 535–41.

Bullock, D. and Grossberg, S. (1989). VITE and FLETE: neural modules for trajectory formation and postural control. In W.A. Hershberger (ed.). *Volitional Action*. Amsterdam: Elsevier Science.

Button, C., Bennett, S.J. and Davids, K. (1998). Co-ordination dynamics of rhythmical and discrete prehension: implications for the scanning procedure and individual differences. *Human Movement Science* **17**, 801–20.

Button, C., Bennett, S.J. and Davids, K. (2001). Grasping a better understanding of the intrinsic dynamics of rhythmical and discrete prehension. *Journal of Motor Behavior* **33**, 27–36.

Button, C. and Davids, K. (1999). Interacting intrinsic dynamics and intentionality requires co-ordination profiling of movement systems. In J. Thomson, D.N. Lee and M. Grealy (eds) *Studies in Perception and Action V*. Mahwah, NJ: Lawrence Erlbaum Associates.

Button, C., Davids, K., Bennett, S.J. and Tayler, M. (2000). Mechanical perturbation of the wrist during one-handed catching. *Acta Psychologica* **105**, 9–30.

Carson, R.G., Thomas, J., Summers, J.J., Walters, M.R. and Semjen, A. (1996). The dynamics of bimanual circling drawing. *Quarterly Journal of Experimental Psychology* **50A**, 664–83.

Clark, J.E. (1995). On becoming skillful: patterns and constraints. *Research Quarterly for Exercise and Sport* **66**, 173–83.

Davids, K. and Button, C. (2000). The cognition–dynamics interface and performance in sport. Commentary on Seiler, R. 'The intentional link between environment and action in the acquisition of skill'. *International Journal of Sport Psychology* **31**, 515–21.

Davids, K., Williams, A.M., Button, C. and Court, M.L.J. (2001a). An integrative modeling approach to the study of intentional movement behavior. In *Handbook of Sport Psychology* (2nd edn) (2001). New York: John Wiley and Sons.

de Rugy, A., Montagne, G., Buekers, M.J. and Laurent, M. (2000). The control of human locomotor pointing under restricted informational conditions. *Neuroscience Letters* **281**, 87–90.

Fitts, P.M. and Posner, M.I. (1967). *Human Performance.* Belmont, CA: Brooks/Cale.

Flash, T. and Hogan, N. (1985). The co-ordination of arm movements: an experimentally confirmed mathematical model. *Journal of Neuroscience* **5**, 1688–703.

Freeman, W.J. (2000). A proposed name for aperiodic brain activity: stochastic chaos. *Neural Networks*, **13**, 11–13.

Gentilucci, M., Castiello, U., Corradini, M.L., Scarpa, M., Umiltà, C. and Rizzolatti, G. (1991). Influence of different types of grasping on the transport component of prehension movements. *Neuropsychologia* **29**, 361–78.

Goodale, M.A. and Humphrey, K.G. (1998). The objects of action and perception. *Cognition* **67**, 181–207.

Guiard, Y. (1997). Fitts' law in the discrete vs. cyclical paradigm. *Human Movement Science* **16**, 97–131.

Haken, H. (1983). *Synergetics, An Introduction: Non-Equilibrium Phase Transitions and Self-Organisation in Physics, Chemistry, and Biology* (2nd edn). Berlin: Springer-Verlag.

Haken, H., Kelso, J.A.S. and Bunz, H. (1985). A theoretical model of phase transitions in human hand movements. *Biological Cybernetics* **51**, 347–56.

Hoff, B. (1994). A model of duration in normal and perturbed reaching movement. *Biological Cybernetics* **71**, 481–8.

Hoff, B. and Arbib, M.A. (1993). Models of trajectory formation and temporal interaction of reach and grasp. *Journal of Motor Behaviour* **25**, 175–92.

Hubbard, A.W. and Seng, S.N. (1954). Visual movement of batters. *Research Quarterly of American Association of Health and Physical Education* **25**, 42–57.

Jakobsen, L.S. and Goodale, M.A. (1991). Factors affecting higher-order movement planning: a kinematic analysis of human prehension. *Experimental Brain Research* **86**, 199–208.

Jeannerod, M. (1981). Intersegmental co-ordination during reaching at natural visual objects. In J. Long and A. Baddeley (eds.), *Attention and Performance* Vol. IX. Hillsdale, NJ: Lawrence Erlbaum Associates.

Kelso, J.A.S. (1981). Contrasting perspectives on order and regulation in movement. In J. Long and A. Baddeley (eds) *Attention and Performance* Vol. IX. Hillsdale, NJ: Lawrence Erlbaum.

Kelso, J.A.S. (1995). *Dynamic Patterns: The Self-Organization of Brain and Behaviour.* London: MIT Press.

Kelso, J.A.S. and Jeka, J.J. (1992). Symmetry breaking dynamics of human multilimb co-ordination. *Journal of Experimental Psychology: Human Perception and Performance* **18**, 645–68.

Kelso, J.A.S., Buchanan, J. and Wallace, S.A. (1991). Order parameters for the neural organisation of single, multijoint limb movement patterns. *Experimental Brain Research* **85**, 432–44.

Kelso, J.A.S. and Scöner, G. (1988). Self-organisation of coordinative movement patterns. *Human Movement Science*, **7**, 27–46

Kugler, P.N., Shaw, R.E., Vicente, K.J. and Kinsella-Shaw, J. (1990). Inquiry into intentional systems I: Issues in ecological physics. *Psychological Research* **52**, 98–121.

Latash, M. (1993). *Control of Human Movement.* Champaign, IL: Human Kinetics.

Laurent, M., Montagne, G. and Savelsbergh, G.J.P. (1994). The control of one-handed catching: the effects of temporal constraints. *Experimental Brain Research* **101**, 312–22.

Lee, D.N. (1976). A theory of visual control of braking based on information about time-to-collision. *Perception* **5**, 437–59.

Lee, D.N. and Young, D.S. (1986). Gearing action to the environment. In H. Heuer and C. Fromm (eds) *Generation and Modulation of Action Patterns*. Berlin: Springer-Verlag.

McLeod, P. and Jenkins, S. (1991). Timing accuracy and decision time in high-speed ball games. *International Journal of Sport Psychology* **22**, 279–95.

Michaels, C.F. and Beek, P. (1995). The state of ecological psychology. *Ecological Psychology* **7**, 259–78.

Milner, D. and Goodale, M. (1995). *The Visual Brain in Action*. Oxford: Oxford University Press.

Newell, K.M. and Slifkin, A.B. (1998). The nature of movement variability. In J.P. Piek (ed.) *Motor Behavior and Human Skill: A Multidisciplinary Perspective*. Champaign, IL.: Human Kinetics.

Peper, C.E., Bootsma, R.J., Mestre, D.R. and Bakker, F.C. (1994). Catching balls: how to get the hand to the right place at the right time. *Journal of Experimental Psychology: Human Perception and Performance* **20**, 591–612.

Rosenbaum, D.A., Loukopoulos, L.D., Meulenbroek, R.G.J., Vaughan, J. and Engelbrecht, S.E. (1995). Planning reaches by evaluating stored postures. *Psychological Review* **102**, 28–67.

Saltzman, E. and Kelso, J.A.S. (1987). Skilled actions: a task-dynamic approach. *Psychological Review* **94**, 84–106.

Savelsbergh, G.J.P., Whiting, H.T.A. and Bootsma, R.J. (1991). Grasping tau. *Journal of Experimental Psychology: Human Perception and Performance* **17**, 315–22.

Schmidt, R.C., Carello, C. and Turvey, M.T. (1990). Phase transitions and critical fluctuations in the visual co-ordination of rhythmic movements between people. *Journal of Experimental Psychology: Human Perception and Performance* **16**, 227–47.

Scholz, J.P. and J.A.S. Kelso, (1989). A quantitative approach to understanding the formation and change of coordinated movement patterns. *Journal of Motor Behavior* **21**, 122–44.

Schöner, G. (1990). A dynamic theory of co-ordination of discrete movement. *Biological Cybernetics* **63**, 257–70.

Schöner, G. (1994). Dynamic theory of action–perception patterns: the time-before-contact paradigm. *Human Movement Science* **13**, 415–40.

Schöner, G. and Kelso, J.A.S. (1988). A synergetic theory of environmentally-specified and learned patterns of movement co-ordination. II. Component oscillator dynamics. *Biological Cybernetics* **58**, 81–9.

Smyth, M.M. and Marriott, A.M. (1982). Vision and proprioception in simple catching. *Journal of Motor Behavior* **14**, 143–52.

Sparrow, W.A. (2000) (ed.). *Energetics of Human Ativity*. Champaign, IL: Human Kinetics.

Sternad, D., Dean, W.J. and Schaal, S. (1999). Interaction of discrete and rhythmic dynamics in single-joint movements. In M. Grealy and J. Thomson (eds) *Studies in Perception and Action V*. Mahwah, NJ: Lawrence Erlbaum Associates.

Summers, J. (1998). Has ecological psychology delivered what it promised? In J.P. Piek (ed.) *Motor Behavior and Human Skill: A Multidisciplinary Approach*. Champaign, IL: Human Kinetics.

Tresilian, J.R. (1999). Analysis of recent empirical challenges to an account of interceptive timing. *Perception and Psychophysiology* **61**, 515–28.

Tuller, B. and Kelso, J.A.S. (1990). Phase transitions in speech production and their perceptual consequences. In M. Jeannerod (ed.) *Attention and Performance XII*. Hillsdale, NJ: Erlbaum.

Turvey, M.T. (1990). Coordination. *American Psychologist* **45**, 938–53.

Tyldesley, D. and Whiting, H.T.A. (1975). Operational timing. *Journal of Human Movement Studies* **1**, 172–7.

Van Dieen, J.H., van der Burg, P., Raaijmakers, T.A.J. and Toussaint, H.M. (1998). Effects of repetitive lifting on kinematics: inadequate anticipatory control or adaptive changes? *Journal of Motor Behavior* **30**, 20–32.

Wallace, S.A. (1996). Dynamic pattern perspective of rhythmic movement: an introduction. In H.N. Zelaznik (ed.) *Advances in Motor Learning and Control*. Champaign, IL: Human Kinetics.

Wallace, S.A., Stevenson, E., Spear, A. and Weeks, D.L. (1994). Scanning the dynamics of reaching and grasping movements. *Human Movement Science* **13**, 255–89.

Walter, C. (1998). An alternative view of dynamical systems concepts in motor control and learning. *Research Quarterly for Exercise and Sport* **69**, 326–33.

Whitall, J. and Clark, J.E. (1994). The development of typical interlimb co-ordination. In S.P. Swinnen (ed.), *Interlimb Co-ordination: Neural, Dynamical and Cognitive Constraints*. London: Academic Press.

Whiting, H.T.A. (1986). Isn't there a catch in it somewhere? *Journal of Motor Behavior* **18**, 486–91.

Williams, A.M., Davids, K. and Williams, J.G. (1999). *Visual Perception and Action in Sport*. London: E & FN Spon.

Young, M.P. (1992). Objective analysis of the topological organization of the primate cortical visual system. *Nature* **358**, 152–5.

Zaal, F.T.J.M., Bootsma, R.J. and van Wieringen, P.C.W. (1999). Dynamics of reaching for stationary and moving objects: data and model. *Journal of Experimental Psychology: Human Performance and Performance* **25**, 149–61.

Zanone, P.G. and Kelso, J.A.S. (1992). Evolution of behavioral attractors with learning: nonequilibrium phase transitions. *Journal of Experimental Psychology: Human Perception and Performance* **18**, 403–21.

14 Bimanual co-ordination in catching behaviour

Martin A. Tayler

Research into the co-ordination of bimanual movements has been dominated by the use of static interceptive actions such as manual aiming (e.g. Schmidt, Zelaznik, Hawkins, Frank and Quinn, 1979; Marteniuk and MacKenzie, 1980; Sherwood, 1994) and rhythmical tapping tasks (e.g. Kelso, 1984; Heuer, 1985). There has been limited work on the co-ordination of dynamic interceptive actions such as two-handed catching. Two contrasting explanations of bimanual co-ordination receiving considerable attention in the past are those proposed by Kelso, Southard, and Goodman (e.g. 1979), and Marteniuk and MacKenzie (e.g. 1980). Considerable debate still exists over the underlying mechanism(s) responsible for interlimb co-ordination. The critical issue concerns whether the brain specifies the states of individual muscles separately in each limb or whether the activity of muscle groups across limbs is co-ordinated as part of one functional structure. Marteniuk and colleagues proposed a neural cross-talk model emphasising the role of a symbolic movement representation within the central nervous system (CNS) (see for example, Cohen, 1970; 1971; Marteniuk and MacKenzie, 1980; Marteniuk, MacKenzie and Baba, 1984). It was suggested that temporal and spatial outcomes of bimanual movements are a function of neural cross-talk between motor command centres. It was argued that neural cross-talk could occur at cortical and/or subcortical levels of the CNS via the descending contralateral/ipsilateral neural pathways. Kelso and colleagues (1979; 1983) proposed an alternative model of bimanual co-ordination to argue that the brain sends signals to functional muscle groupings superimposed across the two limbs. Their data demonstrating high levels of inter-limb synchrony have been interpreted as support for the idea of actions being controlled via co-ordinative structures (Turvey, 1977), proposed as an answer to the degrees of freedom problem (Bernstein, 1967).

In this chapter, the major existing models of bimanual co-ordination are first outlined in some detail for the reader. Next, the implications for the co-ordinative structure model of bimanual co-ordination for the study of dynamic interceptive actions, such as two-handed catching, are discussed. Finally, the issue of the development of stability in co-ordinative structures for bimanual co-ordination as a constraint on two-handed catching performance in young children is considered.

Models of bimanual co-ordination

Kelso and colleagues (e.g. 1979; see also Kelso, Putnam and Goodman, 1983) investigated bimanual aiming movements to static targets over different distances (6 and 24 cm). In the first of three experiments reported, participants were required to move index fingers from a centrally-located position to touch lateral targets as quickly and accurately as possible. No other instructions were provided on how to organise the movements. Evidence that the limbs were functioning as a single unit was observed when participants initiated two-handed movements 'virtually simultaneously' according to the authors, with the largest interlimb difference in reaction time (RT) being 8 ms. Within-subject correlations for RTs between left and right hands in the two-handed conditions ranged from 0.95–0.97. Moreover, movement time (MT) data also showed that the participants' hands moved at different speeds to different target endpoints. Perhaps the main outcome from that study was that, even when each limb was required to move different distances to the targets, times to peak velocity (TPV) and acceleration (TPA) for each limb showed a synchronous pattern, despite the fact that both limbs travelled at entirely different speeds. The mean time difference in peak velocity for each hand, calculated over six trials for each subject, was 9 ms. Similarly, remarkably low levels of interlimb variability were shown in the positive peak acceleration phases (14 ms) and negative peak acceleration phases (4 ms) of the aiming movement.

These findings led Kelso and colleagues (e.g. 1979; 1983) to conclude that the brain sends signals to muscle groupings superimposed across the two limbs. Timing was seen as an essential variable (i.e. a variable that reflects the overall behavioural organisation during action) in the control of bimanual co-ordination. These data have been interpreted as support for the theoretical notion of actions being controlled via co-ordinative structures (Turvey, 1977), proposed as an answer to the degrees of freedom problem in the human motor system (Bernstein, 1967). Rather than the limbs being controlled separately, functional groups of muscles form the significant units of action, thus reducing the cognitive load placed upon the executive system.

An alternative view of bimanual co-ordination was proposed by Marteniuk and MacKenzie (1980; see also Marteniuk, MacKenzie and Baba, 1984). The task in their experiments required participants to aim at a 1 mm target with each hand holding a weighted stylus. As in the experiments of Kelso and colleagues, participants performed aiming movements in conditions where the limbs were required to move the same and different distances to reach the lateral targets (10 and 30 cm distance). Again, participants were instructed to move as quickly and accurately as possible to the targets, and simultaneity of movement was not mentioned by the experimenters. Results from the same distance conditions agreed with those of Kelso, Southard and Goodman (1979) evidencing strong correlations in temporal sequencing between the limbs. However, no such associations were obtained when the limbs were required to travel different distances to the targets. Distance by hand statistical interactions were found for RT and MT data. For example, the left-hand RT was faster than right-hand RT when the left hand was required to move the stylus a greater distance, and MT for the hand moving to the closer target was faster than for the hand moving to the further target. In fact, 25 per cent of the total MT differences between each limb in the disparate distances condition exceeded 50 ms. Although significant within-subject correlations for RT (range of $r = 0.96–0.98$) and MT (range of $r = 0.72–0.82$) for the left and right hands were noted, the authors argued that an examination of individual subject means demonstrated only a consistency of difference in the relationship between the hands. For example, in the condition where the two hands travelled the same distance to the lateral targets, half the participants showed faster MTs with the right hand and half moved faster with the left hand. Finally, kinematic profiles for velocity and acceleration patterns revealed similarity in conditions where each hand had identical displacement requirements with styli of the same weight (average r between hands $= 0.91$). However, varying the mass of the stylus or the distance to the targets for each hand lowered the relationship between the acceleration patterns (range of $r = 0.43–0.70$). The considerable interaction and asymmetrical effects noted between the limbs, when each was required to travel different distances to the targets, led the authors to reject the arguments of Kelso, Southard and Goodman (1979) for a common structure underlying the temporal patterning of the two limbs in bimanual aiming.

The model of Marteniuk and MacKenzie (1980) suggested that temporal and spatial outcomes of two-handed movements are a function of neural cross-talk between motor command centres in the CNS. It was proposed that the neural cross-talk could occur at cortical and/or subcortical levels of the CNS via the descending contralateral/ipsilateral neural pathways. A further suggestion was that motor commands originating in one side of the motor cortex caused movement in the ipsilateral limb *and* interfered with movement in the contralateral limb. When the limbs were required to move the same distance, no interference occurred because identical motor commands were produced for each limb. However, in conditions where the arms moved different distances, the separate motor commands issued for each limb were believed to result in interference in the movement time and spatial accuracy of the bimanual aiming movement. The mechanism behind the interference was hypothesised to exist in the need for separate intensity (i.e. impulse) and spatial endpoint commands for each limb to govern required differences in movement outcomes. High intensities prescribed for one limb (i.e. the limb travelling the greater distance) would inhibit activity in the contralateral limb, while lower intensities would have a facilitative effect.

This aspect of the model, that separate commands are issued to each limb, logically suggests an increase in the cognitive load on the CNS and, thus, exacerbates the degrees of freedom problem for the performer.

Clearly, both the models proposed by Kelso and colleagues (1979; 1983) and Marteniuk and colleagues (1980; 1984) are still incomplete with regards to all types of movement goals in bimanual co-ordination. For example, perhaps the most prevalent bimanual co-ordination requirement in many ball games is for the two limbs to move to intercept dynamic targets in space. It may be argued that catching could be considered as a type of dynamic aiming task (see Sivak and

MacKenzie, 1992). To date, there has been no convincing comparison of the predictive utility of the existing models for explaining the co-ordination of bimanual movements during interceptive actions in sport (e.g. wicket-keeping in cricket, setting in volleyball, receiving a pass in basketball and soccer goalkeeping). It is clear that the existing data from each of the models cannot describe the underlying co-ordination dynamics in an activity where the major task constraint is for the limbs to move over the same and different distances to the same dynamic target endpoint (such as in two-handed catching).

A question raised by the overview of existing models of bimanual co-ordination concerns their utility for understanding performance of common, bimanual dynamic interceptive actions in sport where the target is dynamic and not static, and where the limbs typically have to move to the same endpoint (i.e. two-handed catching). Analysis of the temporal sequencing of the two limbs during the task of two-handed catching affords a relative comparison of the explanatory power of both models of bimanual co-ordination for this particular task. As mentioned above the two models predict different outcomes with respect to the velocity and acceleration traces of the limbs when each is required to move a different distance during the task. If the theory of Kelso and colleagues (1979; 1983) is to be supported then the limbs should demonstrate a synchronous pattern with regards to velocity and acceleration data. Furthermore, the evidence should indicate that movements were initiated simultaneously and that the limbs travelled at different speeds. On the other hand, if the model of Marteniuk and colleagues (e.g. 1984) receives support, it is likely that the limbs moving different distances to perform a catch would demonstrate different points of initiation resulting in few interlimb correlations for velocity and acceleration data.

In order to partly address this issue Tayler and Davids (1997) undertook a kinematic analysis of skilled two-handed catchers. Eleven participants caught tennis balls with both hands in three conditions (25 trials per condition): condition 1, ball projected to the right shoulder area (left hand moved greater distance); condition 2, ball projected to center of the chest area, (both hands moved same distance); and condition 3, ball projected to left shoulder area (right hand moved greater distance). The ball projection speed for each trial throughout the study was held constant at 9 m s^{-1}. The variability of projection was such that the balls fell within a circle 20 cm in diameter centred at a height of 1.7 m above ground height at a distance of 7.20 m from the ball projection machine. A three-dimensional video film analysis (50 Hz) was undertaken for all participants. The main measures of interest from the video analysis were correlations between the limbs in the velocity and acceleration data and movement initiation time (MIT) of the left and right limbs for each individual subject. MIT was defined as the time taken from ball release to the initiation of movement of the limbs. Cross-correlation analyses were performed on the individual trial data and mean values reported for each condition.

Figures 14.1a to 14.3a exemplify typical velocity traces for catches in each condition. As can be seen, the velocity curves follow a similar pattern for both the left and right limb throughout the catch. The peak velocity occurs around 600 ms in both limbs before a reduction in speed in order to catch the ball.

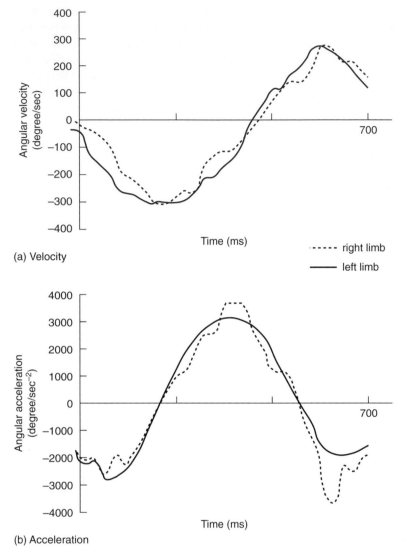

Figure 14.1 Representative velocity (a) and acceleration (b) traces for catches performed in condition 1.

MIT data were collected to allow comparisons to be made with previous research on whether, in such a task as two-handed catching, the limbs initiated movement together or not. Video analysis of MIT data revealed that the limbs appeared to initiate their movements at identical moments in time in all three conditions, 208 (±18) ms, 204 (±22) ms, and 196 (±30) ms for conditions 1, 2, and 3 respectively. Thus, despite the left and right limbs having to move further in conditions 1, and 3 respectively, both limbs set off at the same time when performing the catch.

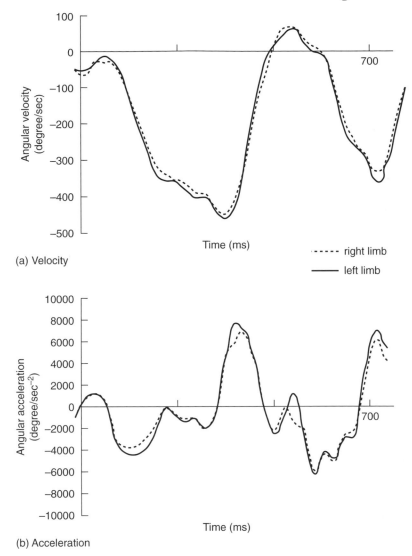

Figure 14.2 Representative velocity (a) and acceleration (b) traces for catches performed in condition 2.

The velocity and acceleration data in that study provided support for the co-ordinative structure theory of bimanual co-ordination examined by Kelso and colleagues (1979; 1983), within the constraints of a dynamic interceptive action. The largest differences between the limbs for TPV data was 5 ms which occurred in condition 2 with velocity traces of the two limbs showing a synchronous pattern throughout the entire movement, whilst the largest difference in TPA data between the limbs was 6 ms for condition 1. Figures 14.1–14.3 also suggest a strong coupling between the limbs for the task of two-handed catching.

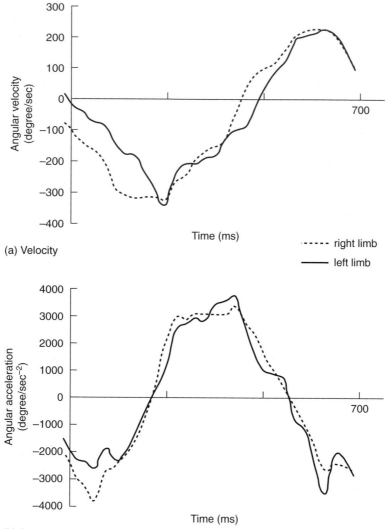

Figure 14.3 Representative velocity (a) and acceleration (b) traces for catches performed in condition 3.

From a theoretical point of view, these findings would suggest that, within these task constraints, rather than the limbs being programmed separately, and individual muscles being controlled by the CNS, a functional group of muscles (co-ordinative structure) would appear to be assembled for the task in hand. This strategy would limit the degrees of freedom to be controlled by the performer to a more manageable number for the CNS and thus realise a more economical solution for the performance of the task. The tasks investigated by Kelso and colleagues

(1979; 1983) required participants to move their limbs to separate (spatially stable) targets. Tayler and Davids (1997) provided further evidence for the co-ordinative structure theory using a different type of task which had hitherto not been investigated in relation to bimanual co-ordination. The kinematic data collected by Kelso, Putnam and Goodman (1983) also showed a strong coupling between the limbs with respect to velocity and acceleration data. Both their data and data from the study of Tayler and Davids (1997) suggest that timing is an essential variable for the co-ordination of tasks in which the limbs are required to move different distances to the same and different targets.

The velocity and acceleration data of that study were contrary to the findings of Marteniuk and MacKenzie (1980) and Marteniuk, MacKenzie and Baba (1984). Their investigations found no such interlimb coupling when the limbs were required to move different distances. They explained the co-ordination of such tasks in terms of intensity and endpoint specifications for each individual limb. When the limbs are required to move different distances, the limb moving the greater distance receives a higher intensity specification than the contralateral limb. Subsequently, there is an interference with the movement topology of that limb, resulting in no apparent interlimb coupling. However, it is possible that for the task investigated by Tayler and Davids (1997), the emergence of the spatiotemporal movement pattern occurred due to the overriding task constraint of the two limbs having to meet the ball simultaneously, thus resulting in the coupling of both limbs.

The velocity data in the present chapter also appear to lend support to the Kelso, Southard and Goodman (1979) explanation of bimanual co-ordination in that, when the limbs were required to move different distances as in conditions 1 and 3, the limb travelling the greater distance moved initially faster than the contralateral limb (Figures 14.1–14.3). If these data were viewed in association with the MIT data, it would appear that both limbs set off at the same time. The limb moving the greater distance travels faster to 'catch up' the opposite limb in order to meet the ball together. Kelso and colleagues (1979; 1983) found no significant differences in RT when the limbs were required to move different distances, whereas Marteniuk, MacKenzie and Baba (1984) found the opposite.

The data from Tayler and Davids (1997) provided further support for the argument that the role of task and environmental constraints should be fully considered in future research into bimanual interceptive actions. The problematic issue of the influence of task instructions in this area of research was circumvented by utilising a real-world interceptive action in which the participant was required to satisfy severe spatiotemporal constraints using both hands. The use of a natural activity provided a valuable insight into the underlying mechanisms for bimanual co-ordination and may be viewed as a preliminary attempt to explore the efficacy of existing theories for the study of dynamic interceptive tasks. Strong support for the co-ordinative structure theory of bimanual co-ordination has been found for such tasks. There is clear evidence that the model of Kelso, Southard and Goodman (1979) may be generalised to the study of highly dynamic, interceptive actions in which the hands are required to arrive simultaneously at the same target endpoint position in order to satisfy rather precise task constraints.

Development of co-ordinative structures for bimanual interceptive actions

An issue related to the Tayler and Davids (1997) study concerns the extent to which a co-ordinative structure for bimanual interceptive actions is a function of organismic constraints (in the form of anatomical design in the human movement system), or develops with task-specific experience. Therefore, a further study was undertaken to assess how the co-ordination involved in two-handed catching develops in children between the ages of five and 11.

Previous studies (e.g. Williams, 1992; see also Strohmeyer, Williams and Schaub-George, 1991) have described the stages of both perceptual and physical development for two-handed catching. For example, Williams (1992) divided children's visual attention and movement strategy into developmental categories based on observations of their catching behaviour. The categories consisted of *retrospective cradling* (early development), *concurrent clamping*, and *predictive grasping* (mature actions). For example, the retrospective cradling stage consisted of the child attending to the point at which the ball was released (thrower's hand) during most of the ball flight, whilst cradling the arms 'hoping' the ball will make contact and be retained. The predictive grasping action constituted an adult-like action in that the child fixated on the early part of ball flight, made a forward movement towards the oncoming ball and 'predicted' the spatiotemporal aspects of ball contact. Results from the Williams (1992) study suggested that only the 10-year-old children consistently used the same visuomotor strategy (predictive grasping) and that the younger children (six to eight years) showed a large degree of variability in the combination of perceptual and motor strategies used. Williams (1992) suggested that 'the participants were "experimenting" with the various ways and means at their disposal to prevent the ball from falling to the ground' (p. 217).

The studies by Williams (1992) and Strohmeyer, Williams and Schaub-George (1991) have provided an insight into the stages that the child undergoes whilst developing catching behaviour. There has been no research, however, investigating the underlying development of the temporal coupling between the limbs during the two-handed catch in children. For example, given the support for the co-ordinative structure model (e.g. Tayler and Davids, 1997), it is necessary to understand whether the temporal coupling observed between the upper limbs is evidence of a physical constraint in the dynamical movement system as argued by Warren (1990). According to Warren (1990), in most movement systems, the potential landscape of stable actions (attractors) is composed of a limited number of solutions. For example, human upright locomotion involves stable task solutions of walking, trotting, cantering and galloping only. That is, during locomotion, human movement systems can search the perceptuo–motor landscape and quickly find a 'functional' attractor, as a physical constraint in the form of a co-ordinative structure. The issue raised by the data in Tayler and Davids (1997) is whether the synchronous behaviour of the upper limbs is evidence of a physical constraint in the developing movement system, or whether the coupling observed was only acquired through extensive task experience and learning. In order to examine this issue the two-handed catching behaviour of children with limited task experience is required.

As the chapters by Temprado and by Button and Summers indicate, Bernstein (1967) suggested that during the early stages of movement skill development the learner freezes the degrees of freedom in order to maintain a manageable number to co-ordinate the limbs. As skill acquisition progresses, the performer gradually releases the degrees of freedom in order to explore his/her environment and to obtain the most efficient co-ordinative state. Some evidence for the freezing of degrees of freedom was found by Vereijken, van Emmerik, Whiting and Newell (1992) who investigated participants attempting to 'learn' a simulated cyclical skiing task. Using inter- and intra-joint cross correlation analyses, findings from the study suggested that early in learning, participants were 'stiffening' their limbs (as evidenced by relatively high cross correlations) before gradually increasing inter- and intra-joint flexibility (evidenced by a significant decrease in the magnitude of the cross correlations), as experience of the task grew. In that study, a kinematic analysis of the joint coupling was not undertaken. These findings, according to the authors, supported Bernstein's (1967) view of motor development in that the high cross-correlations found early in learning suggested that the participants were freezing the relevant degrees of freedom and subsequently releasing them in order to explore the most efficient way of performing the task requirements.

Therefore, the main purposes of the developmental catching study were: (i) to build on the findings on the co-ordinative structure model in Tayler and Davids (1997) by providing a quantitative analysis of two-handed catching in children. This analysis would help (i) to determine whether or not there is evidence of physical constraints in the developing movement system as evidenced by temporal coupling between the limbs (i.e. freezing the degrees of freedom); and (ii) to examine the bimanual co-ordination of children with limited but different experience of two-handed interceptive actions. For example, it would be expected that, generally, with age children would gain more experience of two-handed interceptive actions. Experimental logic suggests that an analysis of groups differing in task experience would facilitate the investigation of the development of a co-ordinative structure for bimanual actions (such as two-handed catching) with task experience.

Thirty children (21 male and nine female) participated in the study. The participants were assigned to three equal groups based on age. Groups 1, 2, and 3 had a mean age of 5.2, 7.9, and 11.4 years respectively. History of ball-game participation was obtained via questionnaire prior to testing in order to control experience in two-handed interceptive activities. Evidence suggested that there were inter-group differences in previous experience of two-handed interceptive actions, but not intra-group differences.

The participants' task was to perform 20 two-handed catches in two different conditions (conditions 1 and 2 above), with the same analytical procedure being undertaken as in Tayler and Davids (1997).

An important aim of the study described in this chapter was to address the issue of the development of temporal synchrony between the limbs in a two-handed catching task. Cross-correlation analyses suggested that early in development (e.g. five years old) the limbs show temporal asynchrony when trying to intercept the ball. For example, cross-correlations were significantly lower for group 1 (C1 and C2, mean $r = 0.47$ and 0.67 respectively) than groups 2 (mean $r = 0.80$ and 0.79 for C1 and C2 respectively) and 3 (C1 and C2, mean $r = 0.85$ and 0.89 respectively). This finding suggests that a co-ordinative structure emphasising the close temporal synchrony between the upper limbs, under the task constraints of two-handed catching, is not the only solution available to the developing movement system. Clearly, given the relative differences between the groups in experience of two-handed catching, the suggestion is that close temporal synchrony between the upper limbs has to be acquired with (a small amount of) task experience.

It would appear that even the younger children in this study improved their performance in condition 2 (balls projected directly at the body with the limbs moving the same distance). Group 1 were, on average, successful in 12 trials out of 20 in this condition. Cross-correlation analyses support these findings in that correlations were significantly higher in condition 2 (group 1) than condition 1, suggesting greater temporal coupling in these conditions when the limbs are required to move the same distance (see also Figure 14.4a and b; Fig 14.5a and b; Fig 14.6a and b). Therefore, when the ball is thrown to a midline position of the body, the lower temporal coupling available in children with limited experience of two-handed catching is enough to satisfy the task constraints. These findings agree with the manual aiming literature in which the limbs are required to move the same distance to static targets (see Kelso and colleagues, 1979, 1983). They also augment findings from previous research in two-handed catching (e.g. Strohmeyer, Williams and Schaub-George, 1991) showing that younger children are more successful when they are required to catch balls thrown directly at them.

However, in condition 1 in this study, children in group 1 found the task constraint of catching the ball projected to the side of the body significantly more difficult to satisfy (group mean $r = 0.47$). In the descriptive analyses of children's two-handed catching, Williams (1992) suggested that younger (six- to seven-year-old) children showed more variability in their catching action, and caught fewer balls, when they were projected away from the body due to them exploring their spatiotemporal possibilities in order to (sometimes) achieve the task goal. The data in this chapter supported this view to an extent in that lower cross-correlations in condition 1 suggest lower interlimb coupling.

The lack of temporal coupling between the upper limbs observed early in development supports the view that the physical constraint of a co-ordinative structure for bimanual co-ordination of the limbs moving together to the same endpoint is weakly developed. The temporal asynchrony observed suggests that, although this particular co-ordinative structure is one of a number of movement solutions to the task constraints of two-handed catching, it needs to be attuned

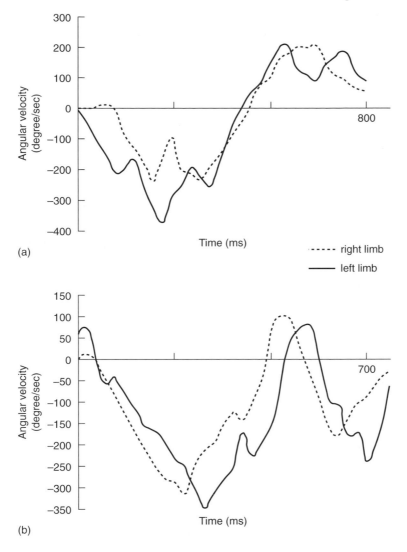

Figure 14.4 Representative left and right limb velocity profiles for group 1 in condition 1 (a) and condition 2 (b).

through specific task experience. The relatively greater amount of experience of two-handed catching in the older groups could account for the increasing magnitude of the cross-correlations with age. This argument is supported by the final peak velocity data (FPV, i.e. the time difference in peak velocities between the left and the right limbs) in this study. The values of these data were significantly higher in

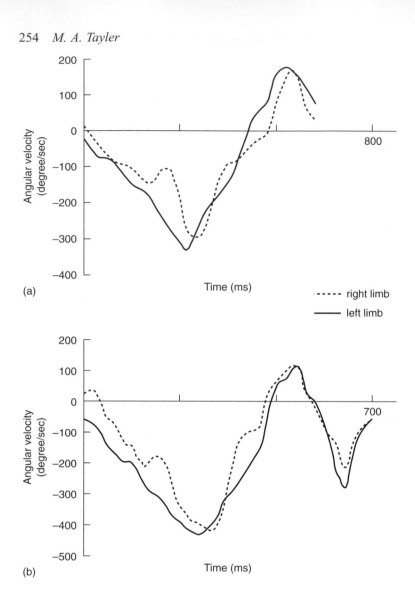

Figure 14.5 Representative left and right limb velocity profiles for group 2 in condition 1
(a) and condition 2 (b).

group 1 (C1) than in the corresponding condition in groups 2 and 3 (e.g. mean
FPV data for group 1 (C1), 145 ms, was significantly higher than group 2 (C1),
mean = 77 ms and group 3 (C1), mean = 14 ms). The interlimb synchrony evidenced
in the older children (and also in Tayler and Davids, 1997) suggested that a transient,
task-specific muscle synergy has been developed as a task solution to the constraints
of co-ordinating two-handed interceptive actions, thus supporting the co-ordinative
structure viewpoint proposed by Kelso and colleagues (1979; 1983).

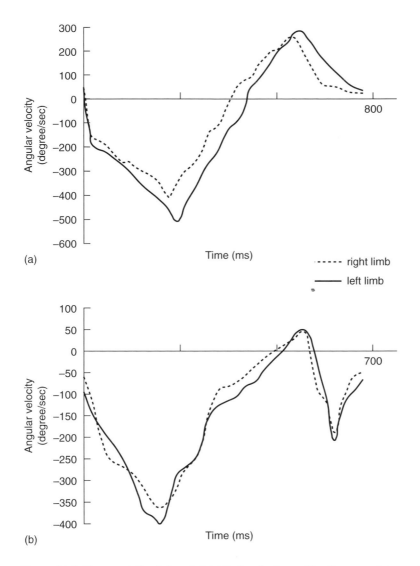

Figure 14.6 Representative left and right limb velocity profiles for group 3 in condition 1 (a) and condition 2 (b).

How may these findings from group 1 and from groups 2 and 3 be explained in terms of the overall development of two-handed catching? One theory proposed from the dynamical systems perspective is based on the notion of the human motor system as a number of separate, but related, subsystems that develop at different rates (e.g. Kamm, Thelen and Jensen, 1990; Thelen, 1995). That is, the motor system is comprised of many interacting subsystems such as for perception, postural control, reaching and grasping, bimanual co-ordination and locomotion. It has been argued that some need to reach a critical stage of development before particular behavioural solutions can emerge to satisfy task constraints on the developing movement system (Thelen and Smith, 1994).

For example, Thelen and Fisher (1983; see also Corbetta and Thelen, 1996) manipulated the weight-to-muscle ratio in four-week-old infants who showed the ability to perform a kicking movement when held upright, suggesting that the CNS was sufficiently developed to co-ordinate such actions. When small weights were attached to the legs of the infant, the ability to kick decreased dramatically, even after a sustained period. Their preferred explanation for this finding was based on the idea that, although the CNS was sufficiently developed to perform kicking movements, the added weight acted as a constraint on the movement solutions available to the movement system. It was not sufficiently developed in order to perform the kicking action under the new (organismic and task) constraints. In the study by Thelen and Fisher (1983), the muscle–fat ratio of the lower limbs was said to be a 'rate limiter' that held back the development of an action at a point in time.

In the context of the developmental study therefore, cross-correlation data, in particular for group 1 in condition 1, suggest that the temporal synchrony between the upper limbs is not sufficiently developed in order to allow participants to consistently catch the oncoming ball. The magnitude of the cross-correlations in the younger groups suggested that the upper arms were capable of being loosely coupled at that stage of development. A high level of temporal synchrony between the arms characterises only one possible stable attractor for bimanual movements, which is developed with specific experience under the task constraints of two-handed interceptive actions. The data on the inter-group differences support the view that the co-ordinative structure for two-handed catching can develop in functionality, most probably as a result of increasing task experience.

In conjunction with the development of the timing between the limbs, as evidenced in the present chapter, the development of other subsystems, such as the perceptual or postural control subsystem, needs to be considered. For example, regarding the perceptual subsystem, in the case of group 1 and perhaps group 2, it is possible that the participants may not have been accurately perceiving ball-flight characteristics in order to successfully intercept the ball. It is unclear at this stage to what extent increased functionality in the perceptual subsystem was responsible for the increased stability of the synchrony between the upper arms for two-handed interceptive actions. Evidence for this idea was provided by Williams (1992) who identified that younger children fixated on the throwers hand for much of the ball flight instead of tracking the flight of the ball later on in its trajectory (see also Davids, 1988 on developmental differences in the role of peripheral vision in two-handed catching in children).

Interestingly, the developmental data in this chapter suggests that analysis of the two arms in isolation during the two-handed catch rejects the notion of freezing degrees of freedom early in development (e.g. Vereijken, van Emmerik, Whiting and Newell, 1992). There is some evidence that the two arms are not physically constrained to move with a high level of temporal synchrony from a very early age. Rather the temporal synchrony between the two arms, for the purposes of two-handed catching, seems only weakly co-ordinated and can be increased significantly with specific task experience. The evidence supports the notion of different states of stability (attractors) being available in movements of the upper arms. Moreover, in this chapter it was intended to analyse the movements of the two arms only and the role of posture control and stability as evidenced in lower limb movements cannot be ignored. For example, for younger children, the legs may well be relatively rigid (frozen out) in such actions in order to allow for the release of the upper limbs in order to explore task solutions.

In conclusion, the developmental data suggested that the temporal coupling between the upper limbs is not sufficiently developed in order to consistently catch a ball, and that this, in conjunction with perceptual development, is a limiting factor in a children's ability to perform such interceptive actions. However, it appears that temporal coupling can develop, most probably as a result of increasing task experience, to reach adult levels by the age of 11 to 12 years. Further work is needed to tease out the extent to which the differences in the co-ordination patterns between the age groups examined in this study were due to differences in the functioning of the perceptual and postural control subsystems, rather than task experience.

References

Bernstein, M. (1967). *The Co-ordination and Regulation of Behavior.* Oxford: Pergamon Press.

Cohen, L. (1970). Interaction between limbs during bimanual voluntary activity. *Brain* **93**, 259–72.

Cohen, L. (1971). Synchronous bimanual movements performed by homologous and non-homologous muscles. *Perceptual and Motor Skills* **32**, 639–44.

Corbetta, D. and Thelen, E. (1996). The developmental origins of bimanual co-ordination: a dynamic perspective. *Journal of Experimental Psychology: Human Perception and Performance* **22** (2), 502–22.

Davids, K. (1988). Developmental differences in the use of peripheral vision during catching performance. *Journal of Motor Behavior* **20**, 39–52.

Heuer, H. (1985). Intermanual interactions during simultaneous execution and programming of finger movements. *Journal of Motor Behavior* **17** (3), 335–54.

Kamm, K., Thelen, E. and Jensen, J.L., (1990). A dynamical systems approach to motor development. *Physical Therapy* **70** (12), 763–74.

Kelso, J.A.S. (1984). Phase transitions and critical behavior in human bimanual co-ordination. *American Journal of Physiology: Regulatory, Integrative, and Comparative Physiology* **15**, 1000–4.

Kelso, J.A.S., Putnam, C.A. and Goodman, D. (1983). On the space–time structure of human interlimb co-ordination. *Quarterly Journal of Experimental Psychology: Human Experimental Psychology* **35A**, 347–75.

Kelso, J.A.S., Southard, D.L. and Goodman, D. (1979). On the co-ordination of two-handed movements. *Journal of Experimental Psychology: Human Perception and Performance* **5** (2), 229–38.

Marteniuk, R.G. and MacKenzie, C.L. (1980). A preliminary theory of two-handed coordinated control. In G.E. Stelmach and J. Requin (eds), *Tutorials in Motor Behavior*. Amsterdam: North Holland.

Marteniuk, R.G., MacKenzie, C.L. and Baba, D.M. (1984). Bimanual movement control: information processing and interaction effects. *Quarterly Journal of Experimental Psychology: Human Experimental Psychology* **36A**, 335–65.

Schmidt, R.A., Zelaznik, H.N., Hawkins, B., Frank, J.S. and Quinn, J.T. (1979). Motor-output variability: a theory for the accuracy of rapid motor acts. *Psychological Review* **86**, 415–51.

Sherwood, D.E. (1994). Interlimb amplitude differences, spatial assimilations, and the temporal structure of rapid bimanual movements. *Human Movement Science* **13**, 841–60.

Sivak, B. and MacKenzie, C.L. (1992). The contribution of peripheral vision and central vision to prehension. In L. Proteau and D. Elliott (eds), *Vision and Motor Control*. Amsterdam: North Holland.

Strohmeyer, H.S., Williams, K. and Schaub-George, D. (1991). Developmental sequences for catching a small ball: a prelongitudinal screening. *Research Quarterly for Exercise and Sport* **62** (3), 257–66.

Tayler, M.A. and Davids, K. (1997). Catching with both hands: an evaluation of neural cross-talk and co-ordinative structure models of bimanual co-ordination. *Journal of Motor Behavior* **29** (3), 254–62.

Thelen, E. (1995). Motor development: a new synthesis. *American Psychologist* **50**, 79–95.

Thelen, E. and Fisher, D. (1983). The organization of spontaneous leg movements in newborn infants. *Journal of Motor Behavior* **15**, 353–77.

Thelen, E. and Smith, L.B. (1994). *A Dynamic Systems Approach to the Development of Cognition and Action*. Cambridge, MA: Bradford Books, MIT Press.

Turvey, M.T. (1977). Preliminaries to a theory of action with reference to vision. In R. Shaw and J. Bransford (eds), *Perceiving, Acting, and Knowing. Toward an Ecological Psychology*. Amsterdam: North-Holland.

Vereijken, B., van Emmerik, R.E.A, Whiting, H.T.A. and Newell, K.M. (1992). Free(z)ing the degrees of freedom in skill acquisition. *Journal of Motor Behavior* **24**, 133–42.

Warren, W.H. (1990). The perception–action coupling. In H. Bloch and B.I. Bertenthal (eds), *Sensory-Motor Organizations and Development in Infancy and Early Childhood*. Dordrecht: Kluwer.

Williams, J.G. (1992). Catching action: visuomotor adaptations in children. *Perceptual and Motor Skills* **75**, 211–19.

15 Co-ordination in the volleyball serve

Expert–novice differences

Jean Jacques Temprado

In the last decade or so, the number of research investigations devoted to the study of motor co-ordination has increased considerably, as pointed out in the chapter by Button and Summers in this text. This effort has reflected an increasing desire to understand the mechanisms involved in mastering the redundant degrees of freedom of the neuro–musculo–skeletal system when assembling stable but flexible patterns of co-ordination during goal-directed movements (Bernstein, 1967). For a long time, the theoretical constructs proposed to explain the mechanisms sub-serving movement co-ordination in living systems was built exclusively on the hypothesis of the existence of motor programmes or hard-wired central pattern generators (CPG) stored in the nervous system (e.g. Schmidt and Lee, 1999). More recently, the dynamical systems approach has been successfully applied to the task of identifying stable states and transitions in movement co-ordination. To recall from the chapter by Button and Summers, empirical work has shown that the dynamics of the order parameter (e.g. relative phase in many of the tasks of previous work) allows the identification of stable states that constitute the intrinsic co-ordination dynamics of the movement system. These co-ordination tendencies express the preference of an individual to adopt specific movement patterns, rather than others, because these forms are more stable, efficient or functional for the system (see Sparrow, 2000).

This chapter explores the issue of how the intrinsic dynamics of a movement system may serve as a frame of reference for the evaluation of qualitative transformations in patterns of co-ordination during learning (see Zanone and Kelso, 1992). From this perspective, learning a new skill, exemplified here by a self-paced, interceptive movement involving an element of extrinsic timing (the volleyball serve), is viewed as the transition from one stable state towards another, as a modification of the existing intrinsic dynamics of the movement system. This modification could consist of 'dismantling' an existing state of co-ordination, already well defined in the motor system's intrinsic dynamics, and creating a new functional pattern in order to achieve the goal of serving the ball.

This approach to the acquisition of co-ordination in interceptive movements sees the learning process as the sequential elaboration and stabilisation of different states of co-ordination. Comparing co-ordination characteristics at different levels of expertise constitutes one possible strategy to identify the various stable states of co-ordination that the system could seek and exploit during goal-directed behaviour (Beek and van Santvoord, 1992). However, this approach presumes the identification of the order parameter(s) of the co-ordination pattern. This task can be problematic, due to the absence of a usable systematic procedure for the *a priori* identification of order parameters. Such a variable has to characterise the relationships between the components that are functional in performing the task, and it therefore has to be defined within a framework that is relevant to the task (Saltzman and Kelso, 1987). Moreover, in the context of this book, and as already outlined in the chapter by Button and Summers, there have been few previous attempts to model discrete movements, such as interceptive actions, from a dynamical systems perspective.

For this reason, the research described in this chapter was concerned with developing an understanding of motor co-ordination sub-serving a complex interceptive timing task: the volleyball serve (Figure 15.1a and 15.1b). This self-paced, extrinsic timing task illustrates the different types of co-ordination that need to be mastered in many sport skills: 1) participant–environment co-ordination (e.g. striking the ball); 2) multilimb and intralimb co-ordination (e.g. tossing the ball with the non-striking arm and co-ordinating the movement of the striking arm with the ball's trajectory); and 3) between-player co-ordination (e.g. directing the ball to a particular point in relation to a player in the opposite court). As proposed in the chapter by Handford, the learner has to find and assemble a stable solution to these different co-ordination problems from the huge number of available perceptual and motor degrees of freedom in the action system. It can be hypothesised that the reduction of this high-dimensional system, in order to assemble successful co-ordination patterns, results from the configuration of different physical and psychological characteristics, previous experiences and tasks constraints. These various interacting constraints shape the perceptual–motor landscape sub-serving, for each individual learner, the search for stable co-ordination solutions to a task problem (Newell, 1986).

The research programme

This chapter describes a research programme that was restricted to the multijoint co-ordination of the striking arm. In this programme of work, our first goal was to identify the essential variable(s) of the interjoint co-ordination. Another goal was to determine whether the development of expertise corresponded to an 'all or none' process or to the successive stabilisation of different co-ordination states.

Our experimental groups involved experts performers from a volleyball team in the highest division of the French national league each of whom had at least 10–12 years of experience in playing volleyball with two or three training sessions per week. Also, a novice group consisted of 14 students from the Faculty of Sciences in Marseilles who declared that they had never previously played volleyball or that they had not played it for several years.

Participants were asked to perform volleyball services of the overhand type, which is a common skill in competitive volleyball (see Figures 15.1a and 15.1b).

Figure 15.1a   The ball is tossed into the air with the non-striking hand and preparation
begins for the striking phase.

The experiment was carried out in a covered gym on a regular volleyball court,
the two halves of which were separated by a net placed at senior male level height.
The participants had to strike the ball to hit a cylindrical target placed 16 m away,
on the other side of the net. The instructional constraints were to try to hit the
target while keeping the ball as close to the net as possible. All participants threw
the ball with the left hand and hit it with the right.

The participants were filmed from the side with a video camera and markers
were placed at four locations on their bodies: (1) the wrist of the throwing arm,

Figure 15.1b   After the ball reaches the zenith of its flight it is struck with the striking arm.

(2) the shoulder of the serving arm, (3) the elbow of the serving arm, (4) the wrist of the serving arm. In addition, the ball was considered as a marker and the position of its centre was digitised. The starting point of the image analysis was the time at which the hand holding the ball started its ascent, i.e. the start of the ball-throwing movement by the left arm. The end of the striking movement was taken as the moment at which the right hand made contact with the ball.

The performances of the experts and novices were compared to determine their effectiveness at the task. The following variables were compared: amplitude of the ball's trajectory, the height at which the ball was struck, the ball's angle of departure, and the initial linear velocity of the ball's departure. We also analyzed the co-ordination of the volleyball serve in the environment-centred space, considering that a macroscopic dimension relevant to the task was the linear position of each component (shoulder, elbow, wrist) in the saggital plane[1] (Jöris *et al.*, 1985). We assumed that the essential variables could be sought in the pattern of spatio–temporal relations between the linear positions of various components, i.e. in the nature of the coupling between the components of the striking system that has to be controlled. For this reason we analyzed the co-ordination between shoulder, elbow, and wrist components via the trajectory of each of these joints along the x-axis (i.e. in the forward–backward direction).

Expert–novice differences

Comparison of the times of the maximum backward displacements of each component revealed differences between the co-ordination patterns of the experts and the novices. More detailed analyses of joint couplings were carried out using cross-correlations of the three joint-pairs (shoulder/elbow, elbow/wrist, shoulder/wrist). The signs of the correlation coefficients revealed the types of coupling (in-phase or anti-phase), the absolute values of the coefficients indicated the strengths of the couplings, and the variability of the coefficients indicated the stability of the co-ordination patterns. Finally, we examined the distribution of the different co-ordination patterns within each group to determine how co-ordination is transformed as a result of expertise.

Task performance was extrapolated from the height of strike, the angle of the ball's departure, and the initial ball velocity. These variables were calculated and then inserted into the formula given by Hay (1985) to compute the 'theoretical' distance covered by a ball launched at a greater height than its point of arrival (see Table 15.1).

The calculated performances of both groups suggested that, under these specific task constraints, they concentrated more heavily on the precision of the serve trajectory than on the force of the strike. For all experts, we observed an 'under-shoot' with respect to the target. The small intra- and inter-participant variability indicated the homogeneity of the group. The participants of the novice group had a different performance profile. We observed a large undershoot, accompanied by high intra- and inter-participant variability. More precisely, three distinct patterns of performance were distinguished in the novice group: (1) participants who systematically 'overshot' the target, (2) participants who performed at the same mean level as the experts, and (3) participants whose mean performance did not clear the net.

There was a significant difference between the experts and the novices with respect to the ball's angle of departure and the height at which the ball was struck. The experts struck the ball at a lower height than the novices and with a more acute angle of departure with respect to the horizontal. The linear velocity of the ball after departure did not differ significantly between the expert and novice servers. These results suggest that, as regards the height at which the ball was struck and its angle of departure, the novice group was homogeneous and significantly different from the experts, but that this was not the case for the ball's linear velocity. Considering the importance of velocity in performance (the amplitude of the ball's trajectory is a function of the velocity squared), such a

Table 15.1   Means and standard deviations (between parentheses) of the variables determining the amplitude of the ball trajectory.

Subjects	Angle (°)	Ball velocity (m/s)	Height of the strike (m)	Amplitude of the trajectory (m)
Experts				
S1	14.1 (0.75)	13.13 (0.22)	2.35 (0.02)	13.7 (2.12)
S2	18.3 (4.95)	11.89 (0.15)	2.36 (0.02)	13.04 (1.56)
S3	17.6 (1.59)	11.72 (0.65)	2.34 (0.02)	12.42 (1.94)
S4	17.3 (2.1)	11.73 (0.7)	2.43 (0.01)	12.64 (1.66)
S5	13.7 (3.78)	12.59 (0.47)	2.46 (0.03)	12.97 (1.99)
S6	24.2 (5.86)	11.34 (1.23)	2.26 (0.01)	13.26 (2.92)
Mean	17.53 (3.78)	12.07 (0.66)	2.37 (0.07)	13.01 (0.45)
Novices				
S1	17.4 (3.07)	16.78 (0.93)	2.49 (0.03)	21.9 (1.16)
S2	21.3 (1.68)	14.63 (0.84)	2.45 (0.02)	19.22 (3.46)
S3	21.3 (7.75)	11.78 (0.76)	2.2 (0.05)	13.36 (2.39)
S4	10.3 (3.58)	14.4 (0.99)	2.13 (0.04)	13.65 (2.58)
S5	17.5 (6.98)	7.92 (0.4)	2.11 (0.04)	7.03 (0.92)
S6	23.7 (2.36)	7.15 (0.8)	2.33 (0.03)	6.73 (0.56)
S7	21.8 (2.56)	6.86 (0.46)	1.97 (0.06)	5.94 (10.93)
S8	31.8 (9.44)	4.55 (0.45)	2.07 (0.04)	3.92 (0.61)
S9	33.4 (9.07)	4.97 (1.01)	2.19 (0.09)	4.07 (3.51)
S10	37.01 (9.86)	4.83 (0.79)	2.2 (0.05)	3.91 (4.12)
S11	26.12 (14.08)	11.56 (2.21)	2.2 (0.07)	13.59 (4.26)
S12	23.63 (7.59)	11.98 (1.85)	2.18 (0.08)	14.12 (3.71)
S13	27.42 (5.52)	12.12 (1.63)	2.18 (0.04)	15.42 (3.23)
S14	32.14 (7.19)	10.78 (1.18)	2.11 (0.04)	12.91 (2.09)
Mean	24.63 (7.28)	10.02 (3.98)	2.2 (0.14)	11.13 (5.86)

result can be attributed to the lack of homogeneity in terms of velocity of the novices' performances.

Analysis of the performances thus confirmed that the two groups differed in their capacities to perform the task. Level of expertise is, therefore, a variable that allows us to distinguish the two groups, at least for task performance. We then went on to consider the variables relevant to co-ordination.

The trajectories of the shoulder, elbow, and wrist of the serving arm in the anterior–posterior dimension, i.e. on the *x*-axis, were analysed. Observation of the trajectories of the three components suggested the existence of important differences between the experts and the novices, in particular for the times of the trajectories' turning points at the start of the forward hitting motion (Figure 15.2). This turning point corresponded to the maximum backward displacement of each component. It indicated a change in the direction of the linear velocity of the

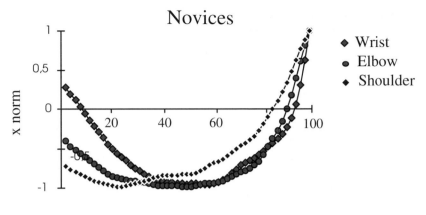

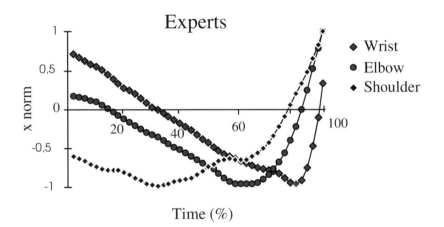

Figure 15.2 Time series of the shoulder, the elbow and the wrist of the striking arm for both the experts and the novices. Normalised co-ordinates on the *x*-axis are plotted as a function of the normalised time.

component in question, which indicated the beginning of the striking phase for each of the components.

For the experts, peak shoulder amplitude was at 38 per cent of mean movement time. It preceded peak elbow amplitude (70 per cent) and peak wrist amplitude (82 per cent). The tests revealed significant differences between the times of peak amplitude of the shoulder and elbow, elbow and wrist, and shoulder and wrist. For the novice group, peak shoulder amplitude occurred at 42 per cent of mean total movement time. It was followed by elbow and wrist peak amplitude, which both occurred at 69 per cent of mean total movement duration (see Figure 15.2). Pairwise comparisons showed significant differences between the times of peak amplitude of the shoulder and elbow, the shoulder and wrist, but not the elbow and wrist.

Next, the type of co-ordination was analysed. The time of the change from backward to forward movement, though a useful measure, is a discrete variable that only gives limited information on the co-ordination of the different components. To analyse the co-ordination pattern between the shoulder, elbow, and wrist, we calculated the cross-correlation coefficients (with zero time lag) for the three pairs formed: shoulder/elbow, shoulder/wrist, and elbow/wrist. The type of co-ordination is reflected in the sign of the correlation coefficient, whereas the intensity or strength of coupling is reflected in the absolute value. A correlation close to +1 indicates a strong in-phase co-ordination; a coefficient close to –1 indicates a strong anti-phase co-ordination; a coefficient close to 0 indicates that the joints function independently of one another.

In order to determine the co-ordination pattern that was representative of each level of expertise, we calculated the frequency of trials performed with an in-phase relationship (i.e. a positive correlation) of each joint-pair for each participant. A qualitative difference in the co-ordination pattern of each group should be reflected in a significant difference in the frequency of positive correlations (see Figure 15.3). The data revealed significant main effects of expertise, joint-pair, and an interaction between these two variables. The decomposition of the interaction into simple effects showed that the influence of expertise was manifested in a modification – from positive to negative – of the sign of the correlation coefficient of the shoulder–wrist coupling. The mean frequency of trials for which the shoulder–wrist coupling was in-phase was 6.7 per cent for the experts and 63.6 per cent for the novices. The proportions of in-phase couplings were similar for the shoulder–elbow (experts: 80 per cent, novices: 93.6 per cent) and elbow–wrist joint-pairs (100 per cent for both groups).

The strength of relationships between the joints was then analysed. The values of the correlation coefficients were lower among the experts than among the novices for the shoulder–elbow and the elbow–wrist relationship, but not for the shoulder–wrist relationship. The absolute mean value of the correlation of the elbow–wrist decreased from 0.79 among the novices to 0.67 among the experts; that of the shoulder–elbow relationship decreased from 0.65 to 0.27. The mean value of the shoulder–wrist correlation was equivalent for both groups (novices: 0.46; experts: 0.51), though correlation was negative for the experts and positive for the novices (see analysis of type of coupling).

Comparisons of the strengths of the relationships between the three joints within each level of expertise showed that for the novice group, the strength of the relationship between the shoulder and the elbow (0.65) did not differ from that between the elbow and the wrist (0.79). However, the relationship between the shoulder and the wrist (0.46) was weaker than those of the other two joint-pairs. For the expert group, however, the shoulder–elbow (0.27) and elbow–wrist (0.67)

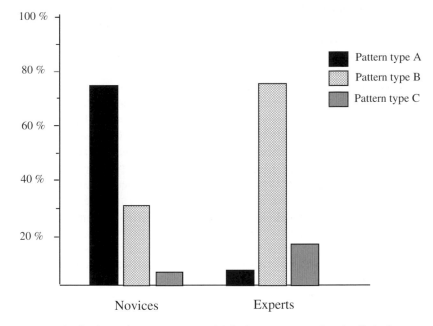

Figure 15.3 Distributions of patterns A, B and C in the two groups. See details in the text.

relationships did differ, and the shoulder–wrist relationship (0.51) also differed from that between the shoulder and elbow. There was no difference in strength between the elbow–wrist (0.51) and shoulder–wrist (0.67) relationships.

To analyse the stability of the strength of the relationships between the different joints, we calculated the within-participant variability of the absolute values of the correlation coefficients for each of the joint-pairs. The experts were more stable than the novices whatever the unit used (experts = 0.15, novices = 0.36). Analysis of the sign of the correlation coefficients indicates the representative type of coupling for each joint-pair for each group, but it does not tell us how the joint-pairs were combined into overall co-ordination patterns. To determine the extent to which different patterns were used, we took each participant group as a whole and looked at the different overall co-ordination patterns used. In other words, we considered the novices and the experts as two systems and calculated the frequency of the different patterns observed in each sample. Following this analysis, three different patterns can be easily identified:

1 Pattern A, in which all three joints-pairs were coupled in-phase (+ + +).
2 Pattern B, in which both the elbow–wrist and shoulder–elbow joint-pairs were in-phase, but the shoulder–wrist joint-pair was coupled out-of-phase (+ + –).
3 Pattern C, in which only the elbow–wrist pair was in-phase (+ – –).

Calculation of the frequency of each co-ordination pattern relative to the total number of trials performed by each group showed the presence of two dominant profiles. For the novices, pattern A was observed in 75 per cent of the trials, pattern B in 20 per cent of the trials, and pattern C on 5 per cent of the trials. For the experts, pattern A was observed in 7 per cent of the trials, pattern B in 75 per cent of the trials, and pattern C in 18 per cent of the trials. These results show that the co-ordination pattern representative of the experts (B) existed at a low frequency among the novices, and that the co-ordination pattern representative of the novices (A) persisted among the experts even after several years of extensive practice. A third pattern, C, also existed at low frequency in both groups. For the expert and novice groups, a participant-by-participant analysis showed that, except for two experts, all three patterns existed in the repertoire of each participant.

The analysis of the percentages obtained for each pattern suggests that the increase in the frequency of pattern B among the experts was the result of the diminution in the number of pattern A trials seen among the novices via modification of the essential variable, i.e. from in-phase to anti-phase coupling of the shoulder and wrist.

What do the data from this programme of work tell us about intra-limb co-ordination processes in an interceptive task? Analysis of the nature of the inter-joint couplings within the hitting arm showed that the co-ordination pattern of the volleyball serve differed qualitatively between the novices and experts, presumably as a result of the development of expertise. Analysis of the times of direction change (from backward motion to forward motion) of the three components suggested that expertise is characterised by a dissociation of the displacements of the shoulder, elbow, and wrist. Among the novices, the dominant co-ordination pattern was that of an in-phase relationship of all three joint-pairs. In contrast, among the experts, the dominant co-ordination pattern was of an *in-phase* relationship of the shoulder–elbow and elbow–wrist joint-pairs, and an *anti-phase* relationship between the shoulder and the wrist. Thus, the nature of the coupling between the shoulder and the wrist constitutes a variable that indicates a qualitative difference between the co-ordination patterns of the experts and the novices. Clearly, it presents itself as a good candidate for the essential variable in the intra-limb co-ordination of the serving arm.

Among the experts, the analysis of the value of the correlation coefficients showed a reduction in the strength of coupling for the shoulder–elbow and elbow–wrist joint pairs, but not for the shoulder–wrist pairing. Moreover, it appears that, to control the relationship between the shoulder and the wrist, the novices treated the arm as a single dynamic unit by rigidly fixing ('freezing') the shoulder–elbow and elbow–wrist joint-pairs. In contrast, the experts dissociated the proximo–medial components (shoulder–elbow) and medial–distal components (elbow–wrist) and coupled them with a phase offset. Thus, a significant feature of expertise was typically manifested in a releasing of degrees of freedom of the motor system. These results are compatible with Bernstein's (1967) hypotheses as well as other studies carried out over a shorter time scale than that used here (McDonald *et al.*, 1989; Sparrow and Irrizary-Lopez, 1987; Vereijken *et al.*, 1992). In these studies it was observed that practice typically results in a freeing of the degrees of freedom of the action system that underlie co-ordination.

The strength of the coupling between the shoulder and wrist was the same for both novices and experts, but the type of co-ordination was different (i.e. in-phase versus anti-phase). The modifications observed in the type of co-ordination takes the form of both a changing of the type of relationship between shoulder and wrist from in-phase to anti-phase and of a freeing of proximal, medial and distal degrees of freedom which is manifested in a reduction in the strength of the couplings. These adaptations are in agreement with the requirements of effective performance illustrated by biomechanical principles of throwing tasks (Atwater, 1979; Chapman and Sanderson, 1990). However, from a dynamical systems perspective, it is not argued that the nervous system has knowledge of the mechanical characteristics of muscle or, even, knowledge of mechanical outcomes of activating muscles (Chapman and Sanderson, 1990). Rather, the type of coupling between the proximal (shoulder) and distal (wrist) components is assumed to summarise, at a macroscopic level, the emerging pattern resulting from the evolution of the interaction between task, organismic and environmental constraints in the course of practice[3] (Newell, 1991). The type of coupling between the different components of the co-ordination may be a functional variable around which the dimensional reduction of the degrees of freedom of this particular action system is organised.

It appears that the development of expertise in interceptive actions, as reflected in the intra-limb co-ordination of the serving arm, is not an 'all or none' process, but involves transitions between a succession of qualitatively different but stable states of co-ordination. This finding is consistent with a dynamical systems viewpoint of conceptualising the acquisition of new motor skills as resulting from the transition of one stable state to another (Zanone and Kelso, 1992). Consideration of each participant group as a system whose behaviour could be analysed with respect to the total number of trials performed, allowed the examination of the distribution of the different co-ordination patterns and the acquisition of additional information on the nature of the changes that underlie the development of co-ordination. The distributions observed among both the experts and the novices were trimodal and composed of the same co-ordination patterns. In other words, the co-ordination pattern of the expert existed among the novices, although at a lower frequency, and the pattern of co-ordination of the novices existed among the experts, even after extensive practice (see Chapter 1 for an explanation). Indeed, trimodality was observed in the repertoire of each participant in each group (except for two experts). From a dynamical systems view of learning, one can equate the novices' repertoire, consisting of three qualitatively different co-ordination patterns, to an initial 'intrinsic dynamic' from which expertise develops. Viewed in this light, expertise consists of the strengthening of a co-ordination pattern that exists intrinsically in the repertoire of the novice rather than in the creation of a completely new pattern.

Thus, the modification of the distribution of the two co-ordination patterns present in the original distribution corresponds to a change in their relative powers of attraction in the repertoire of the participants. However, it is impossible to determine here whether the intrinsic dynamics of the intra-limb co-ordination of the serving arm (i.e. natural tendencies of the system to adopt certain modes of co-ordination) consists of a single co-ordination pattern (i.e. pattern A) or of three different patterns. If it consists of a single pattern, the existence of the expert pattern in the repertoire of novices could be interpreted as resulting from a tension between the spontaneous co-ordination tendencies of the participants and intended patterns during the course of practice (Corbetta and Thelen, 1996). From this viewpoint, one could interpret the presence of both novice and expert patterns as reflecting an interaction between the spontaneous tendency toward in-phase coupling of the components of the action system and what the participant has to do to perform the task comfortably or efficiently. For novices, co-ordination tendencies dominated intentional goals so that maintaining (unstable) pattern B was difficult. In the course of the development of expertise, it seems that participants could disrupt these spontaneous tendencies and establish a new stable pattern. However, the effect of spontaneous tendencies remains, explaining the persistence of the novice' pattern. Be that as it may, the results of the programme of work demonstrated that the novice participants did not come to the task as a 'tabula rasa'. Although having little or no specific practice in the volleyball service, all the novices exhibited a characteristic and identifiable co-ordination pattern.

The programme of work described in this chapter confirms the benefit of the approach of comparing co-ordination processes in experts and novices, and the conceptual and methodological utility of the dynamical systems approach to the study of the development of motor co-ordination during interceptive actions. By and large, it is apparent that the concepts of intrinsic dynamics, order parameters and coupling contribute to our understanding of how co-ordination patterns form, stabilise and change in the development of expertise. However, currently its scope is restricted to multijoint co-ordination of the striking arm. As argued in the chapter by Handford, a future challenge in the study of co-ordination processes during interceptive actions, is to determine how the different co-ordination patterns can be coupled to perceptual information from the projectile to be struck in such self-paced extrinsic timing tasks. From this perspective, it could be interesting to build on the work of Handford and analyse in detail the simultaneous processes of learning both intra-limb and hand-projectile co-ordinations.

Notes

1   Jöris *et al.* (1985), using an overarm throwing task, showed that front–back dimension is a relevant dimension to analyse movement kinematic and kinetic properties. In the present study, a preliminary observation of the movement patterns, reflected in x–y position diagrams suggested that the main dimension of the shoulder, elbow and wrist displacements occurred in the sagittal plane. It was the case because, at the start of the movement, participants positioned the hand of the serving arm in front of them at about shoulder height. At the beginning of the serve (backward displacement), they positioned their hand very quickly at about the height where the ball would be struck and maintained this level throughout the entire movement duration. This strategy resulted in a large movement amplitude in the x-axis and a small movement amplitude on the y-axis.

2   To improve the clarity of the text and to reduce the length of this chapter, we deleted the details of statistical analyses (Anova). These analyses can be found in Temprado *et al.* (1997). However, only the significant differences are reported here.

3 An illustration of this constraints-led perspective is provided by Davids *et al.* (1999). The results obtained by Davids *et al.* – a strong coupling between joint pairs – seem inconsistent with those reviewed in this chapter, suggesting that the release of the degrees of freedom in expert performers permits the exploitation of inertial properties of the movement system. Though the absence of any releasing of intra-limb degrees of freedom with expertise is surprising (see Vereijken *et al.*, 1992), the key point proposed by Davids *et al.* (1999) is that the differences may be best interpreted in light of the (neo-Darwinian) theoretical framework emphasising the specificity of task constraints – type of target, speed–accuracy instructions given to the participants, level of expertise – that determine the emergent characteristic of movement co-ordination. Nevertheless, this plausible interpretation needs to be confirmed by systematic manipulations of task constraints imposed on the participants.

References

Atwater, A.E. (1979). Biomechanics of overarm throwing movements and of throwing injuries. *Exercise and Sport Science Reviews* 7, 43–85.

Beek, P.J. and van Santvoord, A.A.M. (1992). Learning the cascade juggling: a dynamical systems analysis. *Journal of Motor Behavior* 24 (1), 85–94.

Bernstein, N. 1967. *The Co-ordination and Regulation of Movements*. Oxford: Pergamon Press.

Chapman, A.E. and Sanderson, D.J. 1990. Muscular co-ordination in sporting skills. In: J.M. Winters and S.L.-Y. Woo (eds), *Multiple Muscle Systems: Biomechanics and Movement Organization*. Berlin: Springer-Verlag.

Corbetta, D. and Thelen, E. (1996). The developmental origins of bimanual co-ordination: a dynamic perspective. *Journal of Experimental Psychology: Human Perception and Performance* 22 (2), 502–22.

Davids, K., Bennett, S.J., Handford, C. and Jones, B. (1999). Acquiring co-ordination in self-paced, extrinsic timing tasks: a constraints-led perspective. *International Journal of Sport Psychology* 30, 437–61.

Hay, J.G. 1985. *The Biomechanics of Sports Techniques*. Third edition . Englewood Cliffs, NJ: Prentice-Hall.

Jöris, H.J.J., van Muyen, A.J.E., van Ingen Schenau, G.J. and Kemper, H.C.G. (1985). Force, velocity and energy flow during the overarm throw in female handball players. *Journal of Biomechanics* 189 (6), 409–14.

McDonald, P.V., van Emmerik, R.E.A. and Newell, K.M. (1989). The effects of practice on limb kinematics in a throwing task. *Journal of Motor Behavior* 21, 245–64.

Newell, K.M. (1986). Constraints on the development of co-ordination. In: M.G. Wade and H.T.A. Whiting (eds), *Motor Development in Children: Aspects of Co-ordination and Control*. Boston: Martinus Nijhoff.

Newell, K.M. (1991). Motor skill acquisition. *Annual Review of Psychology* 42, 213–37.

Saltzman, E. and Kelso, J.A.S. (1987). Skilled actions: A task dynamic approach. *Psychological Review* 94, 1–23.

Schmidt, R.A. and Lee, T.D. (1999). *Motor Control and Learning: A Behavioral Emphasis*. Third edition. Champaign, IL: Human Kinetics Publishers.

Sparrow, W.A. (ed.) (2000). *Energetics of Human Activity.* Champaign, IL: Human Kinetics.

Sparrow, W.A. and Irrizary-Lopez, V.M. 1987. Mechanical efficiency and metabolic coast as measures of learning a novel gross motor task. *Journal of Motor Behavior* 19 (2), 240–64.

Temprado, J.J., Della-Grasta, M., Farrell, M. and Laurent, M. (1997). A novice–expert comparison of (intra-limb) co-ordination sub-serving the volleyball serve. *Human Movement Science* 16, 653–76.

Vereijken, B., van Emmerik, R.E.A., Whiting, H.T.A. and Newell, K.M. (1992). Free(z)ing degrees of freedom in skill acquisition. *Journal of Motor Behavior* **24** (1), 133–42.

Zanone, P.G. and Kelso, J.A.S. (1992). Evolution of behavior attractors with learning: nonequilibrium phase transitions. *Journal of Experimental Psychology: Human Perception and Performance* **18**, 403–21.

16 Co-ordination and control of kicking in soccer

Adrian Lees and Keith Davids

Soccer is a dynamic ball game in which, typically, a high proportion of players' time is spent attempting to bring about controlled collisions with a moving ball in order to impart an appropriate amount of force, for example, when passing or shooting over long and short distances on the field (Andersen, Dorge and Thomsen, 1999). Consequently, many of the important skills to master are interceptive actions such as kicking with the lower limb, heading or catching/punching the ball (in the case of the goalkeeper). The most widely used (and studied) soccer skill is that of kicking. The scientific sub-discipline of biomechanics has been used to help us to understand the mechanical forces involved, and the kinematics of motion in players differing in age and skill level (e.g. see Wickstrom, 1975; Hatzitaki, 1999; Barfield, 1998; Lees and Nolan, 1998). However, only recently has it been argued that theoretical frameworks from the sub-discipline of motor control need to be linked to biomechanical analyses in order to increase insight into processes of co-ordination and control of movements such as kicking (Sparrow, 1992). A particularly pertinent framework is dynamical systems theory which is relevant to the study of processes of movement co-ordination and control because of its emphasis on how the movement system degrees of freedom become assembled into functional synergies to achieve task goals such as intercepting moving projectiles (see Davids, Lees and Burwitz, 2000).

This chapter will begin by briefly over-viewing how key ideas from dynamical systems theory can aid us in understanding the processes of co-ordination and control of soccer skills. A more detailed treatment of the main ideas of dynamical systems theory can be seen in the chapter by Button and Summers. Following this introduction, we provide an outline of the main biomechanical techniques used to investigate co-ordination and control in soccer kicking. We next review relevant studies that have undertaken biomechanical analyses of kicking, the findings of which can be understood in relation to processes of co-ordination and control. Finally we examine how motor control theory and biomechanical techniques can inform our understanding of the acquisition of co-ordination and control in soccer skills and implications for talent identification, coaching and practice are highlighted.

Kicking in soccer: processes of co-ordination and control

Kicking a soccer ball is a highly complex task, often with severe spatial and temporal constraints of ball flight trajectory. As in other chapters, it has been identified that the multiple degrees of freedom in the movement system need to be co-ordinated and controlled by the performer (e.g. see chapters by Handford, Tayler and Temprado). In successfully satisfying the task constraints of kicking for power and accuracy, the soccer player must master the interaction of information provided by the perceptual system, e.g. relating to the trajectory of the ball, and the motor system components used in interception. This task contains a number of distinct but related constraints to be satisfied. For example, one such constraint involves the design of the musculo–skeletal system. The kicker must acquire the co-ordination of the limb segments involved in the action such that the sequence of muscular innervation optimises foot velocity at the point of contact with the ball (for an example of upper limb interceptive actions see chapters by Handford and Temprado, and Luhtanen (1987)). In transferring joint rotations into high velocities at a distal point (or extension of), the cumulative product of the angular velocity and radius of rotation in each of the contributing segments requires a transfer of momentum during the sequence of movements (Atwater, 1979). The build up of velocity in the segments dictates that large proximal segments with high moments of inertia move first, with smaller segments involving less mass moving later and with higher velocities. Such a sequencing allows proximally located muscles to fully utilise their capacity to do work in contributing to the continued acceleration of the most distal segment (Jöris et al., 1985). Furthermore, the contribution of muscular forces generated during stretch-shortening is facilitated as forward acceleration of the proximal segments causes a type of recoil in the distal segments. Thus both active and passive forces are co-ordinated in a way that is complementary to the movement (see Bober, Putnam and Woodworth, 1987; Heise and Carnwell, 1997). As we shall observe later in this chapter, understanding processes of co-ordination and control in kicking to facilitate skill acquisition, requires a detailed biomechanical analysis of relevant kinematic data, such as limb segment displacements and velocities (Lees and Nolan, 1998).

Dynamical systems theory: a framework for integrating motor control and biomechanics in understanding co-ordination and control of soccer kicking

In this chapter it is argued that an integration of techniques and theoretical ideas from motor control can help us to gain a clearer understanding of processes of co-ordination and control in the human movement system. The movement system is a dynamical system in the sense that its microscopic components (in this chapter we use this term in reference to the muscles, joints and limb segments) are constantly in a state of flux. Given that some estimates have indicated that there are 100 bones in the human body and over 700 muscles, there is enormous potential for disorder in such a complex system (see Williams, Davids and

Williams, 1999). An important task for a movement scientist interested in sport performance is to understand how order emerges in such a complex system that is continually undergoing change (as a result of ageing, learning and training, for example). In fast ball sports, such as soccer, often changes to the organisation of the movement system degrees of freedom are needed within the order of milliseconds as players are required to shoot with the left foot rather than their right foot, for example, or as a ball deviates off the turf. To make sense of these changes in co-ordination over time, we need to be able to view patterns in the organisation of the movement system degrees of freedom. These patterns are important because they represent variables that can be used to describe co-ordination in the movement system.

Biomechanical techniques, outlined later in this chapter, help us to accurately measure key movement variables during an action like kicking a soccer ball. Motor control, particularly dynamical systems theory, can provide us with the theoretical principles needed to explain changes in these variables over short (i.e. milliseconds in terms of performance) and long (days or weeks for processes of learning and months and years for development) timescales (see Schmidt and Fitzpatrick, 1996). There are a number of reasons why the framework of dynamical systems theory can be useful for researchers seeking an integration of motor control theory and biomechanical methods of analyses. These have been outlined in some detail previously (e.g. see Davids *et al.*, 2000; Williams, Davids and Williams, 1999). In this section it is intended to summarise the key reasons before moving on to review the main biomechanical techniques used to measure movement behaviour.

Biomechanical techniques used to investigate movement co-ordination and control

Biomechanics provides the methodology to investigate aspects of movement skill performance. Generally these methods are divided into qualitative and quantitative types. The former rely on observational techniques (often supplemented by a visual recording medium such as video) and careful descriptions of movement to enable a good understanding of the skill to be learned such that the co-ordination and control issues are fully appreciated. The latter rely on the precise measurement of relevant variables from which more detailed descriptions can be obtained so that key characteristics of co-ordination and control of the movement can be quantified.

There are numerous quantitative biomechanical analysis methods available to investigate human motion. From the point of view of co-ordination and control, the most important of these is motion analysis. Motion analysis attempts to directly measure some kinematic characteristic of movement (such as position or angle) and can be used to describe skills and to investigate relationships between parts (or segments) of the body. As we will discuss later, this second aspect is highly relevant to understanding how motor system degrees of freedom become co-ordinated during kicking. Motion analysis can be combined with force analysis to give a much more detailed picture of how the musculo–skeletal system operates. These more complex methods, though, have only infrequently been applied to the soccer kick.

Motion analysis is most commonly conducted by recording displacement measures. Typically these displacement measures are the spatial co-ordinates of a joint centre or reference point. Several of these measures might be recorded to provide a detailed description of a limb (for example toes, ankle, knee and hip for use in soccer kicking). The spatial co-ordinate data can be obtained from digitising a ciné film or video recording of the movement. This task is often done by hand, one point and one frame at a time and so it can be a laborious method for large numbers of recordings or if the sample rate is high, as it needs to be for fast movements such as the soccer kick. The complexity of this task is exacerbated if a three dimensional (3D) analysis is undertaken since a minimum of two views of the movement are required, doubling the number of points to be digitised. From these spatial co-ordinates other variables can be computed. Typically these are limb angles, joint linear and angular velocities and joint linear and angular accelerations. Much effort in biomechanics is devoted to the computational procedures used to overcome the problem of errors of measurement that are an unavoidable by-product of the digitising process. These issues need not be considered here but further information can be found in several biomechanical texts (e.g. Winter, 1990; Bartlett, 1997).

New motion analysis methods have recently become available. These methods are generally referred to as opto–electronic and describe both the optical and electronic nature of their mode of operation. They rely on receiving a light ray from a marker which is recorded by at least two cameras. These cameras are able to scan the field of view and detect the location of the light ray on its light-sensitive surface. The electronic information produced by this event is combined with similar information from other cameras, and computer software is used to compute the three dimensional location of the marker from which the light ray emanated. These methods have the attraction of rapid three dimensional data collection at high speed although the disadvantages are the initial high cost of the system and their restricted use within a laboratory/indoor setting. Opto–electronic systems commonly used in the analysis of sports skills use passive markers (retro-reflective markers are used which reflect light originating from the camera) and have up to six cameras all collecting data simultaneously and sampling complete frames of data at 240 Hz.

With regard to the use of these various methodologies for the investigation of the kicking skill, it should be noted that opto–electronic methods have only recently become available and the vast majority of reports published in the literature have based their investigations on the more traditional ciné film analyses. The popularity of video has had little impact on investigations of the kicking skill due to its relatively low frame rate of 50 Hz (PAL, 60 Hz for NSTM systems) while at the same time increasing costs for the development of ciné film have meant that this medium has become less commonly used. Until more laboratories have access to opto–electronic systems it is unlikely that work in this area will advance substantially. However, this advance should become apparent in the next decade.

Biomechanics provides the means whereby motion data can be combined with inertial and force data collected on a movement to calculate the net muscle moments acting about a joint. The net muscle moment is an estimate of the muscular effort put into changing the motion of a limb segment and is therefore a more directly relevant variable for investigations of co-ordination and control. Net muscle moments have the potential for indicating the relative effort placed into moving different limbs (e.g. what effort is expended by the muscles of the hip, knee and ankle respectively in the soccer kick?) and the timing associated with these efforts (e.g. are the muscles of the hip activated before those of the knee in the soccer kick?). Again, it should be stressed that these methods, while available, have not been applied extensively to investigate aspects of co-ordination and control. However, their availability and application through inter-disciplinary collaboration offers exciting potential for the future.

In terms of both qualitative and quantitative analysis methods, a review of the literature (e.g. Lees and Nolan, 1998) establishes that the instep kick of a stationary ball (simulating a penalty kick) has been the most widely studied variant of the soccer kicking skill. Consequently, the reader should understand the bias in emphasis placed in the analysis of the co-ordination and control of the soccer kick in the following sections.

Qualitative description of the soccer kick

Qualitative methods have enabled the determination of the general characteristics and development of the soccer kick and have permitted a great deal to be learned about the characteristics of kicking and aspects of co-ordination and control of the skill. For example, the mature form of the soccer instep kick is characterised by an angled approach to the ball with one or more steps (Wickstrom, 1975; Bloomfield, Elliott and Davies, 1979; Lees and Nolan, 1998). The steps leading into the kick increase body, and hence foot speed, while the angled approach orientates the body so that the pelvis can rotate through a greater range of motion to ball contact. This orientation also has the effect of tilting the body to one side so as to lift the hip of the kicking leg (see Figure 16.1a–e), and compensate for the flexion of the support leg, which lowers the body, enabling an appropriate foot–ball contact position. The length of the final step also enables the pelvis to be rotated backward: the longer the step, the greater the range of motion. This action enables the foot to be taken back through a greater distance and hence increases the acceleration path of the foot toward the ball. The forward motion of the kicking leg is initiated in a proximal-to-distal sequence of the thigh and shank following the placement of the non-kicking foot. It is notable that this sequence is prevalent in biomechanical analyses of other dynamic interceptive actions, such as volleyball serving (e.g. see chapters by Handford and Temprado)

Forward rotation is initiated by pelvic rotation about the hip of the support leg followed almost simultaneously by rotation of the thigh through hip flexion. The knee of the kicking leg continues to flex until it reaches its minimum angle and then begins to move forward to allow the thigh to approach a vertical orientation. As the shank accelerates forward, the thigh is caused to slow down. Energy flows from the thigh to the shank and increases its angular velocity. In skilled kicking,

Figure 16.1a The instep kick – start of last stride.

Figure 16.1b The instep kick – maximal hip retraction.

Figure 16.1c The instep kick – maximal knee flexion.

Figure 16.1d The instep kick – contact.

Figure 16.1e The instep kick – follow-through.

the peak linear velocity of the foot is achieved just before contact with the ball. The kicking leg is almost fully extended at ball contact and remains extended throughout the early stages of the follow-through until the end of the follow-through, where the knee begins to flex. These actions enable the foot to reach a high velocity, which is the main determinant of ball velocity. Other factors such as ball mass, effective striking mass of the foot, ball pressure and foot deformability, all affect final ball speed (Lees, 1996)

Qualitative analyses of the development of kicking skill

The qualitative analysis method has been useful in describing the developmental characteristics of kicking skill. Wickstrom (1975), in a review of cross-sectional and longitudinal developmental studies of kicking, suggested a four-stage developmental model for children between two and six years of age. The first stage involved a basic pendular motion of the kicking leg with little knee flexion, the second stage exhibited an increase in the preparatory backswing of the kicking leg through hip extension, the third stage demonstrated greater knee flexion and the fourth stage utilised pelvic rotation. In a later study, Bloomfield, Elliott and Davies (1979) identified six stages of development for soccer instep kick in boys between the ages of two and 12 years of age. The stages are similar to those described by Wickstrom (1975). In addition they reported the introduction of a run-up in the fourth stage and an angled approach in the sixth stage to define the full mature form of the skill in which co-ordinated hip hyper-extension and knee flexion during the backswing were demonstrated. The main features of the kicking skill appear to be capable of being developed in some individuals by the age of six years. This finding has implications for talent identification and skill development.

It is worth noting that these largely qualitative analyses have clearly identified features of the kick such as angled approach, tilt of the trunk and pelvis which demand a full 3-D analysis of the movement.

Quantitative analysis of the soccer kick

Quantitative analysis methods can provide the means whereby the co-ordination and control of a movement can be investigated. As noted above, most quantitative analyses have been conducted using 2-D analyses as 3-D analysis methods have only recently become commonplace. Lees and Nolan (2001) briefly reviewed the 3-D studies in the literature. Of the five reported, only two (Prassas, Terauds and Nathan, 1990; Browder, Tant and Wilkerson, 1991) contained data on the genuine three-dimensional aspects of the kick (i.e. pelvic rotation) as described above, and which might be influential in terms of co-ordination and control. This gap in existing research signifies that the information used to explain co-ordination and control of the kicking skill is limited and incomplete. The 2-D kinematic characteristics of the skill are largely defined by the linear and angular data associated with the foot, shank and thigh of the kicking leg. There are extensive normative data for the magnitude of these variables in the literature. However, there is also wide variation in their values due to several factors. These include different levels of skill examined (e.g. collegiate vs. professional players); different experimental task constraints (e.g. the use of a target or not); different variants of the task (e.g. length of approach); different types of footwear, surface and ball (e.g. boots outdoors vs. trainers indoors); and different levels of physical and psychological preparation during testing. Despite these limitations, some biomechanical investigations have reported data or used analysis methods that have a bearing on the co-ordination and control of the kicking skill.

Biomechanical analyses of co-ordination in kicking

Co-ordination is defined by the relative movements between segments of one limb (intra-limb co-ordination), between different limbs (inter-limb co-ordination) or between a limb segment and an intercepted object (Newell, 1985; Turvey, 1990). Co-ordination is mainly determined qualitatively by phase diagrams (e.g. of joint positions or speeds, or segment angles and angular speeds) and quantified by cross-correlational methods (Sparrow *et al.*, 1987; Amblard *et al.*, 1994). Several studies have attempted to comment on the nature of co-ordination for the kicking skill using speed–accuracy and fatigue paradigms, and comparisons between dominant and non-dominant legs, although these investigations have not been specifically designed to investigate co-ordination processes.

Lees and Nolan (2000) used a speed–accuracy paradigm and 3-D analysis to investigate two highly skilled (professional) soccer players kicking a stationary ball in a simulation of a penalty kick. Players were first asked to kick a stationary soccer ball at a target for five trials with an emphasis on speed, and then to repeat the kicks with an emphasis on accuracy. Eighteen dependent variables related to the ball, kicking leg, hip and shoulder displacement and velocity values, were reported. The variability associated with pelvic rotation and thigh motion decreased, as expected, during the accuracy kicks although the variability associated with the distal segment (foot) increased. This unexpected finding was attributed to the need to make late adjustments to the movement in order to produce an accurate outcome and was associated with changes in co-ordination between the trunk, thigh and shank. That is, despite the static nature of this type of interceptive action, there still seemed a need for performers to make ongoing refined adaptations to the movement pattern in order to achieve the task goal. Although the nature of these changes was not reported it might be expected that in some kicks the thigh was co-ordinated with the shank and foot in advance of its normal motion, while in other kicks the motion was retarded.

Barfield (1995) investigated the performance of the maximal instep soccer kick with the dominant and non-dominant leg. Eighteen participants were involved and each was asked to perform 10 kicks with each leg. Although 115 variables were identified for inclusion within a correlational matrix with ball velocity, only the mean and standard deviation from 11 kinematic variables were reported. Of these, six differed significantly (including ball velocity) and in each case the mean values were lower for the non-dominant foot. However, only two of these cases showed greater variability in the non-dominant compared to the dominant foot. Barfield concluded that the kick made on the non-dominant side was a less skilful and more poorly co-ordinated movement, although no further data were reported to support this view. It should be noted that, under these experimental task constraints, two movements may be equally well co-ordinated but the faster movement will generally be viewed as more functional. In the data reported there was little evidence for a poorer co-ordination although the lower ball speed on the non-dominant foot would suggest a less skilled action.

Lees and Davies (1987) investigated the effects of fatigue on the performance of the maximal instep soccer kick. Five skilled male participants were investigated and each performed three kicks while fresh. Each participant undertook a fatigue exercise protocol for six minutes and then immediately performed a fourth kick. The participant then exercised for a further minute followed by performance of a fifth kick. Each kick was filmed in the sagittal plane and 14 ball and kicking leg displacement, velocity and acceleration variables were reported. The inter-participant coefficients of variation ranged from 5.1 per cent to 21.2 per cent (mean = 12.0 per cent) in the fresh state and 2.9 per cent to 27.8 per cent (mean = 15.4 per cent) in the fatigued state. However, only five variables showed greater variability in the fatigued state indicating that the pattern of co-ordination used by the players was highly stable and not easily perturbed by increasing fatigue. Interestingly, the foot velocity was higher in the fatigued state than in the fresh state although the ball velocity was lower. The latter could have occurred due to the fatigued state providing a less rigid foot surface at ball contact, in which the energy transfer from foot to ball will be less effective. Lees and Davies (1987) hypothesised that there may have been components of the co-ordination pattern that changed as a result of the fatiguing protocol, but stopped short of quantifying these changes. It is apparent that some aspects of co-ordination are not evident from recording of motion characteristics of the segments only, requiring a more detailed understanding of the muscular effort generated at any stage in the movement.

Luhtanen (1987) reported net muscle moments for the soccer instep kick The relative magnitude of effort applied was observed in the net hip moment, which was more dominant than that of the knee, which in turn was more dominant than that for the ankle. The hip reaches its peak early in the kick while the knee and ankle reach their peaks later, indicating that a controlled sequence is operational. It is likely that the ankle joint moment is more influential in the control of impact between foot and ball, resulting from the inter-joint co-ordination processes involved. All joints reduce their net moment at or just before impact. While this investigation was not specifically designed to investigate aspects of co-ordination or control, it can be appreciated that this greater level of detail (of how muscles are acting) has great potential for investigating co-ordination strategies in kicking.

There have been no reports in the literature that have attempted to specifically quantify intra-limb co-ordination for the soccer kick. This gap in the soccer literature contrasts with the study of other actions in sport and physical activity. For example, co-ordination changes have been quantified using cross-correlation functions in volleyball serving (see chapters by Temprado and Handford), javelin throwing (Morriss, 1998) and relative timing in the triple jump run-up (see chapter by Maraj).

Biomechanical analyses of control in kicking

Control refers to the ability to precisely vary the parameters of movement production as measured by the absolute position, velocity or acceleration of a limb or limb segment during performance (Newell, 1985). The degree of precision in skilled performance can be established by quantifying the variability associated with repeated trials of the movement. There have been several attempts to determine the nature of this variability for the kicking skill using skilled performers from different football codes, manipulation of kick distance requirements and a speed–accuracy paradigm.

Phillips (1985) investigated the variability associated with kicking a stationary ball to a maximal distance using skilled participants from different codes. Two players (one highly skilled American football place kicker, the other a skilled soccer player) were each asked to kick a stationary ball (assumed to be an American football) five times. Each participant was filmed in the sagittal plane and 14 ball and kicking leg displacement, velocity and temporal variables were reported. The coefficients of variation ranged from 1.1 per cent to 8.3 per cent (mean = 5.4 per cent), and in 12 of these variables the standard deviation of the highly skilled football place kicker was lower than that of the soccer kicker. Phillips (1985) concluded that the data provided evidence of invariance in performance, reflecting a highly sophisticated and precisely timed neuromuscular pattern. However, she also noted that participants used a different approach speed that might explain the difference in variability between the players. Another probable cause of the differences in variability may have been the specificity of the previous experience of the participants (for illustrative data on specificity effects during the volleyball serve in two groups of experts see Davids, Bennett, Handford and Jones, 1999). Individual differences may have occurred because the soccer player had less experience of kicking an American football, or because in soccer the task constraints typically require performance under static conditions of place-kicking a ball, and so it is practised less. Finally, Phillips (1985) did not test the statistical significance of the variability between participants and as a result was not able to conclude on the nature of the control mechanisms operating. From a motor control perspective, it is apparent how these findings support the notion that specificity of task constraints influences the stability of a co-ordination pattern, even within generic task categories such as interceptive actions.

Zebas and Nelson (1990) also investigated the consistency in kinematic variables from one highly skilled participant when kicking an American football from different distances to goal. Anecdotal reports from players have suggested that kicking skill should be highly stable regardless of the location of the field the kick is taken from. The participant was asked to kick a ball three times from each of 20, 30 and 50 yards while being filmed in the sagittal plane and 15 ball and kicking leg displacement, velocity and temporal variables were reported. Interestingly, the distance restriction had little effect on mean ball speed values of 33.9, 36.8 and 35.6 m s^{-1} from each distance respectively. There were no consistent trends noted in either the means or the standard deviations of the data reported for each series of kick. This finding suggests that the player had developed an ability to kick maximally but consistently from any distance, and preferred to perform the skill in a stable manner, rather than to reduce the speed of the kick at shorter distances in order to gain greater accuracy. For this player at least there appeared to be no speed–accuracy trade off. This finding might be an important feature of highly skilled kicking which has not been investigated either in a biomechanical or motor control context. However, it is worth noting that in golf, players elect to use different clubs which presumably enables them to retain some consistency in their swing. One final point made by Zebas and Nelson (1990) was to advise players and coaches to concentrate on the development of consistency in the positioning of the knee at ball contact in the last step and lower leg angular velocity before impact.

In relation to the findings of the previous study by Phillips (1985), this advice clearly represents a prescriptive approach to the performance of the skill and should be interpreted with caution until a range of task constraints in kicking is examined to ascertain the nature of the specificity effects in their study. It was observed earlier in this chapter (i.e. Lees and Nolan, 2000) that the variability associated with pelvic rotation and thigh motion decreased during place kicking for accuracy, in a speed–accuracy paradigm, indicating greater control required under those task constraints, although the variability associated with the distal segment (foot) increased. The results of this study suggest that soccer players can fine-tune the control of an established pattern of co-ordination under static task constraints.

A new view of movement variability

It has to be noted that these studies were not primarily conducted to investigate the problem of movement co-ordination and control, although the authors seem to have intuitively expected that skilled performance is associated with low levels of movement variability. As discussed in Chapter 1, this expectation may be associated with the prevailing assumptions of the information processing paradigm. However, technological advances are now providing sport scientists interested in motor control with a new view of movement variability. From a dynamical systems perspective it has been argued that movement variability observed in the motor co-ordination of skilled and unskilled performers now needs careful interpretation (e.g. Newell and Slifkin, 1998; Slifkin and Newell, 1999). Depending on the nature of the task and individual constraints, the same levels of variability reported by researchers may be functional or dysfunctional in relation to the achievement of task goals (see Williams, Davids and Williams, 1999).

This new view of variability has important implications for the design and interpretation of biomechanical analyses of movements like interceptive actions. Typically, many sport biomechanical studies have attempted to identify a common optimal movement pattern which can act as a model or a 'reference value' for imitation by learners and developing athletes (Bauer and Schöllhorn, 1997). However, in dedicated studies, common optimal kinematic patterns have proved difficult to identify, and furthermore, in training studies, performers preferred to use a performance template based on an individualised personal best rather than the 'objective' best performance by a skilled performer. This preference was well demonstrated in a study of kinematic performance on a simulated interceptive action, in which a row of LEDs was activated sequentially to act as an object in apparent motion (Brisson and Alain, 1996). The task for participants was to move a lever to an appropriate point in the trajectory of the lights in order to 'intercept' them. A common optimal kinematic pattern for this coincident timing task could not be identified. This was despite the fact that the interceptive movement with the lever involved only a single degree of freedom. The authors noted that the performance outcome 'scores could not be predicted by any kinematic characteristics of the movement pattern used' (Brisson and Alain, 1996, p. 222). These findings have been supported in studies of throwing by national and international athletes in which a variety of individual movement styles were identified, with a higher level of performance variation in the international group (Bauer and Schöllhorn, 1997).

A true picture regarding the applicability of biomechanical techniques for investigating co-ordination and control of movements in sport will not be gained until a wider range of studies have been conducted, including those with less skilled participants, so that the intra-participant variability in movement can be distinguished from the error associated with measurement. Nevertheless, the studies reviewed above provide useful normative data on the intra-participant variability associated with skilled kicking performance and some of the factors affecting co-ordination and control. Previous data have suggested that: (i) highly skilled performers attempt to adopt a strategy which promotes relative stability of movement regardless of the task demands; (ii) the task constraints of football are highly specific in that skilled performers from one code of football are initially less able to perform a similar skill in another code; and, (iii) the relative demands of speed and accuracy appear to affect movement organisation by influencing patterns of co-ordination.

Summary

Biomechanical methods have been widely used to describe and define many aspects of kicking skills. The progress made has been restricted due to equipment and methodological limitations. These limitations are primarily to do with the difficulty of obtaining a sufficient quantity of accurate data. Sophisticated motion analysis systems are now becoming available and these enable rapid 3D data to be collected. It is likely that these systems will be used in the near future to collect further data on kicking, and other soccer skills, and enable aspects of co-ordination and control to be better understood. This progression is an exciting development that will enable the generality and explanatory power of existing theoretical models of motor control to be fully explored through the vehicle of 'real world' interceptive actions, such as those in soccer.

References

Andersen, T.B., Dorge, H.C. and Thomsen, F.I. (1999). Collisions in soccer kicking. *Sports Engineering* **2**, 121–5.

Atwater, A.E. (1979). Biomechanics of overarm throwing movements and of throwing injuries. *Exercise and Sport Science Reviews* **7**, 43–85.

Barfield, W.R. (1998). The biomechanics of kicking in soccer. *Clinics in Sports Medicine* **17**, 711–28.

Bartlett, R. (1997) *Introduction to Sports Biomechanics*. London, E & FN Spon

Bauer, H.U. and Schöllhorn, W. (1997). Self-organizing maps for the analysis of complex movement patterns. *Neural Processing Letters* **5**, 193–9.

Bloomfield, J., Elliott, B.C. and Davies, C.M. (1979). Development of the soccer kick: a cinematographical analysis. *Journal of Human Movement Studies* **5**, 152–9.

Bober, T., Putnam, C.A. and Woodworth, G.G. (1987). Factors influencing the angular velocity of a human limb segment. *Journal of Biomechanics* **20**, 511–21.

Brisson, T.A. and Alain, C. (1996). Should common optimal movement patterns be identified as the criterion to be achieved? *Journal of Motor Behavior* **28**, 211–23.

Browder, K.D., Tant, C.L. and Wilkerson, J.D. (1991) A three dimensional kinematic analysis of three kicking techniques in female players. In *Biomechanics in Sport IX* (edited by C.L. Tant, P.E. Patterson and S.L. York). Ames, IA: ISU Press.

Davids, K., Bennett, S.J., Handford, C. and Jones, B. (1999). Acquiring co-ordination in self-paced extrinsic timing tasks: a constraints-led perspective. *International Journal of Sport Psychology*: **30**, 437–61.

Davids, K., Lees, A. and Burwitz, L. (2000). Understanding and measuring coordination and control in soccer skills: implications for talent identification and skill acquisition. *Journal of Sports Sciences* **18**, 703–14.

Hatzitaki, V. (1999). The role of dynamic equilibrium in instep kicking performance of young soccer players. *Journal of Human Movement Studies* **36**, 273–88.

Hay, J.G. (1985). *The Biomechanics of Sports Techniques*. Englewood Cliffs, NJ: Prentice-Hall.

Jöris, H.J.J., van Muyen, A.J.E., van Ingen Schenau, G.J. and Kemper, H.C.G. (1985). Force, velocity and energy flow during the overarm throw in female handball players. *Journal of Biomechanics* **189**, 409–14.

Lees, A. (1996). Biomechanics applied to soccer skills. In *Science and Soccer* (edited by T. Reilly). London: E & FN Spon.

Lees, A. and Davies, T. (1987). The effects of fatigue on soccer kick kinematics. *Journal of Sports Science* **6**, 156-157.

Lees, A. and Nolan, L (1998) Biomechanics of soccer – a review. *Journal of Sports Sciences* **16**, 211–34.

Lees, A. and Nolan, L. (2001). 3-D kinematic analysis of the instep kick under speed and accuracy conditions. In *Science and Football IV* (edited by T. Reilly *et al.*). London: E & FN Spon.

Luhtanen, P. (1987). Kinematics and kinetics of serve in volleyball at different age levels. In *Biomechanics XI-B* (edited by G. de Groot, A.P. Hollander, P.A. Huijing, G.J. van Ingen Schenau). Amsterdam: Free University Press.

Maraj, B.V., Elliott, D., Lee, T.D. and Pollock, B.J. (1993) Variance and invariance inexpert and novice triple jumpers. *Research Quarterly for Exercise and Sport* **64**, 404–12.

Morriss, C.J. (1998) Co-ordination patterns in the performances of an elite javelin thrower. *Journal of Sports Sciences* **16**, 12–13.

Newell, K.M. (1985). Co-ordination, control and skill. In *Differing Perspectives in Motor Learning, Memory, and Control* (edited by D. Goodman, R. Wilberg and I. Franks). Amsterdam: North Holland.

Newell, K.M. (1986). Constraints on the development of co-ordination. In *Motor Development in Children: Aspects of Co-ordination and Control* (edited by M.G. Wade and H.T.A. Whiting). Dordrecht: Nijhoff.

Phillips, S.J. (1985). Invariance of elite kicking performance. In *Biomechanics IX-B* (edited by D. Winter). Champaign, IL: Human Kinetics.

Prassas, S.G., Terauds, J. and Nathan, T. (1990). Three dimensional kinematic analysis of high and low trajectory kicks in soccer. In *Proceedings of the VIIIth Symposium of the International Society of Biomechanics in Sports* (edited by N. Nosek, D. Sojka, W. Morrison and P. Susanka). Prague: Conex.

Schmidt, R.C. and Fitzpatrick, P. (1996). Dynamical perspective on motor learning. In *Advances in Motor Learning and Control* (edited by H.N. Zelaznik). Champaign, IL: Human Kinetics.

Sparrow, W.A. (1992). Measuring changes in co-ordination and control. In *Approaches to the Study of Motor Control and Learning* (edited by J.J. Summers). Amsterdam: North Holland.

Summers. J.J. (1998). Has ecological psychology delivered what it has promised? In *Motor Control and Skill: A Multidisciplinary Perspective* (edited by J. Piek). Champaign, IL: Human Kinetics.

Turvey, M.T. (1990). Co-ordination. *American Psychologist* **45**, 938–53.

Wickstrom, R.L. (1975). Developmental kinesiology. *Exercise and Sports Science Reviews* **3**, 163–92.

Williams, A.M., Davids, K. and Williams, J.G. (1999). *Visual Perception and Action in Sport*. London: Routledge.

Winter, D.A. (1990). *Biomechanics and Motor Control of Human Movement*. New York: John Wiley.

Zebas, C.J. and Nelson, J.D. (1990) Consistency in kinematic movement patterns and prediction of ball velocity in the football placekick. In *Biomechanics of Sports VI. Proceedings of the VIth symposium of the International Society of Biomechanics in Sports* (edited by E. Kreighbaum and A. McNeil). Montana: Montana State University.

17 Strategy and practice for acquiring timing in discrete, self-paced interceptive skills

Craig Handford

The fundamental problems facing the performer when aiming to co-ordinate and control discrete self-paced interceptive actions have been discussed in the chapters by Button and Summers and by Temprado, both of which focus on the assembly of the effector (action) system during performance. Of equal interest (and importance) are the strategies employed by performers to ensure the successful timing of such actions with an external object or perceptual event, in this case the trajectory of a tossed ball. The essence of this timing problem for the server is the same in a number of sports including: squash, racketball, badminton and table-tennis. However, it is in the sports of tennis and volleyball where most comment can be found relating to the determinants of successful serving. This chapter will examine the nature of co-ordination during serving in volleyball, as a self-paced extrinsic timing task, with a specific view to investigating the implications for the design of practice.

Coaching the volleyball serve

Most coaching texts in volleyball consistently highlight the importance of invariant ball placement during the toss phase with particular emphasis given to the height of toss (e.g. see Crisfield (1995) and McGehee (1997)). Serving accuracy is considered to be improved with increased consistency of placement in the forward–backward and left–right dimensions with the ball tossed in front of and above the hitting shoulder (see Scates, 1984 and Nicholls, 1994). The significance of the height of ball placement has also been emphasised as an important factor for two apparent reasons. First, it has been suggested that the higher the point of impact above the court, the more easily the ball can be directed towards the intended target across the net. Second, the successful co-ordination of the striking arm and ball toss is considered to be more likely if the ball has little or no vertical velocity at the point of impact (Crisfield, 1995). In other words, if the ball is rising or falling, its position in space at a given point in time is less predictable due to continual changes in velocity. Consequently, a number of authorities warn against over-extension of the ball toss suggesting that varied ball toss over performances will lead to problems in timing and a greater chance of error (see Bertucci, 1979 and Banachowski, 1983).

However, with regard to absolute values of peak height of ball placement, there are two noticeable features of the coaching literature. First, expert coaches tend to be rather prescriptive about the precise height of the ball toss required for successful serving. Second, there is a large degree of discrepancy amongst authors on the absolute value of ball toss height. Cox (1980), Scates (1984) and Nicholls (1994) suggested that the ball should be tossed to about 1 m above the head, whilst Bertucci (1979), Neville (1994) and Crisfield (1995) advocate 8–18 inches above the extended tossing hand. Gambardella (1987) preferred 50–70 cm above eye level. This level of disparity reflects well the absence of a detailed scientific understanding of the specific underlying mechanisms that are responsible for the co-ordination and control of these types of dynamic interceptive actions.

Interceptive timing in ball games

Since the classical work on baseball batting by Hubbard and Seng (1954) a number of studies have proposed similar control strategies for discrete interceptive type activities where movement initiation is geared to externally-paced events. More recently, several authors have provided evidence to support the notion that a variety of optical information sources (see Chapter 1 and Chapter 7 by Montagne and Laurent), could provide the visual information necessary for timing behaviour in dynamic interceptive actions (see Bootsma and Peper, 1992; Williams, Davids and Williams, 1999 for detailed reviews). A dynamical systems approach to the problems of interceptive timing has preferred to focus on tasks that are continuous and internally paced, as Button and Summers (Chapter 13, this volume) highlight. This perspective advocates the identification of macroscopic variables that describe the patterns of co-ordination which emerge from motor system degrees of freedom (Kelso, 1994; Whiting and Vereijken, 1993). The essential variables or order parameters, described in the chapter by Button and Summers, act to compress the number of movement system degrees of freedom involved in the action and are often specific to the constraints involved. In dynamic interceptive actions, control parameters, which guide the organisation of order parameters, are rarely either entirely performer-based or entirely task-based, but capture the essence of the co-ordination between the performer, the task and the environment (see Wallace, 1996). Typical candidate variables have been shown to exhibit characteristics of both the perceptual and movement subsystems and display minimal levels of variation, often despite considerable fluctuation in the individual component parts (Beek and Van Santvoord, 1992).

In the context of serving, a series of investigations using cascade juggling as the task vehicle is of particular interest due to use of a self-paced extrinsic timing task where a ball must be intercepted during some point in its vertical trajectory. Beek (1989) suggested that the solution to the problem of timing in cascade juggling could be found in the spatial constraint introduced by the placement of the ball. A consistent peak in the ball's trajectory was interpreted as an attractor point around which the performance workspace could be organised. In other words, the fixed height of the ball's peak would ensure that the flight times of the balls remained relatively stable, thus providing informational support in the form of a time base to co-ordinate hand movements during the ball transport and toss phase of juggling. In this way performers are able to exploit the stability afforded by the force of gravity on ball flight. Additional work on cascade juggling by Van Santvoord (1995) provided further support for this notion, that stability in flight time was maintained under both temporally and spatially constrained conditions. While this simple yet eloquent account was derived from a continuous, rhythmical interceptive action an interesting question concerns whether a similar mechanism could operate for a single, discrete action, such as serving in ball sports.

A dynamical systems perspective on timing in the volleyball serve

In recent investigations, we have attempted to examine if such an explanation could be offered for co-ordination in the self-paced extrinsic timing task of the volleyball serve (see Davids, Bennett, Handford and Jones, 1999; Davids, Kingsbury, Bennett and Handford, 2001). We investigated whether consistency of ball placement was used by skilled servers, in light of the common belief that successful servers exhibit highly stable characteristics during the toss phase. The intention was to assess the potential of spatio–temporal parameters as possible essential variables in a dynamical systems framework for explaining co-ordination of the serving action. Of particular interest was the extent to which skilled servers utilised consistency in ball placement to set up a type of discrete 'spatial clock' for the timing of subsequent actions. Using a methodology similar to that of Temprado (Chapter 15, this volume), the serves of international level female performers were analysed using three-dimensional video and kinematic analysis techniques.

A summary of the findings of the spatial analysis revealed that highly consistent placement of the ball in the left–right and forward–backward dimensions was not essential for successful serving. In fact, variability in the location of the ball in these planes tended to increase from the initial movement of the tossing arm to the moment of hand–ball contact. The importance placed on the vertical location of the ball was substantiated by the results showing relatively stable spatial locations for both zenith and contact. Taken together these findings suggested that, whilst performers are willing to compensate for variances in the x and y directions, they preferred to stabilise the vertical position of the ball at its zenith and contact, despite a range of initial conditions and ball flight trajectories (see Figure 17.1). On the basis of these results it seems that practice of the serve should emphasise the development of a stable peak height of ball toss rather than consistency in the left–right and forward–backward directions. The spatio–temporal nature of the information from ball toss height, as a constraint on serving, was supported by the key finding that spatial stability led to high levels of temporal stability during both the ascent and descent phases of the toss. The suggestion was that consistency in the flight time of the ball is important to the overall success of satisfying the demands of the task. In particular, the presence of a constant delay between zenith and contact indicated that the ball was being struck at the same point in time following its zenith and when it had some

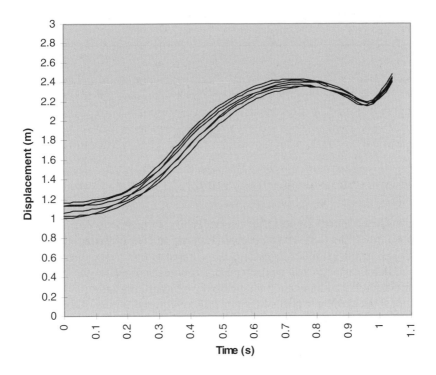

Figure 17.1 Typical inter-trial time–displacement profiles for ball placement in the vertical
(*z*) plane exemplified by one participant in the experimental analysis.

degree of negative vertical velocity. This finding contradicts the common belief by
many coaches and players that the contact of the ball should occur when the ball
reaches its peak point (i.e. zero velocity).

Taken together, the findings from the spatial and temporal analyses suggested
that by fixing the zenith of the tossed ball in the vertical plane, skilled servers
were attempting to secure fixed temporal characteristics of the ball's trajectory,
particularly the time of descent (T_d). How then do these findings relate to a strategy
for co-ordinating the timing of the striking action with ball toss? Our findings
from a previous analysis on co-ordination patterns in volleyball serving showed
that the within-subject variation in total movement time was relatively small with
average deviations ranging from 12 to 39 ms (see Davids, Bennett, Handford and
Jones, 1999). Moreover, the timing of the change in direction of the hip joint
centre from back-swing to fore-swing occurred at an average of 76 per cent of
total movement time and was highly invariant (± 0.5 per cent). On the basis of
these results it would seem that skilled servers prefer to maintain a consistent
movement time and initiate force production at a specific moment during the
movement sequence. An analysis of the relationship between the time of ball
zenith and initiation of forward hip movement showed that the occurrence of
these two events was extremely invariant and strongly coupled (Table 17.1).

Table 17.1   Means and standard deviations for the times of ball zenith, initiation of the striking action and differences between the two events.

Subject	Ta (s) M (S.D.)	Th (s) M (S.D.)	Difference (Ta–Th) M (S.D.)
1	0.624 (0.018)	0.610 (0.028)	0.0 14 (0.011)
2	0.689 (0.054)	0.691 (0.056)	−0.003 (0.016)
3	0.496 (0.029)	0.485 (0.045)	0.010 (0.023)
4	0.638 (0.024)	0.638 (0.031)	0.000 (0.010)
5	0.657 (0.022)	0.640 (0.034)	0.021 (0.018)
6	0.730 (0.041)	0.725 (0.049)	0.005 (0.010)
M	0.639	0.631	0.008
(S.D.)	(0.073)	(0.076)	(0.008)

Pearson product correlation confirmed a significantly strong relationship ($r = 0.99$, $p < 0.001$). It seemed that servers were attempting to control the height of ball zenith to ensure that, if the fore-swing was initiated at this point, then the time remaining before contact was equivalent to the time required for the proximo–distal unfolding of the kinematic chain involved in the striking action. Apparently, the relationships between a stable height at ball zenith, and timing of the interval between the initiation of the serving movement at zenith and the point of ball–hand contact, for co-ordinating a successful serve, is discovered during extensive practice.

This relationship was shown to hold true despite a degree of individual variability in absolute peak height and time of ball peak, suggesting that these values were somehow geared to personal anatomical characteristics to ensure successful interception of hand and ball. A consideration of the equation describing the displacement of a descending ball shows how servers using the timing strategy described above may derive the magnitude of the peak height of toss from a sensitivity to their individual reach height and movement time:

Since,

Peak height = Contact height + Displacement of descending ball (d)

where $d = V_i t + \frac{1}{2} g t^2$

and V_i = initial velocity = 0, g = acceleration due to gravity (9.8 m s^{-2}) and t = time from peak to contact = fore-swing time.

Therefore,

$d = \frac{1}{2} g t^2 = 4.99 \text{ (fore-swing time)}^2$ and so

Peak height = Contact height + 4.99 (fore-swing time)^2

Implications for acquisition of co-ordination in the volleyball serve

Examination of the performance of the group of international players provided practical support for the explanatory theoretical framework outlined above. Performances showed a significant correlation between peak height and fore-swing time ($r = 0.66$) with an even stronger relationship demonstrated with contact height ($r = 0.93$). This latter finding is not completely unexpected as contact height is relatively fixed in adults, given the task constraint of hitting the ball with arm extended, and, as such, represents a kind of anatomical constraint with fore-swing time somewhat more flexible.

From the observations above, it is apparent that the required co-ordination for volleyball serving is defined by information residing in the physical organism–environment system. That is, parameterisation of ball toss could occur using an intrinsic metric in units relative to the performer's body parts and capacity for movement, so called body-scaled information (Konczak, 1990). Such an approach links dimensions of the task and environment to relevant anatomical properties of the performer and so the key relationships that describe successful co-ordination are expressed across persons of different body sizes and dimensions (Davis and Burton, 1991). This explanation may account for the apparent discrepancies in the coaching literature on recommendations for specific height of ball placement during serving. In fact, if this line of reasoning is followed, then practical advice should advocate a less prescriptive, 'hands off' approach to coaching where this aspect is concerned. In other words, as much as possible, performers should be allowed to discover and develop their own particular solution to the problem of timing that is uniquely scaled to their personal anatomical characteristics (see Handford, Davids, Bennett and Button, 1997).

From a dynamical systems perspective, the relative phasing of ball zenith and forward hip movement was found to be an appropriate essential (collective) variable around which co-ordination of the serve was organised (Davids, Bennett, Handford and Jones, 1999; Davids, Kingsbury, Bennett and Handford, 2001). According to proponents of this approach, any account of co-ordination should also consider the parameters which influence the relationships defined by collective variables (Wallace, 1996). The validity of the hypothesis above is further strengthened by the identification of potential control parameters via well-established physical principles derived mathematically. Examination of classical mechanics governing projectile motion in the vertical direction provides useful insight into the factors that determine aspects of spatial (and consequently temporal) behaviour leading to ball zenith. From the height and moment of release:

$$\text{Vertical displacement} = \frac{(V_{\sin}\theta)^2}{2g}$$

Where V = Velocity at release, θ = Angle of release and g = acceleration due to gravity

Since during the toss θ tends towards $90°$ (and sin 90 = 1) and g remains constant, it becomes apparent that the displacement of the ball during its ascent is primarily determined by its velocity at release. Thus, it is possible to see how the force imparted to the ball during the early portion of the toss may act as a control parameter on the system by determining the vertical velocity at release and consequently the absolute height of ball zenith. In summary, a picture of successful co-ordination in the volleyball serve emerged where movement system order is shaped by regulation of the force applied to the ball in order to get it to stable zenith, the specific location of which may be informed by sensitivity to body-scaled information that is unique to each individual at a given time in skill/physical development. These ideas support a description of skilled behaviour which, according to Schmidt and Fitzpatrick (1996), involves two dynamics, one nested within the other. The first is associated with the assembly of a co-ordinative structure at the level of body segments that is responsible for producing the required action (e.g. see Chapter 15 by Temprado). This dynamic, however, is nested within a higher order dynamic that is linked to the successful achievement of the task goal and is associated with aspects of learning. In this way, a one-to-one mapping of the ball zenith and the striking action may be conceptualised as a stable attractor state towards which the system moves as skilled performance develops.

With this in mind, the solutions to the problem of serving offered in this chapter provide a formal basis for examining some of the effects of organismic constraints on motor development that have been predicted. In his seminal paper, Newell (1986) discussed the consequences of child growth and the impact of changing body size on biomechanical constraints. Particular emphasis was given to the changes in segment moment of inertia and the (re)organisation of co-ordination that follows (see also Corbetta and Vereijken, 1999; Van der Kamp, Vereijken and Savelsbergh, 1996). If we consider that the goal for developing games players is the preservation of system order (i.e. successful co-ordination) in complex, dynamic environments, then a change in absolute peak height of ball placement during serving can be expected in young performers as contact height increases due to physical growth and development, and skill acquisition. In other words, the vertical force applied to the ball during the toss phase (control parameter) is a dynamic variable influenced by changes to organismic constraints in order to satisfy task demands at any given time during development. Furthermore, as learners improve intra-limb co-ordination of the striking action, the time required for the proximo–distal unfolding of the kinematic chain during fore-swing is likely to decrease and influence ball placement accordingly.

Future research should attempt to track the changes in these two co-ordination dynamics as novice/young performers acquire these key relationships over time. In addition, practice conditions which best facilitate the development of these essential aspects of co-ordination should be investigated. An understanding of the timing relationship and the ability to predict optimum ball placement for a given individual may be used to assist learners in successfully attaining co-ordination and to make more efficient use of practice time. Furthermore, since peak height is so closely linked to the serving movement, traditional approaches to practice, emphasising the breakdown of the movement into its component parts, should be re-examined in this new light. It is here that attention is now focused.

Part-practice: a question of investigating task dynamics

Traditional views

A particularly thorny problem facing sports coaches and teachers has been the fundamental question of whether a complex motor skill should be decomposed into smaller parts or left as a whole for the purpose of practice. Theoretical support for such a proposal can be found largely within a more traditional approach, viewing the performer as a processor of information with a limited attentional capacity (Chamberlin and Lee, 1993). The *principles* by which a skill might be decomposed for the purpose of part practice are, however, less clear. Traditional views in sport pedagogy have focused on subjective assessment of skill in terms of 'appropriate units of action' and their perceived relationship with one another. More specifically, methods of instruction have relied on subjective assessments of the complexity and organisation of the component parts of a skill to determine whether practice is best organised as a breakdown of the parts or as a whole (see Magill, 1998). However, it has long been pointed out (e.g. Stammers, 1980) that there have been very few direct examinations of this prediction and those that come closest, although not direct, actually show little support.

An interesting issue concerns the provision of a theoretically coherent account of this common practice dilemma. Meaningful practical guidance has not been forthcoming from the literature. Evaluation of previous approaches highlights the arbitrary and unsystematic method by which skills are formed into parts (e.g. see Wightman and Lintern, 1985; Chamberlin and Lee, 1993; Burton and Davis, 1996). In fact, Newell (1981) suggests that such decisions to practice tasks decomposed on the basis of very broad generalisations are 'not founded on strong evidence and theoretical interpretations of their effects are even more hazardous' (p. 218). Magill (1998) sidesteps the issue by suggesting that 'the critical part to making the decision about whether certain parts can be practised separately or together with other parts is dependent on the instructor's knowledge of the skill itself' (p. 299). Clearly the success of this approach presupposes the existence of shared understandings and in-depth analyses of the key factors that influence the dynamics of skills to be acquired. The problem is, as Newell (1989) argued, detailed, objective scientific analyses of task constraints do not exist. Lintern (1991) drew attention to the dangers of following subjective beliefs in partitioning complex tasks for the purposes of practice and suggested that significant limitations in current knowledge relating to the underlying mechanisms involved continues to restrict the development of practical methods. The result may be that many accepted practices in sport are presently implementing task decompositions using a tentative and unprincipled foundation.

The dynamical systems approach

Having highlighted the limitations of traditional approaches it is apparent that the development of procedures dealing with task decomposition should be firmly established on the basis of a principled analysis of the task and not intuitive or anecdotal accounts (Lintern, 1991). Several authors have argued that an ecological/

dynamical approach to examining tasks in terms of organising practice has a number of potential advantages (Davis and Burton, 1991; Williams, Davids and Williams, 1999). One of the benefits of adopting this theoretical framework is the inclusion of both performer and environment-based constraints within the same analytical framework. Moreover, the ecological/dynamical agenda is clearly committed to uncovering the underlying relationships that describe the essence of co-ordination and control of skilled movement. Following this approach, a detailed understanding of exactly what is to be learned could provide a more accurate and valid basis for evaluating the likely contribution of practice regimes believed to be complementary (Newell, 1985). Furthermore, a description of skilled behaviour using an ecological approach allows an evaluation of the potential for transfer of learning in coaching/ training environments where related tasks or specific phases of a movement are practised in isolation.

The relationship between task constraints and transfer of learning

Contrary to the concerns expressed by Davis and Burton (1991), the decomposition of skills from an ecological perspective may be considered as a successful framework for practice, assuming that certain conditions are maintained. Using this approach, the breakdown of skills may be informed by a comparison of the proposed component parts in terms of the constraints involved and the impact on the key parameters/relationships that represent order in the 'to-be-acquired' movement pattern. Measures of the effects on known patterns of variability associated with these key parameters can then be used as a sensitive index of 'transferability' to a criterion task. For example, if the change in constraints brought about by task decomposition is too large, a disruption of the characteristic variability profile over time can be expected. In this case the amount of disturbance will determine the extent of the transfer, with the possibility that high levels of variability will represent a fundamental shift to a co-ordination pattern that is somewhat removed from that to be acquired. In other words, the constraints present in the part task will have changed so much from the original criterion task that the goals of each of the movements will be essentially different and improvements in performance of the criterion would not be predicted (Goodman and Kelso, 1980). However, if the characteristic stability is maintained then it may be assumed that constraints on movement are sufficiently similar and successful transfer of the part practice would seem likely.

Is perception–action coupling a principle for practice organisation in dynamic interceptive actions?

What is proposed here is an alternative framework, based on established theory, for assessing the effects of task decomposition on the acquisition of stable move-ment patterns. In general terms, the preservation of key dynamical relationships between joint segments or between information sources and system components is presented as a potential guiding principle with the prediction of weak or negative transfer should this principle be violated. Clearly the need for a detailed understanding of the task constraints of the motor skill to be acquired remains a priority for the re-organisation of practice. In a recent study we utilised the dynamic description of timing in the volleyball serve outlined earlier in assessing the compatibility of a commonly used part practice regime for ball placement (see Davids, Bennett, Handford and Jones, 1999; Davids, Kingsbury, Bennett and Handford, 2001). With a view towards evaluating the potential for transfer of learning to the criterion task it was proposed that the separation of toss and strike phases in the part-practice regime would disrupt the key relationship shown to be essential to the success of the skill. In particular, a comparison of the absolute magnitude and variability of the ball zenith should provide useful estimations of transferability.

The serving performance of expert volleyballers was filmed and analysed in a ball placement-only condition and a serve-and-toss condition. In the former, the instructions were to practise the ball-placement phase of the serve and to toss the ball without the strike, but stopping short of contact and allowing the ball to drop (part-practice condition). The displacement characteristics of the ball's trajectory during this condition were compared with the trajectory profiles from task constraints when performers actually served the ball. Two key differences were revealed: i) the variance of ball peak height was greater for the placement-only condition; and ii) the mean value of peak height was also greater for the placement-only condition. Figure 17.2. shows the time–displacement profiles for ball placement during the serving (top) and placement only (bottom) conditions exemplified by data from one typical participant.

The differences in profile, particularly the variability in absolute toss height and the location of the ball at zenith, suggested that a manipulation of the task constraints appeared to have caused an adaptation in the spatial pattern of ball placement. In other words, the constraints imposed on ball placement whilst serving were qualitatively different to those present when tossing the ball in isolation. It follows that decomposition of the task for the purposes of part-practice would not predict positive transfer to the criterion task. The implication is that for successful transfer of part-practice regimes to occur, manipulation of task constraints should proceed taking care to preserve the key relationships that describe co-ordination. This implication does of course depend on a basic but non-trivial premise that these relationships are known to the practitioner in the first instance. Such a finding lends credence to the use of ecological approaches for describing tasks demands and leads to questions over the validity of this type of part-practice; in particular for the improvement of serving, but also in general terms for other tasks and in other sports.

In summary, strategies and practices for acquiring timing in the volleyball serve may be understood and enhanced with reference to a dynamical systems approach. Fundamental to such a description is an understanding of the mechanisms that underlie co-ordinated movement and specifically the discovery of the essential relationships between performer, environment and task constraints. The potential for such an approach to shed new light on contemporary principles of practice

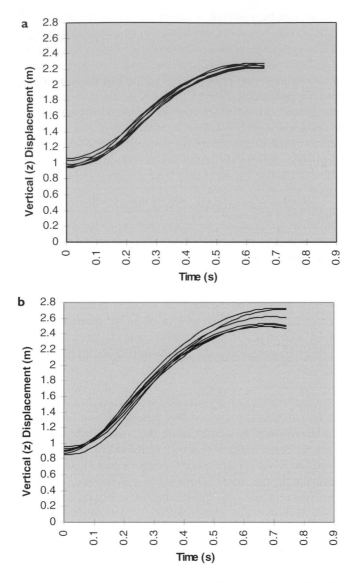

Figure 17.2 Typical inter-trial time-displacement profiles for ball
displacement in the vertical (*z*) plane for a) serving and b)
toss only conditions exemplified by one participant in the
analysis.

organisation has been clearly demonstrated in the area of task decomposition and
may have much to offer in other aspects of skill acquisition. Future research would
do well to examine the implications of a framework that emphasises the manipulation of constraints in other areas such as instruction, observational learning and
feedback provision.

References

Banachowski, A. (1983). *Power Volleyball*. Sarasota, FL: Athletic Institute Publications.

Beek, P.J. (1989). Juggling Dynamics. PhD Thesis. Vrije Universiteit Amsterdam. Amsterdam: Vrije Universiteit Press.

Beek, P.J. and Van Santvoord, A.A.M. (1992). Learning the cascade juggling: a dynamical systems analysis. *Journal of Motor Behaviour* **24**, 1, 85–94.

Bertucci, B. (1979). The overhand floater serve. In *Championship Volleyball by the Experts* (edited by B. Bertucci). New York: Leisure Press.

Bootsma, R.J. and Peper, C.E. (1992). Predictive visual information sources for the regulation of action with special emphasis on catching and hitting. In *Vision and Motor Control* (edited by L. Proteau and D. Elliot). Amsterdam: Elsevier Science Publishing Company, Inc.

Burton, A.W. and Davis, W.E. (1996). Ecological task analysis: utilizing intrinsic measures in research and practice. *Human Movement Science* **15**, 285–314.

Chamberlin, C. and Lee, T. (1993). Arranging practice conditions and designing instruction. In *Handbook of Research on Sport Psychology* (edited by R.N. Singer, M. Murphy and L.K. Tennant). New York: Macmillan Publishing.

Corbetta, D. and Vereijken, B. (1999). Understanding development and learning of motor co-ordination in sport: the contribution of dynamic systems theory. *International Journal of Sport Psychology* **30**, 507–30.

Cox, R.H. (1980). *Teaching Volleyball*. Minnesota: Burgess Publishing Company.

Crisfield, D.W. (1995). *Winning Volleyball for Girls*. Vancouver: Mountain Lion Inc.

Davids, K., Bennett, S.J., Handford, C. and Jones, B. (1999). Acquiring co-ordination in self-paced extrinsic timing tasks: a constraints-led perspective. *International Journal of Sport Psychology* **30**, 437–61.

Davids, K., Kingsbury, D., Bennett S.J. and Handford, C. (2001). Information–movement coupling: implications for the organisation of research and practice during acquisition of self-paced extrinsic timing skills. *Journal of Sports Sciences* **19**, 117–27.

Davis, W.E. and Burton, A.W. (1991). Ecological task analysis: translating movement behavior theory into practice. *Applied Physical Activity Quarterly* **8**, 154–77

Goodman, D. and Kelso, J.A.S. (1980). Are movements prepared in parts ? Not under compatible (naturalized) conditions. *Journal of Experimental Psychology: General* **109**, 475–95.

Handford, C., Davids, K., Bennett, S. and Button, C. (1997). Skill acquisition in sport: some applications of an evolving practice ecology. *Journal of Sports Sciences* **15**, 621–40.

Hubbard, A.W. and Seng, C.N. (1954). Visual movements of batters. *Research Quarterly* **25**, 42–57.

Kelso, J.A.S. (1994). Elementary co-ordination dynamics. In *Interlimb Co-ordination: Neural, Dynamical and Cognitive Constraints*, (edited by S. Swinnen, H. Heuer, J. Massion and P. Casaer). New York: Academic Press Inc.

Konczak, J. (1990). Toward an ecological theory of motor development: the relevance of the Gibsonian Approach to vision for motor development research. In *Advances in Motor Development Research 3* (edited by J. Clark and J. Humphrey). New York: AMS Press.

Lintern, G. (1991). Instructional strategies. In *Training for Performance: Principles of Applied Human Learning* (edited by J.E. Morrison). Chichester: John Wiley and Sons.

Magill, R. (1998). *Motor Learning: Concepts and Applications* (5th edn). New York: McGraw Hill.

McGehee, R. (1997). The virtual wall: a key to learning the basic tennis serve. *Journal of Physical Education, Recreation and Dance* **68**, 7, 10–12.

Neville, W. (1994). *Serve it Up: Volleyball for Life*. San Francisco: Mayfield Publishing Company.

Newell, K.M. (1981). Skill learning. In *Human Skills* (edited by D. Holding). Chichester: John Wiley and Sons Ltd.

Newell, K.M. (1985). Co-ordination, control and skill. In *Differing Perspectives in Motor Learning, Memory, and Control* (edited by D. Goodman, R.B. Wilberg and I.M. Franks). Amsterdam: Elsevier Science Publishing Company, Inc.

Newell, K.M. (1986). Constraints on the development of co-ordination. In *Motor Development in Children: Aspects of Co-ordination and Control* (edited by M.G. Wade and H.T.A. Whiting). Dordrecht: Nijhoff.

Newell, K.M. (1989). On task and theory specificity. *Journal of Motor Behavior* **21**, 92–6.

Nicholls, K. (1994). *Volleyball: The Skills of the Game*. Swindon: The Crowood Press.

Scates, A. (1984). *Winning Volleyball*. Boston, MA: Allyn and Bacon.

Schmidt, R.C. and Fitzpatrick, P. (1996). Dynamical perspective on motor learning. In *Advances in Motor Learning and Control* (edited by H.N. Zelaznik). Champaign, IL: Human Kinetics.

Stammers, R.B. (1980). Part and whole practice for a tracking task: effects of task variables and amount of practice. *Perceptual and Motor Skills* **50**, 203–10.

Van der Kamp, J., Vereijken, B. and Savelsbergh, G. (1996). Physical and informational constraints in the co-ordination and control of human movement. *Corpus, Psyche et Societas* **3**, 2, 102–18.

Van Santvoord, A.A.M. (1995). Cascade Juggling: Learning, Variablity and Information. PhD Thesis. Vrije Universiteit Amsterdam. Amsterdam: Vrije Universiteit Press.

Wallace, S.A. (1996). Dynamic pattern perspective of rhythmic movement: an introduction. In *Advances in Motor Learning and Control* (edited by H.N. Zelaznik). Champaign, IL: Human Kinetics.

Whiting, H.T.A. and Vereijken, B. (1993). The acquisition of co-ordination in skill learning. *International Journal of Sport Psychology* **24**, 343–57.

Wightman, D.C. and Lintern, G. (1985). Part-task training for tracking and manual control. *Human Factors* **27**, 267–83.

Williams, A.M., Davids, K. and Williams, J. (1999). *Visual Perception and Action in Sport*. London: E & FN Spon.

18 Control of grip force in interceptive sport actions

François-Xavier Li and Yvonne Turrell

What is the main task of a player involved in an interceptive sport? Typically one has to hit a ball or a shuttle with a racket, a bat, a club or a stick to a certain location, for instance on the other side of a net. A naïve spectator usually just watches the ball and sees only whether the ball is on target, e.g. in or out of the court, and sometimes whether the ball has been struck fast or slow. Accuracy of the movement and its outcome has been the focus of attention of a large body of the movement science literature (e.g. Bootsma and Van Wieringen, 1990), and examples can be found in several chapters of this book. However, a good coach would also notice whether the player was relaxed or tense during performance.

Although this ability for producing a fluid movement has attracted less research attention, it has important consequences for the quality of the shot and endurance of the player. When a tennis player hits a ball, the energy required to send the ball across the net is generated entirely, in the case of a serve, or essentially, for most other shots, by the contraction of the player's muscles. This energy is then transferred to the ball via the racket. The grip of the hand on the handle constitutes the interface between the player and the racket. The second main task the hand has to accomplish is to control the racket in such a way that a shot is performed accurately. The goal of a tennis shot is of course to send the ball to the other side of the net with enough speed but also with enough force and accuracy to pass an opponent. Control is essential for the second task. So, what are the requirements for a good interface for bat–ball contact?

To maintain control of the racket and transfer energy to it, the hand has to grasp the racket. A brief analysis of the biomechanical constraints shows that two main forces have to be taken into account. First, the *load force* (LF) is the resultant or net force that acts on an object, e.g. a racket. Of special interest here is the load force tangential to the surface which acts to make the racket slip. Note that load force can be caused by a collision with external objects or the environment (e.g. impact of the ball), or without contact (e.g. gravity, inertia). The impact of the ball is largely determined by its momentum (velocity × mass) prior to the collision. The load force is also partly dependent upon the player. For instance, when the player swings a racket, it generates inertial forces proportional to the acceleration, as discussed in Chapter 11 by Davids, Bennett and Beak on haptic information for wielding rackets. Second, when the hand grips a handle, it produces a frictional force or *grip force* (GF), classically defined as the force applied through the fingers and the palm normal to the handle's surface. To maintain control of the racket, the hand has to produce enough frictional force to overcome the load force. The ratio of load force over grip force constitutes the friction coefficient and determines the outcome of the collision. If the grip force is too low, the racket will slip in the hand and the quality of the transfer of energy will be poor. The result may be an ineffective bat–ball contact, and a poor shot or even a dropped racket. The simple solution to overcome this problem is to increase the grip force. Increasing the grip force ensures that the racket stays firmly in the hand. However, this is not inconsequential: as muscles produce more grip force, more energy is used and fatigue and cramps can occur rapidly, particularly towards the end of a long competitive match. It is therefore essential to reach a compromise between the energy expenditure and the task requirement: a player has to be efficient[1] in gripping the racket.

Research on grip force

An extensive body of knowledge on grip force has been developed over the last two decades. Effects of texture (e.g. Westling and Johansson, 1984; Flanagan and Wing, 1997), size (e.g. Gordon, Forssberg, Johansson and Westling, 1991), weight (e.g. Johansson and Westling, 1988b) and shape (e.g. Jenmalm and Johansson, 1997) of the object to be grasped has been the subject of extensive work. The influence of development (Forssberg, Eliasson, Kinoshita, Johansson and Westling, 1991) and ageing (Cole, 1991; Cole and Beck, 1994) on precision grip have also been studied. Of particular interest to interceptive actions in sport is the load force of a hand-held object, which varies with the movements of the arm. For instance, when the racket cyclically moves up and down, the load force successively increases and decreases. Flanagan and Wing (1995) have shown that there is a tight coupling between grip force and load force. It has also been demonstrated that anticipatory control strategies are employed to adjust grip force with such variations of load force.

The literature reveals that grip force is roughly twice the minimal value required to prevent the hand-held object from slipping (see Flanagan and Wing, 1995). This finding suggests that participants tested in laboratory-based experiments have not tended to adopt an efficient strategy. However, it is noteworthy that grip force values are usually relatively low (less than 20 N). It is possible that this low level of task constraint has not pushed participants to adopt an efficient strategy. It is also interesting to note that most of the studies have been conducted using tasks where the load force was applied progressively. This is dramatically different from the impact of a ball on a racket's surface, which is a discrete and explosive affair.

During a collision between a ball and a racket, the load force applied on the racket's handle increases very rapidly, almost instantaneously. This sudden burst creates specific challenges to the problem of maintaining control of grip force. An interesting question concerns how performers deal with this control problem. One potential strategy for dealing with this explosive burst, could be to wait until the collision occurs and increase grip force only if a slip is detected. Long latency reflexes observed 60–100 ms after impact have been reported in the literature (e.g. Johansson and Westling, 1988a). However, this strategy is limited: if the impact is very high, then the reflex would be insufficient to compensate the sudden increase of load force and the racket would slip out of control, with dire consequences for the competitor. An alternative, the 'over-gripping strategy' has been previously evoked, and its limitations discussed above (inefficiency and muscle fatigue). Finally, a player could anticipate ball flight and contract his/her muscles before the collision. The inevitable neuro–motor delays imply that in order to adequately apply the right grip force at the moment of impact the muscles have to be contracted in advance of the collision. Although this problem is partly encountered in most of the task constraints where hand-held objects are manipulated (e.g. Johansson and Westling, 1988a), the very short duration of collision imposes the use of accurate anticipatory mechanisms. During a collision, there is no time available to re-adjust an inadequate grip force.

Receiving vs. producing a collision

In tennis, hitting a ball from the back of the court is different from waiting for a ball at the net. The nature of the task constraints requires a different type of stroke. In a classic forehand drive, the player typically moves the racket backwards and then towards the ball, and his/her swinging actions produce the source of energy. When hitting a ball in front of the net, the main aim is to intercept a ball and provide little time for the opponent to recover. Being closer to the net, the player moves the racket mainly laterally with a small forward displacement, and a large component of the exchange of energy can be attributed to the ball hitting a relatively static racket.

From experience, it is noticeable that often the racket vibrates after the collision in the latter case. The question is whether this empirical sensation can be observed in a more controlled environment. Turrell, Li and Wing (1999) examined this issue by asking 21 participants to hold a manipulandum to hit a pendulum to a certain angle (producing condition). The other task was to remain immobile while the pendulum was hitting the manipulandum held by the participants (Figure 18.1a–c). Participants were seated facing the pendulum, which swung in a fronto–parallel plane. The manipulandum was equipped with a load cell to record the grip force (for details of the apparatus see Turrell, Li and Wing, 2001). A goniometer and another load cell recorded the movements of the pendulum and the force of impact.

Participants were tested in three experimental conditions. In the producing task (A) participants were asked to hit the pendulum to a certain angle (5, 15 or 25 degrees). The starting position was standardised (40 cm from the pendulum), and an auditory signal indicated the start of the trial. In the two receiving conditions (B and C), participants were asked to place the manipulandum against the stationary pendulum. Then the experimenter raised the pendulum by 5, 15 or 25 degrees. An auditory signal indicated the start of the trial and the pendulum was released.

Participants were asked to hold the manipulandum so that it would not slip out of grasp, and a screen prevented them from seeing the pendulum. The difference between conditions B and C was the availability of information on the forthcoming collision. In B, the experimenter indicated verbally the magnitude of the angle from which the pendulum was released, therefore allowing some anticipatory adjustments (receiving with verbal information). However, in C, no indication on the magnitude of the forthcoming impact was provided (receiving without verbal information).

The results showed clearly that producing and receiving a collision are two different actions reflecting the different task constraints. The verbal information given in condition B allowed some preparatory scaling of the grip force prior to impact, compared to condition C in which very little adjustment was observed before the collision. Most of the changes of grip force were observed immediately after contact. In both receiving conditions B and C, while the grip force increased before impact, there was an important burst of force just after the impact (Figure 18.1a–c). This is consistent with previous work (Johansson and Westling, 1988a) and is interpreted as a late latency reflex to prevent a slip of the hand-held manipulandum. The producing condition yielded different results. The anticipation of the collision occurred more smoothly. Grip force increased with a lower rate of change, and peaked at impact. The timing of the grip force was clearly well timed, even if the situation was rather new for the participants and little practice was given. Moreover, the post-impact burst of grip force, if any, was very small or often not observed at all. This finding suggests that the reflex was either inhibited or not triggered. Finally, grip force was scaled to load force with a higher gain. Participants' predictions of the forthcoming collision seemed to be more accurate in the production rather than in the receiving task. We can conclude that anticipatory adjustments of grip force are used to stabilise a hand-held object exposed to impulsive self-generated or externally-imposed load force arising in collisions.

Role of vision in grip force scaling

The experiment discussed in this chapter indicates that producing and receiving a collision led to two different behaviours. Why does the producing task lead to better anticipation in participants? There were two differences between the producing (task A) and receiving task constraints (task B). First, in the producing task, participants generated the movement. Haptic information produced by inertial characteristics of the swinging movement could be used to anticipate the forthcoming collision and scale grip force (for a discussion see chapter by Davids, Bennett and Beak). Second, visual information of the trajectory of the pendulum was available in the producing condition. Can this visual information be the main cause of the difference between the two experimental conditions? What is the role of vision for the control of grip force in the context of interceptive action? Vision has been emphasised as the essential sensory system used to perceive the approach of an object, and consequently to anticipate a forthcoming collision (for a review see Williams, Davids and Williams, 1999). However, little is known about how

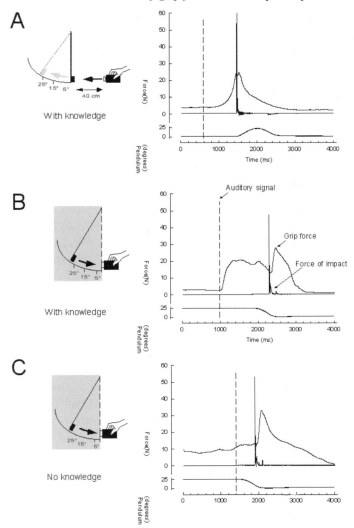

Figure 18.1 Depicts two typical trials from the production task (A) and the receiving task
(B) (adapted from Turrell, Li and Wing, 1999).

vision is used to scale grip force in anticipation of a collision. This question was
investigated in another experiment.

Turrell, Li and Wing (2000) asked 36 participants to produce and receive a
collision in the same set-up, but this time vision was manipulated. Participants
wore liquid crystal glasses during all trials and either had full vision of the set-up
and their hand (vision group) or no-vision (no-vision group). For the no-vision
group the glasses were closed (translucent) 1 s before the beginning of each trial.

The correlation between grip force and load force was studied as an indicator
of the accuracy of the participants' prediction of the magnitude of impact. If

participants were able to perfectly anticipate the collision, grip force to load force scaling should be constant. Analysis of variance on the Pearson correlation coefficients showed that there was a significant main effect for task constraints, with the precision of the anticipation being better for producing than receiving. However, the effect of vision was not significant. The slope of the regression lines was also examined. This is another way to examine the accuracy of judgement (see Flanagan and Wing, 1995), in that the steeper the regression line, the more accurate the prediction. Again the main effect of task constraint was significant, with the producing task allowing more accurate prediction than the receiving task. The visual manipulation again showed no significant effect.

These results confirm the difference between the producing task and the receiving task. Participants were more accurate in their predictions in the producing task. However, the analysis of the data failed to show any effect of vision. This finding indicates that vision is not the source of the difference between the two tasks observed by Turrell, Li and Wing (1999). Moreover, the absence of an effect of visual condition suggests that vision is not essential for the anticipation of the magnitude of a collision between a moving object and a static hand (receiving) or a hand moving toward a static object (producing). Therefore, it can be concluded that other sources of information are used. As the chapter by Davids, Bennett and Beak shows, proprioceptive information is the obvious candidate. When we manipulate an object, our proprioceptive system provides haptic information on the momentum and inertia of the limb and the hand-held object, which can be used to predict the magnitude of the forthcoming collision. Vision does inform on the kinematics of the movement. As the uncertainty of this experimental environment was low (constant amplitude of the movement), information on kinematics was not essential to predict the future collision.

Learning efficiency

We have seen that participants managed to anticipate the magnitude of a forthcoming collision, and did so particularly well in the producing condition. However, most of the time grip force was higher than what was minimally required. An excess of grip force is also known as a 'safety margin' (Johansson and Westling, 1984; Flanagan and Wing, 1993) and is defined as the difference between grip force and load force, expressed in percentage. Participants were over-gripping the manipulandum on average by roughly 50 per cent, and no slip was recorded. To recall, three strategies to control grip force in collisions were presented. The first and simplest but energetically expensive approach was to over-grip; the second was to rely on post-impact reflexes; the third was to adjust as accurately as possible the grip. In our experiments, we observed a mixture of all these strategies. In the receiving condition without verbal information (C), most of the adjustments were attributed to post-collision reflexes (second strategy). In receiving with verbal information (B), some adjustments were made before impact (third and second strategy). In the producing task, virtually no reflex was observed and overall participants were over-gripping (first strategy).

In summary, participants were not using a very efficient strategy. When all information was available, they were still over-gripping. The disadvantages of such strategy have been mentioned: waste of energy, risk of fatigue and cramps. All participants were sport sciences students with quite a lot of experience in sport. So why were they so inefficient? It is clear that the set-up was completely new for them, and this novelty, added to the small number of trials, may explain their lack of efficiency in grip force. However, their timing was good and peak velocity of the hand's movement occurred generally at impact. Therefore, on some aspects of the task they were rather proficient. The novelty of the set-up was clearly not a problem for timing their movement. Is it that grip force requires more time (more trials) for discovery of the kinetic properties of the environment (manipulandum + pendulum)? How long do participants need to become efficient? It was typical to observe that novices over-gripped the object they had to manipulate, whether it was a pen for a child or a racket – for indeed any age group. Can we train athletes to improve both the accuracy of their shots and the grip force? This question was addressed in another experiment.

Turrell, Wing and Li (submitted) asked eight participants to perform a producing task (hit the immobile pendulum with a manipulandum). During a first session, 20 trials were performed to determine a baseline. Then in two experimental sessions on two consecutive days, participants had to perform 500 trials (Day 1: 300 trials, Day 2: 200 trials). They were given knowledge of results (KR) regarding their accuracy and efficiency in grip force. Finally, a short-term retention test (30 min) and a long-term transfer test (1 week) were performed. During the transfer test the set-up and instructions were identical but the surface of the manipulandum was manipulated making this hand-held object more (silk) or less (sandpaper) slippery. This change of texture modified the coefficient of friction and imposed an adaptive constraint on the production of grip force. The instructions were to be accurate *and* efficient. Accuracy was measured in term of degrees of pendulum swing. Efficiency was assessed in percentage of excess grip force (safety margin). Two methods of analysis were used. First, analyses of variance were run to assess the differences between groups of trials, at the beginning, middle and end of practice, as well as the retention sessions. Time series analyses (TSA) were employed to assess the variations between trials. Time series analysis has been used in a few studies (e.g. Spray and Newell, 1986) and has revealed to be efficient in describing the effect that one trial has on the succeeding trials. This is a relatively new approach, which can give interesting insights into the influence of immediate experience and on the learning processes. The first five trials of the pre-test, the first, middle and last five trials of each training session, and the first and last five trials of each retention session were averaged and analysed.

The analyses of variance revealed that the accuracy of the pendulum swing improved with practice. However, although efficiency improved between the baseline and the beginning of the first training session, no significant changes were observed during the first training session and it was only at the end of the last training sessions (last 100 trials) that some improvement was observed. During the retention session, knowledge of response (KR) was removed and some loss of performance (accuracy of pendulum swing) was observed. However, the efficiency (safety margin) continued to improve. In the transfer task, no KR was given, and the accuracy of the pendulum swing remained similar to that observed during retention sessions. Furthermore the safety margin decreased, i.e. efficiency improved, both with silk and sandpaper. As a whole these findings suggested that participants had learned to be more efficient and that changing surface did not affect their performance (accuracy of pendulum swing).

The time series analyses revealed that after 300 practice trials participants had established a stable performance on accuracy of pendulum swing and that the KR given by the experimenter was not used anymore. For movement efficiency, the analyses showed that participants were not able to adjust adequately grip force in anticipation of the collision. These trial-to-trial variations suggested that they were unable to predict accurately the kinetic outcome of the collision. Although they were able to accurately hit the pendulum, they were still not very good at anticipating the magnitude of the impact and its consequences on the manipulandum. This outcome was observed in spite of the strict and clear instruction to be both accurate and efficient. Why could participants not manage to use proprioception to decrease their grip force and why did they have to rely on KR provided by the experimenter? As mentioned above, over-gripping is also called a safety margin. The role of a safety margin is to provide a cushion to absorb most mistakes in the prediction of the magnitude of the collision. If the collision is always of exactly the same magnitude, then there is no need for a substantial safety margin. On the other hand, if there is a large amount of variability in the force of impact, then it is useful to adopt a consequent safety margin to prevent the manipulandum from slipping. Therefore, one should not decrease dramatically the safety margin before the collision becomes very consistent and predictable. It seems that reducing the variability of the impact is a pre-requisite for the diminution of the safety margin. This finding would explain why participants decreased the safety margin only late in the second practice session, long after the accuracy had been improved and stabilised.

Learning step by step

The three experiments presented in this chapter provide some insight into the control of grip force in interceptive actions. Grip force is an important part of any interceptive task where an object, e.g. a racket, is manipulated. The type of task constraint, receiving versus producing, determines what type of information is available and what mode of control is used. The large burst of grip force immediately following the impact observed in receiving and absent in producing, shows that anticipation of a collision is better in the latter condition. One wonders what kind of effect this sudden very large contraction has on one's body. It is possible that risks of injuries increase in these conditions. If this hypothesis were proven to be correct, it would be advisable to take into account this risk in the planning sessions of practice volleys at the net in tennis.

The role of vision, crucial in anticipating the trajectory and timing of a ball, seems to be of a lesser importance in the prediction of a self-generated collision with a stable and predictable target. Finally, it seems that we cannot fully relax the grip on a racket before a certain level of accuracy is reached. Changes in grip force due to relaxation may be a more advanced performance strategy, and it may not be the most appropriate approach to ask a novice player to concentrate both on relaxing the grip and hitting more accurately during the same practice session. A pure novice should first be asked to concentrate on accuracy, without spending too much attention on the grip itself. Then, when a certain level of accuracy is reached in the specific task, instructions regarding the manipulation of the grip could be introduced. Of course this process can be repeated indefinitely. A step-by-step approach to learning seems appropriate: a stage of improvement of accuracy can be followed by a period of concentration on relaxation. Then another level of accuracy can be targeted, followed again by an attempt at decreasing the over-gripping. This kind of staircase learning, step-by-step, is probably more efficient in the long run than splitting the attention on two important technical points: being accurate *and* efficient.

Note

1 Efficiency can have several meanings depending on the context. In the present paper efficiency will refer to *energetic* efficiency.

References

Bootsma, R.J. and van Wieringen, P.C.W. (1990). Timing an attacking forehand drive in table tennis. *Journal of Experimental Psychology: Human Perception and Performance* **16**, 21–9.

Cole, K.J. (1991). Grasp force control in older adults. *Journal of Motor Behavior* **23**, 251–8.

Cole, K.J. and Beck, C.L. (1994). The stability of precision grip force control in older adults. *Journal of Motor Behavior* **26**, 171–7.

Flanagan, J. and Wing, A.M. (1995). The stability of precision grip forces during cyclic arm movements with a hand-held load. *Experimental Brain Research* **105**, 455–64.

Flanagan, J. and Wing, A.M. (1997). Effects of surface texture and grip force on the discrimination of hand-held loads. *Perception and Psychophysics* **59**, 111–18.

Forssberg, H., Eliasson, A.C., Kinoshita, H., Johansson R.S. and Westling, C. (1991). Development of human precision grip I. Basic co-ordination of forces. *Experimental Brain Research* **85**, 451–7.

Gordon, A.M., Forssberg, H., Johansson, R.S. and Westling, G. (1991). The integration of haptically acquired size information in the programming of precision grip. *Experimental Brain Research* **83**, 483–8.

Jenmalm P. and Johansson R.S. (1997). Visual and somatosensory information about object shape control manipulative fingertip forces. *Journal of Neuroscience* **17**, 4486–99.

Johansson R.S. and Westling, C. (1984). Roles of glabrous skin receptors and sensorimotor memory in automatic control of precision grip when lifting rougher or more slippery objects. *Experimental Brain Research* **56**, 550–64.

Johansson R.S. and Westling, C. (1988a). Programmed and triggered actions to rapid load changes during precision grip. *Experimental Brain Research* **71**, 72–86.

Johansson R.S. and Westling, C. (1988b). Coordinated isometric muscle commands adequately and erroneously programmed for the weight during lifting task with precision grip. *Experimental Brain Research* **71**, 59–71.

Spray, J.A. and Newell, K.M. (1986). Time series analysis of motor learning: KR versus non-KR. *Journal of Human Movement Studies* **5**, 59–74.

Turrell, Y.N., Li, F.-X. and Wing, A.M. (1999). Grip force dynamics in the approach to a collision. *Experimental Brain Research* **128**, 86–91.

Turrell, Y.N., Li, F.-X. and Wing, A.M. (2000). Effect of vision on the efficiency of grip force scaling in collisions. In *Transactions of the First International Conference on Sports Vision*, I. Cockerill (ed.). Sports Vision Association.

Turrell, Y.N., Li, F.-X. and Wing, A.M. (2001). Estimating the minimum grip force required when grasping objects under impulsive load conditions. *Journal of Behavior Research Methods, Instrument and Computers* **33**, 1, 38–45.

Turrell, Y.N., Wing, A.M. and Li, F.-X. (Submitted). Sequential effects revealed through time series analysis in a force production task.

Westling, G. and Johansson, R.S. (1984). Factors influencing the force control during precision grip. *Experimental Brain Research* **53**, 277–84.

Williams, A.M., Davids, K. and Williams, J.G. (1999). *Visual Perception & Action in Sport*. London: E & FN Spon.

19 Grip force dynamics in cricket batting

Paul Glazier, Keith Davids and
Roger Bartlett

Previous review articles of scientific research in cricket have focused upon biomechanics and injuries in fast bowling (see Bartlett *et al.*, 1996; Elliott *et al.*, 1996 and Elliott, 2000 respectively), cricket injuries in general (Finch *et al.*, 1999), and the physiological requirements of the game (Noakes and Durandt, 2000). Regarding batting in cricket, a recent review (i.e. Stretch *et al.*, 2000) has argued that all the sub-disciplines of sports science are necessary to understand the mechanisms underpinning skilled performance. Crucially, the affinity between the biomechanics of movement patterns and the underlying motor control mechanisms appears to be the most important factor in understanding effective stroke production, but one that has yet to be fully explored. The ecological approach to the study of processes of perception and action offers a viable platform for integrating motor control and biomechanics in the study of dynamic interceptive actions in sport. This notion clearly advocates the need for multidisciplinary or interdisciplinary research, as prioritised by Stretch *et al.* (2000).

Cricket batting is an example of a dynamic interceptive action, placed by Whiting (1969) in his third, most complex, category of ball skills – encompassing task constraints where a ball has to be received and sent away within the same movement. Batting in cricket requires players to select the most appropriate shot from a wide repertoire of attacking and defensive strokes against a variety of different bowlers – fast, spin, seam and swing. Successful interception of the cricket ball by the batsman[1] requires the cricket bat to be manoeuvred into the right place at the right time, so that the ball can be struck with the required force to send it in an appropriate direction (Savelsbergh and Bootsma, 1994). To achieve this goal, research described in many chapters of this text suggest that skilled batsmen require a combination of unobtrusive footwork, co-ordinated limb movements and precision gripping to deal effectively with the severe task constraints encountered when batting.

The grip is a key facet in successful batting as it is the only interface between the batsman and the cricket bat, through which all force and energy must be transmitted. The importance of precise control of grip forces can be illustrated in limited-overs cricket, where batsmen often have to improvise by 'working' the ball into gaps in the field. Additionally, skilled batsmen frequently manipulate grip firmness to play with 'hard' and 'soft' hands to control rebound velocity, particularly when surrounded by fielders in close catching positions, or when playing on slow or fast pitches. Clearly, therefore, merely intercepting the ball by intersecting the flight path with the bat is not enough in competitive cricket. It would appear that variation in grip firmness is needed to place the ball strategically into gaps, in front of or behind fielders. Such a task requires the scaling of grip forces based on the use of visual information obtained from ball flight characteristics.

The purpose of this chapter is to provide an insight into the mechanisms underpinning skilled cricket batting, with the main emphasis on grip force dynamics. We begin by describing existing biomechanical investigations into this component of the cricket batting technique, highlighting the contributions and limitations of this line of research. We then discuss a theoretical account of cricket batting from an ecological approach in which we explore how batsmen manage visual search strategies and how visual information is used to modulate grip force during stroke play in competitive cricket. Theoretical understanding of the co-dependent relationship between perception and movement systems, outlined in the chapters by Montagne and Laurent, by Benguigui, Ripoll and Broderick, by Michaels and Zaal, and by Scott, along with considerations of biomechanical constraints, will be used to describe grip force dynamics before, during and immediately after bat–ball impact.

Biomechanical analysis of grip forces during batting

In Chapter 18 by Li and Turrell, the relationship between load force and grip force, in the task of striking a ball, was outlined. They reviewed the psychology literature on grip force and made the point that very few sport-related research programmes have been conducted into the ratio of load force and grip force during striking actions. One exception to this gap in the literature is the programme of work by Richard Stretch and colleagues in South Africa during the 1990s. They instigated the first scientific investigations into grip force dynamics in cricket batting. The main aim of that body of research was to verify empirically and evaluate the effectiveness of information outlined previously in pertinent coaching literature. Their results offered unequivocal support for the coaching literature, revealing that the top hand was indeed the most dominant hand during both the drive (*D*) and forward defensive (*FD*) strokes, with the bottom hand reinforcing at impact. Similar grip force patterns were evident during the initial part of both strokes, with greater forces applied by the top and bottom hands just before impact in the drive.

Manipulation of task constraints: effects of surface and bowling type

Data from their research programme suggest that task constraints such as pitch characteristics and bowling type seem to influence grip force dynamics during batting (Stretch, 1993; 1994). Stretch (1993) reported differences in the grip forces when batting on different surfaces and against different paced bowlers. Although

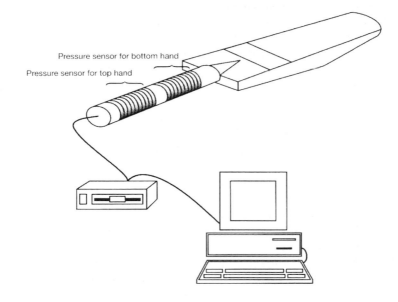

Pressure sensor for bottom hand

Pressure sensor for top hand

Figure 19.1   Diagram of the experimental bat showing the positions of the pressure sensors (adapted from Stretch *et al.* 1998, with permission).

results for the comparison of artificial and turf pitches and spin and medium-paced bowlers were collected from only two batsmen, both were experienced elite cricketers. A purpose-built cricket bat equipped with pressure sensing transducers in the handle was used to measure top and bottom hand grip forces (see Figure 19.1).

Smaller forces were generated by the top hand when the batsmen played the drive against medium-paced bowlers on an artificial pitch compared to a turf pitch. In the drive, grip forces at impact of 195 N were recorded (*FD* = 94 N) with the peak force of 195 N reached 0.02 s post-impact (*FD* = 102 N at 0.04 s pre-impact). The force patterns for the bottom hand before and at impact were similar to those when batting on turf, while a relaxation and re-gripping of the bat during the follow-through was demonstrated when batting on the artificial pitch. The drive played on a turf pitch against a spin bowler demonstrated a peak force (158 N), which occurred 0.02 s post-impact for the top hand. A similar grip-force pattern was demonstrated for the bottom hand (peak force of 102 N at 0.02 s pre-impact), except that after impact a slight re-gripping of the bat occurred as the necessary hand forces were generated to regain control of the bat and to control the inertia of the bat during the follow-through. When playing the forward defensive, the peak forces for the bottom hand (58 N) occurred 0.08 s after impact (Stretch, 1993).

When playing the drive against a spin bowler on an artificial surface, the top hand demonstrated a similar, although smaller, grip-force pattern to when batting on turf, with the exception that the peak forces were reached 0.04 s post-impact (*FD*: peak force 74 N at 0.06 s post-impact). The grip-force pattern for the bottom hand showed similar, although smaller, forces than those for the top hand, with a relaxation and then re-gripping post-impact to control the bat during the follow-through. In the forward defensive, the bottom hand showed little change in grip forces throughout the stroke with a force at impact of 30 N, reaching a peak force of 34 N at 0.06 s post-impact (Stretch, 1993). Stretch *et al.* (2000) attributed the observed differences to the artificial pitch being faster than turf, with a more consistent and predictable bounce and with the ball not spinning or seaming as much as on turf.

How grip forces and load forces are coupled to the inertia and acceleration of the cricket bat during the backswing and downswing has yet to receive research attention, as does the analysis of the optimal range of grip forces. Stretch *et al.* (1995) measured maximal grip forces for both the top and bottom hands using a Takei grip dynamometer. These forces were 552 ± 75 N and 531 ± 74 N for the left and right hands respectively. The authors found no significant relationship between these maximum forces and the forces of the top and bottom hands exerted 0.02 s before impact. However, the mean forces, 0.02 s pre-impact of the top and bottom hands as a percentage of their maximum, were 36 ± 8 per cent (range 23–48 per cent) and 17 ± 8 per cent (range 5–32 per cent) respectively. These normalised values, particularly for the top hand, provide a good fit with the 24–48 per cent maximal voluntary contraction region suggested by Slifkin and Newell (2000) as providing the greatest flexibility for performers in scaling force to a force target in continuous isometric force production tasks. One may speculate that, on this basis, gripping the bat in this range may provide the required variability to enhance flexibility in tailoring force production to the specific task requirements and perturbations in the environment. Clearly, the application of these results from experimental studies of isometric force production, to such a dynamic task as cricket batting, warrants further investigation.

Limitations of the work of Stretch and colleagues

Although the work of Stretch and colleagues has provided some preliminary insights into grip force dynamics during front foot stroke production, there are some apparent limitations associated with their research. Their work needs to be extended due to its descriptive nature and the use of limited sample and trial sizes in a cross-sectional approach, particularly in the investigations into the effects of different bowling types and surface conditions. Future research in this area should emphasise longitudinal designs, investigating the use of individual-specific grip force strategies for specific task constraints. The atheoretical nature of the research, particularly the lack of input from theories of motor control, is also a major limiting factor in the applicability of the existing research. In this chapter, and in Chapter 16 by Lees and Davids, an integrated approach is proposed for the study of dynamic interceptive actions. In Chapter 16, the emphasis is on the integration of dynamical systems theory and biomechanics in an analysis of processes of movement co-ordination and control in soccer kicking. Later in this chapter, we argue that an ecological interpretation promises to provide a viable platform for integrating motor control and biomechanics in the modelling of grip force dynamics in cricket batting. But first, in the following section, we review the implications of motor control research on grip force dynamics for an understanding of how cricketers may regulate grip force dynamics during batting.

Grip force dynamics at bat–ball impact: evidence from motor control research

The nature of grip force dynamics during bat–ball impacts requires clarification. This is a particularly important issue in the exploration of controlling reaction impulse and rebound velocity in the implementation of 'hard' versus 'soft' hands batting tactics, as previously discussed. The review of the grip force data produced by Stretch and colleagues revealed that peak grip force occurs before impact and reduces through the impact period in both the forward drive and defensive strokes. One may speculate that this feature facilitates the transfer of angular velocity to the cricket bat and thus is a mechanism for increasing its horizontal impact velocity. However, this is not necessary in the forward defensive stroke as the aim is often to play with a 'dead' bat, using solely the momentum of the ball. Additionally, the results revealed that the peak horizontal velocity of the cricket bat coincided with peak grip forces in both strokes. Similar findings have been found in other striking activities such as golf (Shibayama and Ebashi, 1983), softball (Messier and Owen, 1984) and baseball (Race, 1961; Breen, 1967; McIntyre and Pfautsch, 1982). The consensus is that the body segments slow down just before contact in preparation for the force of impact during these dynamic interceptive actions (Plagenhoef, 1971).

Contrasting evidence can be found in the motor control literature where a limited body of experimental research has been devoted to the regulation of grip forces when approaching a collision (e.g. see Chapter 18 by Li and Turrell; Turrell *et al.*, 1999) and the role of vision in the scaling of grip forces (e.g. Turrell, 2000). The chapter by Li and Turrell reviews how, using a novel laboratory experiment, Turrell *et al.* (1999) found fundamental differences between receiving and producing a collision. When receiving a collision, little change in grip force occurred before impact. The largest change in grip force occurred after impact. This is consistent with previous research (Johansson and Westling, 1988), which suggested this effect to be due to a late latency reflex to prevent slippage of the striking implement in the hand. When asked to produce a collision, however, the participants were able to increase grip forces at a lower rate of change, peaking at impact. The post-impact burst that occurred in the producing condition was very small or often not observed at all. Grip force was scaled to load force with a higher gain in the producing condition and predictions about forthcoming collisions were seemingly more accurate.

Li and Turrell's suggestions, in Chapter 18, of a tight coupling between grip and load forces during the production of a collision needs to be substantiated under task constraints more closely related to cricket batting because their pendulum was stationary. Under these specific task constraints, direct collisions between the centre of percussion of the striking implement and the pendulum might result in minimal or no increase in load force during impact (Bartlett, 1997). As greater accuracy is inevitable during the producing condition, this task constraint might account for the lack of a burst of grip force post-impact. Conversely, inaccurate striking might simply cause the relatively high post-impact bursts in the receiving conditions rather than a lack of grip force scaling during the pre-impact phase.

The research outlined in the chapter by Li and Turrell provides some valuable insights from a motor control perspective for the analysis of grip force characteristics when intercepting the ball during attacking and defensive strokes in cricket, but similar research is required under more dynamic task constraints. The inter-relationship between the accuracy of bat–ball impact in relation to the centre of percussion of the bat, rebound velocity, recoil impulse and grip forces needs research attention to provide information about how cricketers of various skill levels can manipulate force and directional properties of impacts during batting.

Cricket batting: the role of biomechanics and the ecological approach

To date, the coalition of motor control and biomechanics in cricket research has yet to be realised, largely because of the tendency for the underlying control processes in cricket batting to be modelled from an information-processing standpoint (e.g. Abernethy, 1981; Abernethy and Russell, 1984; Penrose and Roach, 1995). In Chapter 16, Lees and Davids argue that the emphasis of the ecological approach, on the co-ordination and control of degrees of freedom of the movement system in forming a perception–action coupling, presents a greater opportunity for the integration of biomechanics and motor control research. It certainly fits with the idea, raised and discussed in many chapters in this book, that movements can be continuously regulated by information to provide fine-grained adjustments in line with the changing demands of dynamic performance contexts (Savelsbergh and Bootsma, 1994; Bootsma *et al.*, 1997).

Information sources: identification and utilisation

In Chapter 1 it was argued that, although other perceptual mechanisms are at work (i.e. haptic, auditory, proprioceptive), much of the perceptual information used to regulate movement behaviour during cricket batting is provided by the visual system. Energy in the form of light reflected from important surfaces and objects, such as the ball and the fielders, creates an optic flow field that geometrically specifies the exact layout of the environment at any instance. The optic array contains veridical, or invariant, information sources such as motion parallax, texture density gradients and gradient of image size (Bruce *et al.*, 1996), which the perceptual system 'resonates' to, autonomously characterising them in terms of their possibility for action, or affordances (Williams *et al.*, 1992, 1999). The alliance between invariants and affordances means that a tight coupling exists between the state of the environment and system dynamics, allowing the batsman to regulate motor activity 'on-line' right up until the point of bat–ball impact.

In Chapters 1 and 7 of this book it has been outlined how, from an ecological perspective, a relevant property of the perceptual flow can act as information to steer, guide or regulate key movement parameters (e.g. force) throughout the course of the action. A lot of recent evidence was reviewed in support of the prospective control strategy and one particular model, the required velocity model, has seen compelling empirical support. The required velocity model emphasises that the performer regulates the amount of acceleration of an implement such as a cricket bat, produced on the basis of the perceptually specified difference between the required velocity and the current velocity of the implement for interception. The implications of the required velocity model for cricket batting is that the instantaneous distance/velocity of a cricket ball approaching the hand–bat movement axis is divided into the distance a hand–bat system has to move sideways to reach the interception point. Research (e.g. Peper *et al.*, 1994; Montagne *et al.*, 1999; Montagne *et al.*, 2000) has supported the predictions of the required velocity model in the context of ball catching.

Eye movement studies

Results from a recent study of eye movement behaviour during cricket batting by Land and McLeod (2000) can also be interpreted as providing some evidence in support of the use of optical information sources for regulating batting. This study is discussed at some length in Chapter 1 of this book. To briefly re-iterate: using a head-mounted video camera operating at 50 Hz, Land and McLeod (2000) monitored the direction of gaze of three cricket batsmen of various expertise. The batsman's task was to execute attacking and defensive, front- and back-foot cricket strokes based on the line and length of medium-paced (25 m s^{-1}) deliveries produced by a bowling machine. The main findings of this study were that batsmen facing fast bowlers do not keep their eye on the ball throughout its flight and, despite their widely different skill levels, all three batsmen used similar eye movement strategies. The gaze of the fovea was initially focused on the point of delivery, remaining stationary for a period while the ball dropped into the field of view. A key observation discussed in Chapter 1 was that a saccade was then made to bring the focal point of the fovea below the ball, close to the point where the ball would subsequently bounce. All three batsmen tracked the ball for up to 200 ms after bouncing before both the eye and head moved rapidly down in an attempt to track the latter part of the ball's flight.

While the authors preferred to interpret these findings as evidence against the use of a perception–movement coupling to regulate the striking action, they did not rule out the existence of image expansion and changing binocular disparity as a viable means of refining time and position of contact during the post-bounce period. They were reluctant to accept it as the principal method for predicting time-to-contact, particularly during early ball flight. However, there are several good reasons for reconsidering the idea that optical information is not used throughout ball flight to regulate batting action.

Role of the image-retina system

First, it is possible that this eye movement strategy may simply reflect the severe task constraints of batting against fast bowling speeds. Although batsmen may not look directly at the cricket ball throughout the period between release and ball pitching, this finding does not signify that visual information was not used during this period. The image of the cricket ball may have been allowed to wash across the retina until it reaches the bounce location. Although this strategy is less sensitive than focusing directly on the ball, it is probably sufficient to estimate the direction, length and speed of the delivery, providing enough information to direct footwork, select the appropriate stroke and give an approximation of the time and location of impending ball pitch. This would appear to be a more suitable mechanism for counteracting the severe spatio–temporal constraints of fast bowling where pursuit eye tracking would be impossible. Moreover, focusing on the cricket ball throughout early ball flight has been shown to be of limited benefit, since early retinal information about absolute distance and speed is considered to be unreliable (Regan, 1997).

Penrose *et al.* (1976) also demonstrated that the cricket ball decelerates between 4 and 9 m s^{-1} from the period between ball release and arrival at the batting end. Such a marked deceleration, particularly during the pitching phase, would fit well with the use of a prospective control strategy (Montagne *et al.*, 1999; Montagne *et al.*, 2000). A far more tangible strategy for successfully intercepting a cricket ball would be to wait until the ball has bounced, using the subsequent unambiguous optical information to prospectively regulate stroke output parameters and impact conditions. This notion is substantiated by the postulation of short visual–motor delays in other ecological accounts of dynamic interceptive activities. For example, Lee *et al.* (1983) postulated visual-motor delays of 55–130 ms in a ball-striking task and Bootsma and van Wieringen (1990) demonstrated visual–motor delays of around 105–122 ms when modifying a forehand drive in table tennis. The use of a prospective control strategy would make timing considerably easier and sufficiently precise to satisfy the small timing windows postulated by Regan (1997) and McLeod (1987) for successful interception of the cricket ball during the hook (2.5 ms) and the leg glance (4 ms) strokes respectively.

Related to this issue is the question: how do eye movement and visual search strategies change with deliveries of different lengths? Land and McLeod (2000) revealed that the bounce length affected gaze movement in two ways. First, the delay before the early downward saccade increased as the ball bounced closer to the batsman and, secondly, the amount of smooth tracking that accompanied the initial saccade increased as the length of the delivery increased. This combination of saccade and smooth tracking allowed the gaze of the fovea to reach the bounce point accurately and well ahead of the ball (Land and McLeod, 2000). Moreover, for over-pitched deliveries, all three batsmen seemed to begin tracking before the ball bounced.

It would appear from these results that cricket batsman look for the most reliable information on which to guide batting actions. Where deliveries are pitched short, the cricket ball, having bounced, is unlikely to deviate laterally, change trajectory or decelerate considerably making pursuit tracking possible. Image expansion information during this extended post-bounce tracking period can then be used to regulate and refine batting mechanics, producing consistent impact conditions. Over-pitched deliveries are also subject to extended tracking periods just before bouncing, where batsman can again use image expansion information. The decrease in ball speed due to air resistance will be small and predictable and, providing the batsman is positioned sufficiently close to the bounce location, the deceleration of the cricket ball due to interaction with the pitch will be nullified. Clearly, further research into the integration of eye and hand movements during cricket batting is needed to clarify how performers pick up and use information for guiding bat movements.

Support from studies of eye movements during manual aiming

A second source of support for the use of visual regulation strategies during cricket batting can be found in recent studies of manual aiming. Manual aiming is a type of interceptive action that is obviously more static than cricket batting. However, there are many similarities between the two types of interceptive action, especially when aiming is with a stylus. Perhaps the main difference is in the amount of movement of the target to be intercepted. Recent studies of rapid manual aiming movements have found that a two-component model (rapid initiation phase of the aiming movement towards the target followed by a homing-in phase) can explain eye and hand movements under these task constraints (e.g. Khan and Franks, 2000). We note how eye movements during manual aiming bear some resemblance to the eye movement strategies of cricketers identified by Land and McLeod (2000). In the manual aiming research, the role of vision in both phases of the movement was seen to increase error correction effectiveness in reaching the target. Essentially, it has been found that hand movements towards a target are initiated under visual control and followed by a visually based corrective phase as the limb approaches the target (e.g. Helsen *et al.*, 1998; Khan and Franks, 2000). The relevant point for this chapter is that eye movements during manual aiming show similar patterns of behaviour to hand movements. Eye movements are launched before hand movements and typically fall short of the target by around three degrees. After that it appears that micro-saccades are used to bring the eye over the target. Most importantly, the initial saccade appears to finish just when the limb reaches the point of peak acceleration, signifying that the movement system is able to use visual feedback in making small adaptive movements of the hand in locating the target. Interestingly, a significant correlation was found between the number of eye corrections and the number of corrective adaptations in joints of the aiming arm. In relation to the findings of Land and McLeod (2000), manual aiming research has found stable temporal associations for the initiation of second eye movements and the start of second finger movements as the target is approached (Khan and

Franks, 2000). The implication, that there is ample time to seek and use visual information to control the initiation and homing in phases of rapid manual aiming movements, needs to be investigated in the context of cricket batting.

Functional variability of grip forces in cricket batting

We hypothesise that relatively small variability in low levels of intra-trial grip forces are apparent during the period between release and ball pitch. This is mainly because of a general organisation of the mechanical degrees of freedom of the more proximal segments of the kinetic chain during the early part of the bi-phasic batting action. Inter-trial variability is likely to be greater because of the different intentions of the batsman to play attacking or defensive strokes depending on the task context, or to play with 'hard' or 'soft' hands. Greater centripetal accelerations, generated by swinging the cricket bat faster, increase load forces. These changes must be counteracted by proportionally increasing the magnitude of grip force to avoid slipping.

Intra-trial grip force variability is likely to increase markedly during the post-bounce period where visual information may be used to modify the position of the bat on the basis of ongoing visual information from the approaching ball. Additionally, co-ordination of the more distal segments in the kinetic chain becomes increasingly more complex as the number of mechanical degrees of freedom increases (Bartlett, 1999). As the grip represents the terminal articulation in the upper body kinetic chain, movement discrepancies produced by preceding body segments must be accounted for and refined to produce accurate bat–ball impacts. In Chapter 1 it has already been noted from studies of national and international throwers that higher than expected levels of intra-individual variability have been reported (Bauer and Schöellhorn, 1997). Higher levels of variation were found within the performance clusters of international athletes, rejecting the idea of common optimal movement patterns, when the last 200 ms of javelin and discus throwing was measured. From these data, it might be concluded that any observed variability in skilled cricket batting is likely to be compensatory, particularly during the final phase of the movement, to allow a tight fit to develop between actor and environment (see also Bootsma and van Wieringen, 1990). McLeod (1987) has previously raised the issue of the large inertia of the cricket bat, suggesting that it could prevent stroke adjustments during the last 180–200 ms of ball flight. However, if the cricket bat were already moving as the ball approached, the problems of inertia could be overcome to a large extent by exploiting existing momentum. Future analyses of grip forces will reveal whether the effector response allows adjustment, based on ongoing visual information, or whether resistance from inertia forces prevents any adjustment from occurring.

Finally, we hypothesise that inter-trial grip forces will vary quite considerably during the follow-through in relation to the momentum of the bat. Stretch *et al.* (1998) reported a slight increase in grip forces during the follow-through, which they attributed to regaining the control of the cricket bat after impact.

Implications for bowlers

Our interpretation of the use of visual information in cricket batting also has profound implications for tactical awareness of cricket bowlers wishing to make life difficult for batsmen. First, bowlers should try to bowl a length that is sufficiently far up the pitch to exploit visual–motor latencies of only 80–100 ms quoted in the literature (e.g. Ballard *et al.*, 1998). By doing this, the time constraints will be severe enough to inhibit late modification of the batting action once the stroke has been initiated. Any deviation, such as the ball 'seaming' off the pitch, will not be easily picked up by the batsman, possibly resulting in the ball being deflected off the edge of the bat and being caught. Secondly, the bowler should also try to bowl 'yorkers' (full-length deliveries that pitch directly beneath the batsman in the area between the popping crease and the stumps). As batsmen find tracking the ball at the end of its trajectory difficult, the bowler should exploit this weakness by making the ball deviate late, possibly using reverse swing (see Barrett and Wood, 1996). Thirdly, the bowler should use strategies, such as holding the ball loosely or hyperextending the wrist at delivery, to vary bowling speed and flight along the same trajectory (Regan, 1997). Manipulating ball release in this way will make identifying the area and time of bounce tenuous, thus restricting the batsman's capacity to adapt the grip and the spatial trajectory of the bat late in performance.

Summary and recommendations for future research

Throughout this chapter, we have promoted the grip on the bat handle as an important technical component of the batting action and discussed how precise control of grip force dynamics is an integral feature of skilled cricket batting. We have explored the biomechanical constraints imposed on grip force dynamics before, during and after bat–ball impact, highlighting the research work undertaken by Stretch and colleagues, and Li and Turrell in describing the effects of manipulating task constraints on grip forces. Following on from this, we argued that the ecological approach is a relevant theoretical framework for understanding the processes involved in controlling grip forces. Gibson's theory of ecological optics (Gibson, 1979) formed the foundation for our discussion of sources of perceptual information available for pick-up by the batsman and we re-evaluated Land and McLeod's (2000) findings on visual search strategies in cricket batting. Our interpretation of their findings reaffirms the potential role of optic invariants, such as image expansion and rate of change of binocular disparity, as probable control mechanisms underpinning cricket batting. On this basis, we hypothesised a functional role for grip force variability, particularly during the latter stages of ball flight, claiming that it has an adaptive quality and that it is an integral component in satisfying task constraints of batting. We also predicted variations in magnitudes of grip forces between trials according to the intentions of the batsman to play either attacking or defensive strokes. Finally, tactical guidelines were postulated that bowlers might seek to exploit to dismiss a batsman. These implications are based on our interpretation of how batsmen pick up and use information sources and the limitations of the perceptual–motor system at adapting to task constraints and environmental perturbations.

We advocate that future research into cricket batting should be interdisciplinary in nature, integrating techniques and theory from biomechanics and motor control. Recommendations for specific avenues of future research have also been made throughout this chapter. We suggest that identifying grip force strategies used by batsmen of different skill levels is a priority. Owing to the inherently large amount of variability predicted in the data, both longitudinal and cross-sectional research designs need to be incorporated to identify individual-specific grip force strategies as well as to generalise to different sub-populations.

Future research designs need to pay particular attention to the statistical methods used to evaluate the variability in force–time data. Traditional summary statistics, such as the within-subject standard deviation, only provide a global, time-discrete estimate of behaviour and neglect the characterisation of the trial-to-trial or moment-to-moment relations of events in performance time series (Newell and Corcos, 1993). The standard deviation only captures the *magnitude* of fluctuations in system output. However, variations in system output can be measured along another dimension independently of the magnitude. By analysing force–time data in the time domain using a time series analysis, the *structure* of system dynamics can be identified (Slifkin and Newell, 1999, 2000). Orderly relations of events in a time series analysis may be interpreted as a functional basis for variability instead of noise in the perceptual–motor system. Furthermore, as cricket batsmen aim to strike the cricket ball near the centre of percussion of the cricket bat (Page, 1978), we suggest that the location of bat–ball impact also needs to be evaluated in addition to the degree of orderliness. A measuring system similar to the one described by McKellar *et al.* (1998) needs to be incorporated to measure the precise location of bat–ball impact. Knowledge of the location of bat–ball impact in relation to the centre of percussion will also help to clarify how 'off-centre' collisions affect the control of grip force during the impact phase.

Technological developments in ball tracking devices, such as the Hawk-Eye system (Roke Manor Research, UK), hold great potential and promise to make valuable contributions to this line of research. Such devices are able to calculate the spin and the swerve of the cricket ball during the flight phase and predict future ball flight based on the lateral deviation and rebound characteristics of the pitching phase. Manufacturers claim that these devices can reliably measure the location of the cricket ball at any instant from ball release to bat–ball impact to within 5 mm of its 'true' location. Knowledge of the corresponding time histories also allows accurate velocities and accelerations to be calculated, which are particularly important when evaluating the effects of task constraints (e.g. surface types and conditions and bowling speeds) on grip force dynamics.

Note

1 Owing to the lack of research into women's cricket, this chapter will focus on the existing research into the men's game. For this reason, the traditional terms *batsman* or *batsmen* will be used throughout the text.

References

Abernethy, B. (1981). Mechanisms of skill in cricket batting. *Australian Journal of Sports Medicine* **13**, 3–10.

Abernethy, B. and Russell, D.G. (1984). Advance cue utilisation by skillled cricket batsmen. *Australian Journal of Science and Medicine in Sport* **16**, 2–10.

Ballard, D.H., Salgian, G., Rao, R. and McCallum, A. (1998). On the role of timing in brain computation. In *Vision and Action* (edited by L.R. Harris and M. Jenkin). New York: Cambridge University Press.

Barrett, R.S. and Wood, D.H. (1996). The theory and practice of 'reverse swing'. *Sports Coach* **18**, 28–30.

Bartlett, R.M. (1997). *Introduction to Sports Biomechanics*. London: E & FN Spon.

Bartlett, R.M. (1999). *Sports Biomechanics: Reducing Injury and Improving Performance*. London: E & FN Spon.

Bartlett, R.M., Stockill, N.P., Elliott, B.C. and Burnett, A.F. (1996). The biomechanics of fast bowling in men's cricket: a review. *Journal of Sports Sciences* **14**, 403–24.

Bauer, H.U. and Schöellhorn, W. (1997). Self-organizing maps for the analysis of complex movement patterns. *Neural Processing Letters* **5**, 193–9.

Bootsma, R.J. and van Wieringen, P.C.W. (1990). Timing an attacking forehand drive in table tennis. *Journal of Experimental Psychology: Human Perception and Performance* **16**, 21–9.

Bootsma, R.J., Fayt, V., Zaal, F.T.J.M. and Laurent, M. (1997). On the information-based regulation of movement: what Wann (1999) may want to consider. *Journal of Experimental Psychology: Human Perception and Performance* **16**, 21–9.

Breen, J.L. (1967). What makes a good hitter? *Journal of Health, Physical Education and Recreation* **38**, 36–9.

Bruce, V., Green, P.R. and Georgeson, M.A. (1996). *Visual Perception: Physiology, Psychology, and Ecology*, 3rd edition. London: Lawrence Erlbaum.

Elliott, B.C. (2000). Back injuries and the fast bowler in cricket. *Journal of Sports Sciences* **18**, 983–91.

Elliott, B.C., Burnett, A.F., Stockill, N.P. and Bartlett, R.M. (1996). The fast bowler in cricket: a sports medicine perspective. *Sports, Exercise and Injury* **1**, 201–6.

Finch, C., Elliott, B.C. and McGrath, A. (1999). Overview of measures to prevent cricket injuries. *Sports Medicine* **28**, 263–72.

Gibson, J.J. (1979). *An Ecological Approach to Visual Perception*. Boston, MA: Houghton-Mifflin.

Helsen, W.F., Elliott, D., Starkes, J.L. and Ricker, K. (1998). Temporal and spatial coupling of point of gaze and hand movements in aiming. *Journal of Motor Behavior* **30**, 249–59.

Johansson, R.S. and Westling, C. (1988). Programmed and triggered actions to rapid load changes during precision grip. *Experimental Brain Research* **71**, 72–86.

Khan, M.A. and Franks, I.M. (2000). The effect of practice on component submovements is dependent on the availability of visual feedback. *Journal of Motor Behavior* **32**, 227–40.

Land, M.F. and McLeod, P. (2000). From eye movements to actions: how batsmen hit the ball. *Nature Neuroscience* **3**, 1340–5.

Lee, D.N., Young, D.S., Reddish, D.E., Lough, S. and Clayton, T.M.H. (1983). Visual timing in hitting an accelerating ball. *Quarterly Journal of Experimental Psychology* **35**, 333–46.

McIntyre, D.R. and Pfautsch, E.W. (1982). A kinematic analysis of the baseball battings-wings involved in opposite-field and same-field hitting. *Research Quarterly for Exercise and Sport* **53**, 206–13.

McKellar, D.K., Nurick, G.N. and Stretch, R.A. (1998). The measurement of the position of a ball striking a cricket bat. In *The Engineering of Sport: Design and Development* (edited by S.J. Haake). Oxford: Blackwell Science.

McLeod, P. (1987). Visual reaction time and high speed ball games. *Perception* **16**, 49–59.

Messier, S.P. and Owen, M.G. (1984). Bat dynamics of female fast pitch softball batters. *Research Quarterly for Exercise and Sport* **55**, 141–5.

Montagne, G., Fraisse, F., Ripoll, H. and Laurent, M. (2000). Perception–action coupling in an interceptive task: first-order time-to-contact as an input variable. *Human Movement Science* **19**, 59–72.

Montagne, G., Laurent, M., Durey, A. and Bootsma, R.J. (1999). Movement reversals in ball catching. *Experimental Brain Research* **129**, 87–92.

Newell, K.M. and Corcos, D.M. (1993). Issues in variability and motor control. In *Variability and Motor Control* (edited by K.M. Newell and D.M. Corcos). Champaign, IL: Human Kinetics.

Noakes, T.D. and Durandt, J.J. (2000). Physiological requirements of cricket. *Journal of Sports Sciences* **18**, 919–29.

Page, R.L. (1978). *The Physics of Human Movement.* Wheaton: Exeter.

Penrose, T., Foster, D. and Blanksby, B. (1976). Release velocities of fast bowlers during a cricket test match. *Australian Journal for Health, Physical Education and Recreation* **71** (suppl.), 2–5.

Penrose, J.M.T. and Roach, N.K. (1995). Decision making and advanced cue utilisation by cricket batsmen. *Journal of Human Movement Studies* **29**, 199–218.

Peper, C.E., Bootsma, R.J., Mestre, D.R. and Bakker, F.C. (1994). Catching balls: how to get the hand to the right place at the right time. *Journal of Experimental Psychology: Human Perception and Performance* **20**, 591–612.

Plagenhoef, S. (1971). *Patterns of Human Movement.* Englewood Cliffs, NJ: Prentice Hall.

Race, D.E. (1961). A cinematographic and mechanical analysis of the external movements involved in hitting a baseball effectively. *Research Quarterly* **32**, 394–404.

Regan, D. (1997). Visual factors in hitting and catching. *Journal of Sports Sciences* **15**, 533–58.

Savelsbergh, G.J.P. and Bootsma, R.J. (1994). Perception–action coupling in hitting and catching. *International Journal of Sports Psychology* **25**, 331–43.

Shibayama, H. and Ebashi, H. (1983). Development of a motor skill using the golf swing from the viewpoint of the regulation of muscle activity. In *Biomechanics VIII* (edited by H. Matsui and K. Kobayashi). Champaign, IL: Human Kinetics.

Slifkin, A.B. and Newell, K.M. (1999). Noise, information transmission, and force variability. *Journal of Experimental Psychology: Human Perception and Performance* **25**, 837–51.

Slifkin, A.B. and Newell, K.M. (2000). Variability and noise in continuous force production. *Journal of Motor Behavior* **32**, 141–50.

Stretch, R.A. (1993). A biomechanical analysis of batting in cricket. Unpublished doctoral dissertation, University of Port Elizabeth, Port Elizabeth, South Africa.

Stretch, R.A. (1994). A biomechanical analysis of the double-handed grip forces. In *Science and Racket Sports* (edited by T. Reilly, M. Hughes and A. Lees). London: E & FN Spon.

Stretch, R.A., Bartlett, R.M. and Davids, K. (2000). A review of batting in men's cricket. *Journal of Sports Sciences* **18**, 931–49.

Stretch, R.A., Buys, F.J. and Viljoen, G. (1995). The kinetics of the drive off the front foot in cricket batting: hand grip force. *South African Journal for Research in Sport, Physical Education and Recreation* **18**, 83–93.

Stretch, R.A., Buys, F.J., Du Toit, E. and Viljoen, G. (1998). Kinematics and kinetics of the drive off the front foot in cricket batting. *Journal of Sports Sciences* **16**, 711–20.

Turrell, Y.N. (2000). Grip force adjustments in collisions. Unpublished doctoral dissertation, University of Birmingham.

Turrell, Y.N., Li, F-X. and Wing, A.M. (1999). Grip force dynamics in the approach to a collision. *Experimental Brain Research* **128**, 86–91.

Whiting, H.T.A. (1969). *Acquiring Ball Skill: A Psychological Interpretation.* London: G.Bell.

Williams, A.M., Davids, K. and Williams, J.G. (1999). *Visual Perception and Action in Sport.* London: Routledge.

Williams, A.M., Davids, K., Burwitz, L. and Williams, J.G. (1992). Perception and action in sport. *Journal of Human Movement Studies* **22**, 147–204.

20 Visual regulation of the long jump approach phase

Mark A. Scott

The effectiveness of the long jump approach phase is determined by the athlete striking the take-off board accurately with minimum loss of velocity but also in an optimum body position for take-off (Hay, 1988). In order to achieve success in the long jump it is important that the athlete is able to satisfy these requirements repeatedly over trials. Typically, it has been believed by coaches that due to the need to consistently produce an accurate stereotyped approach, the experienced athlete should practise running from a carefully measured out start mark. Lee, Lishman and Thomson (1982) initially investigated the degree to which experienced long jumpers were able to reproduce a stereotyped run-up. The findings of their research provided a valuable insight into the nature of the action and also contributed to the development of a theoretical understanding of how goal-directed gait may be controlled. This chapter aims to review the research that has been conducted on the long jump approach phase and to discuss some of the theoretical and practical issues involved with control of gait in the run up.

Do trained long jumpers display a consistent approach?

In order to access the consistency of the approach phase Lee, Lishman and Thomson (1982) filmed three trained long jumpers.[1] Their foot placement for each step of their run-up was determined. This method of analysis allowed the variability of the foot placement over trials to be quantified. If the athletes were using a stereotyped approach it would be predicted that the variability in foot placement would be very low, i.e. their feet would be striking the floor in the same places for every run-up performed. This procedure of analysing the variability in foot placement has since been termed the inter-trial method (see Montagne, Cornus, Glize, Quaine and Laurent, 2000).

The results of Lee, Lishman and Thomson (1982) showed that the trained long jumpers did not demonstrate a highly consistent run-up (see Figure 20.1). Instead, they displayed a pattern of variability with an ascending/descending trend. In light of this finding, it appears that the approach phase is not solely controlled by running off a series of pre-programmed commands without recourse to feedback. Instead, Lee, Lishman and Thomson (1982) identified two distinct phases of the approach run: an acceleration phase and a zeroing-in phase. The ascending portion of the

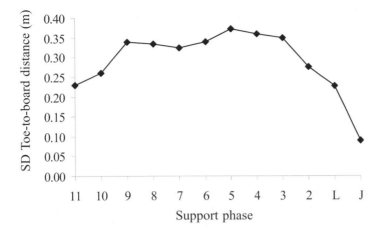

Figure 20.1   Mean standard deviation of toe-board distance in the approach
phase for an elite long jumper. Data adapted from Lee *et al.*
(1982): L = last; J = jump.

footfall variability curve represents the acceleration phase, ending at about 6 m
from the take-off board, and the descending portion of the curve represents the
zeroing-in phase. Lee, Lishman and Thomson (1982) suggested that, during the
acceleration phase, the athletes were trying to maintain a constant stride pattern.
However, small inconsistencies in the stride lengths had a cumulative effect, which
resulted in the build up of footfall variability. In order to adjust their stride length
to deal with this variability, Lee, Lishman and Thomson (1982) suggested that
during the zeroing-in phase, vision was used to regulate stride length, resulting in
the reduction of footfall variability over the final strides.

Visual regulation of step length

Lee, Lishman and Thomson (1982) suggested that the visual regulation of stride
length was achieved by the modulation of one kinetic variable, namely, the vertical
impulse. They performed correlations between step length and the following step
parameters: flight speed, thrust time, flight time and landing time. The suggestion
was that a high positive correlation would indicate which parameter was being
adjusted. The highest correlations in the zeroing-in phase were between step length
and flight time. This finding led Lee, Lishman and Thomson (1982) to propose
that the approach phase was controlled by keeping flight time constant during the
acceleration phase and adjusting it to alter stride length during the zeroing-in
phase. It was argued that changes in the observed flight time were directly related
to changes in the vertical impulse imparted during the thrusting phase of each
foot–ground contact. They suggested that vertical impulse was used to increase
the flight time component of the step without greatly affecting the other parameters
to which horizontal velocity was considered to be too sensitive.

The suggestion by Lee, Lishman and Thomson (1982) that the regulation of goal-directed gait could be achieved by the modulation a single kinetic parameter has become a contentious issue. Warren Young and Lee (1986) found evidence to support this notion when they examined the kinematics of experienced athletes ($n = 2$) stepping on targets taped to the belt of a treadmill. They found that the vertical impulse accounted for 99 per cent of the variance in the data on stride length changes. However, Patla, Robinson, Samways, and Armstrong (1989) argued that the horizontal impulse of the step could account for as much as 40 per cent of the variation in the stride adjustments in novice runners ($n = 20$). Warren and Yaffe (1989) rebutted the arguments of Patla, Robinson, Samways and Armstrong (1989) but still found a contribution of 20 per cent for the horizontal impulse. The discrepancies between these studies may be due to a number of methodological reasons. Warren, Young and Lee (1986) investigated experienced runners and inferred changes in kinetic parameters from kinematic data, whereas Patla, Robinson Samways and Armstrong (1989) examined novice runners but recorded kinetic data more directly by using a force-plate.

Optical information for regulating gait

In addition to claiming that gait in the zeroing-in phase was adjusted on the basis a single kinetic parameter, Lee, Lishman and Thomson (1982) also proposed that the expert long jumpers were regulating their vertical impulse through the use of a single source of optical information. As the athletes were regulating their stride lengths by adjusting their flight times, they suggested that the athletes were 'using information about how far in time they were from the board' (p. 456). They suggested that the athletes adjusted the flight times of their remaining strides so that they fitted the required time-to-contact with the take-off board.

Previously, as indicated in the chapters by Montagne and Laurent, and by Benguigui, Ripoll and Broderick, Lee (1976) showed that, in principle, the remaining time-to-contact of an object travelling directly towards the eye with a constant velocity can be specified by the inverse of the relative rate of dilation of any two points on the surface texture on the object. This optic variable has since become known as local tau (see Tresilian, 1990, 1991). Regarding the zeroing-in phase of the long jump approach, Lee, Lishman and Thomson (1982) argued that 'time-to-contact is specified directly by a single optical parameter, the inverse of the rate of dilation of the image of the board' (p. 456). However, questions have arisen over this account of how time-to-contact information is picked up. Kaiser and Mowafy (1993) mathematically demonstrated how large differences could occur between the actual time-to-contact and the time-to-contact provided by the local tau of a non-spherical object when it does not directly approach the eye. As the take-off board does not directly approach the eye, but instead passes some distance under the eye, it appears that the relative rate of expansion of the board would not provide veridical time-to-contact information.

However, Williams, Davids and Williams (1999) have suggested that Tresilian's (1990, 1991) description of global tau may still be an appropriate definition of how time-to-contact information may be picked up in the long jump approach phase. When a jumper is moving forwards, all texture points in the environment flow out from a single point known as the focus of expansion (Gibson, Olum and Rosenblatt, 1955). Tresilian (1990, 1991) described a form of global tau, where the relative rate of expansion of the distance between the focus of expansion and any texture point could provide veridical time-to-contact information. In the context of the long jump approach, therefore, it is possible for the remaining time-to-contact to be specified by global tau information from the inverse of the relative rate of dilation of the distance between the take-off board and the focus of expansion of the optic flow field. This would appear a more applicable definition of how the remaining time-to-contact with the take-off board could be picked up by the long jumper. However, it is clear that the actual optical information used in the visual regulation of the approach phase has yet to be determined.

Skill differences in footfall variability

Although the proposal of the vertical impulse being modulated on the basis of tau as an explanation of the regulation of stride length remains a contentious issue, the use of vision (in some form) in the regulation of the approach phase has gained considerable support. Using an increased sample size compared to the study by Lee and colleagues, Hay (1988) examined the approach phase of both male and female world-class long jumpers. The results supported Lee, Lishman and Thomson's (1982) notion of visual control during the final steps of the approach, with males showing an average maximum footfall variation of 23 cm, and females 24 cm. This variability was reduced to 4 cm for males and 5 cm for females by the end of the approach (see Figure 20.2). These findings infer that highly skilled world-class athletes still use vision in order to regulate their stride patterns as they run towards the take-off board.

Berg Wade and Greer (1994) recorded long jump performance at high school track and field competitions (grades 9–12; age range = 15–18 years). The novice male long jumpers displayed a similar ascending–descending trend in variability of footfall placement over trials compared to the variability demonstrated by more experienced athletes. This finding suggested that the novice long jumpers also used a visual control strategy. To extend understanding, Glize and Laurent (1997) and Scott, Li and Davids (1997) investigated participants who had received no training or instruction at the long jump. These participants were described as 'non-long jumpers' and still displayed a pattern of variability for footfall placement that inferred visual regulation, i.e. a descending pattern of variability in the final strides of the approach. In light of these investigations into skill differences, it appears that the conclusion of Berg, Wade and Greer (1994), that 'the manner in which gait is visually regulated in the LJA is less a specially trained skill than a natural means of controlling gait in this task' (p. 862),[2] seems appropriate.

The investigation of Scott, Li and Davids (1997) found that non-long jumpers, on average, accumulated a maximum footfall variation of 58 cm (see Figure 20.2). This value is considerably larger than that found in previous research, including

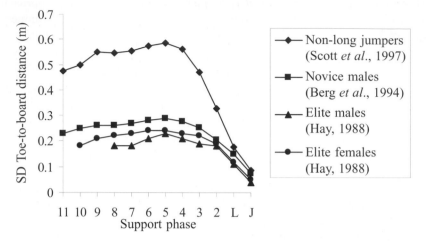

Figure 20.2   Mean standard deviation of toe-board distance in the approach phase for non-
long jumpers, novices and elite long jumpers. Data adapted from Hay (1988)
and Berg et al. (1994) and Scott *et al.* (1997): L = last; J = jump.

Glize and Laurent (1997). Lee, Lishman and Thomson (1982) originally suggested
that small inconsistencies in stride length, which accumulated over the approach,
were responsible for the build up in footfall variability. The larger value in the
investigation by Scott, Li and Davids (1997) may have been partly due to variations
in the adopted start position for each trial in addition to the inconsistencies in
stride length. This conclusion is supported by the finding that the non-long jumpers
in the investigation of Glize and Laurent (1997) displayed a maximum footfall
variability value of approximately 28 cm when using a consistent startmark.

Skill differences in accuracy of hitting the take-off board with the foot

Although the use of vision appears to be consistent across skill levels, skill
differences appear to exist in the level of accuracy achieved for the foot placement
at take-off. A high degree of accuracy at take-off is crucial, overstepping the board
results in a foul, whereas not stepping close enough reduces the effective measured
distance of the jump. Hay (1988) reported average error values of 11 cm and 8 cm
for the final foot placement of male and female world-class athletes, whereas
Berg and Greer (1995) found that novice male jumpers had an absolute error value
of 15 cm at take-off for legal trials. The non-long jumpers of Glize and Laurent
(1997) and Scott, Li and Davids (1997) had accuracy scores of 21 cm and 25 cm,
respectively. In light of these findings it is clear that the more experienced jumpers
achieved a greater degree of accuracy in the final foot placement. These findings
suggest that task-specific practice of the approach phase could improve accuracy
of hitting the take-off board with the foot in this interceptive action.

Where does the onset of visual guidance occur?

Initially, the onset of visual regulation was considered to coincide with the highest value of the standard deviation of the footfall placement. In light of this operational definition, Lee, Lishman and Thomson (1982) suggested that the onset of visual guidance occurred about 6 m from the board. However, Berg, Wade and Greer (1994) argued that using the highest value of the standard deviation of the footfall placement as the indicator of the start of the zeroing-in phase was inappropriate. Instead, they proposed that the point of onset of visual guidance is best identified as a marked and systematic reduction in the footfall variability. When comparing novice and expert data using this definition, Berg, Wade and Greer (1994) suggested that the average onset of visual control occurs at around the fourth step from take-off, regardless of skill level. Scott, Li and Davids (1997) also reported similar findings for non-long jumpers, although it is worth noting that variability exists both between- and within-participants for the point at which visual control emerges. High levels of variability in the point at which visual control emerges have, indeed, been found in many previous studies in the area. For example, Berg, Wade and Greer (1994) stated that novice participants displayed a large degree of between-individual variability for the point at which visual control occurs. Hay (1988) also reported data showing that variability also exists between expert participants for the onset of visual control. By performing a meet-to-meet comparison of expert participants, Hay (1988) found that individual participants varied across jumping sessions for the step at which visual guidance appeared to occur.

Is there an ascending–descending trend to footfall variability?

Later research suggests that using the inter-trial method of looking for a marked and systematic reduction in the footfall variability as the identification of the onset of visual guidance may be inappropriate. Glize and Laurent (1997) developed a trial-by-trial method of analysis. This approach required the calculation of an index of variation for each step during the run up. The index of variation was defined as the difference between the magnitude of stride length of a given stride and the mean magnitude of length for that stride across all trials. Using the trial-by-trial analysis, Glize and Laurent found that both skilled and unskilled jumpers were making early adjustments in their stride lengths. On average the highest value for the index of variation occurred after six strides from the start of the run-up. This finding suggests that adjustments in the approach phase may occur much earlier than previously thought.

Lee, Lishman and Thomson (1982) originally postulated that the larger the build up of footfall variability during the acceleration phase, the earlier the onset of visual regulation would appear in the approach. However, this suggestion initially received no support. Both Hay (1988) and Berg, Wade and Greer (1994) found that the location point of visual regulation was not a function of the magnitude of error accumulated during the acceleration phase.

Montagne, Cornus, Glize, Quaine and Laurent (2000) have questioned the proposal of a two-phase approach. They suggest that instead of having an invariant step at which the control mode switches, an athlete may only produce systematic adjustments in step length when the need for adjustment is perceived. Following on from the research of Glize and Laurent (1997), they employed a trial-by-trial method in analysing the approach phase of mixed experience long jumpers.[3] To identify the initiation of regulation a 4 per cent difference in the step length when compared to the average length of that step over trials was used, rather than using a marked and systematic reduction in the footfall variability. Using this new criterion the initiation of the visual regulation appeared to be spread over the final six steps. A linear relationship was identified between the total amount of adjustment made and the step at which adjustment was initiated. This finding suggests that the larger the total adjustments made in step length, the earlier regulation was initiated. They also found significant relationships between the amount of adjustment required and the amount of adjustment produced for the final four steps of the approach. These findings support their proposal that instead of visual regulation occurring at an invariant number of steps, the initiation of adjustments is made on the basis of the perceived requirement for adjustment within each performance.

Practical applications of visual regulation to the approach phase

Notwithstanding the previous research on the long jump approach, athletes place a great emphasis on getting the run-up right. It is common for an athlete to use various methods in order to develop their proficiency in the approach phase. As mentioned previously, experienced long jumpers typically practise running from a carefully measured out start mark. The adoption of a consistent start mark was thought to aid in the development of a consistent run-up. A comparison of the findings of Scott, Li and Davids (1997) and Glize and Laurent (1997) shows that this assumption has some validity. It appears that the adoption of a consistent start mark does aid in the early development of a consistent run up. Lower footfall variability is clearly observed when non-long jumpers are constrained to use a consistent start mark. In the very early stages of practice the use of a start mark also serves to ensure that learners' foot placements are consistent enough to ensure that they strike the board with their preferred take-off leg.

Since the approach phase is not highly consistent, Glize and Laurent (1997) proposed that there should be a shift away from trying to stereotype the action towards a more continuous control of strides. They suggested that one method for promoting this shift of emphasis could be to vary the position of the start mark (by several centimetres) over trials without the athlete's knowledge. Glize and Laurent (1997) suggested that the variation in start position over trials should increase the need for continuous guidance in the regulation of stride length, forcing the athlete to practice continuous adjustment of stride length. It may be useful if other methods for promoting continuous control of strides can be identified and investigated in future research.

Another common method employed by athletes to improve their accuracy in the approach phase is to make use of run-throughs. A run-through in the long jump can be considered a run-up with no jump. The athlete runs straight over the board and into the pit. On the basis of their findings, Lee, Lishman and Thomson (1982) questioned the value of run-throughs as a training aid for the approach phase. They noted that two of the three participants spread the adjustments of their stride lengths differently in run-throughs when compared to actual jumps. This difference was attributed to the constraints of the task, as in run-throughs the athlete does not have to adopt the take-off posture required for actual jumps (Williams, Davids and Williams, 1999).

Glize and Laurent (1997) provided further evidence against the use of run-throughs. They compared experienced long jumpers' and non-long jumpers' kinematics on a sprinting task with their kinematics for the long jump approach phase. They found that footfall variability was higher in the early part of the long jump approach phase when compared to sprinting, indicating that the athlete was producing a different pattern of footfall placement in response to the different task constraints of sprinting and running to jump. They concluded that as sprinting appeared to be controlled in different way to the approach phase, the 'performance of a run-up without the final jump appears to be of little pedagogic value' (p. 188). On the basis of the limited amount of data available so far, the indications are that the different phases of the task of long jumping should be practised together in order to take advantage of the athlete's capacity to use perception–action coupling as a means of regulating gait (for a similar conclusion regarding the triple jump, see Chapter 21 by Maraj).

Summary

In conclusion, it seems that, regardless of the skill level of the athlete, the approach phase of the long jump is visually regulated. Current understanding is that the onset of visual regulation of step length appears to be based on the athlete's perceived need for adjustment rather than visual regulation being initiated at a specific step away from the take-off board. This explanation denotes a functional explanation for the onset of visual regulation, harmonious with an ecological perspective on the use of perception and action processes to support behaviour.

Although visual regulation occurs across all skill levels, skill differences still exist in the level of accuracy achieved at take-off, with the literature showing that more highly skilled athletes achieve a greater level of accuracy in their final foot placement. In light of this finding, it is apparent that specific practice at the approach phase in conjunction with the performance of a jump should improve take-off accuracy, although this is yet to be empirically verified over a longitudinal study.

One major issue with regard to the visual regulation of the approach phase remains unresolved. The underlying mechanism of control in the approach phase needs to be identified. The original proposal of one optical variable (tau) coupled to one kinetic parameter (vertical impulse) remains a contentious description of control in the limited number of experimental investigations that have been carried out. Clearly, further research is required to determine the exact mechanism by which visual regulation is achieved in the long jump approach phase.

Notes

1   The three female participants were described as a British International of Olympic standard, a Scottish International and a good club long jumper.
2   LJA = long jump approach.
3   The average jump distances of this sample were comparable to those of the novice jumpers described by Berg *et al.* (1994).

References

Berg, W.P. and Greer, N.L. (1995). A kinematic profile of the approach run of novice long jumpers. *Journal of Applied Biomechanics* **11**, 142–62.

Berg, W.P., Wade, M.G. and Greer, N.L. (1994). Visual regulation of gait in bipedal locomotion: revisiting Lee, Lishman, and Thomson (1982). *Journal of Experimental Psychology: Human Perception and Performance* **20**, 854–63.

Gibson, J.J., Olum, P. and Rosenblatt, F. (1955). Parallax and perspective during aircraft landings. *American Journal of Psychology* **68**, 372–85.

Glize, D. and Laurent, M. (1997). Controlling locomotion during the accleration phase in sprinting and long jumping. *Journal of Sports Sciences* **15**, 181–9.

Hay, J.G. (1988). Approach strategies in the long jump. *International Journal of Sport Biomechanics* **4**, 114–29.

Kaiser, M.K. and Mowafy, L. (1993). Optical specification of time-to-passage: Observer's sensitivity to global tau. *Journal of Experimental Psychology: Human Perception and Performance* **19**, 1028–40.

Lee, D.N. (1976). A theory of visual control of braking based on information about time-to-collision. *Perception* **5**, 437–59.

Lee, D.N., Lishman, J.R. and Thomson, J.A. (1982). Regulation of gait in long jumping. *Journal of Experimental Psychology: Human Perception and Performance* **8**, 448–59.

Montagne, G., Cornus, S., Glize, D., Quaine, F. and Laurent, M. (2000). A perception–action coupling type of control in long jumping. *Journal of Motor Behavior* **32**, 37–43.

Patla, A.E., Robinson, C., Samways, M. and Armstrong, C.J. (1989). Visual control of step length during overground locomotion: task-specific modulation of the locomotor synergy. *Journal of Experimental Psychology: Human Perception and Performance* **15**, 601–15.

Scott, M.A., Li, F.-X. and Davids, K. (1997). Expertise and the regulation of gait in the long jump approach phase. *Journal of Sports Sciences* **15**, 597–605.

Tresilian, J.R. (1990). Perceptual information for the timing of interceptive action. *Perception* **19**, 223–39.

Tresilian, J.R. (1991). Empirical and theoretical issues in the perception of time to contact. *Journal of Experimental Psychology: Human Perception and Performance* **17**, 865–76.

Warren, W.H. and Yaffe, D.M. (1989). Dynamics of step length adjustment during running: a comment on Patla, Robinson, Samways and Armstrong (1989). *Journal of Experimental Psychology: Human Perception and Performance* **15**, 616–21.

Warren, W.H., Young, D.S. and Lee, D.N. (1986). Visual control of step length during running over irregular terrain. *Journal of Experimental Psychology: Human Perception and Performance* **12**, 259–66.

Williams, A.M., Davids, K. and Williams, J.G. (1999). *Visual Perception and Action in Sport*. London: E & FN Spon.

21 Control and co-ordination in the triple jump

Brian K. V. Maraj

Horizontal jumping events in track and field include both the long and the triple jumps. Each event consists of an approach run followed by a take-off from a board (20 cm long and 1 m wide) located on a runway and landing into a sand-filled pit. Unlike long jumping, described in Chapter 20 by Scott, which involves one dynamic explosion at take-off, the triple jump sequence is comprised of (as the name implies) three separate take-offs. The hop phase (take-off and landing on the same foot), the step phase (take-off and landing on the opposite foot), and jump phase (take-off from one foot to landing on both feet into a sandpit) comprise the ordered sequence of events following the approach run to the take-off board. The function of the approach run is to propel the jumper down the runway, at a high but controlled velocity, in preparation for the hop phase at take-off. Previous research has shown that the horizontal velocity attained in the approach run is a critical factor in the performance of jumps for distance and directly influences the distance that can be achieved (Hay, 1988; Hay and Koh, 1988; Miller and Hay, 1986).

As with other types of interceptive actions involving locomotion towards a target in space, such as in all horizontal jumps, a major task constraint of the triple jump event is the interceptive action that occurs at the conclusion of the approach run. The jumper is required to place their foot on the take-off board and position it such that it does not exceed the 20 cm limit in preparation for the initial hop phase. This task must be accomplished with a minimal loss of horizontal velocity as the jumper nears the board. Given a jumper's desire to attain the best possible distance coupled with the constraints imposed by the board (i.e. not exceeding the 20 cm limit), accurate foot placement at take-off is at a premium. While it may be possible to have beautiful running form, and a great flight trajectory after each of the three take-offs, if the foot placement exceeds the 20 cm boundary, even a world record jump would go for naught!

How do triple jumpers regulate the stride pattern of their approach run in order to cope with the task constraints discussed? As outlined in the chapter by Scott, many researchers in visuo–motor control have explored the use of visual information to guide and regulate movement to accurately arrive at a particular location in space (e.g. Berg *et al.*, 1994; Lee *et al.*, 1982; Maraj *et al.*, 1998). The regulation of gait in the triple jump allows an insight into the factors that affect movement control and co-ordination in a complex task. One means by which processes of co-ordination and control can be explored is by examining the variability in footfall positions of the jumper in the approach run. The approach run is a highly practised skill for triple jumpers. The regulation of gait toward the take-off board is a component of the task that athletes and their coaches strive to make as exact and repeatable as possible. The belief is that a highly repeatable run up is necessary for the jumper when faced with different competition and weather conditions.

However, it has been proposed in early work that two distinct phases exist in the performance of the approach run of the long jump (e.g. Lee *et al.*, 1982; Berg *et al.*, 1994) and the triple jump (Maraj *et al.*, 1998). The first phase has been described as a very stable phase in which the jumpers try to produce as consistent an approach as possible. Some research has also suggested that the second phase may be under visual control as the jumper uses the take-off board to guide him/ herself to an accurate take-off position on the board (see chapter by Scott).

As outlined in Chapter 1 of this book, previous investigations have examined the manner in which the jumpers utilised visual information in the performance of their approach run in order to regulate their strides and arrive accurately on the take-off board. Specifically, some researchers wanted to know the extent to which the run up (20–30 m) to the take-off board (20 cm wide) was stereotyped by the athlete to achieve the goal of stability and consistency over trials. That is, do the jumpers simply run off a prepared movement sequence in the performance of the approach run? If this were not the case, were the athletes using vision to regulate their gait and, if so, where in the approach was the visual regulation strategy most important?

Footfall variability

In past work, it has been generally accepted that variability in footfall position over repeated trials is the dependent measure that best captures how an athlete completes the run up phase when repeating a number of trials in the horizontal jumps (see Hay, 1988; Lee *et al.*, 1982; Maraj, 1995). As Scott argues in this text, using the inter-trial method of analysis, it seems apparent that the pattern of footfall position variability increases during the initial portion of the approach run and then rapidly decreases as the jumper gets nearer to the take-off board. While trying to produce as stable a run up as possible, it appears that the jumpers cannot help but produce small inconsistencies in their stride pattern. These inconsistencies were reflected by the increasing variability of the footfall position that the athletes displayed as the strides approached the take-off board. The accepted wisdom has been that, if athletes continued in this fashion, the foot position on the board could result in either a foul trial by exceeding the 20 cm limit or in a jump where the take-off position occurred well before the board reducing the total distance measured.

In fact, it has been shown that athletes are generally able to compensate for these inconsistencies in the approach by regulating their gait. The pattern of the approach run that has been reported is an increase in the variability of each foot's

Triple jump

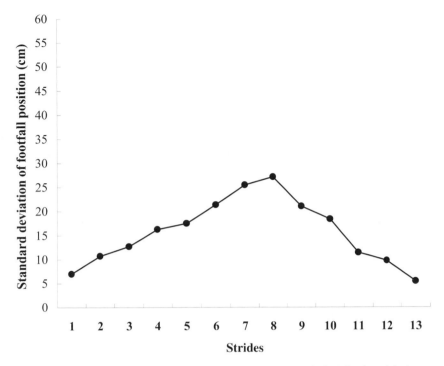

Figure 21.1 Typical pattern of footfall variability (standard deviation) in the triple jump approach across strides leading to take-off (adapted from Maraj *et al.* 1998).

landing position *across trials* up to a specific point in the run up, after which there is a steady decline in variability. This robust finding has been generally taken as support for vision being used to direct the jumpers to accurately hit the take-off board (see Figure 21.1). As outlined in the chapter by Scott, the point at which visual control emerges has been suggested to occur at a point of systematic reduction of variability of footfall position (Berg *et al.*, 1994). That is, it does not have to be the highest point of variability, but instead the point at which the footfall position variability begins to systematically decrease as the take-off board is neared.

Given the specific statements in the literature about the relevance of the optical information from the take-off board discussed Chapter 1, some effort has been directed to examining whether the take-off board plays an integral role in driving the variability seen in the approach run (e.g. Maraj, 1999). Obviously, one way to ascertain the role of the take-off board is to engage in experimental analysis of the run up with and without its presence. In fact, with such a manipulation, primacy of the information from the take-off board was evidenced by the sharp contrast of the stride patterns produced when jumps are performed in the presence or absence of the take-off board. Use of the board/no-board manipulation provided some

Triple jump

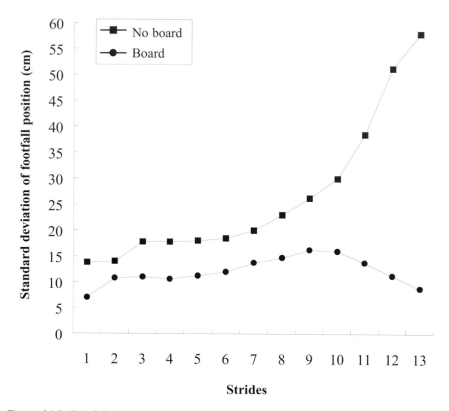

Figure 21.2   Footfall variability across strides in the triple jump in the presence and absence of a take-off board (from Maraj, 1999).

evidence for the point at which visual control seemed to emerge (see Figure 21.2). This manipulation assisted in developing understanding of the visual control mechanisms that have been suggested to occur during the approach run. Triple jump participants do seem to use optical information from the board, in some way to guide their action leading to take-off. Were the run up simply a pre-prepared response, regardless of information sources present, then footfall variability would not show the divergent pattern seen in the two conditions. Of course, the nature of the relevant information source(s) to regulate stride pattern has yet to be ascertained. A key issue raised by Scott in this book, is whether information from the take-off board acts as a texture element in relation to a focus of expansion point (Gibson, 1979) to regulate gait.

Stride by stride statistical analysis revealed that, in the execution of the approach run in skilled triple jump performance, a portion of the run seems to display highly stable characteristics, but only to a point. The highly stable portion showed no significant differences between the board and no-board conditions for approximately 80 per cent of the approach run. The critical difference between the two conditions appeared approximately two strides before take-off. One interpretation is that this is the point at which the jumpers visually guided themselves by using the board in preparation for take-off (although see Montagne *et al.* (2000) for a different interpretation). This is an important element in the understanding of visuo–motor control of the approach run, because the point at which visual control of the approach run is effected has been suggested previously as being the point of maximum standard deviation of footfall variability (e.g. Berg *et al.*, 1994; Hay, 1988).

Several researchers have shown that the pattern of footfall variability seen in the horizontal jumps is the same regardless of the ability level of the performers. Hay (1988) has demonstrated this for elite long jumpers and Berg *et al.* (1994) have done the same with novice level jumpers. While the pattern may stay virtually the same, novices tend to be more variable in the initial phase of the approach run. However, research needs to clarify how much this finding has to do with the use of changing starting points by novices, rather than any systematic difference between the skill groups. Once a starting point has been established, novices and experts in the triple jump tend to show the same pattern of footfall variability as has been previously demonstrated (see Scott *et al.*, 1997).

Effects of situational constraints on triple jumping performance

While the changes seen in the footfall position may seem to be a stable feature of performance of this type of interceptive action, regardless of skill level, it appears that there are other factors that can play a role in the execution of the take-off into the jump. For example, it is clear that jumpers may face situations in competition that act as constraints in the production of different types of jumps. For example, in competition, jumpers are faced with an assortment of constraints, such as intentionality, which guide the way that their jumps need to be performed (for a discussion of the influence of intentionality on co-ordination dynamics see Chapter 13 by Button and Summers). Studies have rarely measured jumpers' performances under 'real life' competitive situations since the different scenarios of competition occur with insufficient frequency to allow for a reasonable number of trials to be obtained for study. However, one such study has focused on the role of situational constraints in the performance of the triple jump (e.g. Maraj *et al.*, 1998). Jumpers can be faced with a situation where accuracy is at a premium, because the specific competition goal is not to produce a jump that exceeds the 20 cm limit of the take-off board (i.e. a foul). It has been shown that jumpers do make accommodations at take-off in compliance with situational (tactical) constraints. Interestingly, it appears that presence of footfall variability stays the same regardless of the context.

Notwithstanding the robustness of the footfall variability data, there are other components that can influence the overall motor performance. The context in which the jump is performed can have a profound effect on the execution of the movement.

For example, when approach velocity and horizontal velocity at take-off are examined in relation to the situational constraints of the jump, there are some very interesting performance features to note. The first is that when maximum jump distance was at a premium, the velocities increased for both approach and take-off. Conversely, when accuracy was required (i.e. not exceeding the limits of the board and fouling) the horizontal velocity decreased in correspondence with the demands of this context (Maraj et al., 1998).

Changes in horizontal velocity commensurate with the situational constraints of the jump (e.g. the need to ensure the highest levels of accuracy in footfall placement) also have implications for the type of jump that is utilised. Hay (1999) has outlined the degree to which jumpers used different styles at interception with the take-off board. The three phases of the triple jump produce performances that can be categorised in three different ways depending on the emphasis placed on different phases by the jumpers. These phases can be classed as hop-dominated, jump-dominated or balanced. It has been demonstrated that regardless of the type of jump strategy that is employed, the jumpers' footfall pattern remains basically the same. The interesting point, however, is that these differing strategies call for very different approach and take-off velocities. The changes in velocity at these two different points are very dramatic in terms of the type of jump strategy that is to be employed.

The velocity changes seen as a function of the jumpers' intent can be interpreted as changes made in response to the constraints placed on the participants. Thus, horizontal velocity at take-off was increased in competitive settings that required the participant to achieve greater distance. Horizontal velocity at take-off was decreased in response to demands of having to be more accurate at the take-off board. The coaching intervention suggested by such research manipulations is that advanced learners should be encouraged to engage in functional changes of the run up in response to the competitive demands likely to be faced by the jumper.

Fouled jumps

The interception of the take-off board by the jumper is not always performed successfully. It should be noted that, although it is quite possible that optic variables play a role in determining the time-to-contact and the requisite changes necessary to hit the take-off board, the reality of triple jumping is that fouling of jumps still occur regularly. In an analysis of the horizontal jumps at the 1987 and 1991 World Athletics championships, an overall average of 28 per cent of the trials in these events resulted in fouls (see Maraj, 1995). It is likely that a greater proportion of jumps will be fouls when the situational constraints emphasise distance and if the jumper is hop-oriented in the triple jump. In analyses of the triple jump approach run, jumps that were fouled were not eliminated from the overall data analysis. Moreover, it has been demonstrated that fouled jumps do not have an impact on the footfall variability pattern seen and the pattern is not an artifact of the removal of fouls from consideration (Maraj, 1995).

Practical application

The data discussed in this chapter suggest that the take-off board is important in visually guiding jumpers in preparation of horizontal jump performance. This finding highlights the fact that in the performance of motor skills, regulatory stimuli (such as the take-off board) play an important role in guiding behavior (Gentile, 1972). One implication is that coaches should facilitate practice sessions that can enhance the athlete's performance and utilise the components of stable and visually controlled phases in the approach run. The practical application of this work for coaches would be to place an emphasis on attaining a consistent pattern of striding to minimise errors in the early portion of the approach run. While this is a part of the regime of many coaches in the horizontal jumps, there is little attention given to the visual regulation of the approach run. In keeping with the data from this study and others (e.g. Hay and Koh, 1988), it is important to incorporate drills that address the visual regulation function. Drills which will assist the athlete in perception of distance and in making accommodations (in stride length) to arrive at a given target position would be very helpful in addressing the visual regulation function.

In practising the approach run, there need not be an emphasis on the demanding exactness often prescribed by most coaches. This implication relates to practice of the 'run-throughs' as well, discussed in the chapter by Scott. In a 'run-through' the jumper practises the approach run but does not go into at take-off phase once the take-off board is reached. This practice strategy can sometimes be used to assist jumpers in finding the point from which the take-off should start, leading to adjustments in the run up length as necessary. The data presented for footfall variability in this chapter, allied to those reported in the chapter by Scott, suggest that this is an unnecessary procedure and that the jumpers utilise more on-line control even in the practice with 'run-throughs'.

Conclusions

Coaching has been described as a bastion of habitual behaviour in which coaches have often not utilised the information that science has to offer. Instead they opt for the comfort of what others have done and what has been known to work in the past (regardless of cause). While in many cases coaches have been correct in their intuitions, such is not the case with the interceptive action seen in the control and co-ordination of the triple jump approach run. This is because this interceptive action is one in which the visual control is utilised to hit the take-off board with a high degree of precision. While there are aspects of the approach that need to be rehearsed, the degree to which it is a stable, pre-prepared response is minimised by the visuo–motor interaction that dominates and guides the movement of the jumper during the run up.

Start point consistency does not decrease the footfall variability seen in the approach run. While triple jumpers strive for a consistent approach run, the reality is that typically it is not. As such, more emphasis in practice needs to be placed on running speed, take-off and flight mechanics in preparing a jumper for the triple jump.

References

Berg, W.P, Wade, M.G. and Greer, N.L. (1994). Visual regulation of gait in bipedal loco-motion: revisiting Lee, Lishman, and Thomson (1982). *Journal of Experimental Psychology: Human Perception and Performance*, **20**, 854–63.

Gibson, J.J. (1979). *The Ecological Approach to Visual Perception*. Mahwah, NJ: Lawrence Erlbaum Publishers.

Gentile, A.M. (1972). A working model of skill acquisition with application to teaching. *Quest* **17**, 3–23.

Hay, J.G. (1988). Approach strategies in the long jump. *International Journal of Sport Biomechanics* **4**, 114–29.

Hay, J.G. (1999). Effort distribution and performance of Olympic triple jumpers. *Journal of Applied Biomechanics* **15**, 36–51.

Hay, J.G. and Koh, T.J. (1988). Evaluating the approach in the horizontal jumps. *International Journal of Sport Biomechanics* **4**, 372–92.

Lee, D.N., Lishman, J.R. and Thomson, J.A. (1982). Regulation of gait in long jumping. *Journal of Experimental Psychology: Human Perception and Performance* **8**, 448–59.

Maraj, B.K.V. (1995). The effect of environmental and cognitive constraints on the approach run of the triple jump. *Dissertation Abstracts International* **57**–01A, 150.

Maraj, B.K.V. (1999). Evidence for programmed and visually controlled phases of the triple jump approach run. *New Studies in Athletics* **14**, 51–6.

Maraj, B.K.V. and Allard, F. (1997). Variability in the triple jump approach run. *Research Quarterly for Exercise and Sport* **68**, A-63.

Maraj, B.K.V., Allard, F. and Elliott, D. (1998). The effect of non-regulatory stimuli on the approach run of the triple jump. *Research Quarterly for Exercise and Sport* **69**, 129–35.

Maraj, B.K.V., Elliott, D., Lee, T.D. and Pollock, B.J. (1994). Variance and invariance in expert and novice triple jumpers. *Research Quarterly for Exercise and Sport* **64**, 404–12.

Miller, J.A. and Hay, J.G. (1986). Kinematics of a world record and other world class performances in the triple jump. *International Journal of Sport Biomechanics* **2**, 272–88.

Montagne, G., Cornus, S., Glize, D., Quaine, F. and Laurent, M. (2000) A perception–action coupling type of control in long jumping. *Journal of Motor Behavior*, **32**, 37–43.

Scott, M.A., Li, F.-X. and Davids, K. (1997) Expertise and the regulation of gait in the long jump approach phase. *Journal of Sport Sciences* **15**, 597–605.

Index